p42 - 1 line summary

When Movements Anchor Parties

ed reform DPers
8, 43 [187] 196
"generous benefits"
151, 152
"union bosses" 153
"overpaid pub employees" 179

a bunch of post 2015
changes in generalizations
eg 197, 198, 249

annoying prevalence of
methodological throat clearing

graveyards of the
movements

parts on labor - DP standard
left labor history w/ focus
on politics & occasional nod
to methodological premises

"intrusion"

154 private & public
welfare state

164 CRA 1964

166 UAW assessed - yes but
UAW democracy missing

165 14(b) repeal

PRINCETON STUDIES IN AMERICAN POLITICS:
HISTORICAL, INTERNATIONAL, AND COMPARATIVE PERSPECTIVES

Ira Katznelson, Eric Schickler, Martin Shefter, and Theda Skocpol, Series Editors

A list of titles in this series appears at the back of the book

When Movements Anchor Parties

Electoral Alignments in American History

Daniel Schlozman

PRINCETON UNIVERSITY PRESS

Princeton and Oxford

Published by Princeton University Press, 41 William Street,
Princeton, New Jersey 08540
In the United Kingdom: Princeton University Press, 6 Oxford Street,
Woodstock, Oxfordshire OX20 1TW
press.princeton.edu

ISBN 978-0-691-16469-4
ISBN (pbk.) 978-0-691-16470-0
Library of Congress Control Number: 2015935301
British Library Cataloging-in-Publication Data is available
This book has been composed in Sabon Next LT Pro

10 9 8 7 6 5 4 3 2 1

In what will the history of a party consist? Will it be a simple narrative of the internal life of a political organization? . . . Clearly it will be necessary to take some account of the social group of which the party in question is the expression and the most advanced element.

—Antonio Gramsci, *Selections from the Prison Notebooks*

All the New Right has done is copy the success of the old left.

—Richard Viguerie, *The New Right: We're Ready to Lead*

Contents

Acknowledgments

As I have toiled for far too long on this book, let me begin with a round of appreciation to absolutely everyone who has pointedly, and often reproachfully, asked me when I might finally finish. Extraordinary scholars supervised the dissertation from which this book arose. Theda Skocpol, my advisor, trained me that thinking historically and thinking rigorously go hand in hand. She has watched over this project since its gestation. Without her, it would have been done badly—or not at all. Andrea Campbell, ever supportive, taught me to turn concepts into prose, not least by learning what should get left on the cutting-room floor. Eric Schickler combines deep knowledge about American political history, wide-ranging interests in political science, and remarkable good cheer. Sid Verba has rare wisdom about many subjects academic and otherwise. I would be a better scholar and person if I took all his advice—at least I've now followed his dictum to "get it done."

My thinking on religion owes much to the Saguaro Seminar, and particularly to Valerie Lewis and Robert Putnam. My colleagues at Johns Hopkins University have provided a wonderful environment in which to complete this book. I thank Bentley Allan, Joe Cooper, Matt Crenson, Ben Ginsberg, Adam Sheingate, Lester Spence, Steve Teles, Chloe Thurston, and Emily Zackin for all their thoughts on the manuscript.

Over the years, more discussants, panelists, and friends than I can recount have offered thoughts or have read particular sections. Dorian Warren offered detailed notes on the labor chapters. Paul Frymer and David Karol traveled to Baltimore for an extremely stimulating book conference that helped me to clarify the argument. Entirely unbidden, several special people read the entire manuscript: John Corcoran (every liberal should have so steadfast a right-wing friend), Colin Moore (who also provided a beachside tutorial on the political development of Hawaii), Sam Rosenfeld (whose combination of political historian and editor gave this book its title), and Kay Schlozman (thanks, Mom). Dan Galvin and an anonymous reviewer provided extensive and helpful comments for Princeton University Press. As only those who saw early drafts could possibly understand, the concepts and the prose alike owe much to their now-virtual red pencils. At the press, the editor, Eric Crahan, Jenny Wolkowicki, and Joseph Dahm skillfully brought the book into print.

For more than a decade, I spent my spare hours doing party politics, and even served a term as chair of the Cambridge (Mass.) Democratic City Committee. I count all the mornings holding signs in the cold, and all the nights on folding chairs in storefront offices, as my real education in politics. So many mentors taught me how to play the game—and, still more important, why it's worth the good fight—among them Mo Barbosa, Jarrett Barrios, Donna Barry, Larry Field, Helen Glikman, Avi Green, Elaine Kistiakowsky, Gerry McDonough, Jesse Mermell, K.D. Mernin, Mark Puleo, Trellis Stepter, and Alice Wolf. I especially remember Brian Murphy, whom we lost far too soon.

Finally, I thank my family. My sister, Julia, bucked up my spirits and listened to tale after tale of political intrigue. My parents, Kay and Stan Schlozman, offered equal and opposite contributions: my mother has always taken me and my ideas seriously; my father has never taken me too seriously. In the fall of 1934, at the tender age of fifteen, my grandfather, Elliot Lehman, moved from one seedbed of the New Deal to the other. After graduating from DeWitt Clinton High School in New York City, he headed off to the University of Wisconsin. His father thought that Elliot would be looked after in Madison by a cousin on the faculty, the labor economist Selig Perlman. (That very spring, I recently learned, Perlman had supervised the senior thesis of Wilbur Cohen, soon to become "Mr. Social Security.") As it transpired, Cousin Selig was too busy writing about the job consciousness of American trade unions—a concept that returns in the pages that follow—to pay Elliot much heed. However, Elliot soon met a whip-smart Chicagoan named Frances Mecklenburger, and they recently celebrated their seventy-fourth anniversary. So, as the circle comes round, I dedicate this book to my grandparents, lifelong New Deal Democrats all: to the memory of Mary and Morris Schlozman, and to Frances and Elliot Lehman.

Abbreviations

ABL	American Bimetallic League
ACTV	American Coalition for Traditional Values
ACWA	Amalgamated Clothing Workers of America
ADA	Americans for Democratic Action
AFL/AF of L	American Federation of Labor
AFL-CIO	American Federation of Labor and Congress of Industrial Organizations
AFSCME	American Federation of State, County & Municipal Employees
AFT	American Federation of Teachers
ALP	American Labor Party
CBN	Christian Broadcasting Network
CIO	Congress of Industrial Organizations (from 1935 to 1938, Committee for Industrial Organization)
CIO-PAC	CIO–Political Action Committee
CNP	Council for National Policy
COPE	Committee on Political Education (of the AFL-CIO)
CP	Communist Party of the United States of America
CSFC	Committee for the Survival of a Free Congress
DNC	Democratic National Committee
EFCA	Employee Free Choice Act
ERA	Equal Rights Amendment
ERLC	Ethics & Religious Liberty Commission (of the Southern Baptist Convention)
FEPC	Fair Employment Practices Committee

ILGWU	International Ladies' Garment Workers' Union
ILWU	International Longshoremen's and Warehousemen's Union
IUE	International Union of Electrical, Radio and Machine Workers
LLPE	Labor's League for Political Education
LNPL	Labor's Non-Partisan League
NAACP	National Association for the Advancement of Colored People
NC-PAC	National Citizens Political Action Committee
NCPAC	National Conservative Political Action Committee
NEA	National Education Association
NIRA	National Industrial Recovery Act
NLRA	National Labor Relations Act
NLRB	National Labor Relations Board
NRTWC	National Right to Work Committee
PAC	Political Action Committee
PATCO	Professional Air Traffic Controllers Organization
PCA	Progressive Citizens of America
RAVCO	Richard Viguerie Company
RNC	Republican National Committee
SBC	Southern Baptist Convention
SEIU	Service Employees International Union
SP	Socialist Party of America
UAW	United Automobile Workers
UE	United Electrical, Radio and Machine Workers of America
UMW	United Mine Workers of America
UPWA	United Public Workers of America
USWA	United Steelworkers of America
YAF	Young Americans for Freedom

When Movements Anchor Parties

CHAPTER 1

Introduction

THE MAKING OF ANCHORING GROUPS

"CLEAR IT WITH SIDNEY." THE TIME WAS JULY 1944, A WEEK BEFORE THE Democratic National Convention in Chicago. The Sidney was Sidney Hillman, president of the Amalgamated Clothing Workers of America and chairman of the Congress of Industrial Organizations' Political Action Committee. The speaker was said to be Franklin Delano Roosevelt, instructing Robert Hannegan, chairman of the Democratic National Committee and a St. Louis pol, to get Hillman's approval before selecting a vice presidential nominee to replace the erratic Henry Wallace. As a Republican catchphrase, the slogan aimed to show FDR in the pocket of sinister elements sympathetic to communism. Exactly what Roosevelt told Hannegan remains frustratingly out of reach; the evidence is stronger that Hillman quashed the nomination of Jimmy Byrnes, a conservative from South Carolina, than that he affirmatively approved Harry Truman.

Whatever the particulars, granting something like a veto over the year's most important political decision to the leader of a small men's clothing union, an immigrant with a thick Eastern European accent, confirmed major shifts in both the Democratic Party and the labor movement. Wallace having become unacceptable to southern conservatives, the party regulars—Hannegan and his pals in other big-city organizations—sought a candidate who would satisfy all factions, including labor. The new reality was clear. As a leftist magazine explained, "there was a deeper reason for the choice of Senator Truman: he was the only candidate on whom both the conservative pro-Roosevelt elements and the most advanced labor groups could agree."[1] For the labor movement, the moment marked a turning

[1] A. B. Magil, "Why They Chose FDR, Truman," *New Masses*, 1 August 1944, 6.

point: the breakaway CIO had abandoned organized labor's long-standing practice and, through CIO-PAC, embraced party politics to press for broad social legislation that would benefit all workers.

"I know you can't endorse *me*. But . . . I want you to know that I endorse *you*." The date was 22 August 1980. The speaker was Ronald Reagan. The place was the National Affairs Briefing, a gathering of fifteen thousand conservative evangelicals organized by a who's who of the emergent Christian Right and its allies in the conservative movement. And the line was hardly spontaneous: James Robison, a Fort Worth televangelist who entered politics the previous year when his program had been yanked from the local station after he discussed homosexuals recruiting children, had fed it to Reagan in a meeting on the way from the airport.[2]

The National Affairs Briefing represented a major departure for white evangelicals, who had long shied away from direct engagement in party politics and from alliances that crossed sectarian boundaries. The Dallas event heralded the shift. As Robison told the crowd just before Reagan spoke, "I'm sick and tired of hearing about all of the radicals and the perverts and the liberals and the leftists and the Communists coming out of the closet. It's time for God's people to come out of the closet." Six members of Congress, Republicans all, addressed the crowd; New Right political guru, Paul Weyrich, an Eastern Rite Catholic, spoke on emulating liberals' organization; Phyllis Schlafly, also Catholic, denounced the Equal Rights Amendment; Paige Patterson, a driving force behind the conservative takeover of the Southern Baptist Convention, addressed how "The Bible Sets the Agenda"; and a Georgia judge spoke on "Scientific Creationism."[3] The Republican Party, too, had begun to shift. In the 1970s, surveys show, Republicans favored fewer restrictions on abortion than did Democrats.[4] Yet the party had begun to expand its issue agenda, emphasizing social issues such as abortion, homosexuality, and school prayer, and linking them to the embrace of traditional American values.

Political Parties and Social Movements

Each gathering marked a pivotal juncture in alliance—that is, institutionalized accommodation of mutual priorities—between what I term an

[2]William Martin, *With God on Our Side: The Rise of the Religious Right in America*, rev. ed. (New York: Broadway Books, 2005), 216; Allen J. Mayer, "A Tide of Born-Again Politics," *Newsweek*, 15 September 1980, 28.

[3]Howell Raines, "Reagan Backs Evangelicals in Their Political Activities," *New York Times*, 23 August 1980, 8; Box 4, Religious Roundtable file, unprocessed accretion of September 1986, Papers of Paul M. Weyrich, American Heritage Center, Laramie, Wyo.

[4]Greg D. Adams, "Abortion: Evidence of an Issue Evolution," *American Journal of Political Science* 41 (1997): 730.

"anchoring group" and a major political party. Anchoring groups are organized actors that forego autonomous action to ally with major political parties. Inside parties, anchoring groups exercise broad influence on national politics by virtue of the money, votes, and networks that they offer to the party with which they have allied. Just as other influential actors may keep would-be anchors outside the party, anchoring groups control the entrance into the partisan coalition of new claimants. More than just a logroll, anchoring groups shape parties' long-term trajectories by enacting favored policies and shaping parties' ideological development.

This book offers a new framework for understanding party development from the Civil War to the present day, emphasizing the crucial role of social movements. Repeatedly, movements have redefined the fundamental alignments of political parties and, in turn, the organizable alternatives in national politics. The alliances between labor and the Democrats, and the Christian Right and the Republicans have defined parties' basic priorities, and exerted long-term influence away from the median voter. The two alliances' fates have proceeded in close parallel with each other. Still more important, they diverged sharply from those of major social movements that failed to find and to maintain a stable place inside political parties.

Mass movements and mass parties emerged together at the dawn of modern democracy, as means for ordinary citizens to influence the state. In the United States, these developments define the Jacksonian era; in Europe, they began in the Age of Revolution and quickened through the nineteenth century.[5] Movements and parties share a common history—but they hold very different roles, and operate on different time horizons.

Social movements hold special possibility to disrupt the terms of debate and expand ideological horizons. The movements in this study have all offered public philosophies that reframe basic questions asked since the founding. Each has thrust into party politics conflictual, moralistic traditions of

[5] For macrohistorical context, see Charles Tilly, "Social Movements and National Politics," in *Statemaking and Social Movements: Essays in History and Theory*, ed. Charles Bright and Susan Harding (Ann Arbor: University of Michigan Press, 1984), 297–317; Charles Tilly, *Social Movements, 1768–2004* (Boulder, Colo.: Paradigm, 2004), chap. 2; Ira Katznelson and Aristide R. Zolberg, eds., *Working-Class Formation: Nineteenth Century Patterns in Western Europe and the United States* (Princeton: Princeton University Press, 1986); and Seymour Martin Lipset and Stein Rokkan, "Cleavage Structures, Party Systems, and Voter Alignments: An Introduction," in *Party Systems and Voter Alignments: Cross-National Perspectives*, ed. Seymour Martin Lipset and Stein Rokkan (New York: Free Press, 1967), 1–64. In Tilly's definition ("Social Movements and National Politics," 306), "A social movement is a sustained series of interactions between powerholders and persons successfully claiming to speak on behalf of a constituency lacking formal representation, in the course of which those persons make publicly visible demands for change in the distribution or exercise of power, and back those demands with public demonstrations of support." This definition offers a more concrete understanding of power than that in his 2004 book.

reform, protest, and dissent.[6] Social movements seek radical change—but they cannot simply institutionalize their visions and call it victory. Instead, the American electoral system agglomerates social cleavages inside parties. Given the realities of the Electoral College and a first-past-the-post voting system, movements that seek durable change in the state and its priorities must confront political parties.

"A political party," wrote E. E. Schattschneider in 1942, "is an organized attempt to get control of the government."[7] This venerable definition zeroes in on the goal of parties, and of parties alone. Because political parties organize social conflict—the sine qua non of a democratic party system[8]—they also structure the possibilities for movements to achieve ongoing influence. Movements for fundamental change in American society seek influence through alliance, by serving as anchoring groups to sympathetic parties, because parties hold the special capacity to control the government and its resources, and to define the organizable alternatives in public life.

Through the votes, and networks that they offer to allied parties, anchoring groups gain influence when they ally with a party—but they also gain the power to mold ideological possibilities in republican government. Just as Felix Frankfurter once said of Franklin Roosevelt, anchoring groups "take the country to school" as they inject ideas into partisan politics.[9] So, too, anchoring groups loom largest in coalition management, allowing into parties' orbit only partners whose visions can be rendered compatible with their own. These patterns link together: social movements inject foundational ideas into the party system, which then defines the democratic questions to which partisans offer differing answers.[10]

Movements join with political parties only on terms acceptable to winning coalitions inside those parties. Political parties want to win election. Otherwise, the politicians and interests that constitute them have no hope of wielding power or setting policy. And pragmatists inside party coalitions know this lesson best of all. Parties accept alliance only with the support of a winning coalition inside the party, including hard-nosed realists as well as ideological sympathizers. If the movement threatens the pragmatists' core interests, whether electoral or pecuniary, then the party seeks other paths

[6]Seymour Martin Lipset, "Third Parties and Social Movements," *Dialogue* 5 (1972): 3–8; cf. Gunnar Myrdal, *An American Dilemma: The Negro Problem and Modern Democracy*, vol. 1 (New York: Harper and Row, 1944), chap. 1; Samuel P. Huntington, *American Politics: The Promise of Disharmony* (Cambridge, Mass.: Belknap, 1982), chap. 2.

[7]E. E. Schattschneider, *Party Government* (New York: Rinehart, 1942), lix.

[8]The canonical statement is V. O. Key, Jr., *Southern Politics in State and Nation* (New York: Knopf, 1949), chap. 14.

[9]Quoted in Marc Landy and Sidney M. Milkis, *Presidential Greatness* (Lawrence: University Press of Kansas, 2000), 158.

[10]See Nancy L. Rosenblum, *On the Side of the Angels: An Appreciation of Parties and Partisanship* (Princeton: Princeton University Press, 2008).

to majority. No movements that meet the terms parties set, no alliance. If parties believe that movement radicals imperil their electoral prospects, then movement moderates must jettison their brethren if they want to sustain alliance with a major party. Anchoring groups pay a high price to join together with parties. Yet given the rules of the game, it is a price well worth paying.[11]

In a two-party system, it takes a majority to win election and gain access to the levers of power. Alliance requires parties, including pragmatists as well as strong sympathizers, to believe that they can win an ongoing majority with the movement incorporated. Parties must perceive that movements offer them votes and the resources needed to get votes—time, money, and access to networks—to make alliance a beneficial proposition. When movements knit together effective organizations, often politicizing face-to-face networks and exploiting new technology, then parties will find them attractive partners. When they fall apart, parties will swoop in, and organize their supporters directly.

Parties and movements cannot magically join together. While conditions present the opportunity for elites to forge alliance, the real work falls to brokers, midlevel figures with deep ties spanning party and movement. They build coalitions from neither the top down nor the bottom up, but from the inside out and the outside in, stitching together different blocs of supporters and finding policies and candidates with appeal across them. Brokers lower transaction costs, explaining to parties the deal that makes alliance work for both sides: use of the movement's grassroots networks to offer the party electoral support, in return for the party delivering on the movement's substantive priorities.

Over time, parties have lost their monopoly over political resources. They have relied increasingly on outside partners who provide the money, time, and networks required to win office. Those outside groups, for their part, demand policy payback—what I term "ideological patronage"[12]—in return for their support, pushing parties away from the median voter. Through this dynamic, anchoring groups and their competing ideological agendas lie at the roots of polarized politics.

Two Transformative Alliances

The reciprocal processes by which organized labor came together with the Democratic Party, and the Christian Right joined with the Republican

[11] Cf. Paul Frymer, *Uneasy Alliances: Race and Party Competition in America* (Princeton: Princeton University Press, 1999), discussed in the conclusion.

[12] I have taken the term from Sidney M. Milkis, *The President and the Parties: The Transformation of the American Party System since the New Deal* (New York: Oxford University Press, 1993), 57.

Party demonstrate remarkable similarities.[13] Although the cases may seem disparate—a movement of the left centered on the job site and a movement of the right centered in the church—no other social movements have built such broad and deep relationships with political parties over such a long stretch of time. Religion and work, defining sources of meaning in modern life, have animated these alliances. Rather than taking each in isolation and emphasizing its particular telos, systematic comparison emphasizes their similarities as organizers of political conflict.

Both alliances built on connections and alignments adumbrated in prior campaigns. In 1908 and 1916, the American Federation of Labor supported Democratic presidential candidates in exchange for promises to limit labor injunctions. "Fighting Bob" La Follette's third-party insurgency in 1924 brought together many of the key supporters of labor-liberalism in the coming decade: old Progressives from the West and the settlement houses, moderate socialists, and labor unions. So, too, the networks forged among conservative activists in the Goldwater campaign and the Young Americans for Freedom formed the nucleus of the political New Right. Yet these early efforts hardly resembled full-blown party-group alliance.

In 1936 and in 1980, anchoring groups mounted large-scale, nominally independent, efforts to elect realigning presidents. Group leaders vouched for the candidates, as they gave entrée into voting blocs not yet cemented in their partisan loyalties. Labor's Non-Partisan League, spearheaded by John L. Lewis of the United Mine Workers, spent millions to reelect Franklin Roosevelt. In 1980, Jerry Falwell's Moral Majority, along with other new groups such as Christian Voice, sought to rouse the "sleeping giant" of American evangelicals against the born-again Jimmy Carter, whom they viewed as a failure in office. However unsophisticated in the mechanics of electioneering they may have been, these efforts set out the leading edges of campaigns to reframe electoral coalitions and Americans' expectations of the state.

Amid convulsive social change, midlevel entrepreneurs from both party and movement took advantage of opportunities around galvanizing events to politicize key actors in civil society and meld internal group and broader partisan cleavages. In 1935, John L. Lewis stomped out of the AF of L convention in Atlantic City after punching the Carpenters' "Big Bill" Hutcheson in the jaw. He formed the Congress of Industrial Organizations to embrace

[13] I use the term "Christian Right" as opposed to "Religious Right" to note the movement's particular religion. The term "conservative" has different meanings in religious and political contexts, and in upper- and lowercase, while the term "profamily," often used in movement circles, converts a valence issue—the family—into a position issue. "Christian Right," however imperfect, seems the best shorthand to describe a complex and multifaceted set of leaders and mass publics evolving over decades.

positions long anathema to the federation: to "organize the unorganized" in industrial unions, and to fight for social legislation that would benefit all workers, organized or not. In 1979, conservatives began their takeover of the Southern Baptist Convention, the nation's largest Protestant denomination, committing the SBC to a platform of biblical inerrancy—and also, for the first time, to opposing abortion rights and the Equal Rights Amendment.

More than realigning presidents, midlevel brokers such as Hillman and Weyrich, located at key sites of power across the sprawling American state, made alliance. Young movement loyalists and their intellectual allies moved into government, aggressively staffing up the New Deal administrative state, and decades later attempting to channel hiring, regulations, and rulemaking to new ends. The executive branch followed the dictum of New Right operative turned Reagan aide Morton Blackwell, who expressly emulated Franklin Roosevelt: "personnel is policy."[14]

In Congress, partisan brokers reached out to give the movement space to organize, and to demonstrate the rewards for involvement. The key figure in the Second New Deal of 1935 was Senator Robert F. Wagner of New York, the loyal Democrat who wrote the law guaranteeing most workers the right to bargain collectively. In the late 1970s and 1980s, a passel of congressional conservatives stopped the Carter administration from revoking tax exemptions for discriminatory schools formed in the wake of school desegregation (so-called seg academies) and banned federal dollars for abortions. Later, they enacted a universal child tax credit, and banned abortions by intact dilation and extraction.

Cementing the partnerships between movements and parties took further, less-dramatic rounds of institution building. Labor and the Christian Right routinized the coming together first effected in moments of ideological tumult. As movements sought to prove themselves as responsible partners even in politically unfriendly times, they discarded troublesome voices—communists in the one instance, millennialists and televangelists in the other—and shifted toward maintaining ongoing influence *inside* political parties.

After disillusion and defeat—the devastating 1942 midterm elections, and the collapse of the Moral Majority amid policy drift in the late Reagan years—savvier leaders, with deep ties in party as well as movement circles formed new groups to lead effective political efforts. Supporters and opponents alike tagged them as vote-getting machines. Even as they espoused fundamental visions of social change, many radical elements ultimately accepted the rationale for working inside a political party. Sidney Hillman

[14]Quoted in Becky Norton Dunlop, "The Role of the White House Office of Presidential Personnel," in *Steering the Elephant: How Washington Works*, ed. Robert Rector and Michael Sanera (New York: Universe, 1987), 145.

founded CIO-PAC for the 1944 elections. It matured politically—and was joined by Labor's League for Political Education from the AF of L—in 1948, when labor helped mastermind Harry Truman's unlikely victory. Although Pat Robertson failed to win a single state in his 1988 run for the GOP nomination, he brought hundreds of thousands of evangelicals and Pentecostals into electoral politics for the first time. They served as the base for the Christian Coalition, which he formed in 1989 with the young GOP operative Ralph Reed. CIO-PAC and the Christian Coalition established ties with political parties far closer than those of their predecessor organizations.

In return, the anchoring groups have wielded effective vetoes on important appointments—to the vice presidency or the Supreme Court. Especially when anchoring groups have leveraged other bases of support inside party coalitions, they have achieved victories against long odds. Labor has protected the welfare state and pushed toward full employment. The Christian Right has funneled public dollars into faith-based programs, appointing a phalanx of conservative judges, and gaining a public role for faith. Nevertheless, cherished policy hopes—reformed labor law, a ban on abortions—have remained unmet.

Alliance has always had internal opponents, even in friendly parties. Libertarian-minded conservatives, worried about the loyalties of tolerant young people, may abandon the Christian Right on issues around gay rights.  Similarly, Democrats for Education Reform now seeks to place teachers' unions and their inflexible ways at the center of education policy debates, asking Democrats about the price of some of their most loyal backers.

Courts critically shaped the process of party-group alliance. For unions, the story happened earlier in their life cycle. The labor injunction and restrictions from the Commerce and Due Process Clauses had long constrained both unions and social-welfare legislation. These hostile realities in the late nineteenth and early twentieth centuries nurtured Gompersian voluntarism, with workers extracting benefits directly from employers. When the Supreme Court upheld the National Labor Relations Act in 1937, it opened the door for unions to safeguard the interests of all workers, without fear of losing their special privileges. For its part, anger at Supreme Court decisions on abortion and school prayer helped to mobilize the Christian Right into politics. This focus has remained in the decades since, encompassing both legal strategies through conservative legal organizations, as well as political activism around court decisions, the role of judging, and even the rules for judicial selection.

Albeit in different ways, racial politics centrally shaped the trajectories of both these alliances, whose formation bracketed the civil rights years. Southern opposition to labor, predicated on the fear that strong unions threatened Jim Crow, sharply limited the reach of labor-liberalism, and pushed unions inward to defend their prerogatives and seek benefits through the private welfare state as the conservative coalition in Congress blocked public programs. A generation later, the crumbling of the Solid South and "white backlash" created possibilities for evangelicals regardless of region to ally with the Republican Party. Two critical episodes—the passage of the Taft-Hartley Act over Truman's veto in 1947, with support from southern Democrats as well as Republicans, and the controversy over the IRS's plans to revoke the tax exemptions of racially discriminatory schools in 1978—demonstrate the ways that racial politics impinged on issues of class and religion respectively.

As movements became fully incorporated into partisan politics, they lost the fringes unacceptable to their partisan allies and forswore sweeping notions of a renewed society. Movement moderates—although not, to be sure, moderates in the system as a whole—oversaw multilevel bargains that sprawled across campaigns, appointments, and policies. Anchoring groups have represented, in many instances, the most radical voices included inside the party system. Yet if 1935 and 1979 signaled the rise of ideologues pushing groups into large-scale issues about where society ought to go, then 1948, especially, and 1989 represented victories for accommodation as majorities proved harder to build. Partial victories inside the system prevailed over more sweeping visions of industrial democracy or a Christian America. Despite predictions, in rocky patches, that alliance would soon end in divorce or oblivion, these partnerships continue to shape the Democratic and Republican Parties, and their responses to fundamental questions about the kind of society in which Americans seek to live.

Outline

The coming chapters develop these themes. Part I asks why movements get inside, or remain frozen outside, the party system. Part II then asks why movements stay inside, or are forced outside, the party system. Each part begins with the story of organized labor and the Democrats, moves onto that of the Christian Right and the Republicans, and finally considers "shadow cases" of movements that failed respectively to ally and to consolidate alliance with major parties. The book moves progressively through the process of alliance rather than chronologically through historical time. By moving the narrative forward in alliance time, the sequence highlights how the same mechanisms of party-movement alliance have played out across very different eras.

Chapter 2 lays out a framework to analyze the confrontations of parties and movements. Political parties accept alliance with potential anchoring groups only when winning coalitions inside those parties see the path to ongoing electoral majority with the anchoring group incorporated. They

TABLE 1.1
POTENTIAL ALLIANCES BETWEEN PARTIES AND MOVEMENTS

Movement	Party	Elections	Outcome
Abolitionism	Republicans	1860–96	Incorporated but not consolidated
Populism	Democrats	1892, 1896	Not incorporated
Labor-CIO	Democrats	1936–present	Incorporated and consolidated
Anti–Vietnam War	Democrats	1968, 1972	Not incorporated
Christian Right	Republicans	1980–present	Incorporated and consolidated

see that path, in turn, when the anchoring group does not threaten their core interests, and when it is sufficiently organized so as to offer electoral incentives—votes, money, time, and networks—unavailable to the party if it mobilizes movement supporters directly. When powerful forces inside parties exercise their blocking power to exclude movements, then movements face nearly impossible odds to institutionalize themselves, or to find their ideological visions a place in ongoing political contestation.

The following chapters apply that structure to critical episodes of party development at each major realignment in the American party system. Table 1.1 lists the five potential alliances between movement and party that this book explores, the presidential elections in which movements played a role, and then the ultimate outcome of alliance in the party system.

Part I examines the moments when major social movements mobilized politically quiescent publics and first confronted political parties. Chapter 3 explores the alliance of organized labor and the Democratic Party in the New Deal years. The breakaway Congress of Industrial Organizations reversed the long-standing philosophy of the American Federation of Labor to eschew partisan politics, and simply "reward its friends and punish its enemies." The Wagner Act gave state sanction to labor unions, and required employers to recognize and bargain with representatives of workers' own choosing. Newly emboldened by a sympathetic state, the CIO embraced industrial unionism and the welfare state, and opened its treasury and mobilized its members on behalf of sympathetic candidates, beginning with Franklin Roosevelt's landslide reelection in 1936.

Chapter 4 considers the entrance into Republican Party politics of white evangelicals during the late 1970s. New Right brokers, led by the direct mail wizard Richard Viguerie and the Coors-funded organizer Paul Weyrich, sought out evangelicals as the crucial new component of a lasting conservative majority, culminating in the founding of Jerry Falwell's Moral Majority in 1979. The New Right demonstrated to evangelicals how electoral politics impinged on their religious practice—and then mobilized them on the basis of perceived threat.

Chapter 5 tackles two great failures, movements that fell apart before their remnants ended up in the Democratic fold: Populism in the 1880s and 1890s, and the antiwar movement of the 1960s. In each instance, at the moment of movements' greatest strength, parties would not accept alliance with actors they deemed injurious to their core interests. By the time the parties began to come around, movement organization had dissipated and any possibilities for a national majority had vanished. The Silverite remnants of the Populist crusade merged into the Democrats in 1896, while the antiwar senator George McGovern won the presidential nomination in 1972 only after the movement had splintered and the public had tired of casualties in Vietnam. With Populism died the most serious challenge to corporate capitalism that United States would ever see. Although its personnel occupied positions at the top of the Democratic Party for decades, the antiwar movement failed to restrain American empire or reorient American democracy toward a more authentic politics.

Part II treats parties and anchoring groups further in their life cycle. Over time, movement energy dissipates into the ongoing back-and-forth of ordinary politics. The extraordinary circumstances that propelled initial victories recede, even as fundamental controversies from formative moments remain touchstones of partisan division. Majorities prove evanescent and other actors inside parties grow wary. Movements focus on the imperatives of organizational maintenance, exercising influence inside parties and protecting their policy victories even when they cannot realize their visions for a transformed society. To that end, they attempt to build with their partisan partners virtuous circles that trade policy and influence in exchange for votes and the resources that deliver them. Alliance works when those circles benefit both partners, and when other influencers inside the party accept their legitimacy. Should they break down, so does alliance.

Chapters 6 and 7 examine the long alliance between labor and the Democratic Party in the seven decades since the end of the Second World War. As Chapter 6 explains, organized labor cemented its status in the postwar Democratic order, but only at an enormous price. The CIO and, after 1955, the merged AFL-CIO, buoyed Democratic candidates and pushed them toward liberal priorities. At the peak, unions represented more than a third of American workers. Yet it was not the thirties. Congress passed the strongly antilabor Taft-Hartley Act over Harry Truman's veto. The CIO forced out its left-led unions, home of the most talented organizers, when they would not endorse the staunchly anticommunist Truman. And once

Congress blocked expanded pensions and universal health care, unions negotiated benefits at the bargaining table that foreclosed future possibilities for public provision.

Chapter 7 brings the story to the present. Starting in the late 1960s, labor and the Democrats endured their roughest years, tested by Vietnam and the "New Politics." Since the 1970s, the fragile foundations of the postwar order have eroded. Weak federal labor law and a patchwork welfare state, unresolved issues from the Fair Deal years, have reemerged amid conservative resurgence. The divide between party and movement has healed; labor's structural position continues to worsen. Organized labor seeks the same goals as it has for decades: space to organize, and support from the state for all workers. Labor's influence inside an emasculated Democratic coalition remains robust—for now.

Chapter 8 explores the Christian Right as it has matured. The sharp distinctions between party on the one hand and movement on the other have softened, and group-specific infrastructure has atrophied. A sequence of peak associations—the Moral Majority, ACTV, the Christian Coalition—have flamed out and, with many of the same leaders and direct-mail supporters, re-formed. All the while, Christian conservatives have grown far more influential inside the organizational Republican Party. The GOP, in turn, has increasingly mobilized church-based networks for its candidates directly, without relying on the assistance of group elites. Evangelicals and their allies may eventually serve as a particularly influential party faction rather than as an ongoing anchoring group.

Chapter 9 takes up another case of failed incorporation, albeit from a very different starting point in party politics: after the Civil War and the end of slavery, the abolitionist movement failed to sustain alliance between African Americans and their northern supporters, and a Republican Party dominated by the interests of northern industry. Although perhaps the most consequential alliance in American history, the movement failed to sustain effective infrastructure in the North, nor did it forge effective links between the freedmen and northern supporters of the Union cause. What began as a social movement died in high politics. In Reconstruction and after, alliance frayed as the Republican Party followed the interests of its core industrialist backers, and forsook its founding heritage.

The conclusion, finally, tackles the problem of writing political history in medias res with some speculation on the future. Both the Occupy movement of 2011 and the Tea Party have aimed to remake American politics. Although the framework presented here helps to make sense of their experience, neither one precisely fits the model of a potential anchoring group—and for rather different reasons. Occupy reveled in its rejection of hierarchical organization and lost any infrastructural capacity before it meaningfully confronted the party system. The Tea Party, for its part, should be understood more as a party faction aiming to take control of a party than as a social movement with independent goals and supporters.

And so history will continue on. Parties will look to outside supporters for various baskets of resources, and welcome or fear new claimants. Citizens seeking to change society will join together in social movements. They will call Americans back to their visions of what its founding demands, and make claims for opinions and on behalf of social groups often heretofore invisible. Yet they will do so inside a framework that imposes harsh limits on party and movement alike. Parties will have to cobble together majorities from diffuse collections of minorities. Movements will have to hold specific influence over supporters in order to induce parties to move far from the median and include them in their fold. Whatever the issues and whomever the players, when major social movements confront parties, the stakes will remain high. As long as political parties determine competing alternative visions in public life, the entrance into party politics of social movements making radical claims will play a critical role in determining the organizable alternatives in American public life.

CHAPTER 2

Political Parties and Social Movements

THE FERTILE AND CONTESTED MEETING GROUND BETWEEN POLITICAL PARTIES and social movements has made and remade American politics. As the incentives of parties to win elections have interacted with the incentives of movements to exert influence, would-be anchoring groups have found their place in or out of the party system. Together, these confrontations between party and movement have shaped parties' long-term ideological trajectories, and defined the possibilities and limits in national politics.

Influencers inside parties are made, not born. Movements cannot simply wish themselves to become anchoring groups inside the party system. Instead, their presence inside—or absence from—parties itself requires explanation. Therefore, rather than simply asking *who* has influence inside political parties, we must ask *how* those influencers got their influence. And asking that question, in turn, requires asking about both who didn't get influence and how, and what difference it has made.

This chapter offers a framework to make sense of the circumstances under which parties will—or will not—ally with a particularly critical category of influencers: the major social movements that confront them. To summarize the argument, political parties have achieved durable alliance with social movements when two conditions intersect. First, winning coalitions inside parties perceive that the party can achieve durable electoral majority with the movement incorporated. Not all these partisan actors, and certainly not the pivotal ones, agree with the movement in all its particulars. Rather, they favor alliance over alternative paths to build the coalitions that will win them elections. Second, for parties to pay movements' price of admission, they must believe that movements control resources—votes, money, and networks—unavailable to parties themselves. That judgment in turn requires serious organization building on movements' part, tying together grassroots supporters with elite brokers whom parties trust to deliver on their electoral bargains.

Specifically, I define that parties achieve alliance with movements when winning coalitions of partisan and movement elites accept the bulk, albeit not the totality, of each other's priorities, and when movements wield legitimate vetoes, over partisan priorities in Congress and presidential nomination, that reorient the party's long-term ideological trajectory.

The coming pages make sense of alliance step by step, proceeding through the logic behind each of these concerns. Social movements and political parties each enter into and then maintain alliance under constrained circumstances that have interacted with changing patterns of political conflict across time and between the parties.

Social Movements Meet Parties

The contested meeting point between social movements and political parties, relatively little theorized, comes at a moment in the life cycle after the questions usually asked about social movements, and before the questions usually asked about parties. Yet it crucially determines critical variables for scholars of movements and of parties: the institutionalization (or dissolution) of social movements, and the place of groups in the party system.

By the point in their development when they confront the party system, movements must have already framed issues, catalyzed members, and cultivated allies.[1] Those are tall orders, and research beginning with movements' origins would undoubtedly emphasize different variables. Some movements may, in a relative instant and at critical junctures for a political regime, influence mainstream actors, who preempt, co-opt, institutionalize, or otherwise respond to movement demands. At such moments, structural opportunities hold far more sway than any factors internal to movements. The Townsend movement, which pushed for generous universal pensions in the 1930s, serves as a particularly apt example.[2]

[1] See, e.g., Doug McAdam, Sidney Tarrow, and Charles Tilly, *Dynamics of Contention* (New York: Cambridge University Press, 2001); Doug McAdam, *Political Process and the Development of Black Insurgency*, 2nd ed. (Chicago: University of Chicago Press, 1999); Doug McAdam, John D. McCarthy, and Mayer N. Zald, "Social Movements," in *Handbook of Sociology*, ed. Neil Smelser (Newbury Park, Calif.: Sage, 1988), 695–737; Sidney Tarrow, "States and Opportunities: The Political Structuring of Social Movements," in *Comparative Perspectives on Social Movements: Political Opportunities, Mobilizing Structures, and Cultural Framings*, ed. Doug McAdam, John D. McCarthy, and Mayer N. Zald (Cambridge: Cambridge University Press, 1996), 41–61; Bert Useem and Mayer N. Zald, "From Pressure Group to Social Movement: Organizational Dilemmas of the Effort to Promote Nuclear Power," *Social Problems* 30 (1982): 144–56.

[2] See the important dispute between William Gamson and Jack Goldstone on goals, tactics, and organization, as opposed to structural opportunities, in determining movement outcomes; reprinted in William Gamson, *The Strategy of Social Protest*, 2nd ed. (Belmont,

Nevertheless, the story here continues beyond the point where most scholars of American social movements leave off: as movements struggle to join forces with mainstream allies, win recognition from the state, and find their place in ongoing political contestation. Simply to say that movements institutionalize or that they switch to conventional tactics avoids hard questions about the opportunity structure, conditioned above all by the electoral regime, that they face.[3]

Alliance between parties and social movements represents a particularly consequential outcome for movements seeking to reshape American society, but not the only one. Movements represent a minority; they must make an impact that persuades a majority. Robert Dahl, in the concluding chapter of his 1967 textbook, outlined a trilemma of mutually exclusive and exhaustive options:

- "The movement can organize a separate political party."
- "Although it remains neutral between the two major parties, the movement can act as a pressure group to secure favorable legislation and the nomination and election of sympathetic candidates."
- "By entering into one of the existing parties, the movement can become an element in a major party coalition; it can then use its bargaining power to gain influence for the movement within the party."[4]

Even as movement activists continue to debate these alternatives, the first two strategies offer grave perils to movements seeking major social change that impinges on state policies. If both extant parties prove hostile to movement demands and unwilling to accept alliance, a movement may form a third party to supplant them. Only the Republicans in the 1850s have succeeded in displacing a major party. The People's Party in 1892 tried to

---

Calif.: Wadsworth, 1990); and Edwin Amenta, *When Movements Matter: The Townsend Plan and the Rise of Social Security* (Princeton: Princeton University Press, 2006). Soon, however, the Townsendites confronted the party system. Beginning in the 1936 election (and after their peak influence), they followed a pressure-group strategy, endorsing rural Republicans as well as populist Democrats, as they sought universal old-age annuities.

[3] For important exceptions, see Jack A. Goldstone, "Introduction: Bridging Institutionalized and Noninstitutionalized Politics," in *States, Parties, and Social Movements*, ed. Jack A. Goldstone (Cambridge: Cambridge University Press, 2003), 1–24; and Doug McAdam and Sidney Tarrow, "Social Movements and Elections: Toward a Broader Understanding of the Political Context of Contention," in *The Future of Social Movement Research: Dynamics, Mechanisms, and Processes*, ed. Jacquelien van Stekelenburg, Conny Roggeband, and Bert Klandermans (Minneapolis: University of Minnesota Press: 2013), 325–46. To be sure, the march toward institutionalization is not universal. In a few instances (parts of the New Left, for example) radical cadres may direct movements further toward militant protest. For a typology, see Hanspeter Kriesi, "The Organizational Structure of New Social Movements in a Political Context," in McAdam, McCarthy, and Zald, *Comparative Perspectives*, 157.

[4] Robert Dahl, *Pluralist Democracy in the United States: Conflict and Consent* (Chicago: Rand McNally, 1967), 429–30. Dahl further distinguishes between single-issue third parties such as the Greenbackers and third-party coalitions such as the Progressives of 1924.

disrupt the existing parties, but failed. In the twentieth century, even as maximalists occasionally dreamed of a third party, unconnected outsiders promising to clean up political messes largely supplanted social movements in waving the banner for third parties.[5]

As Dahl warned, "a movement that seeks something more than its own group interests may conclude that as a pure pressure group it will exert too limited an influence over the policies of the American republic."[6] And so it was for each of these atypically consequential movements. The vast majority of groups eyeing the American party system debate trade-offs between strategies that emphasize, in various measure, working inside a single party or else lobbying both parties.[7] Although minimalists advocated incremental lobbying strategies, movement leaders in every instance explored here recognized the power of the party system to enact policy and define alternatives. Instead, the real challenge has come not in choosing strategy but in implementing it, as movements have struggled to find the allies and build the infrastructure that allows them to attain and maintain a place in the party system.

Maximalists who prize movement autonomy and confrontational tactics may also wish to elide the trilemma altogether, and continue to agitate from the outside.[8] Such a decision augurs enormous risk. No social movement has sustained effective militancy on a society-wide basis—rather than inside a single organization—over decades. Passions fade; radicals and moderates split; organizations collapse.[9] Windows to enter the party system often open and close quickly.[10] Movements' legacies influence politics even if the movement cannot effectuate alliance, by changing the policy agenda and leaving behind an activist core, but should movements miss their opportunity to

[5] Steven J. Rosenstone, Roy L. Behr, and Edward H. Lazarus, *Third Parties in America: Citizen Response to Major Party Failure*, 2nd ed. (Princeton: Princeton University Press, 1996).

[6] Dahl, *Pluralist Democracy*, 454.

[7] On the relation between parties and interest groups, see E. E. Schattschneider, *The Semi-Sovereign People* (New York: Holt, Rinehart, and Winston, 1960), 54–60; E. E. Schattschneider, "United States: The Functional Approach to Party Government," in *Modern Political Parties: Approaches to Comparative Politics*, ed. Sigmund Neumann (Chicago: University of Chicago Press, 1956), 213–14; V. O. Key, Jr., *Politics, Parties & Pressure Groups*, 5th ed. (New York: Crowell, 1964), 155–61; John Mark Hansen, *Gaining Access: Congress and the Farm Lobby, 1919–1981* (Chicago: University of Chicago Press, 1991), 222–27; and Mildred A. Schwartz, "Interactions between Social Movements and US Political Parties," *Party Politics* 16 (2010): 587–607. For a comparative review, see Elin H. Allern and Tim Bale, "Political Parties and Interest Groups: Disentangling Complex Relationships," *Party Politics* 18 (2012): 7–25.

[8] Frances Fox Piven and Richard A. Cloward, *Poor People's Movements: Why They Succeed, How They Fail* (1977; repr., New York: Vintage Books, 1979).

[9] Albert O. Hirschman, *Shifting Involvements: Private Interest and Public Action* (Princeton: Princeton University Press, 1982).

[10] John W. Kingdon, *Agendas, Alternatives, and Public Policies*, 2nd ed. (New York: Longman, 2003), chap. 8.

transform politics, it rarely comes again. The trilemma is both a choice and an iron cage.

Political Parties Meet Movements

Political parties require resources in order to secure ongoing majorities. Those resources come from other actors, increasingly organized across diffuse "party networks" that link together party organizations, ideologically driven party factions, and pressure groups.[11] Organized groups offer specific influence through social networks that encompass activists and supporters, and resources in money and time beyond the reach of individual activists. Yet those groups, like many issue activists in their ranks, hold views distant from the median, and demand that parties move closer to them in order to access their votes and resources. As Doug McAdam and Karina Kloos write, "When challenged by sustained, national movements attuned to electoral politics, 'playing to the base' can come to be seen as more important strategically than courting the 'median voter.'"[12]

To gain the collective benefits, including party identification and shared electoral resources, that parties provide, politicians accept demands from off-median actors as they compete to win office.[13] Hence, parties seek alliance with movements because movement leaders, with the power to direct resources and frame issues, have access to resources that political parties covet but cannot control directly. Those movement elites, therefore, may use their influence—through access to votes, and the money, time, and networks that help in winning votes, or else the threat of disruptive protest—as ransom with parties seeking to hold and maintain power. In return for providing parties with this access, movements bargain to extract off-median concessions. These may include policy ("ideological patronage"), vetoes over key appointments and positions, public jobs for supporters, esteem and prestige, and access to ongoing state policies. It is a mutually beneficial exchange relationship.[14]

[11] Gregory Koger, Seth Masket, and Hans Noel, "Partisan Webs: Information Exchange and Party Networks," *British Journal of Political Science* 39 (2009): 633–53; Matt Grossmann and Casey B. K. Dominguez, "Party Coalitions and Interest Group Networks," *American Politics Research* 37 (2009): 767–800; Michael T. Heaney, Seth E. Masket, Joanne M. Miller, and Dara Z. Strolovitch, "Polarized Networks: The Organizational Affiliations of National Party Convention Delegates," *American Behavioral Scientist* 56 (2012): 1654–76.

[12] Doug McAdam and Karina Kloos, *Deeply Divided: Racial Politics and Social Movements in Post-war America* (Oxford: Oxford University Press, 2014), 10.

[13] John H. Aldrich, *Why Parties? The Origin and Transformation of Political Parties in America* (Chicago: University of Chicago Press, 1995), 50; he expands on Anthony Downs, *An Economic Theory of Democracy* (Boston: Addison-Wesley, 1957).

[14] John D. May, "Opinion Structure of Political Parties: The Special Law of Curvilinear Disparity," *Political Studies* 21 (1973): 151–73; Thomas Quinn, "Block Voting in the Labour Party: A Political Exchange Model," *Party Politics* 8 (2002): 207–26.

TABLE 2.1
PARTISAN SUPPORT, MOVEMENT CAPACITY, AND ALLIANCE

Alliance	Strength of allies in party	Independent movement capacity	Outcome
Abolition-GOP	Medium (1868) then low	Medium (1868) then low	Incorporated but not consolidated
Populism-Dems	Low	High (1892) then low (1896)	Not incorporated
Labor-Dems	High	High	Incorporated
Antiwar-Dems	Low (1968) then high (1972)	Medium (1968) then low (1972)	Not incorporated
Christian Right-GOP	Medium	High	Incorporated

In such a world, a party develops as a group-oriented, policy-demanding long coalition; this is the powerful insight of research from the past decade.[15] Yet a theory that places high-demanders front and center cannot simply bracket the question of who becomes a high-demander, or of how the answer has changed. Rather, to understand movements and parties fully, we must study them together as they have developed jointly over time.

Table 2.1 applies this framework to the episodes of party development explored in the coming chapters. The second column summarizes the strength of movements' allies—that is, the organized actors inside the party who favor alliance over alternative paths to building a majority, whether for reasons of deep sympathy with the movement's project or pragmatic desire for victory and its spoils. The third column offers a capsule assessment of movement elites' capacity to overcome collective action problems and mobilize supporters on behalf of partisan allies. Each anchoring alliance—between organized labor and the Democrats, and the Christian Right and the Republicans—combined support inside the party with strong mobilization capacity.

The other would-be anchoring groups did not achieve that combination, and they could not consolidate long-term incorporation inside parties. The position of the freedmen and their northern allies inside the Republican

[15] Kathleen Bawn, Martin Cohen, David Karol, Seth Masket, Hans Noel, and John Zaller, "A Theory of Political Parties: Groups, Policy Demands and Nominations in American Politics," *Perspectives on Politics* 10 (2012): 571–97; and Martin Cohen, David Karol, Hans Noel, and John Zaller, *The Party Decides: Presidential Nominations Before and After Reform* (Chicago: University of Chicago Press, 2008). See also David Karol, *Party Position Change in American Politics: Coalition Management* (Cambridge: Cambridge University Press, 2009), which emphasizes group allies' leverage over members of Congress.

Party deteriorated as their Radical allies lost sway, and as abolitionist organizations and the Freedmen's Bureau alike folded up their tents, rendering far more difficult the process of mobilization apart from partisan patronage channels. The other two movements never found a stable place inside parties. Populism threatened the Democratic Party, which embraced only its Silverite fringe. The movement transformed itself into a third party in 1892, but by the time it sought fusion (in this book's parlance, alliance) with the Democrats, the cooperatives that sustained it had collapsed, and the Democrats, on their way to an epochal defeat, swooped in to attract its voters while freezing out movement elites. The antiwar movement in 1968 faced a hostile Democratic Party still under the control of hawkish regulars. By 1972, with reformers in the ascendance and the dovish George McGovern the nominee, the movement had splintered apart. Again, albeit on more favorable terms, the party appealed directly to supporters. Only when parties accept movement allies, and movement allies deliver resources, can both sides effectuate durable partnership.

Parties not only link elites and masses, but also shape the contours of political conflict. Together, the "lines of cleavage" that divide and "the outer boundaries" that demarcate parties' positions mark the organizable alternatives at a given historical moment.[16] Realignment theory at its grandest sought to explain both electoral outcomes and the basic issues over which the parties grappled.[17] For a generation, scholars emphasized the former claims, and examined the American party system principally in terms of candidates and elections. Yet the attempt to identify particular critical elections has fallen out of academic favor.

[16]Quotes from respectively James L. Sundquist, *Dynamics of the Party System: Alignment and Realignment of Political Parties in the United States*, rev. ed. (Washington, D.C.: Brookings Institution Press, 1983), 23; and Walter Dean Burnham, *Critical Elections and the Mainsprings of American Politics* (New York: Norton, 1970), 10.

[17]On realignment, see V. O. Key, Jr., "A Theory of Critical Elections," *Journal of Politics* 17 (1955): 3–18; V. O. Key, Jr., "Secular Realignment and the Party System," *Journal of Politics* 21 (1959): 198–210; Schattschneider, *Semisovereign People*, chaps. 4 and 5; Burnham, *Critical Elections*; Jerome M. Clubb, William M. Flanigan, and Nancy H. Zingale, *Partisan Realignment: Voters, Parties, and Government in American History* (Beverly Hills, Calif.: Sage, 1980); Sundquist, *Dynamics*; David Brady, *Critical Elections and Congressional Policy Making* (Stanford: Stanford University Press, 1988); Larry M. Bartels, "Electoral Continuity and Change, 1868–1996," *Electoral Studies* 17 (1998): 301–26; David R. Mayhew, *Electoral Realignments: A Critique of an American Genre* (New Haven: Yale University Press, 2002). For an intellectual history, see Theodore Rosenof, *Realignment: The Theory That Changed the Way We Think about American Politics* (Lanham, Md.: Rowman & Littlefield, 2003). Note that Mayhew attacks principally the claims about critical elections. He interprets partisan alignment primarily in terms of parties' ideological self-presentation (drawing on John Gerring, *Party Ideologies in America, 1828–1996* [Cambridge: Cambridge University Press, 1998]), rather than their representation—or nonrepresentation—of groups or interests. The emphasis on alignments emerges especially from Schattschneider, *Semisovereign People*, chap. 4; and Sundquist, *Dynamics*, chap. 2.

This book takes up the other side of realignment theory, and focuses on alignments—that is, on political parties' competing positions, rooted in coalitional interests.[18] It reinterprets party development through the movement origins of partisan alignments. In every realignment since the 1850s, a potential anchoring group has sought entrance into politics demanding, in the context of the prior political order, radical change. Alignments privilege and discourage conflict along certain issues; they are vulnerable to disruption along some lines but not others. Together alignments define the ideas and interests represented (or nor represented) in the party system. As Samuel Beer wrote of the New Deal years, "one side says 'yes,' the other 'no,' but they are trying to answer the same question."[19]

The era of polarization raises questions of alignment anew. The parties have nationalized, divided on ever more issues, and grown more internally coherent. Activists inside, on the penumbra of, and outside formal parties have forged our conceptions of liberalism and conservatism.[20] Given their size and importance in coalition management, anchoring groups have a special role among the polarizers who have built the contemporary coalitions. Even if the underlying ideas originated earlier and the ultimate effects in roll calls appeared later, anchoring groups have reified substantive disagreements into ideology, and chained them to partisan priorities. The CIO retooled liberalism for the urban worker and injected race into the Democratic coalition, while the Christian Right offered social conservatism in a form maximally acceptable to big and small business alike. Above all anchoring groups have muscle behind their pronouncements: they deploy resources to favored candidates, forcing politicians to respond to these alternative bases of authorities. Anchoring groups are, in short, polarizers with troops.

Patterns of Alliance and American Political Development

As movements have sought allies inside parties and resources to offer to those allies, however, they have done so under highly variant circumstances.

[18]On changing alignments over time, see Sundquist, *Dynamics*; A. James Reichley, *The Life of the Parties: A History of American Political Parties*, updated ed. (Lanham, Md.: Rowman & Littlefield, 2000); Mark D. Brewer and Jeffrey M. Stonecash, *Dynamics of American Political Parties* (Cambridge: Cambridge University Press, 2009).

[19]Samuel H. Beer, "In Search of a New Public Philosophy," in *The New American Political System*, ed. Anthony King (Washington, D.C.: American Enterprise Institute, 1978), 6.

[20]For recent treatments, see Hans Noel, *Political Ideologies and Political Parties in America* (Cambridge: Cambridge University Press, 2013); Katherine Krimmel, "Special Interest Partisanship: The Transformation of American Political Parties" (PhD diss., Columbia University, 2013); and Sam Rosenfeld, "A Choice, Not an Echo: Polarization and the Transformation of the American Party System" (PhD diss., Harvard University, 2014).

Over time, parties have lost their monopoly over the electoral process and become increasingly reliant on resources from outside partners. The available alternatives for would-be anchoring groups have been largely sequential. In the nineteenth century, parties controlled politics, from slating candidates to printing ballots to mobilizing voters. When movements sought to exercise influence inside existing parties, they held few cards against internal opponents—and with little room inside existing parties, often looked instead to form third parties.

After 1896, party competition declined in most regions. Movements harnessed new organizational forms to create pressure groups that lobbied both parties. Since the New Deal, traditional political organizations have receded and the parties hollowed out. Since the 1970s, the parties have divided as supporters sorted themselves into rival camps and conflict diffused across institutional boundaries. With their reach exceeding their grasp, parties have looked to movements to gain resources and reach out to supporters. A surfeit of alliances between parties and movements uniquely define the warring camps in contemporary politics.

These patterns have abraded against consistent differences between the major parties.[21] Alliances between movements and the diffuse, fractious Democrats have generally emerged from grassroots pressure to which elites have responded. For the relatively more homogeneous Republicans, state sponsorship and party elites' search for a mass base have proven more important. Some history helps to make sense of these trends.

Nineteenth-century politics was party politics.[22] The Jacksonian era established the pattern for mass-based parties eager to reap the rewards of office and fill appointments through the spoils system. Popular enthusiasm sustained the system. Voters turned out in the decades after the Civil War at rates never again equaled, even in a vastly better educated country. Given weak national institutions, parties stitched politics together. State and local bosses and their organizations, with varying institutional bases, jostled against one another, newspaper editors in the partisan press, and the interests that bankrolled them. State legislatures chose senators, who in turn oversaw patronage relationships in the post office and customs house, and into state and local government.

[21] Karen Orren and Stephen Skowronek, *The Search for American Political Development* (Cambridge: Cambridge University Press, 2004).

[22] Joel H. Silbey, *The American Political Nation, 1838–1893* (Stanford: Stanford University Press, 1991); Richard L. McCormick, *The Party Period and Public Policy: American Politics from the Age of Jackson to the Progressive Era* (New York: Oxford University Press, 1986); Michael Holt, "Change and Continuity in the Party Period: The Substance and Structure of American Politics, 1835–1885," in *Contesting Democracy: Substance and Structure in American Political History, 1775–2000*, ed. Byron E. Shafer and Anthony J. Badger (Lawrence: University Press of Kansas, 2001), 93–115.

The tight networks in the nineteenth-century party dominated every facet of American elections, from slating candidates to funding campaigns to printing ballots. Because parties controlled all the resources necessary to wage electoral combat, movements had few inducements to tempt parties into alliance. Groups like the Grand Army of the Republic, veterans of the Union Army, spread the party's message out every bit as much as they applied pressure to it.[23] Just as women, Native Americans, often African Americans (a more complicated case, as Chapter 9 explains), and the organized working class fell outside the parameters of party-led distributive politics, so, too, movement claimants either remained excluded from mainstream politics, or had to enter it on unfavorable terms that rendered them vulnerable when other influential forces in the party clashed with their priorities.

Shut out from major parties, movements typically formed third parties. To prove their bona fides, they displayed the full trappings of party, with national and state officers, and candidates at all levels of government. That is the story of the Free Soil Party—which bolted precisely because a faction of New York Democrats disapproved of its rivals' disposition of patronage—the American Party (the Know Nothings), the nascent Republican Party, the Prohibition Party, and the People's Party (the Populists). For a generation of reformist causes, the Republicans' emergence as a new party exploiting sublimated issue cleavages served as a model, however chimerical. As agricultural prices fell in the decades following the Civil War, third parties moved West, and a series of agrarian radical parties proposed inflationary policies designed to aid indebted farmers.

The defeat of Populism and the victory of the corporate-dominated Republicans in 1896 shifted earlier patterns. Sectionalism and federalism explain much of the puzzle. Elite dominance by the Republicans in the North and the Democrats in the South forestalled party-based mass mobilization. For the American Federation of Labor, as for other advocates—suffragists, prohibitionists—one-party dominance in most states posed a common challenge. Groups' natural allies appeared on both sides of the fence, and paths to systemic change seemed blocked. In states and cities, national alliances could preclude useful local relationships. "To local unionists, a policy of national nonpartisanship meant they could be Democratic in Democratic cities, and Republican in Republican cities."[24]

[23]Theda Skocpol, *Protecting Soldiers and Mothers: The Political Origins of Social Policy in the United States* (Cambridge, Mass.: Belknap, 1993), chap. 2; Mary R. Dearing, *Veterans in Politics: The Story of the G.A.R.* (Baton Rouge: Louisiana State University Press, 1952); Stuart McConnell, *Glorious Contentment: The Grand Army of the Republic, 1865–1900* (Chapel Hill: University of North Carolina Press, 1992).

[24]Michael Rogin, "Voluntarism: The Political Functions of an Antipolitical Doctrine," *Industrial and Labor Relations Review* 15 (1962): 535.

Parties fell from their pedestal, and lost control over basic tasks. The voter initiative, party primary, civil service, and secret (Australian) ballot all served to weaken party organization, dismantle the spoils system that sustained it, and shift campaigns from mass spectacle to individual persuasion. National committees, close to large corporations and the growing executive establishment, centralized fundraising while local organization attenuated.[25]

New actors filled the void as parties retreated. Pressure groups developed new techniques and organizational forms to lobby officials and persuade voters.[26] The Anti-Saloon League, for instance, pioneered direct mail and the voter guide as it worked with sympathetic officials, Republicans in the North and Democrats in the South, first for the local option and then for national prohibition.[27] The Progressive movement, individualistic, led from the upper-middle class, was, by the standard definitions, hardly a social movement at all. While industrial violence flared up from Ludlow to Lawrence, an insulated political system responded more to reformism than to mass agitation.

The New Deal realignment decisively changed these patterns. The Rooseveltian coalition rested on a "three-legged stool." The administrative state, directed by the presidency, placated, sometimes uneasily, the South, big-city bosses, and organized labor. Yet only labor, especially in the CIO, swelled with the children of new-stock immigrants, fully shared the goal of a robust federal government devoted to a modicum of protection against what Roosevelt termed "the hazards and vicissitudes of life." The New Deal state protected workers' rights through the National Labor Relations Board, while labor proved an able defender of programs outside the reach of the traditional, state and locally oriented Democratic organizations.[28]

[25] Michael McGerr, *The Decline of Popular Politics: The American North, 1865–1928* (New York: Oxford University Press, 1986); Harold Gosnell, "Thomas C. Platt—Political Manager," *Political Science Quarterly* 38 (1923): 443–69; Mark Kornbluh, *Why America Stopped Voting: The Decline of Participatory Democracy and the Emergence of Modern American Politics* (New York: New York University Press, 2000); Daniel Klinghard, *The Nationalization of American Political Parties, 1880–1896* (Cambridge: Cambridge University Press, 2010).

[26] Elisabeth S. Clemens, *The People's Lobby: Organizational Innovation and the Rise of Interest Group Politics in the United States* (Chicago: University of Chicago Press, 1997), 17–31. The reforms' ultimate impact—whether as demobilizers of mass politics or creators of responsive government—is a more complicated question.

[27] Peter H. Odegard, *Pressure Politics: The Story of the Anti-Saloon League* (New York: Columbia University Press, 1928); Joseph R. Gusfield, *Symbolic Crusade: Status Politics and the American Temperance Movement*, 2nd ed. (Urbana: University of Illinois Press, 1986), 107–9.

[28] See Sidney M. Milkis, *The President and the Parties: The Transformation of the American Party System since the New Deal* (New York: Oxford University Press, 1993). Milkis suggests a direct link between the growth of ideological patronage and the atrophy of state and local party organizations, but a comparative look at union-party relations in the postwar decades suggests a more complicated story. The UAW's near takeover of the Michigan Democratic Party contrasts with fluid factionalism in New York City and segmentation between pliant

Racial tensions formed under the surface once the Democratic Party married egalitarian commitments with an activist, national state, and first burst out with the Dixiecrat bolt of 1948. By the 1960s, the three-legged stool had collapsed. Civil rights nationalized politics. Sectionalism and federalism, the old confounders, retreated. Traditional political organizations, labor's friends and rivals both across the New Deal era, finally expired. Professional advocacy in Washington exploded. When new groups sought to enter politics, first on the left and then on the right, they found ample funding and leverage points from subcommittees to courts.[29]

Initially, politics seemed disorganized amid an individualized Congress and postreform nominating process. "Political parties," Hugh Heclo observed in 1983, "have traditionally served as grand simplifiers. People mobilized through the new group politics, in contrast, serve as grand complicators."[30] Contrary to expectations among political scientists and New Right operatives alike, groups and coalitions have not replaced political parties but increasingly define them.[31]

Instead, the advocacy explosion of the 1960s interacted with the New Deal divide over the size and scope of government and the new group politics became partisan. Just as their opponents in the Christian Right anchored the Republican Party, cultural liberals emerging from the feminist and gay rights movements exercised increasing influence in the Democratic Party.[32] Yet parties failed to regain their preeminence, and new space opened for movements. Parties needed group allies to reach voters and fund cam-

crafts unions and frustrated industrial unions in machine Chicago. Cf. J. David Greenstone, *Labor in American Politics* (New York: Knopf, 1969).

[29] See, from perceptive analysts at best ambivalent about these shifts, James Q. Wilson, "American Politics, Then and Now," *Commentary*, February 1979, 39–46; and Martha Derthick, "Crossing Thresholds: Federalism in the 1960s," *Journal of Policy History* 8 (1996): 64–80.

[30] Hugh Heclo, "One Executive Branch or Many?," in *Both Ends of the Avenue: The Presidency, the Executive Branch, and Congress in the 1980s*, ed. Anthony King (Washington, D.C.: American Enterprise Institute, 1983), 38.

[31] See McAdam and Kloos, *Deeply Divided*.

[32] See Jo Freeman, "Whom You Know versus Whom You Represent: Feminist Influence in the Democratic and Republican Parties," in *The Women's Movements of the United States and Western Europe: Consciousness, Political Opportunity, and Public Policy*, ed. Mary Fainsod Katzenstein and Carol McClurg Mueller (Philadelphia: Temple University Press, 1987), 215–44; Christina Wolbrecht, *The Politics of Women's Rights: Parties, Positions, and Change* (Princeton: Princeton University Press, 2000); John Gallagher and Chris Bull, *Perfect Enemies: The Religious Right, the Gay Movement, and the Politics of the 1990s* (New York: Crown, 1996); Kira Sanbonmatsu, *Democrats, Republicans, and the Politics of Women's Place* (Ann Arbor: University of Michigan Press, 2002). The gender gap in partisan voting that has arisen since the 1970s has had more to do with support by women for the welfare state, and with men abandoning the Democratic Party, than with divergent preferences about "women's issues." Indeed, men and women have notably similar views on abortion. See Karen M. Kaufmann and John R. Petrocik, "The Changing Politics of American Men: Understanding the Sources of the Gender Gap," *American Journal of Political Science* 43 (1999): 864–87.

paigns. Without sufficient resources on their own to appeal to an electorate whose loyalties had frayed and attenuated, they paid movements' price. It was one they could afford: given the vast expansion in the role of government, they also controlled ideological patronage to dole out to supporters.

The parties' organizational hollowing out and ideological separation simultaneously widened the scope for and narrowed the explicitly partisan role in political conflict. Groups both polarized parties, and took advantage of new opportunities.[33] Fights traverse institutional boundaries that once served to separate presidency, Congress, courts, and agencies. In venues from independent expenditures to confirmation hearings to policy proposals, group allies—including para-organizations such as super PACs, public interest organizations, and business associations, as well as the movements here—search for "a piece of the action" in no-holds-barred conflict.[34] As in much of the nineteenth century, the parties stand deeply divided—but where once those parties controlled the electoral process and defined the contours of American political life, the new elite-led, group-oriented coalitions messily strain to match their long-lost forebears as organizers of democratic politics.

Democratic and Republican Alliances

The divergent coalitional imperatives of Democrats and Republicans have shaped their strategies in ways that have remained largely constant across time. The Federalists, Whigs, and Republicans have continued to ally with the preponderance of big business. So, too, even as alignments and geographies have shifted, the modal American has remained in the Republican

[33]On polarization, see, in a large literature, Alan I. Abramowitz, *The Polarized Public? Why Our Government Is So Dysfunctional* (Upper Saddle River, N.J.: Pearson, 2013); Morris P. Fiorina, *Culture War? The Myth of a Polarized America*, 3rd ed. (Boston: Longman, 2011); William Galston and Pietro S. Nivola, "Delineating the Problem," in *Red and Blue Nation? Characteristics and Causes of America's Polarized Politics*, ed. Pietro S. Nivola and David W. Brady (Washington, D.C.: Brookings Institution Press, 2006), 1–47; Nolan McCarty, Keith T. Poole, and Howard Rosenthal, *Polarized America: The Dance of Ideology and Unequal Riches* (Cambridge, Mass.: MIT Press, 2006); Andrew Gelman, *Red State, Blue State, Rich State, Poor State: Why Americans Vote the Way They Do* (Princeton: Princeton University Press, 2008).

[34]This is the world described in Benjamin Ginsberg and Martin Shefter, *Politics by Other Means: Politicians, Prosecutors, and the Press from Watergate to Whitewater*, 3rd ed. (New York: Norton, 2002). On interest group and party campaign activity, see Michael M. Franz, *Choices and Changes: Interest Groups in the Electoral Process* (Philadelphia: Temple University Press, 2008). For an historical schema, see David C. W. Parker and John J. Coleman, "Pay to Play: Parties, Interests, and Money in Federal Elections," in *The Medium and the Message: Television Advertising and American Elections*, ed. Kenneth M. Goldstein and Patricia Strach (Upper Saddle River, N.J.: Prentice Hall, 2004), 147.

fold, consistently white and Christian and less conflicted over sectionalism. Since the Civil War, Democrats have assembled their coalition through agglomerating diffuse minorities, and been more heterogeneous and prone to internal schisms than Republicans.

The march from the party period to the networked party continues, refracted through distinctive coalitional biases. Both parties have grown more permeable and more dependent on outside groups, but in different ways. Barriers to entry into the Democratic camp have always been lower as the party has cobbled together its coalition, and have grown even more so as traditional organization collapsed. No party has ever contained quite so many disparate elements as the contemporary Democrats, and the relations among them define partisan priorities. Republicans have often reached out to their allied movements rather than simply confronting them, while existing players have effectively wielded vetoes to stop would-be entrants that confront them at the coalition's gate. Yet, as the Tea Party shows, even there the old blocking power has dissipated.

Republicans have sought to energize allies and to politicize groups with sympathetic agendas. Relatively homogeneous parties can protect their borders, but face danger in failing to create resonant allegiances among supporters. Hence, political entrepreneurs seek to tap deeper, prior loyalties, as Republicans did with the Grand Army of the Republic, and New Right leaders with gun owners as well as evangelicals in the 1970s. So, too, the acquiescence of business interests, the party's bulwark since its founding, looms larger for would-be Republican allies. The GOP's centralized structure and emphasis on leaders hashing out differences behind closed doors encourages movement activists to move, as social conservatives from Phyllis Schlafly to Ralph Reed have done, directly into party positions, rather than relying solely on public pressure as a way to carry on party-group negotiations.[35] For all its antiestablishment rhetoric and divisive primary challenges, even the party faction of the Tea Party carefully maintained ties with Republican official-dom.[36]

Democrats, by contrast, have been the more permeable party, seeking to build majorities through a coalition of out-groups jostling to control the party's agenda. Group claimants, seemingly representing geological strata of movement activity, have emerged more from movements making demands on the state than from elites cultivating associational allies, and have played a larger role in the party's coalitional development. Small farmers, industrial workers, African Americans, women, and gays were all deeply

[35] Jo Freeman, "The Political Culture of the Democratic and Republican Parties," *Political Science Quarterly* 100 (1986): 327–56; Freeman, "Whom You Know."

[36] See, e.g., Robert Costa, "Conservatives Seek to Regain Control of Republican Agenda," *Washington Post*, 16 May 2014, 1.

marginalized in American politics as collective actors (even if their members were variously excluded as *individuals*) prior to joining with the Democrats. Yet these different players have often failed to congeal into a partisan whole above its parts. In the party's darkest years in the last century—the 1920s and, on a presidential level, the 1980s—these divisions have become endemic.[37] Indeed, accounts of the two decades can sound notably similar, with cultural and economic divisions fought out almost as bitterly within the Democratic Party as between it and the GOP. Democratic elites and the professionals surrounding them have sought maneuvering room—and often coziness with powerful economic interests—to the detriment of movement and party building.[38]

Winning Partisan Coalitions

From these overviews of parties, movements, and their interactions across American history, we now turn to the inner dynamics within political parties. Pivotal players inside party coalitions, around whom winning coalitions must be built, determine the posture that parties take toward movements. Parties accept movement insurgencies inside their ranks only with the assent of a winning coalition inside those parties.[39] In turn, that assent comes only if a winning coalition finds the movement consonant with its basic ideological interests, and if it believes that incorporating the movement will make the party better placed to achieve ongoing electoral majority. It is a multilevel game. A majority inside the party must see a path, with the movement incorporated, that betters its own position and that delivers an ongoing majority in the electorate as a whole. Should party elites doubt that movements will deliver them such a majority, those movements will be forced outside the party-political order.

[37] David Burner, *The Politics of Provincialism: The Democratic Party in Transition, 1918–1932* (New York: Knopf, 1968); Thomas Byrne Edsall with Mary D. Edsall, *Chain Reaction: The Impact of Race, Rights, and Taxes on American Politics* (New York: Norton, 1991); William Mayer, *The Divided Democrats: Ideological Unity, Party Reform, and Presidential Elections* (Boulder, Colo.: Westview, 1996).

[38] Daniel J. Galvin, *Presidential Party Building: Dwight D. Eisenhower to George W. Bush* (Princeton: Princeton University Press, 2010); Philip A. Klinkner, *The Losing Parties: Out-Party National Committees, 1956–1993* (New Haven: Yale University Press, 1994).

[39] A few regional "party-movements" have blunted the basic dichotomy here, but they have had relatively little impact in national politics—and virtually none since the nationalization of politics in the New Deal. See Mildred A. Schwartz, *Party Movements in the United States and Canada: Strategies of Persistence* (Lanham, Md.: Rowman & Littlefield, 2006); Richard M. Valelly, *Radicalism in the States: The Minnesota Farmer-Labor Party and the American Political Economy* (Chicago: University of Chicago Press, 1989); and, on the merits of pressure-group or alliance strategies even for a party-movement, Samuel P. Huntington, "The Election Tactics of the Nonpartisan League," *Mississippi Valley Historical Review* 36 (1950): 613–32.

TABLE 2.2
STRENGTH OF PLAYERS IN PARTIES

Alliance	Movement supporters	Pivotal players	Movement opponents
Abolition-GOP	Medium then low (Radicals)	High (Stalwarts)	High (northern business)
Populism-Dems	Low (none)	High (Silverites)	High (Goldbugs, Bourbon Democrats)
Labor-Dems	High (urban liberals)	High (northern machines)	High (southern Democrats)
Antiwar-Dems	Low then high (doves)	Low then high ("New Politics" reformers)	High then medium (hawks, regulars)
Christian Right-GOP	Medium (conservative insurgents)	High (big business)	Low (moderate Republicans)

Table 2.2 summarizes the views of key party factions to disaggregate partisan actors, and assess for each case—generally and subjectively, to be sure—the strength of partisan actors who determined movements' fate. The second column in Table 2.2 is the same as in Table 2.1, and the additional columns add the strength of other key actors inside the party. The pivotal players are the actors whose choices decide whether or not alliance holds a winning coalition inside the party. When supporters are stronger than opponents, then pivotal players acquiesce to alliance.

Supporters inside the party actively desire alliance; opponents hope to stop it. Either way, they understand that the new entrants will disrupt existing cleavages.[40] Partisan brokers who seek to lower the costs to alliance emerge from the former group. Partisans in the latter group, their core interests threatened, seek to freeze out the movement and highlight the costs of alliance at every turn. For both sets of actors, the party's long-term ideological trajectory hangs in the balance, fundamentally affecting their own status as high-demanders inside the party coalition and, ultimately, their ability to win goodies from the state. Yet in every instance, neither strong supporters nor implacable opponents have held a majority inside parties. If the former had held true, then the movement would hardly have brought new and radical sentiments into parties; if the latter, then it would have had

[40] Cf. William H. Riker, *The Art of Political Manipulation* (New Haven: Yale University Press, 1986).

to abandon mainstream politics and head to the streets, or else into hearts and minds, to have any chance of success.

Pivotal players favor alliance if they perceive (whether correctly or not, if such an objective determination might even be possible) that new group allies will offer a higher probability of continued electoral majority than will other available coalitional alternatives. Under this model, pivotal players inside parties do not necessarily seek to maximize votes or seats, potentially weakening candidates in marginal districts, but they do seek majorities so they can wield power and implement policies. Since opponents of alliance can be expected to defect or to sit on their hands should unwanted guests gain entrance to the partisan club, the pivotal players back alliance only when its supporters are, in their judgment, more influential in the party than its opponents.

If pivotal players acquiesce to movement incorporation, they exercise power subtly and sometimes invisibly as they negotiate and renegotiate the terms of trade in alliance, gaining resources—votes, money, time, and networks—from movements in exchange for ideological patronage. When movements are weak, however, and offer few resources to tempt partisans, pivotal players will abandon any such compromises, and mobilize group supporters without paying the ideological price. Silverites nominated William Jennings Bryan on the ruins of Populist insurgency, and liberal reformers took from the antiwar movement its spirit of openness more than its opposition to American empire. In turn, when those pivotal players find the arguments of opponents more compelling, then movements find themselves in the cold. Loyal Republicans in the 1870s and 1880s turned against abolition-republicanism when they feared the costs to core supporters in northern business.

Above all, partisan power is blocking power. Elites keep unwanted elements out of parties, or else feast on their remains when those movements cannot bargain for a better deal. They exercised this blocking power against abolition-republicanism, Populism, the left-led unions in the CIO, and the radical elements in the antiwar movement. Once excluded from mainstream party politics, their alternative visions disappeared from national life.

In each instance, the pivotal players controlled the central party organs, and held sway over its presidential and congressional wings; if we may speak of a party outside of its constituent elements, these players are it. These swing voters have relatively weak ex ante views on the movement's core demands, but they want victory and its spoils. Far more than for movement radicals, for whom ideas matter, the goal-oriented assumptions of rational choice well describe pivotal players' behavior. Paradoxically, even as anchoring groups inject into politics ideas far from the mainstream, their success depends on acquiescence by hard-boiled regulars.

Successful alliance emerges typically reflects what Eric Schickler, in explaining the coalitions behind congressional rules changes, terms "common carriers": policies that a multiplicity of interests support for sometimes dissimilar reasons.[41] American parties are diverse, heterogeneous coalitions, not, even in polarized periods, simple unidimensional entities. A first-past-the-post system and, especially, the Electoral College force parties to persuade majorities in a system that sometimes uneasily aggregates cleavages. The impetus for pivotal players emerges from a complicated mixture of material and purposive incentives, sometimes linking sympathies in one venue with policymaking seemingly far afield. Democrats' alliances with women's and gay rights groups in recent decades have endeared them to Hollywood, which in turn has managed to get Democrats to take relatively restrictive stances on issues of piracy and intellectual copyright. Brokers must construct those logrolls, and demonstrate to pivotal players the electoral viability of their newly constructed coalitions.

In the two anchoring alliances, the pivotal players favored alliance. Northern machine Democrats faced powerful New Deal liberals aligned with organized labor, and southerners deeply (and correctly!) fearful that labor would push their Democratic Party to abandon Jim Crow. Because even progressive unions offered at least a modicum of support to Democratic organizations in their own states, keeping themselves and their pals in office, urban bosses, most prominently in the 1944 vice presidential selection, went with labor. At a time of weak parties, movement conservatives, working alongside their New Right and Christian Right allies, constructed coalitions across the Sun Belt with increasingly assertive business interests, attacking high taxes and a meddlesome federal government. Accommodationist Republican moderates, on the ropes in an increasingly assertive party, soon faded away.

The other potential anchoring groups found fewer friends among partisan decisionmakers. As Radicalism waned, Republican pragmatists found ideological appeals to "the very idea of Republicanism" less appealing than fealty to business interests, who feared that a strong southern policy would threaten cheap cotton and incite northern labor. Populism had virtually no real supporters inside the parties. In its stead, the Silverite center mobilized its supporters directly. The antiwar movement faced a changing pivot. In 1968, party regulars could still freeze out the antiwar movement. By 1972, a sympathetic reform coalition controlled the party center—but no longer had a meaningful movement partner.

Successful anchoring groups make common cause with important segments of the business community. Mere reference to "party elites" fails to capture this dynamic, by which such elites serve as agents rather than solely as principals. In a direct sense, should capitalist elites decide that a

[41] Eric Schickler, *Disjointed Pluralism: Institutional Innovation and the Development of the U.S. Congress* (Princeton: Princeton University Press, 2001).

movement threatens their core interests, they will use their influence to ensure that parties remain hostile, and to freeze the movement out of the political system.[42] The pattern holds with particular strength in the Republican Party. Abolition-republicanism after the Civil War failed to forge the same *modus vivendi* with corporate capitalism inside the GOP fold that the Christian Right achieved a century hence. Yet even among the catch-all Democrats, similar pressures apply. Populism, bereft of any funding save the silver mining interests with the coming of fusion, became a supplicant to Democratic priorities in the summer of 1896. The extrusion of CIO radicals tells a similar story.

On the other hand, parties—instruments of social control as well as inclusion—often insulate themselves from mass pressure, with Republicans particularly choosy. Parties, under the right circumstances, may prosper even without movement allies. The extraordinary success of the post-1896 Republicans came precisely as industrial elites organized politics so as to protect themselves from agitation, especially on the "social question." To reiterate the essential argument, because party-movement alliance can fundamentally disrupt the political landscape, it takes place only on terms acceptable to political parties and the coalitions behind them. Yet determining *why* parties deem movements to be good electoral bets requires exploring movements' own organizations and incentives as they attempt to mobilize supports, demand policies and recognition from the party system, and broker with partisan elites.

Influence and Organization

Unlike most "resource donors" to political parties, movement elites exercise much of their influence indirectly, as they principally activate and persuade other supporters.[43] Whether for material, solidary, or purposive incentives, when effective movements have established channels to disseminate information around person-to-person interaction, followers will look up to group leaders for political cues. Those cues offer movements leverage when dealing with American parties, which must reach out to disparate constituencies in search of electoral majority. Group-specific appeal serves as a mechanism to explain both conversion of those who would have voted (or

[42] See Thomas Ferguson, *Golden Rule: The Investment Theory of Party Competition and the Logic of Money-Driven Political Systems* (Chicago: University of Chicago Press, 1995), esp. 61–79 and 205–26.

[43] I have taken the phrase from Seth E. Masket, *No Middle Ground: How Informal Party Organizations Control Nominations and Polarize Legislatures* (Ann Arbor: University of Michigan Press, 2009), 34.

otherwise behaved politically) differently absent party-movement alliance, and mobilization of those who would not have voted (or been politically involved) at all.[44] As Anna Harvey explains in a rational-choice account of why the women's movement proved unable to shift from lobbying to electoral mobilization, at which the parties had a built-in advantage, following women's suffrage: "Group members will likely have more information than nonmembers on the development of shared expectations of appropriate behavior within any given group; benefit-seeking group elites will thus likely have an informational advantage over office-seeking party elites who are not group members in initiating electoral mobilization."[45]

To make parties accept alliance, movements need more than informational advantage about supporters. Movements also need the special infrastructural capacity to mobilize them. Movement infrastructure with deep roots in civil society serves as a necessary if insufficient condition for successful incorporation. If that infrastructure atrophies, parties will have less incentive to work through movement elites. Movement loyalties come and go, but party identification endures as a lifelong guide to individuals' political behavior.[46] Without the need to give ideological patronage in exchange for support, parties will either seek to mobilize movement supporters directly or else build their majorities elsewhere.

Organization building to leverage votes, time, money, and networks requires stitching together into national politics grassroots networks grounded in face-to-face, personal organization. These efforts have constituted movement building on a vast scale. Potential anchoring groups have almost all had forums for face-to-face organizing. They have combined avowedly political and nonpolitical functions, providing supporters with purposive and solidary incentives to come together.[47] They have also had to link national elites with grassroots leaders and then neighborhood-level

[44]On mobilization and conversion in the New Deal elections, see Kristi Andersen, *The Creation of a Democratic Majority, 1928–1936* (Chicago: University of Chicago Press, 1979); and Gerald Gamm, *The Making of New Deal Democrats: Voting Behavior and Realignment in Boston, 1920–1940* (Chicago: University of Chicago, 1989).

[45]Anna L. Harvey, *Votes without Leverage: Women in American Electoral Politics, 1920–1970* (Cambridge: Cambridge University Press, 1998), 55. The attribution of motive to "benefit-seeking" and "office-seeking" elites sometimes obscures as much as it reveals. Movement elites typically hold, and behave so as to keep, organizational office, sometimes to the detriment of extracting policy benefits. On the other side, party elites who back alliance to the hilt often push their views on issues beyond the limits of pure reelection-seeking or vote-maximizing caution.

[46]For an incisive demonstration of this proposition in practice, see Michael T. Heaney and Fabio Rojas, *Party in the Street: The Antiwar Movement and the Democratic Party after 9/11* (Cambridge: Cambridge University Press, 2015).

[47]James Q. Wilson, *Political Organizations* (1973; repr., Princeton: Princeton University Press, 1995), chap. 3.

TABLE 2.3
MOVEMENT CAPACITY TO PROVIDE RESOURCES

Alliance	Independent movement capacity	Locus of movement capacity
Abolition-GOP	Medium (1868) then low	Freedmen's Bureau and Union League Clubs (1868 only)
Populism-Dems	High (1892) then low (1896)	Farmers' Alliance, movement press
Labor-Dems	High	Union halls
Antiwar-Dems	Medium (1968) then low (1972)	Mass demonstrations
Christian Right-GOP	High	Churches, para-organizations

organizers.[48] Movements that try to build their own infrastructure, rather than to politicize extant networks and organizations, face deep vulnerabilities. No meeting hall, no movement, no influence.

Table 2.3 shows where movements have based their face-to-face organizing. The second column is repeated from Table 2.1, and the third column identifies the locus of movement building for each case. The labor-Democratic partnership has benefited from automatic dues deduction, and launched millions of canvasses from the local union halls that also coordinate ice cream socials and worker trainings. Despite tensions among them only partially ameliorated through joint efforts, international unions follow a classic federated model, zipping information back and forth from local to state to national offices. The Christian Right, like other social movements beginning with abolitionists in the 1830s and on through temperance and the civil rights movement, has based itself in the most common voluntary associations in the United States: churches. As Chapter 8 discusses, congregation-based local supporters, embedded in direct-mail lists, helped the Christian Right to overcome the successive implosions of its premier national organizations.

Problems of organizational maintenance crippled other movements' ability to enter the party system. In an era when parties dominated politics, abolition-republicans worked through Republican organization more

[48]Theda Skocpol, *Diminished Democracy: From Membership to Management in American Civic Life* (Norman: University of Oklahoma Press, 2003).

than they offered resources to it. In 1868, the Freedmen's Bureau and Union League Clubs served as adjuncts to the party apparatus, reaching out to African American voters, but they soon disbanded, and factional fights over patronage doomed efforts to build stable organizations. The last two movements make the point particularly sharply. The Populists worked through the Grange, the reform press, and a vast network of alliances and cooperatives centered in rural communities. Yet the institutions that sustained the Farmers' Alliance atrophied during the explicit move to electoral politics following the launch of the People's Party. The antiwar movement eschewed the seamy backrooms it associated with hawkish compromisers. Democracy, it proclaimed, is in the streets. But when the fragile leadership coordinating mass protests splintered, the movement had no organizational base from which to regroup.

Networks and Brokers

The work of making alliance has fallen to brokers, midlevel actors with ties spanning party and movement, who patiently work with both sides to explain and achieve the benefits of alliance. The narrative chapters that follow represent a kind of "lives of the brokers" as they search for power, and puzzle through complicated and imperfect choices.[49] Although the boundary between party and movement may seem crisp here, in the case histories it seems far more fluid and contested.

From the movement side, brokers make movements political and sharpen their goals. They lead movements to see why alliance, among all orientations toward politics, will help them achieve the society for which they yearn. Brokers help to define goals as compatible (or incompatible) with partisan activity, and then assist the party in targeting the relevant populations. They help to shape worldviews so that partisan goals encompass the movement, and the movement links its struggles with the party. Jesse Helms, in a speech at Jerry Falwell's Baptist Fundamentalism '84 conference, captured the rhetoric of alliance, warning preachers that "They are the same people after me who are after you: the atheists; the homosexuals; the militant woman's groups; the union bosses; the block [*sic*] voters."[50] This joint project, embedded in dense issue networks, transcends policy and ideological patronage, as well as electioneering.

[49] Brokers play the same role as bureaucrats in Hugh Heclo, *Modern Social Politics in Britain and Sweden: From Relief to Income Maintenance* (New Haven: Yale University Press, 1974).

[50] W. Craig Bledsoe, "The Fundamentalist Foundations of the Moral Majority" (PhD diss., Vanderbilt University, 1985), 182.

At the same time, brokers clarify for parties why those parties will achieve majorities with movements inside their coalitions, and then cement those alliances with ideological patronage, and access. Precisely because the long-term calculus of the expected number of votes to be gained from group affiliation as against the cost in would-be supporters repelled and the opportunity cost of potential supporters elsewhere foregone is so fraught, brokers have tremendous autonomy in shaping partisan response.

The structural conditions behind alliance emerge directly from the American electoral system, which agglomerates cleavages in a pluralistic society. Yet rather than claiming omniscience for groups and parties incapable of independent judgment, brokerage provides a contingent, individual mechanism to ascribe decisions about partisan electoral strategy and movement goal definition. Even as structural factors—urbanization and the policymaking revolution of the New Deal; later, the unfreezing of southern political cleavages and the social dislocations of the 1960s—set the stage for transformations in the party system, only the actions of determined brokers opened the windows of historical opportunity.

Given their differing incentives, political transformations emerge from midlevel elites more than from presidents or their immediate circle. Because presidents need support from actors across a panoply of issues, strident presidential advocacy for divisive causes threatens either to split the coalitions they have assembled, or else to engender such immense hostility that other parts of their program fall into jeopardy.[51] Franklin Roosevelt and Ronald Reagan, without whose dominance of the national agenda potential anchoring alliances would never have congealed into historically meaningful blocs, flit only fitfully across the stage in the pages to follow. Their image-makers to the contrary, neither had great personal commitment to the anchoring groups that still incant their names in party battles. In the making of alliance, direct presidential leadership is notable principally for its absence. As the partisan presidency has developed, the executive establishment has become increasingly important in brokerage. Still, brokers, often reaching out to old pals from earlier battles, have operated out of the cabinet, lower-level White House staff, or the national committees, much more than from the nerve centers of presidents' own personalistic initiatives.[52] Members of Congress, too, figure prominently. As long as they can win reelection, they have freedom to expand beyond their geographic

[51] For a similar conclusion reached from very different evidence, see Elizabeth Sanders, "Presidents and Social Movements: A Logic and Preliminary Results," in *Formative Acts: American Politics in the Making*, ed. Stephen Skowronek and Matthew Glassman (Philadelphia: University of Pennsylvania Press, 2007), 223–40.

[52] See the discussion of Reagan and the Christian Right in Sidney M. Milkis, Daniel J. Tichenor, and Laura Blessing, "'Rallying Force': The Modern Presidency, Social Movements, and the Transformation of American Politics," *Presidential Studies Quarterly* 43 (2013): 641–70.

constituencies. Investigations, symbolic resolutions, and awkward votes on riders all offer targeted tools that can be directly linked to ongoing electoral mobilization.

Movements, Groups, and Cases

Meaningful comparison requires variance across the dependent variable.[53] Rather than drawing faulty inferences from the primary cases alone, the coming chapters also explore three other defining episodes when social movements in a fairly literal sense confronted political parties. The abolitionist, Populist, and antiwar movements were all *potential* anchoring groups—but given external opposition and internal turmoil, none produced the durable partnerships of organized labor and the Democrats, or the Christian Right and the Republicans. In ways the primary cases alone cannot, their stories together show just how rare, consequential, and historically patterned have been long-running alliances between political parties and social movements.

The movements that shaped the party system at critical episodes in American political development look, in a universe either of social movements or of group influencers on parties, quite atypical.[54] Yet American politics would have developed vastly differently without them. Among the myriad groups seeking to influence parties, I focus only on the subset that are social movements, and then only on movements that carried with them the potential, whether realized or not, to anchor major-party coalitions. Not all anchoring groups emerge from social movements; not all social movements try to become anchoring groups. Let us take these issues in turn, first separating social movements from other group claimants on the party system, and then dividing the potential anchoring groups from other social movements.

The movements explored here have all sought systemic change that threatened to upend other policy demanders and extant commitments inside a party, and that required intense back-and-forth with those demanders for successful alliance. Movements with such possibilities are rare birds; anchoring alliance, to belabor the point, deserves attention precisely as a consequential exception to ordinary patterns in American politics. Their

[53]Gary King, Robert O. Keohane, and Sidney Verba, *Designing Social Inquiry: Scientific Inference in Qualitative Research* (Princeton: Princeton University Press, 1994), 137.

[54]In David Karol's helpful definition, a group is "a self-aware collection of individuals who share intense concern about a particular policy area" (*Party Position Change*, 9). For these purposes, their concern need not encompass policy per se, but the distribution of goods and status in public life.

particular issue concerns and priorities spring from an ideology—whether free labor or industrial democracy—that spans policy concerns, and frames particular issues in the context of foundational principles.

These movements make appeals not just to a set of definable movement beneficiaries, but outward to wide swaths of the electorate insufficiently represented in the extant political order. As Chapter 4 outlines, New Right brokers took particular issues threatening white evangelicals, especially around tax exemptions for church schools, and transformed them into an ideology with concerns from the role of the state to personal morality to American exceptionalism. Such movements represent more than congeries of voters, circles of elites, or interests in civil society. They possess leaders who seek to mobilize a mass base, and a structure embedded in face-to-face contact by which to do so. And they confront the party system in ways that shake it to the core.

More typically, social movements cannot reorder the extant party system, and alliance takes place in the context of issues already consonant with larger partisan priorities. Under these circumstances, movements decide strategies conditional on expected partisan response. Over time, as parties have divided across ever-more issues and required resources from outsiders, they have looked with greater favor on movement claimants.

When their would-be supporters crosscut the extant cleavages, movements pursue pressure group strategies, working with allies on both sides of the aisle and avoiding offense to either major party on core issues. They may find supporters in different places—as the Anti-Saloon League worked with Republicans in the North and Democrats in the South—or else for different parts of a multi-issue agenda. Or else they follow the strategy common to professional advocacy groups with only disembodied "paper memberships," focusing on the courts and avoiding political organizing.[55]

When movements find their allies in a single party, they organize supporters to offer resources to parties in exchange for ideological patronage, and they win acceptance into the party coalition if partisan elites approve of the deal. At a basic level, then, these narrow alliances operate under the same logic as anchoring groups, trading supporters' resources for policy and prestige. Yet they pose fewer challenges in coalition management. To take a quintessential example of narrow alliance, the National Rifle Association frames a distinctive worldview, emphasizing how individual liberty requires the right to keep and bear arms, interwoven with the philosophy of the Republican Party since the 1970s. It applies this worldview only to issues around firearms. That the NRA has tied itself to the GOP probably makes little difference for most captains of industry.

[55] See Jeffrey Berry, *The New Liberalism: The Rising Power of Citizen Groups* (Washington, D.C.: Brookings Institution Press, 1999).

To be sure, these are ideal types, and some groups straddle boundaries. The environmental movement offers a good example. Although its closest allies have long been liberal Democrats, it deliberately eschewed overt partisanship so as to keep ties with conservation-minded Republicans; Richard Nixon signed the Clean Air and Clean Water Acts and George H. W. Bush the sweeping 1990 Clean Air Act Amendments. The movement has struggled to switch toward a strategy of alliance with Democrats as its Republican friends have dwindled to irrelevance. A stronger movement, with a comprehensive ideology, might have aimed to be an anchoring group, an American equivalent to Green parties in Western Europe.[56]

Even as business and parties engage in the same kinds of exchange as movements and parties, key distinctions separate business from mass movements. Foremost, mass movements, unlike business, face the daunting imperative to keep supporters responsive to group-specific mobilization. If they cannot do so, their influence collapses. Firms certainly influence their employees, shareholders, and customers, but in no way does their power in American politics spring directly from their ability to mobilize a population. Nor, among other group influencers inside American parties, do I consider pure party factions, elite-led subunits from the Mugwumps to the Democratic Leadership Council.[57] I similarly exclude a slew of ethnic groups and lobbies that have worked inside and outside the party system.

The civil rights movement represents a particularly tricky case. Ultimately, however, it represents an instance more of incorporation and mobilization of an already salient group than of alliance along the lines considered here. The exigencies of movement leadership, group definition, and organizational maintenance define the contours of anchoring-group alliance, and none applied in the same way as in the episodes in this book. Like them, the civil rights movement connected movement demands with deep themes in the American promise, brought new issues and voters into party politics, altered partisan alignments, and aimed to exerted influence away from the median voter and toward group priorities. Critically, and in notable contrast to its abolition-republicanist predecessor a century earlier,

[56] Samuel P. Hays, *Beauty, Health, and Permanence: Environmental Politics in the United States, 1955–1985* (Cambridge: Cambridge University Press, 1987), 40–43; Charles R. Shipan and William R. Lowry, "Environmental Policy and Party Divergence in Congress," *Political Research Quarterly* 54 (2001): 245–63; Brian P. Obach, "Labor-Environmental Relations," *Social Science Quarterly* 83 (2002): 82–100; Judith A. Layzer, *Open for Business: Conservatives' Opposition to Environmental Regulation* (Cambridge, Mass.: MIT Press, 2012); Theda Skocpol, "Naming the Problem: What It Will Take to Counter Extremism and Engage Americans in the Fight Against Global Warming" (paper, Symposium on the Politics of America's Fight Against Global Warning, Cambridge, Mass., 14 February 2013).

[57] See Daniel DiSalvo, *Engines of Change: Party Factions in American Politics* (Oxford: Oxford University Press, 2012).

however, no ongoing organized movement mediated between voters and elites. In the North, African Americans had begun to be incorporated into urban municipal regimes, principally as Democrats in the wake of the Great Migration and the New Deal. The links between ethnic and partisan solidarities resembled in degree if not kind the ties between parties and waves of European immigrants. After 1965, the civil rights movement fragmented, just as the Voting Rights Act finally brought universal suffrage to the South. Democrats have received overwhelming support from and catered, if often fitfully, to the demands of African American voters.

Yet they have not had to rely on group intermediaries in the same way, nor have policy demands emerged as the price of mobilization. While Democratic elites mobilized using the black church, it is harder to think of the distinct concessions that the black church has demanded. Nor have elites had to create supporters and politicize their identities in the same way as labor, the Christian Right, or any of the shadow cases. The tie between African Americans and the Democrats, and the subsequent backlash against it, has transformed party politics—but it does not constitute party-movement alliance in the precise sense as the episodes discussed here.

To be sure, business, party factions, and ethnocultural groups have all exercised influence inside—indeed, have anchored—American parties. The mechanisms of exchange between parties and group allies, the process of anchoring inside parties, and the historical context of changing partisan resources and alignments structured their relations, as well. Yet these underlying factors impinged on parties and groups in different ways, and I make no claims that alliance between parties and other group allies proceeded in precisely the same manner as they did for the major social movements considered in these pages. That is the work for researchers who will refine the comparisons, and reframe the concepts deployed here.

For their part, not all movements direct their fire at the national state. Others aim at targets ranging from the local water board to Nike to the World Trade Organization. From utopian communities in the 1840s to open-source software today, scores of movements have had little to do with politics per se. Their supporters seek, instead, to live out their values through the conduct of their lives. So, too, movements change far more than coalitions or policies. "The movement," in Joseph Gusfield's words, "is to be found in the housewife considering entry into the labor force, the relations of blacks and whites in ambiguous situations, the response of parents to knowledge of a child's homosexuality."[58] By considering only formal organizations with aims to affect the authoritative allocation of resources in national politics, this book underplays those social and cultural processes.

[58]Joseph R. Gusfield, "The Modernity of Social Movements: Public Roles and Private Parts," in *Societal Growth: Processes and Implications*, ed. Amos H. Hawley (New York: Free Press, 1979), 297.

Nor do the categories here apply outside the highly idiosyncratic context of the United States. In other democracies, poor as well as rich, alliance between unions and center-left parties tends in most cases to be more formalized, and to take place within an explicit commitment to social democracy; often, it exists alongside various corporatist arrangements.[59] Neither does the relationship between the Christian Right and the Republican Party have any close parallel. It resembles neither once-confessional parties typically formed in the historical response to liberalism, nor other militant Protestant politics, which in Northern Ireland and South Africa have stressed the ties between Calvinism and ethnicity, rather than the issues of moral uplift designed to unite believers across churches and sects common in American politics.[60]

Toward Mature Alliance

As parties and movements seek to consolidate victories won amid early triumphs, the exigencies of coalition building and organizational maintenance sap radical tendencies, but also create substantial incentives to maintain ongoing benefits from the other partner in alliance.[61] The two sides air disagreements internally and attempt to change the other actor's policy

[59]Although ties between trade unions and political parties form an elemental building block of the democratic left, and of comparative political economy, with a large literature to match, no systematic study gathers together the relevant data, or explains legal rules' real-world consequences. Accounts that move across continents would be especially welcome. For a useful list of cross-national variables, see Michael Shalev, *Labour and the Political Economy in Israel* (Oxford: Oxford University Press, 1992), 346–47. On general patterns of left party formation, see Bernard Ebbinghaus, "The Siamese Twins: Citizenship Rights, Cleavage Formation, and Party-Union Relations in Western Europe," *International Review of Social History* 40 (1995): 51–89; and Konstantin Vössing, "Social Democratic Party Formation and National Variation in Labor Politics," *Comparative Politics* 43 (2011): 167–86. Paul Leduc Browne, ed., *Labour & Social Democracy: International Perspectives* (Ottawa: Canadian Center for Policy Alternatives, 2002) offers a rich record of talks from union leaders around the world on their experiences working with center-left parties in and out of government.

[60]Stathis N. Kalyvas, *The Rise of Christian Democracy in Europe* (Ithaca, N.Y.: Cornell University Press, 1996), 255; John Madeley, "Politics and the Pulpit: The Case of Protestant Europe," *West European Politics* 5 (1982): 149–71; Steve Bruce, *Conservative Protestant Politics* (Oxford: Oxford University Press, 1998).

[61]For classic treatments of institutionalization and organizational maintenance, see H. H. Gerth and C. Wright Mills, trans., *From Max Weber: Essays in Sociology* (New York: Oxford University Press, 1946), 297–301; the original critique of bureaucratism in social-democratic parties in Robert Michels, *Political Parties: A Sociological Study of the Oligarchical Tendencies of Modern Democracy*, trans. Eden and Cedar Paul (1915; repr., Glencoe, Ill.: Free Press, 1949), esp. 393–409; and Wilson, *Political Organizations*, chap. 3. For a recent account of interest group development over time, see McGee Young, *Developing Interests: Organizational Change and the Politics of Advocacy* (Lawrence: University Press of Kansas, 2010).

from within, rather than abandoning alliance, in what the colloquial metaphor calls "divorce," and the academic jargon terms "exit."[62]

American politics, built on overlapping coalitions of minorities, holds no permanent majorities. When normal politics resumes, movements and parties repeatedly renegotiate their relationships. Movements shape parties, but parties also shape movements.[63] Across long decades, they experience limits and disappointments. All the same, if partisan elites continue to favor alliance, then the movements may still exercise influence. Governing elites inside parties seek to redistribute power toward favored groups. They receive programmatic resources from the state and then organize on behalf of their political patrons. Indeed, the long-term effects of party-group alliance have emerged less through particular programs than by helping to organize the structure of political conflict around differing responses to those policies. Party-movement alliance has endured not just through issue-by-issue policy feedback, but through long-term ideological feedback.[64]

However, this virtuous circle works only when movements find issues and policies that bring them together with other high-demanders inside the party coalition. When groups find common ground—as fiscal Keynesianism provided a basis for the long labor-Democratic partnership and tax cuts united the Christian Right with other "tribes of the right"—their place is secure. When they fail—as with abolition-republicanism—their place as partisan allies becomes perilous, indeed, and victories won at moments of historical opportunity prove vulnerable to drift, retreat, and counterattack.

The internal opponents of alliance—whether driven by policy goals or vote maximization if the allied group risks sinking a majority—will often seek to substitute new issue cleavages, shine light on repellent features, and point out the electoral danger if nothing is done to right the ship. In some

[62] See Albert O. Hirschman, *Exit, Voice, and Loyalty: Responses to Decline in Firms, Organizations, and States* (Cambridge, Mass.: Harvard University Press, 1970).

[63] Scholars have begun to describe this process as coevolution. The approach here tracks their ideas closely, although I do not use the metaphor because evolution raises questions about agency. See Michael T. Heaney, "Linking Parties and Interest Groups," in *The Oxford Handbook of Political Parties and Interest Groups*, ed. L. Sandy Maisel and Jeffrey M. Berry (Oxford: Oxford University Press, 2010), 568–87; and Clyde Wilcox, "Of Movements and Metaphors: The Coevolution of the Christian Right and the GOP," in *Evangelicals and Democracy in America*, vol. 2, ed. Steven Brint and Jean Reith Schroedel (New York: Russell Sage Foundation, 2009, 337. Karol, *Party Position Change*, 188–89, expresses a similar position to mine.

[64] See Eric M. Patashnik, *Reforms at Risk: What Happens after Major Policy Changes Are Enacted* (Princeton: Princeton University Press, 2008); Andrea Louise Campbell, *How Policies Make Citizens: Senior Political Activism and the American Welfare State* (Princeton: Princeton University Press, 2003); Suzanne Mettler, *Soldiers to Citizens: The G.I. Bill and the Making of the Greatest Generation* (New York: Oxford University Press, 2005); Joe Soss, "Lessons of Welfare: Policy Design, Political Learning, and Political Action," *American Political Science Review* 93 (1999): 363–80.

cases, they oppose alliance outright; more often they want the allied group not to anchor quite so tightly. John McClellan, an archconservative Arkansas Democrat, for instance, shone a spotlight on union corruption in the 1950s, and contemporary Democrats concerned about mediocre schools have emphasized "rubber rooms" and other unattractive pieces of contracts with teachers' unions. Liberal Republicans in the 1980s pointed up Christian Right funding from the Unification Church, famous for its opaque finances and mass wedding ceremonies.

Should would-be anchoring groups unambiguously cause parties to lose elections, however, then office-oriented elites will boot them out and attempt to build a majority on other grounds.[65] If office-oriented elites principally answer to dominant business interests, the party's unwanted guests may be ushered especially swiftly toward the door, rather than tolerated amid intraparty feuds—although parties' authority to do so has atrophied over time. Partisan response, rather than movement choice, determines the ultimate outcome.

Delimiting Radicalism

Incorporation inside a political party defangs movement radicalism as parties seek supporters who will not unduly upset their coalitions. This paradox lies at the heart of alliance. Movement moderates, whom politicians trust not to inflame other supporters, assume leadership and shunt aside their more doctrinaire brethren. To be sure, even many of the winners seem radical in the context of the median voter and the political system as a whole. Thus Sidney Hillman, the "labor statesman" from the Amalgamated Clothing Workers of America, always deferred to Franklin Roosevelt, unlike the fiery coal miner, John L. Lewis, or Lewis's erstwhile allies in the left-led unions, purged from the CIO at the Democrats' behest as the Cold War heated up. Christian conservatives, for their part, have turned away from the jeremiads of Jerry Falwell. The cleavages in the black community after 1965 reveal similar patterns.

In turn, when support is high and the bargain of movement support gained to other votes foregone runs in the movement's favor, then relatively more militant figures will gain legitimacy and influence; Hillman himself stood far to the left of the AF of L. When support runs against the movement, whether because it is unpopular or has dissolved, then parties will ignore even moderates. Martin Shefter, observing the freeze-out of the left-led

[65]The key word is "unambiguously." Voters cast ballots, and pundits may spin them as they please. Movement activists far from the median are especially creative, and so the dangers of alliance may remain obscured.

American Labor Party in postwar New York, describes the process well: "If a group is to gain a position in the regime that is secure, it must be integrated into the system in a manner consistent with the interests of other members of the regime's dominant political coalition. Political parties are the institutions that seek to construct such coalitions."[66]

More generally, movements' confrontations with established power create opportunities but also foreclose possibilities. Alliance is a story of losers every bit as much as winners, of powerlessness as well as power. Movements often bring previously excluded voices into politics. Yet, as abolition-republicans, Populists, and the CIO all learned through bitter experience, when windows of opportunity for fundamental change clang shut, they rarely open so wide again. Janus looks forward and back; this story tells a tale neither of declension nor of Whiggish progress. Across the sweep of history, democratic possibilities have narrowed even as democracy embraced ever more Americans.[67]

Movement Legacies

Social movements with political aims seek to realize their visions for a transformed society, and parties gate-keep them on the way. They aim to inject radical visions into the bloodstream of party politics, and then transform those visions into law. Their legacies differ across those dimensions. Considering only the fate of radical worldviews undersells real-world policy and risks counterfactual nostalgia; looking principally to policy change, a common pattern in political science, misses the extent to which movements have carried with them the potential for more fundamental transformations of the social order.

Even as movements lose their radical edge as they enter mainstream politics—and few observers of George Meany or Ralph Reed would mistake them for genuine insurgents—their power emerges from what were

[66] Martin Shefter, *Political Parties and the State: The American Historical Experience* (Princeton: Princeton University Press, 1994), 231.

[67] For a similar scheme, see Bruce Ackerman, "The Broken Engine of Progressive Politics," *American Prospect*, May 1998, 34–43. Cf. the small-d democratic James A. Morone, *The Democratic Wish: Popular Participation and the Limits of American Government* (New York: Basic Books, 1990); and Aziz Rana, *The Two Faces of American Freedom* (Cambridge, Mass.: Harvard University Press, 2010); and the small-r republican Joseph Cooper, "From Congressional to Presidential Preeminence: Power and Politics in Late Nineteenth-Century America and Today," in *Congress Reconsidered*, 9th ed., ed. Lawrence C. Dodd and Bruce I. Oppenheimer (Washington, D.C.: CQ Press, 2009), 361–91. On multiple orders, see Robert C. Lieberman, "Ideas, Institutions, and Political Order: Explaining Political Change," *American Political Science Review* 96 (2002): 697–712; and Desmond S. King and Rogers M. Smith, "Racial Orders in American Political Development," *American Political Science Review* 99 (2005): 75–92.

Table 2.4
Legacies of Potential Alliances

Alliance	Incorporation of radicals	Ideology in party	Policy
Abolition-GOP	Low-medium (marginalized)	Low-medium	High (Civil Rights Act of 1866, Reconstruction amendments)
Populism-Dems	Low (frozen out)	Low	High (income tax, fiat currency)
Labor-Dems	Low (frozen out)	High	High (Wagner Act, Medicare)
Antiwar-Dems	Medium (some incorporated)	Low-medium	Low (Boland Amendment)
Christian Right-GOP	High (incorporated)	High	Medium (Hyde Amendment, Supreme Court appointments)

movements at the moment they confronted the party system. Whether or not these long-institutionalized actors still deserve the sobriquet of "movement," their ongoing influence represents the consequences of movement-born activity. Cutting short the study when they "go mainstream" fails properly to gauge their long-term impact.

Table 2.4 assesses—again, at a general level, with details of the particular policies in the subsequent chapters—the legacies of each potential alliance in bringing radical visions into or freezing them out from mainstream politics, influencing the ideological trajectory of major parties, and enacting consequential public policies. To begin with the anchoring alliances, the labor-Democratic partnership has stood at the heart of economic liberalism for eight decades, with its fingerprints all over the American welfare state and attempts to create the infrastructure for full employment. But its grander visions of industrial democracy remained unfulfilled. The Christian Right, too, has exerted enormous influence inside the Republican Party, without such painful extrusions of its supporters on the extreme right. Yet its attempts to roll back cultural liberalism have met little success.

Both nineteenth-century movements left concrete legacies before they crumbled. For abolition-republicanism, its brief years as an anchor left a powerful legacy in the Reconstruction Amendments, but one that was buried as its supporters lost influence in the postbellum party and polity.

While Congress and the Warren Court could have eradicated Jim Crow without them, their commandments on the states and egalitarian commitments made the job vastly easier. Populism, by contrast, saw its policy legacy decades later; it was enormously important, but also paled against the movement's goals. Democrats and progressive-minded Republicans in the 1910s, who feared any notions of a "cooperative commonwealth" and often battled Populists in state politics, enacted its proposals to regulate railroads, elect senators directly, and impose a constitutional amendment for an income tax. Over time, the United States even accepted a fiat currency—albeit without the inflationary benefits the Populists had hoped. The antiwar movement brought a generation of into politics, but their own history as influencers in the post-1968 Democratic Party belies the movement's limited ideological and policy legacy as the insurgents came to define the new party establishment. In short, no movement has confronted the party system and realized the totality of its vision, yet even the movements that failed to institutionalize themselves inside political parties have held powerful legacies in American political life.

Together, the factors explored in this chapter provide a framework for social movements in party politics that makes sense of key transformations across American history. Movements and parties will ally only when winning coalitions inside parties accept support from movements, and when movements offer to parties resources otherwise unattainable to them. Alliance has become more likely over time, as parties have divided on the issues that animate movements, and looked to outsiders for resources that allow them to win elections. The consequences at critical junctures have repeatedly shaped the terms of ideological combat. They have defined the contours of partisan cleavage, and marked the outer boundaries for radical possibilities.

Part I explains how this process played out as consequential social movements across American history attempted to enter the party system. For three anchoring groups—abolitionism and the Republicans, organized labor and the Democrats, and the Christian Right and the GOP—Part II examines the histories after party and group join together, showing how only the latter two cases consolidated partnerships forged amid extraordinary circumstances into long-running alliance.

PART I
Forging Alliance

CHAPTER 3

Labor and the Democrats in the New Deal

FUNDAMENTAL REORIENTATIONS IN BOTH THE LABOR MOVEMENT AND THE Democratic Party during the New Deal years produced an enduring alliance that safeguarded the policy achievements of the Rooseveltian era and sharpened the class divide between the parties. Backed by an ambitious new federal bureaucracy and a surge in worker militancy, John L. Lewis and the Congress of Industrial Relations organized mass-production industries, and ventured into politics to support the reelection of Franklin D. Roosevelt. The Democratic Party, with the support of newly mobilized voters, reoriented itself as the protector of the disadvantaged through a strong national state.

Yet the limits of organizable alternatives repeatedly dominate the narrative of labor-Democratic alliance. Labor-liberals never held a national majority. Opportunities for fundamental social change in America would never again swing open as wide as in the heady spring of 1935. Even as Democrats edged toward "an American social democracy that dared not speak its name," they remained dependent on the still-segregated South. Its powerful representatives in Congress excluded African Americans (and many poor whites) from collective bargaining, denied them Social Security, and, after 1938, implacably battled labor unions, lest interracial organizing disturb the economic or political equilibrium behind Jim Crow.[1] Stories of the labor movement ask why the gains of the 1930s have proven evanescent. Stories of the Democratic Party record frustration at the limitations of programmatic

[1]Quote from Nelson Lichtenstein, "The View from Jackson Place," *Labor History* 37 (1999): 149. For an excellent treatment placing this bargain in the foreground, see Ira Katznelson, *Fear Itself: The New Deal and the Origins of Our Time* (New York: Liveright, 2013) and, for more detail on race and labor, Sean Farhang and Ira Katznelson, "The Southern Imposition: Congress and Labor in the New Deal and Fair Deal," *Studies in American Political Development* 19 (2005): 1–30.

liberalism, as the party accommodated business and its traditional constituencies. The story of alliance comes precisely in the intersection between these two partial narratives.

By mobilizing members through group-specific channels, labor traded votes, money, and networks for policy from the divided Democrats. It delivered electoral rewards in northern states where Republicans threatened and where machine loyalists at the party's core, who controlled its formal organs and brokered among the surfeit of influencers inside the party, appreciated its efforts. Even as northern Democrats controlled the party, however, they did not alone control the polity. FDR and his successors held limited maneuvering room to their left. Beginning in the 1937 "Little Steel" strikes, labor experienced the frustrations of zero-sum conflict inside the party coalition and the political system, and found success only when it built bridges to other influential forces inside the Democratic coalition.

For a generation of scholars writing in the confines of Rooseveltian politics, the labor-liberal alliance of the 1930s stood at the apex of the New Deal's triumphs. It settled "the social question," brought dignity to the worker, and paved the way for decades of rising wages. The Democratic Party incorporated "labor's new millions" and built a generation-long majority.[2] To the New Left, by contrast, extraordinary waves of contention organized by militant workers themselves withered away through sclerotic bureaucracies sanctioned by the administrative state, and Democratic politicians' failures to defend gains won on the shop floor.[3]

Most potential anchoring groups, however, *fail* to exercise decisive influence on the state and its role in society. Each story asks too much of movements, and says too little about parties or coalitions. In a country where movements represent minorities and must cobble together majorities, compromise becomes inevitable. When political parties refract those compromises, relations among their constituent elements come to the fore. Moves to the left and conciliation with the South together delineated the possibilities and limits in party-movement alliance.

[2] See Irving Bernstein, *Turbulent Years: A History of the American Worker, 1933–1940* (Boston: Houghton Mifflin, 1969); and J. David Greenstone, *Labor in American Politics* (New York: Knopf, 1969).

[3] See Frances Fox Piven and Richard A. Cloward, *Poor People's Movements: Why They Succeed, How They Fail* (1977; repr., New York: Vintage Books, 1979); Mike Davis, *Prisoners of the American Dream* (London: Verso, 1986); Michael Goldfield, "Worker Insurgency, Radical Organization, and New Deal Labor Legislation," *American Political Science Review* 83 (1989): 1257–82; Peter Friedlander, *The Emergence of a UAW Local, 1936–1939: A Study in Class and Culture* (Pittsburgh: University of Pittsburgh Press, 1975); Alice Lynd and Staughton Lynd, eds., *Rank & File: Personal Histories by Working-Class Organizers*, 2nd ed. (1973; repr., Chicago: Haymarket Books, 2012).

The CIO at its most militant and tactically innovative moment, on the march against the most powerful employers in the land, adopted a political strategy to ally with a flawed major party. The reasons are structural. The Democrats under Roosevelt had transformed, however incompletely. The party had endorsed its issues, however imperfect the ultimate policies, and romanced its leaders with charm, appointments, and, from the president, electoral support even for the non-Democrats.[4]

In a majoritarian electoral system, providing support to a popular liberal-reformist president aided the CIO's long-term goals better than any alternative. Under proportional representation, or even a Westminster system, concentrated preferences at times force parties into coalitions to sustain governments. A movement could form a labor or farmer-labor party and establish a beachhead through an "opening to the left." The Labour Party ultimately supplanted the Liberal Party in the United Kingdom, and the New Democrats pressured the Liberals to adopt universal health care in Canada.[5] The CIO faced no such luxuries. As it confronted the party system, the CIO faced a decision of whether to betray its benefactor—which was no decision at all.

Absent the Congress of Industrial Organizations to institutionalize them, the opportunities from the Depression and the Rooseveltian accession might well have reverted into a kind of North American Perónist or Mexican model as unions simply behaved as high-wage guilds without concomitant links to redistributionist policies, or as pure Gompersian voluntarists. Or else, like wave after wave of labor protest before them, they might simply have flamed out without leaving behind any institutional legacy. As the wreckage of the late nineteenth century should indicate, absent the CIO's move into Democratic politics, the alternative to imperfect alliance was either, as in the exclusionary railroad unions, a limited partnership entrenching guild-like privileges for white unionists, or no durable alliance whatsoever.[6]

[4]See Seymour Martin Lipset, "Roosevelt and the Protest of the 1930s," *Minnesota Law Review* 68 (1984): 284. Katznelson, *Fear Itself*, emphasizes the hard realities of the party coalitions, particularly in the South, more than presidential co-optation. Because Roosevelt conciliated the South, the approaches are entirely compatible.

[5]Richard Oestreicher, "Urban Working-Class Political Behavior and Theories of American Electoral Politics, 1870–1940," *Journal of American History* 74 (1988): 1257–86.

[6]This conclusion broadly matches those of both David Plotke, *Building a Democratic Political Order: Reshaping American Liberalism in the 1930s and 1940s* (Cambridge: Cambridge University Press, 1996), 7–8, who takes a more abstract view of the "Democratic order," and, from a careful review of New Left historiography, Howell Harris, "The Snares of Liberalism? Politicians, Bureaucrats, and the Shaping of Federal Labour Relations Policy in the United States, ca. 1915–47," in *Shop Floor Bargaining and the State: Historical and Comparative Perspectives*, ed. Steven Tolliday and Jonathan Zeitlin (Cambridge: Cambridge University Press, 1985), 148–91.

Neither did the New Deal years solely determine the eventual place of organized labor as an anchoring group. The engorged Roosevelt coalition never faced the wrenching choices among its disparate elements—corrupt bosses and old Progressives, southern conservatives, and radical leftists. Instead, the FDR years built up institutions and loyalties that connected unionists to the Democratic Party, and reinforced their loyalties to the forces that had jointly transformed their lives in the Depression and war years. While the New Right sought consciously to bring party and group together to forge a majority, labor and the Democrats took the opportunities presented in the Depression, and, at some cost, consolidated them into a stable alignment. As Chapter 6 explains, the routinization of labor's place in party politics came only in the 1940s, when the Democrats purged their most left-wing elements and began to push out the most reactionary ones. For alliance to survive that wrenching process, the movement had to build its infrastructural capacity and demonstrate its value to Democrats during the New Deal years.

Beyond Craft Unionism—and Voluntarism

The American Federation of Labor, led from its formation in 1886 until his death in 1924 by Samuel Gompers, was founded to supplant the Knights of Labor and its vision of artisanal republicanism. The AF of L organized skilled workers into exclusive bargaining units by trade, and pushed benefits only for its membership. For Gompers, labor's role in politics was to "support its friends and punish its enemies," in support of "pure and simple" trade unionism. AFL craft unionism and voluntarism set the pattern against which the CIO rebelled in the 1930s as it built industrial unionism and forged alliance with the Democratic Party. Nevertheless, the CIO remained imprisoned inside older patterns that stratified work along ethnic lines, organized trade unions by occupation, and yoked radicalism on the job site to bargaining inside cross-class parties.

Within a decade of its formation—a socialist platform backed by the Machinists nearly won a majority in 1894, and deprived Gompers of the presidency for a year—the AFL had vanquished its rivals, including the Knights and Eugene Debs's industrial American Railway Union.[7] The victories of

[7]See Martin Shefter, *Political Parties and the State: The American Historical Experience* (Princeton: Princeton University Press, 1994), chap. 4. Cf. Philip Taft, *The A.F. of L. in the Time of Gompers* (New York: Harper, 1957), 26–29 and 40–42. On the Knights, see Richard Oestreicher, "Terence Powderly, the Knights of Labor, and Artisanal Republicanism," in *Labor Leaders in America*, ed. Melvyn Dubofsky and Warren Van Tine (Urbana: University of Illinois Press, 1987), 30–61; Leon Fink, *Workingmen's Democracy: The Knights of Labor and American Politics* (Urbana: University of Illinois Press, 1983); Kim Voss, *The Making of American*

the AFL and of William McKinley in 1896 on the ruins of Populism sharply limited workers' organized pressure to change the basic economic or political structures that controlled their lives. Those failures foreclosed alternatives to corporate capitalism, notably for a farmer-laborite or avowedly socialist party.[8]

More than in any peer nation, craft unions dominated the American labor movement in the early twentieth century, accounting for about three-quarters of AFL membership. Craft unions organize skilled and semiskilled workers who perform a common task. They typically control hiring halls that train and assign workers, through which they bargain with employers. By forcing hiring within ethnic enclaves, craft unionism reinforced stratification in the labor market, benefiting old-stock English, German, and Irish Americans to the detriment of immigrants from Asia (banned after 1882 under the Chinese Exclusion Act, which received broad labor support), immigrants from Southern and Eastern Europe, and, especially, African Americans.[9] Industrial unions, by contrast, organized "vertically," bringing together all workers in a given sector. Without control over labor supply, industrial unions were vulnerable to strike-breakers and "forced back on other kinds of leverage, including mass strikes, boycotts, demonstrations—and political pressure."[10]

Exceptionalism: The Knights of Labor and Class Formation in the Nineteenth Century (Ithaca, N.Y.: Cornell University Press, 1993); and Terence V. Powderly, *Thirty Years of Labor, 1859–1889* (Columbus: Excelsior, 1889).

[8]On the politics of the period, see Chapter 5. The literature is vast; a labor intellectual wrote in 1936 of "the ancient refrain of half a million Ph.D dissertations: 'Why a Labor Party Is Slow in Coming to the United States.'" J.B.S. Hardman, "Is a Labor Party on the Way?," *Jewish Frontier*, December 1936, 8. See Werner Sombart, *Why Is There No Socialism in the United States?*, trans. Patricia M. Hocking and C. T. Husbands (1906; repr., White Plains, N.Y.: International Arts and Sciences Press, 1976); Seymour Martin Lipset and Gary Marks, *It Didn't Happen Here: Why Socialism Failed in the United States* (New York: Norton, 2000); Daniel Bell, *Marxian Socialism in the United States* (1952; repr., Princeton: Princeton University Press, 1967); Jerome Karabel, "The Failure of American Socialism Reconsidered," *Socialist Register* 16 (1979): 204–27; Eric Foner, "Why Is There No Socialism in the United States?," *History Workshop Journal* 13 (1984): 57–80; Robin Archer, *Why Is There No Labor Party in the United States?* (Princeton: Princeton University Press, 2007). On socialism and AFL unions, see John H. M. Laslett, *Labor and the Left: A Study of Socialist and Radical Influences in the American Labor Movement, 1881–1924* (New York: Basic Books, 1970). For a historiography, see Michael Kazin, "The Agony and Romance of the American Left," *American Historical Review* 100 (1995): 1488–1512.

[9]Gwendolyn Mink, *Old Labor and New Immigrants in American Political Development: Union, Party, and State, 1875–1920* (Ithaca, N.Y.: Cornell University Press, 1986).

[10]Gary Marks, *Unions in Politics: Britain, Germany, and the United States in the Nineteenth and Early Twentieth Century* (Princeton: Princeton University Press, 1989), 207.

Politically, the AF of L pursued a policy of voluntarism. Through unions' standing on their own two feet, without aid from employers or the state, labor, it argued, should seek to improve conditions for its members alone—but not for the unorganized. For AFL voluntarists, social legislation threatened to substitute the mercies of a state they could not control for workers' own concerted action rooted in their particular concerns at work. American labor was, in the labor economist Selig Perlman's phrase, "job-conscious"—and hence distinct from its putatively class-conscious, socialist brethren in Europe.[11]

The AFL stood against state-funded pensions, as well as unemployment and health insurance. In 1916 when the railway brotherhoods, which stood apart from the federation, won passage of the Adamson Act, which guaranteed an eight-hour day to workers running the trains—the first such federal legislation—the AFL stood on the sidelines.[12] To constrict labor supply and protect male unionists' wages (and status), the federation backed protective legislation limiting work by women and children.

The AFL reached out to the Democrats in the decade prior to the First World War, but its efforts resembled those of a typical pressure group, and foundered by 1920. In 1908, when Gompers mounted his most emphatic effort to elect a presidential candidate, William Jennings Bryan, the AFL spent in real terms only one-seventieth as much as unions spent to reelect Roosevelt in 1936.[13] At the same time, the weakness of ties with national parties opened up opportunities for state and local unions to set their own course. Unions looked most progressive at the state level as state federations endorsed protective legislation, such as unemployment insurance, opposed by the national AFL. In cities, however, weak ties with national parties allowed building trade unions, reliant on municipal patronage, to ally with whatever party held the reins at City Hall. While most bosses were Democrats, in Detroit, Philadelphia, Pittsburgh, and San Francisco machines were, until the New Deal, Republican affairs.[14]

[11] Selig Perlman, *A Theory of the Labor Movement* (New York: Macmillan, 1928); updated in Selig Perlman, "The Basic Philosophy of the American Labor Movement," *Annals of the American Academy of Political and Social Science* 274 (1951): 57–63. For a sharp rejoinder from the CIO tradition, see J.B.S. Hardman, "Power-Accumulation Transcends 'Job-Consciousness,'" *Labor & Nation*, Winter 1951, 46–50.

[12] Julie Greene, *Pure and Simple Politics: The American Federation of Labor and Political Activism, 1881–1917* (Cambridge: Cambridge University Press, 1998), 259.

[13] Greene, *Pure and Simple Politics*, 165; Louise Overacker, "Labor's Political Contributions," *Political Science Quarterly* 54 (1939): 57–59.

[14] Theda Skocpol, *Protecting Soldiers and Mothers: The Political Origins of Social Policy in the United States* (Cambridge, Mass.: Belknap, 1993), 233–45; Michael Rogin, "Voluntarism: The Political Functions of an Antipolitical Doctrine," *Industrial and Labor Relations Review* 15 (1962): 521–35; Gary M. Fink, "The Rejection of Voluntarism," *Industrial and Labor Relations*

Above all, the American electoral system, with its first-past-the-post system and Electoral College, constrained geographically concentrated industrial workers, and favored organization of workers—native-born white, at least semiskilled—whose interests could be made congruent with other established high-demanders in the party system.[15] Urban machine and craft union alike traded on specific benefits for specific populations; neither one agitated for universal state provision of social protection. In many northern cities, they emerged from and reproduced similar ethnic hierarchies through "the tacit alliance constructed between the Irish machines and the Irish-controlled trade unions."[16] Together they demarcated a boundary between work and its occupationally based grievances, and politics based on ethnocultural divides and solution of day-to-day problems.[17] Widespread radical sentiment across the American working class found institutional support neither in trade unions nor in electoral politics.

The Wagner Act

The Great Depression decimated the American labor movement. Its membership declined below a tenth of the American labor force. Franklin Roosevelt gained nomination in 1932 through accommodation with his party's fiefs, accepting John Nance Garner, the House Speaker and a West Texas rancher, as his vice president. Conservative old Wilsonians drafted the Democratic platform. It pledged a balanced budget and, in contrast even to the platitudes in its Republican counterpart, said nothing whatsoever about labor. Roosevelt won in a landslide, but more in repudiation of Herbert Hoover than an affirmative mandate of his own.

To reverse severe deflation wrought by excess competition, the new administration pushed through Congress the National Industrial Recovery Act, premised on business-government partnership to revive the economy through elaborate codes for each industry. Section 7(a) of the act, drafted by Senator Robert F. Wagner, a liberal Democrat from New York, guaranteed

Review 26 (1973): 805–19; see also Herbert Harris, *American Labor* (New Haven: Yale University Press, 1938), 407–8.

[15] Shefter, *Political Parties*; Oestreicher, "Urban Working-Class Political Behavior."

[16] Steven P. Erie, *Rainbow's End: Irish-Americans and the Dilemmas of Urban Machine Politics, 1840–1985* (Berkeley: University of California Press, 1988), 252; see also David Montgomery, "The Irish and the American Labor Movement," in *America and Ireland, 1776–1976: The American Identity and the Irish Connection*, ed. David Noel Doyle and Owen Dudley Edwards (Westport, Conn.: Greenwood, 1980), 205–18; Marc Karson, *American Labor Unions and Politics, 1900–1918* (Carbondale: Southern Illinois University Press, 1958), 219.

[17] Ira Katznelson, *City Trenches: Urban Politics and the Patterning of Class in the United States* (1981; repr., Chicago: University of Chicago Press, 1982).

workers "the right to organize and bargain collectively through representatives of their own choosing," and banned joining a company union as a condition of employment. It was the first protection of the right to organize ever included in federal law—yet it contained no duty for employers to bargain, nor any mechanism of enforcement. Although William Green of the AF of L testified in favor, labor pressure hardly produced the unwieldy compromise.[18]

Armed with the new codes, the few industrial unions aggressively expanded their membership through a wave of organizational strikes. John L. Lewis of the United Mine Workers won an advantageous code in bituminous coal, and quickly brought miners across Appalachia under contract. By April 1935, UMW membership had risen fourfold in two years, to 540,000—and by the end of 1935, its treasury had increased eightfold in two years, to $2.3 million ($39 million in 2013 dollars).[19] Those dues, amazingly modest for so vast a social transformation, would fund the organizing drives of the CIO. Still, captive mines, owned by the steel mills to provide coking coal for their blast furnaces, stymied the UMW. To unionize coal would mean unionizing steel.

The opening to the left also proved opportune for the two garment workers' unions: the International Ladies' Garment Workers Union in women's clothing and the Amalgamated Clothing Workers of America in men's clothing. Each was led by immigrants from Eastern Europe, and their membership was largely Jewish. Through joint boards in their major markets (established by Louis Brandeis in his days as a lawyer), they enjoyed generally good labor relations. The ILGWU, led by David Dubinsky, had deep roots in anticommunist Jewish socialism and the labor movement alike. ACWA sought a broader national profile and a more ecumenical set of allies. Its president, Sidney Hillman, cultivated connections from the settlement houses to the Ivy League. While Dubinsky, a skilled cutter, remained foremost a union president, Hillman threw himself into service for Roosevelt.[20]

[18] Irving Bernstein, *The New Deal Collective Bargaining Policy* (Berkeley: University of California Press, 1950), chap. 3; Lewis L. Lorwin and Arthur Wubnig, *Labor Relations Boards: The Regulation of Collective Bargaining under the National Industrial Recovery Act* (Washington, D.C.: Brookings Institution, 1935), chap. 2; Harry A. Millis and Emily Clark Brown, *From the Wagner Act to Taft-Hartley: A Study of National Labor Policy and Labor Relations* (Chicago: University of Chicago Press, 1950), 21. Much of the language came directly from the Norris-LaGuardia Act passed the prior year, and expanded its ban on labor injunctions.

[19] Walter Galenson, *The CIO Challenge to the AFL: A History of the American Labor Movement, 1935–1941* (Cambridge, Mass.: Harvard University Press, 1960), 193 and 195. On the economics of coal, see David Brody, *In Labor's Cause: Main Themes on the History of the American Worker* (New York: Oxford University Press, 1993), chap. 4.

[20] Robert D. Parmet, *The Master of Seventh Avenue: David Dubinsky and the American Labor Movement* (New York: New York University Press, 2005), chaps. 9 and 10; Steven Fraser, *Labor Will Rule: Sidney Hillman and the Rise of American Labor* (Ithaca, N.Y.: Cornell University

In June 1935, Congress passed the National Labor Relations Act, known then and since as the Wagner Act. It aimed to bring democracy to the vast modern workplace, and also to secure industrial peace and restore aggregate demand. Through representatives of their own choosing (therefore de facto banning company unions) and without employer coercion, workers in a given bargaining unit gained the power to negotiate labor contracts, with employers duty bound to sit at the bargaining table with workers' representatives. A new National Labor Relations Board enforced the act. With the national state now supportive, union membership doubled in five years and quadrupled in fifteen. Still, in a direct sop to the South, the bill excluded agricultural and domestic workers. In April 1935, Wagner wrote to Norman Thomas, then organizing for the Southern Tenant Farmers Union, "that the inclusion of agricultural workers would lessen the likelihood of passage so much as not to be desirable."[21]

"No one, then or later, understood why Congress passed so radical a law with so little opposition and by such overwhelming margins."[22] The basic factual record is disarmingly simple: the Wagner Act was principally the result of one man, Senator Robert F. Wagner, with drafting from his chief aide, Leon Keyserling, then all of twenty-eight. The bill received only minimal attention on the floor of both chambers or from the executive bureaucracy. Franklin Roosevelt signed the law without public ceremony, but failed to understand its significance in realigning the roles of labor and the state. Frances Perkins, the labor secretary who herself paid little heed to the substance, wrote gently that FDR "did not altogether grasp that sense of their being a solid bloc of people united to one another by unbreakable bonds which gave them power and status to deal with their employers on equal terms."[23]

It was an opportune moment. After the devastating 1934 midterms, Republicans held a bare 25 seats in the Senate and 103 in the House. From spark plug workers in Toledo to truckers in Minneapolis, militancy erupted, and bled into indigenous radical politics, from Huey Long's Share Our Wealth campaign to Upton Sinclair's failed EPIC bid for governor of California.

Press, 1991), chap. 11; for a good contemporary synthesis, Benjamin Stolberg, "A Government in Search of a Labor Movement," *Scribner's Magazine*, December 1933, 345–50; for a shrewd view of Hillman from the left, Len DeCaux, *Labor Radical: From the Wobblies to the CIO* (Boston: Beacon, 1970), chap. 11.

[21] Robert F. Wagner Papers, Georgetown University, box 410, folder 7. The record here is much less complex than in the case of Social Security.

[22] William E. Leuchtenberg, *Franklin D. Roosevelt and the New Deal* (New York: Harper & Row, 1963), 151.

[23] "Roosevelt Signs the Wagner Bill as 'Just to Labor,'" *New York Times*, 6 July 1935, 1; Frances Perkins, *The Roosevelt I Knew* (New York: Viking, 1946), 325.

Nevertheless, strike activity peaked in the fall of 1934, and hardly determined the content or form of the state's response.

The Wagner Act hardly emerged as a goody from partnership. While the AF of L advocated the bill as a "Magna Charta for Labor," and passage would have been unlikely had it not been supportive, the federation remained weak. It failed to give the NLRB a tripartite form (business, labor, and public); Wagner, following the policy entrepreneurs close to the New Deal state, stuck with an independent board to adjudicate policy. Nor did the AF of L succeed in importing the practice of railway labor law to accept prior union jurisdictional claims; Wagner insisted on workers' "designation of representatives of their own choosing," so the state itself determined appropriate bargaining units.[24]

The NIRA was declared unconstitutional on 27 May 1935, just after the Senate had passed the first version of the Wagner Act. Business-government partnership stood shattered. In its wake, the Second New Deal articulated a more adversarial and avowedly egalitarian model. With public pressures favorable, skeptical members of Congress voted yes, confident that the law would be struck down. In each chamber, more Republicans voted in favor than against the labor disputes bill, and it won support even from southern conservatives such as Jimmy Byrnes and Walter George, soon to break with labor. In 1937, the Court shifted course to accept economic regulation and by a five to four vote upheld the law on Commerce Clause grounds.[25]

Through Robert Wagner passed most of the liberal currents in the twentieth-century Democratic Party. As I. F. Stone wrote in 1944, "Wagner has plugged away, without demagoguery and without drama, at one task. That is to raise the living standards of the lower-income groups in our society."[26] Wagner was more than just the avatar of a single interest or an

[24]The literature is vast. The factual record in Bernstein, *New Deal Collective Bargaining Policy*, chaps. 7–9, remains unsurpassed. See also Kenneth Finegold and Theda Skocpol, "State, Party, and Industry in America's New Deal," in *Statemaking and Social Movements: Essays in History and Theory*, ed. Charles Bright and Susan Harding (Ann Arbor: University of Michigan Press, 1984), 159–92; Plotke, *Building a Democratic Political Order*, chap. 4; Ruth L. Horowitz, *Political Ideologies of Organized Labor* (New Brunswick, N.J.: Transaction Books, 1978), chap. 5; and, for a perspective emphasizing pressure from below, Goldfield, "Worker Insurgency."

[25]*National Labor Relations Board v. Jones & Laughlin Steel Corporation*, 301 US 1 (1937). For the legal issues, see James A. Gross, *The Making of the National Labor Relations Board: A Study in Economics, Politics, and the Law* (Albany: State University of New York Press, 1974), chaps. 5 and 6.

[26]I. F. Stone, "Robert F. Wagner," *Nation*, 28 October 1944, 507. See J. Joseph Huthmacher, *Robert F. Wagner and the Rise of Urban Liberalism* (New York: Atheneum, 1968); Leon Keyserling, "The Wagner Act: Its Origin and Current Significance," *George Washington Law Review* 29 (1960): 199–233; Jack H. Pollack, "Bob Wagner, Liberal Lawmaker," *Coronet*, April 1946, 36–39; Henry F. Pringle, "The Janitor's Boy," *New Yorker*, 5 March 1927, 24–26.

agent of state capacity. Rather, he and his highly competent staff stood at the center of networks uniting the organizational Democratic Party and its state and local machines, the legislative branch, progressive insurgents, the federal bureaucracy, social reformers from the settlement houses, liberal-minded trade unionists, the intellectual "Brain Trust" around FDR, and Roosevelt himself, whom Wagner had known since their days in the New York state senate.

Born in Germany in 1877, Wagner came to New York at the age of six and began his political career under Charles F. Murphy, the leader of Tammany Hall. Loyal Democratic partisanship stood at the core of Wagner's politics.[27] Although most scholars of social policy would probably contest the claim, Wagner saw an unbroken line from the clubhouse to the welfare state. "Tammany Hall may justly claim the title of the cradle of modern liberalism in America," he declared in a 1937 July Fourth address.[28]

As a state senator in 1911, Wagner chaired a committee investigating the Triangle Shirtwaist fire. The experience impelled him to use government as a means to help the disadvantaged. The same motivations—to raise consumption, to combat inequality, to secure democratic voice for all—run through the National Labor Relations Act and Wagner's other legislative initiatives. In four terms in the U.S. Senate, he shepherded the NIRA through the Senate and chaired its early labor board, saw the Federal Housing Administration into being, and wrote the legislation affirming U.S. participation in the Bretton Woods institutions. His failures pointed the way to the party's future. Southern-led filibusters bottled up his anti-lynching legislation, and for nearly a decade he led the charge for universal health insurance.

These purposes extended to the labor disputes bill. Wagner wanted to stimulate demand as a reflationary measure against the Depression. "The inequality of bargaining power . . . tends to aggravate recurrent business depressions, by depressing wage rates and the purchasing power of wage earners in industry," the findings of fact, drafted by Keyserling, explained. He wanted to expand workers' collective rights to encompass "full freedom of association [and] actual liberty of contract." He wanted to ensure industrial peace through routinizing grievance procedures to limit strikes. He

[27] For instance, Wagner supported his old pal, Jeremiah Mahoney, for mayor of New York in 1937 against Fiorello LaGuardia. My interpretation, although highly sympathetic to both attempts at situating Wagner's extraordinary entrepreneurship, pushes further toward a party-centric account than the state-centered account in Finegold and Skocpol, "State, Party, and Industry," and the ideational account in Mark Barenberg, "The Political Economy of the Wagner Act: Power, Symbol, and Workplace Cooperation," *Harvard Law Review* 106 (1993): 1379–1496.

[28] "Wagner Declares Tammany Cradled Liberalism in U.S.," *New York Times*, 6 July 1937, 1.

wanted, most broadly, to further "a just relationship among the respective forces in modern economic society."[29]

Wagner never viewed collective bargaining simply as a means to enshrine his party at an organizational level but rather saw political advantage in mobilizing sympathetic constituencies on the basis of universal benefits. He stayed out of union squabbles, if only to keep friends in both AFL and CIO. "What the Republican masterminds never seem to understand," he said in a 1938 speech, "is that improvement of the worker's welfare benefits the country at large."[30]

The CIO

The Committee on Industrial Organization formed in the fall of 1935 to "organize the unorganized." At the AF of L convention in Atlantic City, the Mine Workers and the two needle trade unions proposed to issue charters for new unions in mass-production industries. They failed by a margin of nearly two to one.[31] Two days later, John L. Lewis of the Mine Workers punched the conservative "Big Bill" Hutcheson, president of the Carpenters' Union, in the jaw, sending him reeling across the table with blood dripping.[32]

The morning after the convention adjourned, Lewis met with officials from the UMW and the union chiefs on the losing side of the vote over industrial unionism, and sketched his plans for massive organizing drives across basic industry. The following summer, the AF of L expelled the dissidents for practicing dual unionism. The CIO soon formalized itself as the Congress of Industrial Organizations. While personally sympathetic to industrial unionism, William Green, the weak AFL president and a coal miner himself, felt bound to the majority, and to the voluntarists such as Matthew

[29] First two quotes from NLRA Findings and Declaration of Policy, 29 USC 151; last from an April 1937 speech at Yale University, quoted in Keyserling, "Wagner Act," 229. See also (presumably ghostwritten by Keyserling) Robert F. Wagner, "Wagner Challenges Critics of His Act," *New York Times (Magazine)*, 25 July 1937, 1–2, 20, 23. New Left critics often quoted the language about limiting strike activity as evidence of the law's corporate-liberal intent—but as strikes impeded interstate commerce, the language had a clear constitutional purpose.

[30] Wagner Papers, box 404, folder 33.

[31] The issue came on a contract between the Wobbly-influenced and ultimately communist-led Mine, Mill & Smelter Workers and the metal trades over a contract with skilled workers at Anaconda Copper.

[32] Louis Stark, "Fist Fight Puts A.F. of L. in Uproar," *New York Times*, 20 October 1935, 22.

Woll and John Frey who ran the federation bureaucracy, and made few efforts to avert the split.[33]

Behind the personalities lay coherent blocs with divergent interests in the New Deal political economy. Industrial unions would organize vast factories at the vanguard of American industry, regardless of job category. The opponents came principally in unions representing the building trades, urban craftsmen, and white railroad workers. Industrial unionism put at risk their ties to existing local party organizations, including plenty of Republicans. Nor had they any desire to relinquish jurisdictional rights, or to accept into their ranks millions of unskilled workers. Distinctions of pay and status that the AFL had worked tirelessly to build hung in the balance.[34] Frey scoffed at industrial unionism's unbroken record of failure from the Knights of Labor to the American Railway Union to the Industrial Workers of the World (the syndicalist Wobblies). "We have heard this form of organization advocated in the past . . . and there is only a tombstone now to mark the fact that they existed."[35] This time would be different, however, because the American state now protected the new unions.

John Llewellyn Lewis, with his bushy eyebrows, lantern jaw, and predilection for the orotund and the melodramatic, lived in an Alexandria plantation house long in the Lee family, and dined at the Cosmos Club.[36] Yet he felt for his miners an unshakeable loyalty beyond the list of his failings. Lewis lurched hither and yon across the political spectrum during his long career. A midwestern business unionist who supported Herbert Hoover, he seized the opportunities presented by worker insurgency and the New Deal. As he sought autonomous space for his union, he endorsed Wendell Willkie in 1940, disaffiliated the Mine Workers from the CIO, violated

[33]On the split, see Bernstein, *Turbulent Years*, chaps. 8 and 9; James O. Morris, *Conflict within the AFL: A Study of Craft Versus Industrial Unionism, 1901–1938* (Ithaca, N.Y.: Cornell University, 1958), chap. 7; Walter Galenson, *Rival Unionism in the United States* (New York: American Council on Public Affairs, 1940); Melvyn Dubofsky and Warren Van Tine, *John L. Lewis: A Biography* (New York: Quadrangle, 1977), chaps. 10 and 11; and the interpretive framework in David Brody, *Workers in Industrial America: Essays on the 20th Century Struggle*, 2nd ed. (New York: Oxford University Press, 1993), chap. 3.

[34]The division between craft and industrial unions often collapsed in practice. The Teamsters Union, whose president, Dan Tobin, inveighed against the "rubbish" that industrial unionism would bring into labor's house at the same time grew its membership tenfold from 1933 to 1946 by organizing "everything on wheels . . . not only in trucking but in related industries." See Robert D. Leiter, *The Teamsters Union: A Study of Its Economic Impact* (New York: Bookman Associates, 1957), 38; and the strained logic in Daniel J. Tobin, "Editorial," *International Teamster*, January 1936, 9–12.

[35]*Report of Proceedings of the Fifty-Fifth Annual Convention of the American Federation of Labor* (Washington, D.C.: American Federation of Labor, 1935), 556; John P. Frey, "Industrial Unionism, Unsound and Destructive," *Machinists' Monthly Journal*, August 1936, 492–93.

[36]Dubofsky and Van Tine, *John L. Lewis*, 297.

the no-strike pledge in the 1943 captive mines dispute and precipitated the Smith-Connally Act, joined and quickly left the AF of L, and finally used national coal bargaining to build a private welfare state.

Lewis threw himself into the CIO; it was the finest moment in his long career. He rounded up former dissidents from the UMW who had chafed at his iron rule, including the old socialists Adolph Germer and John Brophy, veterans of the Wobblies like Len DeCaux, the occasional Musteites and Trotskyites, crusaders like the journalist Gardner Jackson who had spent the long lonely twenties bounding from lost cause to lost cause. And, at the height of the Popular Front, the old business unionist embraced communist organizers. As Lewis asked David Dubinsky, "Who gets the bird, the hunter or the dog?"[37]

"In industrial unionism," said an early CIO mimeo, "we do not develop craft, trade, religious, political, or race ideas. We develop class solidarity."[38] Low-skilled workers, easily replaceable if they struck, forged bonds with skilled and semiskilled brethren, often the most militant of all. The CIO looked to organize sectors alongside coal in the heavy industrial supply chain: steel, autos, chemicals, electrical manufacturing, and hard-rock mining. Only through this organization could labor meet its adversaries on an equal footing. Arrayed against labor, Lewis saw an opposing bloc that united the titans of industry—Mellons, Du Ponts—with the ultimate source of power in finance capital: the House of Morgan.[39] For all Lewis's demagogy, even the strongest corporate-liberal treatments confirm his interpretation of Morgan-linked industries as the New Deal's most implacable opponents.[40] Executives in iron and steel in 1936 gave twenty-two times more to the Republican than to the Democratic National Committee.[41]

[37] Bernstein, *Turbulent Years*, 783.

[38] Quoted in Max M. Kampelman, "Labor in Politics," in *Interpreting the Labor Movement*, ed. George W. Brooks, Milton Derber, David A. McCabe, and Philip Taft (Madison: Industrial Relations Research Association, 1952), 185.

[39] *UMW Journal*, 1 October 1936, 8, for instance, repeated a rumor "that if Landon is elected President, the Wall Street banking house of J.P. Morgan & Co. will immediately establish a private office in the United States Treasury."

[40] See Thomas Ferguson, *Golden Rule: The Investment Theory of Party Competition and the Logic of Money-Driven Political Systems* (Chicago: University of Chicago Press, 1995), chap. 2; Michael Patrick Allen, "Capitalist Response to State Intervention: Theories of the State and Political Finance in the New Deal," *American Sociological Review* 56 (1991): 679–89; Peter Swenson, "Arranged Alliance: Business Interests in the New Deal," *Politics & Society* 25 (1997): 66–116; Jacob S. Hacker and Paul Pierson, "Business Power and Social Policy: Employers and the Formation of the American Welfare State," *Politics & Society* 30 (2002): 277–325.

[41] Louise Overacker, "Campaign Funds in the Presidential Election of 1936," *American Political Science Review* 31 (1937): 485.

The Mandate of 1936

The 1936 landslide for Roosevelt's reelection brought together for the first time the vast majority of the nation's liberal elements. Robert F. Wagner drafted the Democratic platform. It boasted of the "right to collective bargaining and self-organization free from the interference of employers," and promised "equal economic opportunity for all our people."[42] Behind the president flocked old Bull Moosers like George Norris in Nebraska and Hiram Johnson in California, agrarian radicals in the Upper Midwest, and the right wing of the Socialist Party in New York. The vast Rooseveltian coalition, however, extended to the old small-town party of Bryan and Wilson, to the machines in the industrial and border states, and, most crucially, to the Solid South. Wrote James MacGregor Burns in 1963:

> It was not a radical coalition, for countless conservative Democrats were in it. It was not a Democratic party coalition, for many independents and some Republicans were part of it. It was not a bipartisan coalition, for the overwhelming majority of Republicans were out of it. It was a grand coalition of all the leaders and groups who were sticking with Roosevelt because of, or despite, the leftward direction of his Administration. It was, most simply put, a *Roosevelt* party.[43]

Organizationally, the reelection campaign followed a two-pronged strategy to transcend—but not directly to combat—state and local organizations, and reach out to supporters of the New Deal whether or not they identified as Democrats. A series of para-organizations, such as a Progressive National Committee aimed at farmer-laborites and liberal intellectuals, supported Roosevelt outside the traditional party structure, while the Democratic National Committee served largely as a conduit for more traditional patronage; its chairman, James Farley, mastermind of FDR's first victory, fell from favor and broke with him over the third term.[44]

Yet the national party in 1936 asserted its authority as the arbiter of rules over nomination. At Roosevelt's behest, the convention repealed the two-thirds rule that since Andrew Jackson had mandated a supermajority for nomination. The decision removed from the South its effective veto, and pushed nomination politics into big industrial states where unions were strongest. As a hostile Georgia representative predicted, foreshadowing the 1960s with remarkable accuracy, "The next step will be a demand to

[42] "Democratic Party Platform of 1936," http://www.presidency.ucsb.edu/ws/?pid=29596.

[43] James MacGregor Burns, *The Deadlock of Democracy: Four-Party Politics in America* (Englewood Cliffs, N.J.: Prentice Hall, 1963), 159, italics original.

[44] These groups provided a template for Hillman's NC-PAC in 1944; George Norris served the titular leader of both efforts. See Donald R. McCoy, "The Progressive National Committee of 1936," *Western Political Quarterly* 9 (1956): 454–69.

strip States of the power to control their affairs. This will be followed up with a proposal to outlaw the suffrage laws of the South." In Congress, labor-liberals spent decades trying to open the institutional blockages that preserved southern power. In presidential nomination, they won without a fight.[45]

"The elimination of Roosevelt is a necessary condition of a third party," explained a speaker at a 1935 gathering of assorted radicals. An estimate of vote totals in the spring of 1936 agglomerated third-party support from across sets of supporters; it imagined somewhere between 3.4 and 10.3 million votes, and victories in two to four states, in an election in which 45.6 million Americans ultimately voted. In the United States, such totals could mean only a spoiler candidacy in a critical election—and no third party ultimately emerged.[46]

Instead, John L. Lewis and Sidney Hillman pushed the CIO and its newly mobilized workers into party politics. In the summer of 1936, they formed Labor's Non-Partisan League, with its "sole 1936 objective the re-election of President Franklin D. Roosevelt." The name intentionally postponed questions of a third party. As Hillman told the ACWA board in April 1936, "We are today bound by the decision of our convention to help bring about a labor or farmer-labor party—what is commonly known as independent political action. . . . We know that the defeat of the Roosevelt administration means no labor legislation for decades to come." Lewis appointed as titular chair George Berry of the AFL-affiliated Printing Pressmen, a Tennessean, a New Dealer on government payroll, and a longtime Democrat. Although most AFL unions stayed away, and Dan Tobin of the Teamsters, whom Lewis and Hillman distrusted deeply, worked with Farley in the DNC's small Labor Division, Roosevelt sent a letter of support to the LNPL.[47]

[45]Charles R. Michael, "4 States Back 2–3 Rule," *New York Times*, 25 June 1936, 1; Charles R. Michael, "South Bows to Change," *New York Times*, 26 June 1936, 1; presciently, William Allen White, *What It's All About: Being a Reporter's Story of the Early Campaign of 1936* (New York: Macmillan, 1936), 67–75.

[46]Robert Morss Lovett, "A Party in Embryo," *New Republic*, 24 July 1935, 297; "American Commonwealth Federation," *Common Sense*, April 1936, 23. On the radical milieu, see Arthur M. Schlesinger, Jr., *The Politics of Upheaval* (Boston: Houghton Mifflin, 1960), 142–51; and Eric Leif Davin, "The Very Last Hurrah? The Defeat of the Labor Party Idea, 1934–1936," in *"We Are All Leaders": The Alternative Unionism of the Early 1930s*, ed. Staughton Lynd (Urbana: University of Illinois Press, 1996), 117–71. The poll data in Eric Schickler and Devin Caughey, "Public Opinion, Organized Labor, and the Limits of New Deal Liberalism, 1936–1945," *Studies in American Political Development* 25 (2011), too, suggest the limits of radical, and even prolabor, sentiment.

[47]*Labor's Non-Partisan League: Its Origin and Growth* (Washington, D.C.: Labor's Non-Partisan League, 1938), 1–5; Robert Frederick Carter, "Pressure from the Left: The American Labor Party, 1936–1954" (DSS diss., Syracuse University, 1965), 10; "Text of Roosevelt Letter to Labor," *New York Times*, 11 August 1936, 10. On Berry, see Felix Bruner, "Major Berry—Always Available," *American Mercury*, January 1937, 83–90; Frank R. Kent, "The Great Game of Politics," *Kansas City Times*, 25 August 1936.

Trade unions pumped $770,218 (or $13.2 million 2014 dollars) into the 1936 campaign, totaling about a tenth of total recorded dollars aiming to elect Democrats. Nearly two-thirds of labor's contribution ($470,000) came from the United Mine Workers, with the needle trade unions responsible for half of the remainder. About a third of labor's dollars flowed to Labor's Non-Partisan League, a quarter apiece to the American Labor Party (the LNPL affiliate in New York) and the Democratic National Committee, and the remainder to state and local parties and pro-FDR para-organizations.[48] While LNPL itself maintained a nonpartisan posture, the UMW, its ultimate paymaster, gave both to the party directly and to the new organization. Every union in the nascent CIO offered its support to Roosevelt. He was, the needle trades exulted, "the man who started you back in life with all your dignity and self-respect."[49]

In New York, LNPL used fusion rules to create a full-fledged ballot line for itself as the American Labor Party. Elsewhere, it organized principally in the big industrial states, with a particular focus on coal country in Pennsylvania. Before formal rules on coordination or limits on campaign contributions differentiated partisan from independent spending, it conducted the panoply of campaign activities—posters, palm cards, massive rallies, even a purchase of radio time. All these activities aimed not simply at union members themselves, but outward to influence all voters who could support sympathetic officeholders.

As citizens and as workers, the new unionists and their neighbors in mobilized communities sought to entrench the gains that they had made.[50] The National Labor Relations Act, and the pro-CIO board that administered it, had swiftly rendered the American state into unions' protector. The new social legislation gave jobs to the unemployed and pensions for the aged as rights of citizenship, rather than privileges of employment. The *UMW Journal* explained the logic that discarded voluntarism, and connected industrial unionism with state and party: "Political action will also be increasingly necessary for two reasons: first, to safeguard the fundamental principles and rights of industrial democracy; and second, in order to secure legislative and perhaps constitutional sanctions for its economic program. Success in the basic industries will bring with it the political

[48] Data from *Investigation of Campaign Expenditures in 1936: Report of the Special Committee to Investigate Campaign Expenditures of Presidential, Vice Presidential, and Senatorial Candidates in 1936* (Washington, D.C.: Government Printing Office, 1937), 127–33, and popularly known as the Lonergan Report; summarized in Overacker, "Campaign Funds," and Overacker, "Labor's Political Contributions."

[49] Robert Zieger, *The CIO, 1935–1955* (Chapel Hill: University of North Carolina, 1995), 39; circular from Baltimore Joint Board ACWA, 21 October 1936, collection of the Baltimore Museum of Industry.

[50] On these connections, see Lizabeth Cohen, *Making a New Deal: Industrial Workers in Chicago, 1919–1939* (Cambridge: Cambridge University Press, 1990), chaps. 6–8.

power which the labor movement has hitherto lacked for the attainment of these objectives."[51]

In 1896, Mark Hanna had organized national corporations in the mass-production economy, and made them Republicans. Four decades later, the CIO organized the workers, and Roosevelt made them Democrats. Those two tracks respectively reinvigorated job-site radicalism and reconfigured distributive politics. Yet they coexisted uneasily until the postwar years. The CIO, with its support for integration, its communist-linked elements, and, for a time, the voluble Lewis, stood to the left of the Democratic establishment. The AF of L under William Green, ever sensitive to the niceties of distributive patronage politics, stood to the right of the centralizing New Dealers. It dallied with the antilabor Dies Committee, which investigated leftist bias at the pro-CIO NLRB ("sleeping with the enemy," retorted the CIO). Pragmatic Democrats wondered what exactly their swollen majority might ultimately entail for all its diffuse parts. Still, the parameters had been set, and neither side ever thereafter seriously considered exit. The most salient breaks in the coming decade—John L. Lewis's lonely support for Willkie and southern Democratic participation in the conservative coalition—confirm the links among partisanship, liberalism, labor, and race. The joint inheritance manifest by 1936 still defines alliance between organized labor and the Democrats.

Race, Labor, and New Alignments

Through linked processes centered around class, African Americans embraced both Franklin Roosevelt and, in turn, his party, and also the unions of the CIO, which admitted them as full members. To be sure, neither transformation augured full racial equality. Yet because coalitions structure organizable alternatives and mediate group conflict into principled disagreement, these new alignments presaged the next transformations of the party system. Economic liberalism for all, guaranteed by the federal government, set the stage for racial liberalism.[52] Southern Democrats realized as much when they joined with Republicans to form the conservative coalition that attempted to stop the Fair Labor Standards Act, which "put a ceiling over

[51] *UMW Journal*, 1 February 1936, 9.

[52] Eric Schickler, "New Deal Liberalism and Racial Liberalism in the Mass Public, 1937–1968," *Perspectives on Politics* 11 (2013): 75–98. The argument fits nicely alongside its converse in Farhang and Katznelson, "Southern Imposition." Cf. Edward G. Carmines and James I. Stimson, *Issue Evolution: Race and the Transformation of American Politics* (Princeton: Princeton University Press, 1989).

hours and a floor under wages"—and the CIO blundered into the same truth when it failed to organize the South in Operation Dixie starting in 1946.

In the North, the New Deal after 1935 generally delivered relief without regard to color, despite local officials' intransigence. The Works Progress Administration under Harry Hopkins and the Public Works Administration under Harold Ickes gave jobs to the unemployed (in 1936, African Americans accounted for 64 percent of unskilled workers on WPA payroll), built housing in black neighborhoods, and sponsored artists and composers. Via Ickes and Eleanor Roosevelt, civil rights leaders gained access to the White House unseen in a half century, albeit no firm break with the Jim Crow South. To a greater extent even than northern white Democrats, African Americans consistently supported New Deal policies and labor unions. In a 1938 *Fortune* poll, 87 percent of Negro respondents approved of Roosevelt's economic objectives. Roosevelt won almost three-quarters of the vote in the black precincts of northern cities in 1936, with swings sharpest for young voters without previous party attachments. Union influence worked indirectly: by 1940, Roosevelt's margins proved highest in cities where African Americans had broken into industrial work, usually through the CIO.[53]

On the eve of the Depression, only about eighty thousand African Americans held union membership. By 1939, approximately half a million black workers had joined unions, about four-fifths in the CIO.[54] Black workers often cast their first votes ever in representation elections. To be sure, because the Wagner Act excluded agriculture and domestic work, about two-thirds of African Americans fell outside its protections. All the same, the CIO unions all formally banned racial discrimination, and most welcomed black workers as full participants—even if their internal records never matched the public rhetoric.

Ideology and labor-market realities pressed in the same direction. Industrial unions risk collapse when low-wage strike-breakers, excluded from unions by virtue of ethnicity, cross picket lines. The United Mine Workers had long admitted black members, outside the South in fully integrated locals. Through its organizers, other CIO unions imported the "UMW formula," placing African American workers as officers (albeit rarely president or treasurer) in local unions, and reaching out to elites in the black power structure. In return for CIO support for government action that would ban racial discrimination in hiring, the newly supportive NAACP and the

[53] Harold F. Gosnell, "The Negro Vote in Northern Cities," *National Municipal Review*, May 1941, 278; Nancy J. Weiss, *Farewell to the Party of Lincoln: Black Politics in the Age of FDR* (Princeton: Princeton University Press, 1983), 289; Schickler and Caughey, "Public Opinion," 20.

[54] Ira De A. Reid, *Negro Membership in American Labor Unions* (New York: National Urban League, 1930), 101–3; Ray Marshall, *The Negro and Organized Labor* (New York: John Wiley, 1965), 49.

Urban League refrained from criticizing CIO unions' internal policies. Starting in 1948, racial liberals and labor would form a sometimes-uneasy bloc inside the Democratic Party. That partnership was possible only with African Americans' newfound support for both the Democrats and the CIO in the 1930s.[55]

The Second Term

In the months following Roosevelt's reelection, Lewis pushed his advantage to the hilt. In Flint, a sit-down strike—preventing the use of replacement workers—at the Fisher Body plant forced General Motors to recognize the United Auto Workers. Crucially, when Frank Murphy, the liberal Democratic governor of Michigan, deployed the National Guard, it protected the strikers from GM goons, rather than evicting the strikers from company property.[56] Without Murphy's "Little New Deal" in Michigan, the Flint strike might have remained just a flicker of militancy, rather than the spark for what would become, for a time, the country's largest union and its harbinger for social-democratic possibility.

The U.S. Steel Company controlled two-thirds of steel production. Morgan interests, which hoped to avoid a long organizational strike (a contract for British armaments guaranteed uninterrupted production), directed the company's business in Pittsburgh. Its chief, Myron Taylor, a sometime presidential adviser with a Medici villa above Florence, shook hands with John L. Lewis and, "without a shot," recognized the Steel Workers Organizing Committee.[57] When the CIO struck the smaller, scrappier rivals collectively known as Little Steel later in the spring, Democratic elected officials less committed than Murphy to the New Deal—Ed Kelly, the mayor of Chicago, in the brutal Memorial Day Massacre at Republic Steel, which killed eighteen strikers; and Martin Davey, the governor of Ohio, at Youngstown Sheet & Tube—deployed the National Guard and police on behalf of the steel companies to reopen their plants. "A plague on both your houses,"

[55] Horace R. Cayton and George S. Mitchell, *Black Workers and the New Unions* (Chapel Hill: University of North Carolina Press, 1939); Harvard Sitkoff, *A New Deal for Blacks: The Emergence of Civil Rights as a National Issue* (New York: Oxford University Press, 1978), chap. 7; Herbert R. Northrup, "The Negro and the United Mine Workers of America," *Southern Economic Journal* 9 (1943): 313–26; Sumner M. Rosen, "The CIO Era, 1935–1955," in *The Negro and the American Labor Movement*, ed. Julius Jacobson (Garden City, N.Y.: Anchor Books, 1968), 188–208.

[56] Sidney Fine, *Sit-Down: The General Motors Strike of 1936–1937* (Ann Arbor: University of Michigan Press, 1969), esp. 307–9.

[57] "It Happened in Steel," *Fortune*, May 1937, 91–95, 176–81; Bernstein, *Turbulent Years*, 48 and 466–73.

pronounced Roosevelt, forced to choose between his party's elected officials and his backers in the CIO. "It ill behooves one who has supped at labor's table and who has been sheltered in labor's house," Lewis replied, "to curse with equal fervor and fine impartiality both labor and its adversaries when they become locked in deadly embrace."[58] Less than the class relations in steel, the Democratic Party's own incomplete transformation doomed the Little Steel campaign (the companies unionized only during wartime) and set Lewis and Roosevelt on a collision course.

For his part, Roosevelt mounted an ill-fated campaign in 1938 to purge disloyal Democrats who had turned against the New Deal. It failed completely, toppling only a Tammany hack in New York. Roosevelt hoped to have it both ways, not disturbing the basic structure of locally oriented parties, attacking Jim Crow, or embracing farmer-labor agitation, but instead simply picking favorites in primaries. A purge in 1936 might have succeeded, but by the time frustration at congressional inaction roused FDR to a nationwide whistle-stop, a severe recession, principally of his own making from premature belt tightening, had left the electorate in a conservative mood. Nor did the purge embrace labor. The CIO, badly organized in most of the southern and western states where Roosevelt had targeted recalcitrant incumbents, played little part. Labor's Non-Partisan League had grown somnolent once George Berry (who then turned right himself) accepted appointment to fill a Senate vacancy from Tennessee early in 1937. Most AFL locals had remained loyal to old friends such as Walter George of Georgia and Millard Tydings of Maryland, even when they opposed the wage-and-hour law.[59] Only once CIO-PAC started to work in congressional races in 1944 would the anchoring group shape contests for the House and Senate.

In 1940, Lewis broke with Franklin Roosevelt and returned to the Republican fold to endorse Wendell Willkie. The moment pointed up the limits of group leadership, even in a movement at the height of its powers, to ascend the commanding heights and dictate national policy. In a genuine rivalry,

[58] Benjamin Stolberg, "Big Steel, Little Steel, and the C.I.O.," *Nation*, 31 July 1937, 119–23; Marcus A. Roberto, "Franklin D. Roosevelt, Martin L. Davey, and the 'Little Steel' Strike" (MA thesis, Kent State University, 1960), chap. 4; "Roosevelt Quotes Shakespeare," *New York Times*, 30 June 1937, 1. Davey continued to fulminate against John L. Lewis, and lost his bid for renomination in 1938. In Chicago, the machine, always ideologically adaptable, soon saw votes in alliance with the CIO unions and reversed course. Kelly instructed the police to protect CIO strikers, and won a favorable settlement at a contentious Packinghouse Workers' strike. The CIO then turned out the vote for Kelly in his 1939 reelection. See Barbara Warne Newell, *Chicago and the Labor Movement: Metropolitan Unionism in the 1930's* (Urbana: University of Illinois Press, 1961), 178–79 and 224–25; and Robert A. Slayton, "Labor and Urban Politics: District 31, Steel Workers Organizing Committee, and the Chicago Machine," *Journal of Urban History* 23 (1996): 29–65.

[59] Susan Dunn, *Roosevelt's Purge: How FDR Fought to Change the Democratic Party* (Cambridge, Mass.: Belknap, 2010).

a popular president held all the cards against an unpopular trade unionist unafraid to strike. Nor, personal pique aside, had Roosevelt much running room to accommodate Lewis. The conservative coalition had formed and, after 1938, doomed all New Deal legislation. As he moved toward a more internationalist posture, Roosevelt felt pressure to keep up relations with business, while Lewis, a midwestern isolationist, despaired against war to enrich industrialists.[60] Increasingly, the president turned to Sidney Hillman, president of a Jewish-dominated union, whose ultimate vision proved far more accommodating.

"John Ell," a voice without a movement behind him, exercised little influence in the fall election. The capacity of the labor movement remained with Roosevelt, and his margins saw only modest declines from 1936 in urban working-class neighborhoods and newly organized cities in coal and iron country. Unionists' loyalties to the New Deal had already been cemented. Nor did Lewis bring with him the infrastructure required to influence voters.[61] He never formalized his ties to other isolationists such as Burton Wheeler of Montana. The CIO leadership, including even his lieutenants from the UMW—Phil Murray, Van Bittner, John Brophy—and the LNPL Washington director and every state organization save one, all backed Roosevelt. Lewis's leftist allies worried about the president's belligerence but feared Willkie above all. They remained neutral or sought refuge in the Communist ticket. True to his word, Lewis resigned the CIO presidency for Phil Murray, his loyal deputy and a loyal Democrat. He soon withdrew the Mine Workers from the CIO. "When he marched into the waiting arms of the Girdlers, the Weirs, and the Fords," wrote a Hillman lieutenant, "he marched alone."[62]

War and CIO-PAC

After Pearl Harbor, organized labor fell into line to support the war effort. Unions left to right offered a "no-strike" pledge, and employers promised no lockouts. A powerful new War Labor Board set guidelines to organize production. Under the Little Steel formula, wage increases (but, critically, not fringe benefits) were limited to rates as of January 1941, in exchange for

[60] See, on this theme, Marc Landy, "FDR and John L. Lewis: The Lessons of Rivalry," in *Modern Presidents and the Presidency*, ed. Marc Landy (Lexington, Mass.: DC Heath, 1985), 105–11.

[61] Irving Bernstein, "John L. Lewis and the Voting Behavior of the C.I.O," *Public Opinion Quarterly* 5 (1941): 233–49; impressionistically, see Samuel Lubell, "Post-Mortem: Who Elected Roosevelt?," *Saturday Evening Post*, 25 January 1941, 10–11, 91–96.

[62] "C.I.O. Denunciation Pours on J.L. Lewis," *New York Times*, 27 October 1940; "Wide Split Seen in C.I.O. Over Lewis' Willkie Stand," *Christian Science Monitor*, 28 October 1940; Spencer A. Klaw, "Labor's Non-Partisan League: An Experiment in Labor Politics" (AB thesis, Harvard College, 1941), 27; Jacob S. Potofsky, "Of, By, and For the Union," *Advance*, 5 November 1940, 3.

de facto union shops.[63] While workers in many CIO unions—for instance, in steel, autos, rubber, and radio—simply shifted from industrial and consumer to military production, semiskilled AFL unions—the Machinists and Carpenters, in particular—saw the greatest membership increases during the wartime boom.[64] Midterm elections amid wartime stalemate typically inflict damage on the president's party, and 1942 proved the point. Democrats lost 45 seats in the House, holding only a bare majority with 222 seats. The CIO, preoccupied, had largely sat on its hands.

In early 1943, pressured by internal dissent from wildcat anthracite strikes, John L. Lewis launched a nationwide coal strike, to searing nationwide condemnation. An enraged FDR seized the mines, and placed them under federal control. Southern Democrats, led by the viciously antilabor Howard W. Smith of Virginia (later the scourge of civil rights on the Rules Committee) alongside Republicans and a smattering of northern Democrats, soon passed over Roosevelt's veto the War Labor Disputes Act, better known as the Smith-Connally Act.

The AFL and CIO alike condemned the bill. It arrogated from workers in critical war-related industries the right to strike, and gave the president direct statutory authority to seize plants as a means to continue production. Paving the way for more drastic limits under Taft-Hartley, the law also prohibited direct contributions from union general funds to general election campaigns. Although he accepted its core provisions, Roosevelt objected to the campaign provisions and to restrictions on union leaders' ability to offer new contracts during cooling-off periods.[65] To resist the state, Lewis showed, invited the wrath of labor's opponents in the conservative coalition. What would become a central theme in labor politics over the coming decades emerged first in 1943: labor's position on the shop floor depended upon protection against unfavorable labor laws, which turned it toward Democratic politics.

A month after the passage of Smith-Connally, Sidney Hillman launched the CIO Political Action Committee.[66] PAC embraced not only Roosevelt,

[63] Little Steel decision in *The Termination Report of the National War Labor Board: Industrial Disputes and Wage Stabilization in Wartime, January 12, 1942–December 31, 1945*, vol. 2 (Washington, D.C.: Government Printing Office, 1947), 288–322. Logic, largely drawn from case opinions by a board public member, in Frank P. Graham, "The Union Maintenance Policy of the War Labor Board," in *Yearbook of American Labor*, vol. 1 (New York: Philosophical Library, 1945), 145–61.

[64] As with white workers, most wartime gains in membership for African Americans came in AFL unions—although especially in the low-skill Laborers, and Hotel and Restaurant Employees unions.

[65] Cf. Louis Stark, "More Strikes Expected under Regulatory Bill," *New York Times*, 20 June 1943, E9; and Arthur Krock, "Roosevelt Veto Defeat Traced to Many Causes," *New York Times*, 27 June 1943, E3.

[66] On CIO-PAC (whose name still graces Political Action Committees of all stripe) and its legacy for campaign finance, an issue I sidestep to facilitate comparison across different legal regimes, see Emily J. Charnock, "The Rise of Political Action: Labor Unions and the

but a transformed Democratic Party, establishing a permanent alliance that traded votes, money, and networks for sympathetic state policy. Abolition-republicans and Populists failed to build permanent infrastructure. Labor's Non-Partisan League disappeared with the eclipse of John L. Lewis. Nor did even the Christian Right ever build an organization to last. CIO-PAC succeeded.

"PAC," wrote the journalist Richard Rovere, "wants the fruits, not the means, of political power."[67] The new, legally separate and geographically organized entity would register and turn out liberal-minded voters, including trade unionists, their relatives and neighbors, and progressives from all walks of life. As models, PAC looked to the political machines that served depending on the city or state as friend or rival. Machines often tamped down competition more than they maximized participation, and PAC aimed to best them at their vote-getting game. Sympathetic politicians would then implement Keynesian and welfarist policies and guarantee labor's rights to organize.

PAC had made peace with the Democrats; a memo outlining PAC's operations frankly denied even "the slightest possibility of our achieving influence in the Republican Party." Tellingly, CIO-PAC in 1944 endorsed liberals Claude Pepper of Florida and Lister Hill of Alabama for reelection to the Senate despite their support for Smith-Connally, in a cycle when even the railway brotherhoods withheld support. As the Amalgamated Clothing Workers newspaper wrote, "Though technically the contending parties are the Democrats and the Republicans, in effect it is a division between two sets of forces in American life."[68]

Roosevelt may or may not have actually told Robert Hannegan, chairman of the Democratic National Committee, to "Clear everything with Sidney." Once Henry Wallace, the vice president, lost the confidence of the South and of the bosses who doubted his viability, the CIO influenced the pick of what it deemed an inferior substitute. Hillman at the chaotic 1944 convention certainly scotched the nomination of the South Carolinian, Jimmy Byrnes. Over breakfast in his hotel suite, Hillman indicated to Truman that should Wallace falter, "there was another man labor could be for and 'I'm looking at the other one.'" Northern bosses close to the White House, led by Ed Flynn of the Bronx, signed off on a choice that met the

Democratic Party" (paper, American Political Science Association, New Orleans, La., 30 August to 2 September 2012).

[67] Richard Rovere, "Labor's Political Machine," *Harper's*, June 1945, 597.

[68] James Caldwell Foster, *The Union Politic: The CIO Political Action Committee* (Columbia: University of Missouri Press, 1975), 9; Helen Fuller, "The PAC and the Future," *New Republic*, 27 November 1944, 689; J.B.S. Hardman, "Sidelights on Issues and Campaign Methods of This Election," *Advance*, 3 November 1944, 9.

CIO's test without causing division in home-state delegations. Regardless of exactly who said what to whom when, now lost in the mist of time, the public perception from friend and foe alike marked a turning point in labor's place in party politics.[69]

Hillman and Murray asked for CIO leaders to make political action "a primary concern for 1944 around which your normal trade union activities revolve." Tactically, PAC sought principally to mobilize a war-weary electorate, much of it far from home. The 1944 campaign emphasized registering union members, organized for the first time in lists by precinct, and turning them out to vote. PAC distributed, by its estimate, eighty-five million pieces of literature. The techniques seem, by present lights, primitive, with blizzards of pamphlets, along with the rudiments of door-to-door canvassing, and precious little targeting of key votes, states, or campaigns for congressional endorsees. In proportional terms, labor (including the linked National Citizens PAC of progressive professionals, under the honorary chairmanship of George Norris) contributed more than a fifth of total dollars designed to aid Democrats, almost all from CIO unions save a contribution from the ILGWU—a figure twice as high as in 1936.[70]

PAC itself became a polarizing issue in the presidential race. Seeking to unmask the jaunty president's nefarious backers, the Republican nominee, Thomas Dewey, inveighed against the PAC and its supporters, including communists. Radio ads warned that "the Hillman-Browder Axis know they can handle Harry Truman."[71] Although the Democrats retained their

[69]Initially reported in Arthur Krock, "The Inflammatory Use of a National Chairman," *New York Times*, 25 July 1944, 18; Robert H. Ferrell, *Choosing Truman: The Democratic Convention of 1944* (Columbia: University of Missouri Press, 1994), 53; Turner Catledge, "Democrats Face Many-Sided Battle on Vice-Presidency," *New York Times*, 19 July 1944, 1; cf. Edward J. Flynn, *You're the Boss: The Practice of American Politics* (1947; repr., New York: Collier Books, 1962), 195–98; James F. Byrnes, *All in One Lifetime* (New York: Harper & Bros., 1958), 223–31. On Flynn, who merits a proper biography, see Richard H. Rovere, "Nothing Much to It," *New Yorker*, 8 September 1945, 28–41.

[70]Richard Polenberg, *War and Society: The United States, 1941–1945* (Philadelphia: J.B. Lippincott, 1972), 205; Fraser, *Labor Will Rule*, chap. 14; Louise Overacker, "American Government and Politics: Presidential Campaign Funds, 1944," *American Political Science Review* 39 (1945): 899–925. The data in Foster, *Union Politic*, 208–13, which entirely concern margins of victory (and implicitly persuasion rather than mobilization effects), are unconvincing.

[71]"Text of Gov. Dewey's Speech at Boston Attacking the PAC and the Communists," *New York Times*, 2 November 1944, 14; David M. Jordan, *FDR, Dewey, and the Election of 1944* (Bloomington: Indiana University Press, 2011), 242. Although she does not discuss the case, Dewey's strategy entirely fits with the theory in Lynn Vavreck, *The Message Matters: The Economy and Presidential Campaigns* (Princeton: Princeton University Press, 2009). Dewey had to choose an issue—but Roosevelt was winning the war, which had brought the economy back to full employment, and a frontal assault on the New Deal would have been a disaster. So he chose to emphasize leftist influence. FDR was plainly no communist, and adroitly parried Republican charges that he was simultaneously a one-man dictator and a pawn for foreign

congressional majorities, and Roosevelt won every industrial state save Ohio, barely 150 House Democrats won election from outside the South.

CIO-PAC emerged from internal as well as external threat. Inside the tempestuous CIO, the pragmatic center under Hillman and Murray consistently put as first priority close ties to the Democratic Party, and then tactically joined forces with whichever unions' winds at that moment blew in the same direction. During the wartime Popular Front, the Communist Party and its allies embraced Roosevelt and the CIO leadership, while on the right, staunch anticommunists, many with roots in the Socialist Party or the Association of Catholic Trade Unionists, kept their distance from the Democratic establishment. The roles would reverse again: the socialist heretics of 1944 grew into hard-line Cold Warriors by 1948 while erstwhile Popular Fronters soon lambasted American empire.[72]

CIO-PAC positioned itself as steward of universal prosperity, emphasizing national unity more than class division. "All have an equal right to share in America. . . . It is good to be an American. I love America," its leading pamphlet intoned.[73] The CIO's 1944 plan pivoted directly off of Roosevelt's call for an Economic Bill of Rights, encompassing:

> The right to a useful and remunerative job in the industries or shops or farms or mines of the nation;
>
> The right to adequate medical care and the opportunity to achieve and enjoy good health;
>
> The right to adequate protection from the economic fears of old age, sickness, accident, and unemployment.

These rights would have matched the Beveridgean social protections—although not the nationalization of basic industry—undertaken by the 1945 Labour government in the United Kingdom, obviating the private welfare state that ultimately emerged from collective bargaining. As Hillman realized, policies for industrial workers would need support from other constituent elements in the Democratic coalition and in the polity, including rural and middle-class voters, in order to become law. Far from evincing gauzy retreat from proper, producerist politics, these universal themes, like

---

interests. See Franklin D. Roosevelt, "Address at Fenway Park, Boston, Massachusetts, November 4, 1944," http://www.presidency.ucsb.edu/ws/?pid=16468.

[72]Cf. Nelson Lichtenstein, *Labor's War at Home: The CIO in World War II* (Cambridge: Cambridge University Press, 1982), 171–77.

[73]Joseph Gaer, *The First Round: The Story of the CIO Political Action Committee* (New York: Duell, Sloan and Pearce, 1944), 22. The book is an excellent compendium of PAC propaganda, including the full "People's Program for 1944," a quasi-platform that reprints the Second Bill of Rights, at 185–212. See also Michael Kazin, *The Populist Persuasion* (New York: Basic Books, 1995), 160. John Gerring, *Party Ideologies in America, 1828–1996* (Cambridge: Cambridge University Press, 1998), 233–38, dates a similar shift in the Democratic platform to 1952.

the creation of NC-PAC, responded not only to the particular opportunities and constraints of the moment, but to the realities of coalition building in American politics.[74]

PAC had won a strong victory, yet without congressional majorities, a hollow one.[75] Dewey's attacks had failed. Fat margins across the nation's urban centers convinced observers that PAC had become a political force to which Democrats would have to pay heed—a perception of influence critical in the trading of favors.[76] "The outcome of the national elections," Hillman told the CIO convention weeks afterward in a barely veiled attack on any notions of a third party, "has proved the continued vitality of the two-party system as a framework within which a democratic people can fully express their will."[77] Nevertheless, the CIO stood exposed to the conservative coalition. When movements seek to leverage influence alongside sympathetic parties, they simultaneously expose their vulnerabilities. Such was the story of CIO-PAC in Roosevelt's last campaign.

Heroic accounts to the contrary, alliance between labor and the Democrats emerged from weakness more than strength, but that weakness renders the achievement of alliance all the more remarkable. The American political system requires movements, representing minorities, to cobble together majorities congruent with the interests of other players inside major parties. A social movement led in its formative phase by coal miners and clothing workers secured its place despite opposition from both the vast majority of American industry and a long-dominant faction in the allied party. So, too, the CIO pushed forward, however imperfectly, the joint alignment of racial and economic liberalism that still dominates American politics—if not always to Democrats' or liberals' advantage.

The timing for movement building and party building intersected imperfectly in the New Deal years. The CIO formed only after the extraordinary moment in 1935 that produced the Wagner and Social Security Acts passed, and built an effective political operation only once passage of nearly any progressive legislation proved impossible. Franklin Roosevelt made his

[74]This dilemma goes far back in social-democratic politics, even under proportional representation. See Adam Przeworski and John Sprague, *Paper Stones: A History of Electoral Socialism* (Chicago: University of Chicago Press, 1986).

[75]A particular disappointment came in Ohio's senate race, where Robert Taft squeaked to victory with a margin of less than seventeen thousand out of more than three million votes cast. CIO did its part—turnout rose in the state's largest counties even as it declined in rural areas—but the state Democratic operation was weak and divided. The campaign hardened Taft against Big Labor and its underhanded tactics. See James T. Patterson, *Mr. Republican: A Biography of Robert A. Taft* (Boston: Houghton Mifflin, 1972), 273–80.

[76]See, e.g., Stephen Hill, "PAC Eyes the Democratic Party," *New Leader*, 25 November 1944, 8; "What P.A.C. Did," *Time*, 20 November 1944, 22.

[77]*Final Proceedings of the 7th Constitutional Convention of the Congress of Industrial Organizations* (Washington, D.C.: CIO, 1944), 208.

only attempt to mold the Democratic Party in 1938, at a moment of weakness and without assistance from the anchoring group.

At the same time, the very success that the CIO achieved came despite these long odds. The CIO forged durable organization among unskilled workers, even crossing the color line, where worker militancy had so often dissipated, and translated allegiances from the job site to political action. The panjandrums of a party long based in small towns and dependent on the South accepted industrial workers as keys to electoral majority. In 1932, all those developments would have been unthinkable. By 1944, they reflected the new realities. The most plausible alternative to labor-Democratic alliance was not industrial democracy, but a far less consequential partnership that simply entrenched the prerogatives of white unionists—or no alliance at all.

CHAPTER 4

"We Are Different from Previous Generations of Conservatives"

The New Right and the Mobilization of Evangelicals

In the late 1970s, reciprocal shifts on the part of party and movement led directly to a durable alliance between white evangelicals and the Republican Party. Yet "the New Right was not created by politicians but by organizers."[1] The key moves in forming alliance—finding new supporters to mobilize, and then using them to elect politicians who would deliver on issue priorities—fell to longtime movement operatives. Much more than evangelicals themselves awakening politically, political entrepreneurs from outside evangelicalism made white evangelicals into an organized movement with priorities compatible with other elements in American conservatism, above all through embrace of low taxes.[2] Led by Richard Viguerie and

[1]Frances FitzGerald, "The Triumphs of the New Right," *New York Review of Books*, 19 November 1981, 19.

[2]In contrast to evangelicals' embrace of party politics in the 1970s, early twentieth-century fundamentalism was a cultural much more than a partisan phenomenon. In the first decades of the twentieth century, fundamentalist Protestants sought public action to ban liquor, protect the Sabbath, and prohibit the teaching of evolution. Divisions between fundamentalists and modernizers, especially bitter among northern Baptists and Presbyterians, cued genuine disputes over doctrine, but did not reflect broader social or partisan cleavages. Fundamentalists in the early twentieth century ran the political gamut from a few Christian socialists to William Jennings Bryan to a slew of rock-ribbed northern Republicans. None of their issues divided the two parties (indeed, only prohibition registered in national politics at all), nor did fundamentalists express a particularly coherent approach to political questions either intellectually or strategically. See Paul A. Carter, "The Fundamentalist Defense of the Faith," in *Change and Continuity in 20th Century America: The 1920s*, ed. John Braeman, Robert H.

Paul Weyrich, these tacticians, most of them neither evangelicals nor terribly loyal Republicans, skillfully exploited events to build a diffuse conservative insurgency. They simultaneously forged links between particular policy controversies and conservative ideology, and made evangelicals into an advantageous electoral partner as they marched into the Republican Party.

Although the New Right hoped itself to orchestrate single-issue coalitions that would supplant partisan politics, evangelical leaders increasingly closely tied with the Republican Party itself displaced their former New Right patrons, whose talents lay in agitating and organizing more than in brinksmanship and compromise. The ongoing ideological sort in American politics doomed any notions of "coalitionism" as the movement found its home in a party eager for its votes—if not always ready to go to the mat for its substantive priorities.

Beyond the New Right lay structural changes that set the stage for, but did not determine, the nature of alliance: the growing confidence of American evangelicals; the unfreezing of southern political cleavages; the crisis of postwar Keynesianism; the reassertion, after Vietnam, of American exceptionalism and greatness.[3] Each of these themes plays out across the coming pages. Yet neither the ongoing "rise of the right" in the conservative movement nor an increasingly conservative public mood itself created the Christian Right, or its alliance with the Republican Party. Instead, contingent triggering events crystallized this incipient alliance. The controversy in 1978 over tax-exempt status for Christian schools galvanized evangelicals across the country, helping them to forge a political identity that deemphasized race and focused on threats to their community from meddlesome federal bureaucrats. The evangelical prolife movement, far from springing forth immediately after *Roe*, required careful cultivation. New Right leaders and the theologian Francis Schaeffer worked to cultivate and then to mobilize evangelicals across denominational boundaries.

Bremner, and David Brody (Columbus: Ohio State University Press, 1968), 179–214; George M. Marsden, *Fundamentalism and American Culture*, 2nd ed. (New York: Oxford University Press, 2006); Ferenc M. Szasz, *The Divided Mind of Protestant America, 1880–1930* (Tuscaloosa: University of Alabama Press, 1982), chap. 8. For a general history, see Nancy T. Ammerman, "North American Protestant Fundamentalism," in *Media, Culture, and the Religious Right*, ed. Linda Kintz and Julia Lesage (Minneapolis: University of Minnesota Press, 1998), 55–113.

[3]Cf. Daniel K. Williams, *God's Own Party: The Making of the Christian Right* (Oxford: Oxford University Press, 2010); and Allan J. Lichtman, *White Protestant Nation: The Rise of the American Conservative Movement* (New York: Atlantic Monthly Press, 2008). Williams stresses the first of these factors. Yet his account, which focuses primarily on evangelical elites, elides the differences between ad hoc backing by individuals, such as Billy Graham's support for Dwight Eisenhower and Richard Nixon, and the vastly more consequential ongoing electoral partnership that developed in the following decades. On Graham, whose public witness paved the way for the Christian Right, but who conspicuously declined to join it, see William Martin, *A Prophet with Honor: The Billy Graham Story* (New York: William Morrow, 1991).

The framework in Chapter 2 explains in general terms that parties will ally with movements in anchoring-group alliance when majority coalitions inside parties prefer the movement to other paths toward electoral majority. They do so when the movement has substantial infrastructural capacity to connect with supporters, and when cross-cutting brokers bring party and movement closer to one another and effectuate alliance. Those general rules, for all their usefulness about *what* has happened across American political history, say relatively less about the precise mechanisms through which human beings actually made those determinations. Hence, this chapter shows *how* alliance unfolded at the point when alliance crystallized in its most salient example since the New Deal. Political actors, operating under complex historical and institutional constraints, effectuated each of these underlying factors. They realized and put resources behind the notion that alliance was a good electoral bet. They reframed issues, especially around race, taxes, and abortion, and mobilized extant networks. Above all, they used threat and opportunity to build political coalitions. Each factor played out critically in the moment—and it was just a moment, in 1979—when the Christian Right joined together with the Republican Party. If the structural conditions in Chapter 2 make alliance seem ineluctable, then the bottom-up view of conservative politics in the late 1970s suggest the myriad ways that making parties accept alliance with cohesive movements takes tremendous political skill—and a bit of luck. The more coherent saga of the Christian Right as it matured inside the GOP ambit is the task of Chapter 8.

The New Right and the Party System

The Christian Right assumed its place in the Republican Party with remarkably little resistance, especially considering the ambivalence of key New Right brokers about the GOP itself. With the defeats of George Romney and Nelson Rockefeller, moderate Republicanism had been vanquished. Disorganized, its scattered leaders offered few electoral inducements for would-be coalition brokers instead romanced by the New Right. Older reformist and progressive traditions had already receded; the Equal Rights Amendment, a staple in Republican platforms since 1944, remained in the 1976 GOP text only by a thread. In contrast to the conservative Democrats who long stymied labor-liberalism, Republican moderates neither stopped alliance with the Christian Right at the gate, nor thwarted its ongoing development.[4]

[4]Geoffrey Kabaservice, *Rule and Ruin: The Downfall of Moderation and the Destruction of the Republican Party, From Eisenhower to the Tea Party* (Oxford: Oxford University Press, 2012), esp. chap. 11; Catherine E. Rymph, *Republican Women: Feminism and Conservatism from Suffrage through the Rise of the New Right* (Chapel Hill: University of North Carolina Press, 2006),

Business, as in much of American history the pivotal player in the Republican coalition, had begun to move right as it regrouped from the punishing regulations of the sixties and early seventies. As labor law reform in 1978 evidenced, big and small business increasingly joined together. With depopulation in the Rust Belt, regional political economies shifted. Although business hardly seeded the Christian Right, as white evangelicals in the Sun Belt entered conservative politics, they found easy allies among business interests. New Right brokers worked to direct white evangelicals' grievances toward a business-friendly worldview committed to lowering taxes and defanging liberal bureaucrats. While the Republican National Committee under Bill Brock aggressively expanded its organizational capacity during the late 1970s, the institutional party thought rather less about the process of coalition building, or about the boundaries of membership in a party still reeling from Watergate. That task, instead, fell to the New Right brokers. Party revival, rather, came only indirectly.[5]

The rise of single-issue politics, split-ticket voting, and ad hoc coalitions led analysts to foretell the death of the American political party as a means to link elites and the mass public, and to organize political conflict. Much of the New Right in the 1970s—and Richard Viguerie, especially—sought to replace partisan politics with single-issue coalitions that would draw together conservatives regardless of party identification, region, or views on questions other than the given group's priorities. Austin Ranney, a distinguished student of parties and a veteran of the Democrats' McGovern-Fraser commission, speculated in 1978 that parties would atrophy and "the candidate organizations, the women's caucuses, the black caucuses, the right-to-life leagues, and the like would become the only real players in the game."[6]

That same year Kevin Phillips, a populist journalist, observed the fractured polity, and remarked that "if Ranney is right, and he may well be, the rise of the 'New Right' in American politics will probably be remembered as playing a pivotal role." As it transpired, Ranney was largely wrong—and the New Right ought to be remembered as playing a pivotal role. Rather, what Phillips imagined to be "a post-GOP party" constituted almost precisely what the GOP became. It was the Republican Party shorn of its "upper-middle-income liberal fringe," plus neoconservatives, southern Democrats,

---

chaps. 7 and 8; Bill Peterson, "In Her Farewell, Mary Crisp Blasts GOP 'Sickness,'" *Washington Post*, 10 July 1980, A1.

[5] Philip A. Klinkner, *The Losing Parties: Out-Party National Committees, 1956–1993* (New Haven: Yale University Press, 1994), chap. 7.

[6] Austin Ranney, "The Political Parties: Reform and Decline," in *The New American Political System*, ed. Anthony King (Washington, D.C.: American Enterprise Institute, 1978), 247.

and the New Right.[7] The caucuses became high-demanding players inside networked parties.

Therein lies a critical irony: the movement that sought to supersede the Republican Party ultimately defined and strengthened it. The search for a durable conservative majority brought together the single-issue groups, and forged ideological commonalities across their particular stances. What the New Right termed "coalitionism" was always a label rather than an approach to policymaking. The New Right's fiercest opponents concentrated in the left wing of the Democratic Party. All forty liberals "targeted for defeat" in a 1978 Free Congress mailing were Democrats.[8] Once the 1978 midterm elections put a coterie of New Right–leaning Republicans into office and, especially, after Ronald Reagan's nomination and election, grassroots conservatives and Republicans supplanted the antiestablishment "coalitionism" that Viguerie had advocated.

For their part, the New Right's Republican friends in Congress focused on party building, even as the nominal Democrats favored something like tactical coalitionism. In the House, young conservatives such as Newt Gingrich, Henry Hyde, and Mickey Edwards worked through the Republican Study Group, initially directed by Ed Feulner, later the longtime president of the Heritage Foundation. James McClure, the New Right's point person on energy and land-use issues, ascended to the third-ranking position in the Senate leadership during his first term. In the institutional party, Morton Blackwell, a longtime Viguerie aide at the *New Right Report*, and president of the Leadership Institute, which since 1979 has taught thousands of young conservatives the nuts and bolts of succeeding in politics, is also the acknowledged expert on the rules of the Republican National Committee.[9] After the 1980 landslide, Jesse Helms carefully mentored a string of southern conservative Republicans. By the early Reagan years, however, many of the New Right's favorite Democrats, such as Bob Stump and Phil Gramm, had

[7] Kevin Phillips, "New Right and Two Party System," *Florida Times-Union*, 10 October 1978, A-6; *American Political Report*, 18 August 1978; for a broader critique, Kevin Phillips, "The Balkanization of America," *Harper's*, May 1978, 37–47. Interestingly, Phillips never explicitly mentions evangelicals. He also imagined Scoop Jackson and Pat Moynihan, as well as Irving Kristol and Norman Podhoretz, in his post-GOP party. Cf. Kevin Phillips, *American Theocracy: The Peril and Politics of Radical Religion, Oil, and Borrowed Money in the 21st Century* (New York: Viking, 2006), esp. pt. 2, a much-disillusioned Phillips's jeremiad against what he deemed "America's first religious party."

[8] "CSFC Contributions $300 and Above," accretion of September 1986, Papers of Paul M. Weyrich. On Free Congress scorecards, see Richard Starnes, "Right-Wing Voice Avoids Lunatic Label," *Knoxville News-Sentinel*, 7 November 1977, C1.

[9] See, with explicit reference to party takeover and to supplanting the New Deal coalition, Morton Blackwell, "Building a Conservative Governing Majority" in *Steering the Elephant: How Washington Works*, ed. Robert Rector and Michael Sanera (New York: Universe, 1987), 22–38.

switched parties. The last leading holdout, Larry McDonald, a right-wing Georgia Democrat who served on the John Birch Society board, died in 1983.

New Right Brokers

New Right brokers transcended the divide between party and movement. The phrase "political entrepreneur" has become something of a catchphrase.[10] For men like Viguerie and Weyrich, however, it is a pitch-perfect description of their hybrid roles. The political entrepreneurs of the New Right hoped for a conservative majority that would restore traditional morality, aggressively champion American interests, and roll back the frontiers of the state. Like party elites, they sought new voters to fashion an electoral majority—although they lacked the authority to shape the state. Like movement elites, their goals transcended politicians' immediate exigencies of reelection, officeholding, and coalition management—although they lacked direct influence over members or supporters.

Above all, they were effective *organizers* set on redefining the underlying political terrain through advocacy on behalf of candidates and causes. As Weyrich, an omnipresent, pugnacious son of Racine, Wisconsin, seeded by the Coors family, said in 1978, "We are different from previous generations of conservatives. We are radicals, working to overturn the present power structure. . . . We are the outsiders, very much like the New Dealers of 40 years ago: a group of young people coming and saying 'What's here isn't right and we are going to change it.'"[11] Their conservative-populist vision embraced myriad dissidents from the crack-up of Cold War liberalism and the Democratic political order: hard hats in Youngstown, Ohio, and mothers in South Boston protesting court-ordered busing.[12] They sought careful,

[10] See Adam Sheingate, "The Terrain of the Political Entrepreneur," in *Formative Acts: American Politics in the Making*, ed. Stephen Skowronek and Matthew Glassman (Philadelphia: University of Pennsylvania Press, 2007), 30–31.

[11] William J. Lanouette, "The New Right—'Revolutionaries' Out after the 'Lunch-Pail' Vote," *National Journal*, 21 January 1978, 89; see also L. J. Davis, "Conservatives in America," *Harper's*, October 1980, 21–27. On Weyrich, see Stephen Isaacs, "Coors' Capital Connection," *Washington Post*, 7 May 1975, A1; "Paul Weyrich and Connaught Marshner: People of the Free Congress," *Christian Life*, March 1980, 29–30; Paul M. Weyrich, "Blue Collar or Blue Blood: The New Right Compared with the Old Right," in *The New Right Papers*, ed. Robert W. Whitaker (New York: St. Martin's, 1982), 48–62; Lee Edwards, *The Power of Ideas: The Heritage Foundation at 25 Years* (Ottawa, Ill.: Jameson Books, 1997); Alf Tomas Tønnessen, *How Two Political Entrepreneurs Helped Create the American Conservative Movement: The Ideas of Richard Viguerie and Paul Weyrich* (Lewiston, N.Y.: Edwin Mellen Press, 2009).

[12] See Jefferson Cowie, *Stayin' Alive: The 1970s and the Last Days of the Working Class* (New York: New Press, 2010); Judith Stein, *Pivotal Decade: How the United States Traded Factories for Finance in the Seventies* (New Haven: Yale University Press, 2010); Rick Perlstein, "That Seventies Show," *Nation*, 8 November 2010, 25–34.

selective mobilization of certain issue publics; Weyrich told the National Affairs Briefing in 1980 that "our leverage in the election quite candidly goes down as the voting populace goes up."[13] While it emphasized traditional family and morality, the New Right saw cultural conservatism in nuts-and-bolts rather than civilizational terms. As a paleo-conservative commentator noted drily, "few New Rightists have displayed much interest in literature, the arts, or philosophy."[14]

The hub of the New Right was Richard Viguerie's mail room. Viguerie, a hard-charging vanguard for a new generation of conservatism, looms larger in the historical account of how party-movement alliance took place than he does in demarcating its ultimate nature or successes. Viguerie sought to emulate liberals' successes at forging ideological consensus from disparate single-issue groups.[15] "All the New Right has done is to copy the old left," he wrote in 1981.[16]

A Catholic from Houston, Viguerie in 1961 found himself in New York as executive secretary of Young Americans for Freedom. The YAF served as a prototype for the movement building para-organizations that would sustain the Christian Right. Its goals focused on electoral change—it was not a principled debating society like, say, the American Conservative Union that bore the brunt of so many New Right critiques of the Old Right—but neither was it tied to any particular politician, or the electoral calendar. Especially after the defeat of Barry Goldwater in 1964, when the pragmatic new RNC chair, Ray Bliss of Ohio, purged party ranks, conservatives in party circles congregated in the densely interlocked Young Republicans and YAF.

[13] Mary Barrineau, "Nominee Questions Evolution," *Dallas Times-Herald*, 23 August 1980, 1-A.

[14] Paul Gottfried, *The Conservative Movement*, rev. ed. (New York: Twayne, 1993), 115; similarly, see Chilton Williamson, "Country & Western Marxism: To the Nashville Station," *National Review*, 9 June 1978, 711–16.

[15] Viguerie discovered the tactic from Marvin Liebman, who had learned it as a member of the Popular Front–era Young Communist League. After the Second World War, Liebman moved far to the right, and began a series of single-issue groups with titles like the Committee of One Million to Keep Red China out of the United Nations. Liebman ultimately came out of the closet and broke with the conservative movement over its antigay stands. See Marvin Liebman, *Coming Out Conservative: An Autobiography* (San Francisco: Chronicle Books, 1992); Marvin Liebman, "Independently Speaking," *The Advocate*, 7 February 1995, 41; and a fascinating exchange with William F. Buckley, "Notes & Asides," *National Review*, 9 July 1990, 16–18.

[16] Richard Viguerie, *The New Right: We're Ready to Lead* (Falls Church: Viguerie Company, 1981), 78. See also John Fialka, "Godfather of the 'New Right' Feels the Torch Is Passing," *Washington Star*, 23 June 1975, A-1; John Fialka, "Arch-Conservative's Crusade," *Washington Star*, 24 June 1975, A-4; Phil Galley, "Doubts on Direct Mail Wizard," *Washington Star*, 9 May 1978, A-1; Nick Kotz, "King Midas of the New Right," *Atlantic Monthly*, November 1978, 52–61; Nick Thimmesch, "The Grassroots Dollar Chase—Ready on the Right," *New York*, 9 June 1975, 54–65; and the oft-cited but unsourced Alan Crawford, *Thunder on the Right: The New Right and the Politics of Resentment* (New York: Pantheon, 1980).

A generation of Republican and conservative operatives and politicians, including Gary Bauer, Charlie Black, Morton Blackwell, Pat Buchanan, Phil Crane, David Keene, Buz Lukens, Connie Marshner, Dana Rohrabacher, and Roger Stone, all got their start at the YAF.[17]

In 1965, Viguerie combined the YAF list with the names of Goldwater's donors that he had laboriously hand-copied at the House clerk's office. Soon after, he saved the data on magnetic tapes. Much of his business was with nonprofits, ranging from bread-and-butter charities such as hospitals (often religiously affiliated), to a spate of ideologically minded groups devoted to conservative goals. In 1970, he handled fundraising for G. Harrold Carswell, a Senate primary candidate in Florida whose nomination for the Supreme Court had been voted down after concerns about his views on civil rights and women's rights.[18]

His most important client, however, was George Wallace.[19] Wallace brought Viguerie on board early in 1973 to retire $400,000 in debt from the 1972 campaign. In exchange for unusually lenient terms—Wallace netted half the proceeds, rather than the usual quarter—the Viguerie Company received the three million names on Wallace's mailing list. By the end of 1975, Viguerie had raised $5.6 million for Wallace; it was substantially more than any other 1976 presidential candidate had garnered to that point, although the relationship ended following Wallace's disappointing primary showings. After Ronald Reagan failed to capture the GOP nomination, Viguerie then flirted with backing the remnants of Wallace's old American Independent Party in the fall.[20]

[17] John A. Andrew, III, *The Other Side of the Sixties: Young Americans for Freedom and the Rise of Conservative Politics* (New Brunswick, N.J.: Rutgers University Press, 1997); Wayne Thorburn, *A Generation Awakes: Young Americans for Freedom and the Creation of the Conservative Movement* (Ottawa, Ill.: Jameson Books, 2010); F. Clifton White and William J. Gill, *Why Reagan Won: A Narrative History of the Conservative Movement, 1964–1981* (Chicago: Regnery Gateway, 1981), 76–77. In the early 1970s, many of them also joined the ad hoc coalitions on Capitol Hill through which young staffers at the core of the New Right came together. Edwin J. Feulner, Jr., *Conservatives Stalk the House: The Republican Study Committee, 1970–1982* (Ottawa, Ill.: Green Hill, 1983), chap. 3; "Memorandum for the Files," 1/2/1973, Weyrich papers, accretion of December 1985.

[18] "Carswell Backers Ask Campaign Aid," *New York Times*, 29 May 1970, 59.

[19] Amazingly enough, Morris Dees proposed that Wallace hire Viguerie. Dees, a liberal native Alabamian, had learned about direct mail while in publishing, and then directed George McGovern's 1972 mail operation before founding the Southern Poverty Law Center, which has worked to expose what it deems hate groups on the right. He made the suggestion in response to a query from Wallace aide Charles Snider, an old acquaintance from Montgomery. See Stephan Lesher, *George Wallace: American Populist* (Reading, Mass.: Addison-Wesley, 1994), 462–64; Richard A. Viguerie and David Franke, *America's Right Turn: How Conservatives Used New and Alternative Media to Take Power* (Chicago: Bonus Books, 2004), 149–50; Christopher Lydon, "Credit System Fuels Wallace Fund Drive," *New York Times*, 23 May 1975, 1.

[20] Stephen Isaacs, "Newcomers' Hopes Are Scuttled at 3d-Party Session," *Washington Post*, 29 August 1976, 3; Karen Elliott House, "American Independents Select Maddox, Reducing

Support for Wallace is often described as a way station for disaffected conservative Democrats on the road to the Reagan coalition. Viguerie took grassroots populism, and sublimated us-versus-them themes with racial overtones in favor of a public morality oriented around the traditional family. The relationship forged several critical links among religious, social, and political conservatives. Half the letters sent to Wallace had some kind of religious reference, an aide said. Viguerie saw cultural issues as a bridge to Wallace supporters: "I'm realizing each day that George Wallace and I have more in common than I thought. I'd like to see less government in people's lives than Wallace does, but when it comes to social issues in the public schools, we're together." While Wallace was a thrice-married Methodist more interested in baiting elites than in promoting personal morality, Viguerie soon learned where his supporters went to church. As Viguerie said in 1976, "the next major area of growth for the conservative ideology and philosophy is among evangelical people."[21]

The expansion of Viguerie's activity in the mid-1970s emerged not only from conservative ferment but from rules on fundraising. Just as the history of CIO-PAC and its tactics was deeply entwined with rules on campaign finance, so with the New Right. The Federal Election Campaign Act was amended in 1974 to impose stringent two-thousand-dollar limits on contributions to congressional candidates. Under the new rules, which bit hard in the days before soft money or independent expenditures, Coorses, Pews, and Hunts could no longer single-handedly bankroll candidates on the right. Weyrich noted archly that "the election reformers who are now busy developing ways of taking Richard Viguerie out of the political process have only themselves to blame for putting him there in the first place."[22]

Viguerie married direct-mail technology with red-meat appeals that riled up supporters. Magnetic tape reels allowed him to store contributors' addresses and giving histories electronically, and eased the preparation of extremely large mailings by automating the once-laborious process of labeling and sorting envelopes. In the age of Big Data, his methods appear antediluvian. At the time, they were revolutionary. By cross-feeding lists, he

Right-Wing Challenge to Ford," *Wall Street Journal*, 30 August 1976, 4; William Rusher, *The Rise of the Right* (New York: William Morrow, 1984), chap. 11.

[21] Lesher, *George Wallace*, 463; "Wallace Raises $1.3 Million, Widening Fund Lead," *New York Times*, 15 July 1975, 17; "New York Seeks to Ban Wallace's Fund-Raiser," *New York Times*, 22 December 1975, 17; Warner Stough, "Wallace Campaign Reducing '72 Debt," *Birmingham News*, 28 August 1973, 6; Thimmesch, "Grassroots Dollar Chase," 58; Ted Knap, "Tough New Up-and-Comer Bucks the Conservative Ranks," *Evansville Press*, 1 January 1976, 20; Jim Wallis and Wes Michaelson, "The Plan to Save America," *Sojourners*, April 1976. For a thoughtful discussion on Wallace and the Right, see Michael Kazin, *The Populist Persuasion* (New York: Basic Books, 1995), 252–58.

[22] Paul M. Weyrich, "The New Right: PACs and Coalition Politics," in *Parties, Interest Groups, and Campaign Finance Law*, ed. Michael J. Malbin (Washington, D.C.: American Enterprise Institute, 1980), 73.

established himself as the necessary destination for any conservative candidate or cause. And by advancing funds for early mailings, he ensured that clients owed him massive debts, giving him enormous leverage over them.

Viguerie claimed that he was not just fundraising but hand-delivering tailored messages straight to supporters, adding value whether or not the reply card arrived back with a check. "Direct mail," he explained, "can bypass the monopoly the left has in the media, and let us go directly to the people and tell them what the problem is and what to do about it."[23] He embedded his tactics in a view of resource mobilization that scholars of social movements (few of them sympathetic to his politics) would well understand:

> Any cause that hopes to become a mass movement must have at its core burning issues that motivate people into action. . . . What kinds of issues have this power?
>
> - A perceived crisis that is not being managed by the ruling establishment . . .
> - Threats to a way of life, or to the economic security of a large number of people, such as onerous taxation or regulations that are grinding the economy to a halt . . .
> - Idealistic projections of a better life once the 'bad guys' have been overthrown.[24]

His over-the-top letters expressed this vision. A mailing for Howard Phillips's Conservative Caucus in November 1974, which raised half a million dollars, presaged the themes and style of grassroots conservatism down to the age of Fox News: "Are you as sick and tired as I am of liberal politicians who: force children to be bused; appoint judges who turn murderers and rapists loose on the public; force your children to study from school books that are anti-God, anti-American, and filled with the most vulgar curse words; give your tax money to communists, anarchists and other radical organizations; do nothing about sex, adultery, homosexuality and foul language on television?"[25] The money was often skimmed off twice over before reaching candidates themselves, first by RAVCO (the Viguerie Company) for postage, printing, and profit, and then by a PAC led by a broker with his own agenda, such as Terry Dolan's NCPAC, Paul Weyrich's CSFC-PAC, or Jesse Helms's Congressional Club. Only 11 percent of the fundraising from CSFC-PAC, and 12 percent from NCPAC, in the 1980 cycle went directly to

[23] "Raising Millions of Dollars for Conservatives—The Way It's Done," *US News & World Report*, 26 February 1979, 53.

[24] Viguerie and Franke, *America's Right Turn*, 140–41.

[25] Fialka, "Arch-Conservative's Crusade."

endorsed candidates.[26] In turn, each of these empires operated its own collection of campaign committees, PACs, for-profit consultancies, advocacy arms, and foundations, each designed to wheedle as much impact from dollars in a particular category with as little cost and public scrutiny as its lawyers deemed that the law allowed.[27]

Were the new methods of direct mail genuine game changers, or simply the vehicle to fundraise for causes and candidates whose time had come? The experimental turn in political science came too late to provide any micro-level evidence. The Viguerie Committee purged its archives when it had to sell its building in the late 1980s. And precisely because RAVCO held a near monopoly on New Right direct mail and sold lists to most of the other fundraisers, few prominent grassroots conservative candidates succeeded, or failed, outside his umbrella.

For many candidates, direct mail was plainly a bad deal given the fees that Viguerie collected. Direct mail typically worked best for ideologues and for candidates who had already established a strong national brand.[28] As a way to bring together politicians and movement allies, however, the system of cross-filing succeeded brilliantly despite each mailing's high cost. The New Right leadership, funded by individual campaigns and causes, absorbed the "public good" costs of bringing causes and candidates together.

The Christian Right, the New Right, and Trigger Events

The late 1970s stand out for the sheer number of events that grassroots conservatives exploited. In each case, aggressive attacks took aim at smug, out-of-touch liberal elites. The evangelical political scientist Robert Zwier identified four "trigger events" in the 1970s that led to the creation of the Christian Right: the Supreme Court's 1973 decision in *Roe v. Wade*, the

[26]Tim Wyngaard, "On the GOP Front," *El Paso Herald-Post*, 17 June 1977, D-5; Rich Jaroslavsky, "Mr. Viguerie Collects Funds, Gains Influence in Conservative Causes," *Wall Street Journal*, 6 October 1978; Robert D. Shaw, Jr., "New Right Gave Candidates Little," *Miami Herald*, 29 March 1981.

[27]Larry J. Sabato, *The Rise of Political Consultants: New Ways of Winning Elections* (New York: Basic Books, 1981), 222; Paul Taylor, "Helms Modernizes GOP Political Machine for the Electronic Age," *Washington Post*, 15 October 1982, A2; Robert Timberg, "New Right Campaign Operation Bypasses Election Laws," *Baltimore Sun*, 17 October 1982, A1; Bob Hall with Marcie Pachino, "Jesse Helms: The Meaning of His Money," *Southern Exposure*, January 1985, 14–23.

[28]"Direct Mail Fundraising Roundtable, the Pros Speak," *Campaigns & Elections*, Fall 1980, 20–46; Larry Light, "Direct-Mail Bids Do Not Ensure Pot of Gold," *CQ Weekly Report*, 23 October 1982, 2714–15; Dom Bonafede, "Part Science, Part Art, Part Hokum, Direct Mail Now a Key Campaign Tool," *National Journal*, 31 July 1982; Paul C. Harris, "Politics by Mail: A New Platform," *Wharton Magazine*, Fall 1982, 16–19.

battle against the Equal Rights Amendment, early attempts to limit gay rights, and the 1978 fight over proposed IRS rules to limit the tax exemptions of racially discriminatory private schools.[29]

These events all reflect the New Right's careful framing, taking controversial positions and placing them under a sympathetic "profamily" label. Rates of divorce and out-of-wedlock birth had risen sharply, and traditional families seemed under assault. From Richard Nixon's failed Family Assistance Plan for a guaranteed income to Jimmy Carter's ill-fated White House Conference on Families, policymakers' responses seemed at best uncertain.[30] The New Right, by contrast, took fraught questions at the intersection of family structure, gender roles, and social policy, and refocused them on traditional moral standards.

The IRS controversy and the growing prolife movement loom largest. They cover the institutional origins and signature issue of the Christian Right, and address issues of race and gender respectively. Gay rights has been episodic in its importance to the Christian Right, and the flurry of activity in the late 1970s dissipated; the larger legacy came in defining the "culture wars."[31] Nor did early controversies in states and cities over gay rights—Miami, Minneapolis, California—reach national politics. Gay rights issues have been much more central since 1992, when Bill Clinton sought to end the ban on gays in the military, the Republican platform first mentioned homosexuality, and same-sex marriage surfaced as a state-level issue.

In the summer of 1972, Phyllis Schlafly, a Roman Catholic, a virulent anticommunist and strong Goldwater backer, and a former vice president of the National Federation of Republican Women, formed STOP ERA to defeat the amendment. As it made common cause to stop ERA, a conservative

[29] Robert Zwier, *Born-Again Politics: The New Christian Right in America* (Downers Grove, Ill.: InterVarsity Press, 1982), chap. 2.

[30] On family policy, see Nathan Glazer, "The Rediscovery of the Family," *Commentary*, March 1978, 49–56; Gilbert Steiner, *The Futility of Family Policy* (Washington, D.C.: Brookings Institution Press, 1981), chap. 2; and Kimberly Morgan, "A Child of the Sixties: The Great Society, the New Right, and the Politics of Federal Child Care," *Journal of Policy History* 13 (2001): 215–50. On the "profamily" frame, see Allen Hunter, "Virtue with a Vengeance: The Pro-Family Politics of the New Right" (PhD diss., Brandeis University, 1984), 181.

[31] The political science of issue and coalition formation adds little to questions around sexual orientation, personal morality, and conservative religion—not least the number of men in the Christian Right caught up in gay sex scandals. An unscientific list would include Billy James Hargis, firebrand anticommunist at the American Christian College—and who, a couple discovered on their wedding night, had slept with both the bride and the groom; Bob Bauman, a congressman from Maryland who had sex with a sixteen-year-old prostitute; Terry Dolan, the closeted head of NCPAC who died of AIDS in 1986; and Ted Haggard, the president of the National Association of Evangelicals, who had sex with and took drugs from a prostitute. For a portrait of Dolan, see Perry Deane Young, *God's Bullies: Native Reflections on Preachers and Politics* (New York: Holt, Rinehart, and Winston, 1982), chap. 10.

coalition of Catholics, evangelicals, and Mormons began both to work together for the first time, and to find itself in Republican circles. Yet the leading, male-dominated Christian Right para-organizations arose only after it was clear that the amendment was going down to defeat.[32]

In addition to these four expressly moral controversies, each of which specifically triggered political activity by evangelical Christians, three further events helped to propel the New Right to national prominence, and situated cultural issues within the emergent framework of grassroots conservative backlash. In all three cases, direct mail produced by the Richard Viguerie Company fueled the insurgencies. First, the New Right led opposition to the Panama Canal Treaties; the issue kept Ronald Reagan in the national spotlight after his 1976 loss, gave Richard Viguerie half a million new names on his reels of tape, and arguably helped to elect nearly a dozen acolytes of the New Right to the Senate in 1978.[33] Second, Howard Jarvis's antitax revolt in California led to the passage of Proposition 13 in June 1978, which severely limited property and business tax increases in the nation's most populous state.[34] Third, after extensive lobbying led by the National Right to Work Committee, the Senate failed in 1978 to end a filibuster on labor-law reform, marking the end of the liberal postwar political economy.[35]

Each event heralded themes that conservatives would sound for decades. The Panama Canal Treaties, the quintessential single-issue campaign, signaled an end to bipartisanship on foreign policy through use of the treaty power, and the recrudescence of national sovereignty as a grassroots conservative leitmotif. Proposition 13 ushered in a renaissance in policymaking through initiative and referendum at the state level, a favorite tactic of

[32]Donald T. Critchlow, *Phyllis Schlafly and Grassroots Conservatism: A Woman's Crusade* (Princeton: Princeton University Press, 2005), chap. 9; Jane J. Mansbridge, *Why We Lost the ERA* (Chicago: University of Chicago Press, 1986), esp. chaps. 9 and 10.

[33]Adam Clymer, *Drawing a Line in the Big Ditch* (Lawrence: University Press of Kansas, 2008); Rusher, *Rise of the Right*, 300.

[34]David O. Sears and Jack Citrin, *Tax Revolt: Something for Nothing in California* (Cambridge, Mass.: Harvard University Press, 1985); Clarence Lo, *Small Property versus Big Government: Social Origins of the Property Tax Revolt* (Berkeley: University of California Press, 1990), chap. 8; Isaac William Martin, *The Permanent Tax Revolt: How the Property Tax Transformed American Politics* (Stanford: Stanford University Press, 2008); James R. Dickenson, "How Badly Will Tax Revolt Hurt Brown?," *Washington Star*, 8 June 1978, A1; Adam Clymer, "Co-Author Says Proposition 13 Is No Panacea for Rest of Nation," *New York Times*, 19 November 1978, 26.

[35]See Chapter 7. Although the defeat of labor-law reform owed a great deal to mobilization by corporate America through, for instance, the Business Roundtable, much of the impetus behind right-to-work came from the grassroots right in the Sun Belt. See Kim Phillips-Fein, *Invisible Hands: The Making of the Conservative Movement from the New Deal to Reagan* (New York: Norton, 2009), esp. chap. 9.

grassroots conservatives who distrusted entrenched interests and sought to activate issue publics. It also created a movement that, in combination with skillful use of Watergate-era reconciliation rules, would succeed in unifying the "tribes of the right" around their common distaste for taxes. The defeat of labor law reform brought together big and small business (especially from right-to-work states) to stop "big labor" in its tracks. In each case, evangelicals found common cause with other tribes in American conservatism angry respectively at multilateralism, taxes, and unionism.

Race, Religion, and the IRS Controversy

To what extent did race, class, region, and religion all figure into the rise of the right in the final decades of the twentieth century? In one oft-told tale, white backlash against race reoriented national politics, and religious change simply expressed those cleavages. In another narrative, liberal elites forced religious traditionalists into the public square to defend their values against incursions from courts and bureaucrats. Neither story really addresses the complexities of race, religion, and party. The alliance between conservative evangelicals and the Republican Party emerged from changed racial politics in the wake of desegregation and the civil rights movement. The new racial alignment unfroze regional political cleavages, expanded the issue content in national politics, accelerated ideological sorting, and brought evangelicals in and out of the South together in a common program.

At the mass level, political science has yet to produce a systematic account linking the reorientation of religious divisions with changing partisanship and voting behavior. In particular, accounts focusing on racial context and attitudes to explain voting behavior have rarely examined religion or religiosity. The Dixiecrat bolt of 1948 and the Goldwater and Wallace candidacies began to peel away ancestral Democratic loyalties in the South. Change accelerated with conservatives' shift, especially pronounced toward the top of the white class structure, to identify as Republicans after Richard Nixon's landslide win in 1972. Yet these shifts took place on very different time horizons. Conservative evangelicals became a political force inside the GOP starting in 1980, yet religious polarization in the mass public only peaked in the George W. Bush years, long after the elite-level fights had resolved.[36]

[36]Byron E. Shafer and Richard Johnston, *The End of Southern Exceptionalism: Class, Race, and Partisan Change in the Postwar South* (Cambridge, Mass.: Harvard University Press, 2006); John C. Green, Lyman A. Kellstedt, Corwin E. Smidt, and James L. Guth, "The Soul of the South: Religion and Southern Politics in the New Millennium," in *New Politics of the Old South: An Introduction to Southern Politics*, 5th ed., ed. Charles S. Bullock III and Mark J. Rozell (Lanham, Md.: Rowman & Littlefield, 2013), 291–312; Edward Carmines and Harold Stanley, "Ideological Realignment in the Contemporary South," in *The Disappearing South: Studies*

Race and religion combined with particular force in the 1978 fight over IRS rules for private schools. The immediate threat to their churches and schools politicized evangelicals long suspicious of the public realm. The New Right mobilized to build organizational infrastructure and mount ideological appeals that reoriented public debate on race and religion. Framing, mobilization, issue bundling, and the creation of cross-cutting networks all worked together. In the vein of law-and-order politics in the late 1960s, advocates shifted the gaze away from race and supplied as victims not African Americans but innocent churches.[37]

Yet Republican and New Right elites moved a step further. An attempt to crack down on schools evading integration became a rallying cry against intrusive government. Party and movement leaders found a common language that submerged race to emphasize religious freedom and meddlesome bureaucrats.[38] The debate on the IRS rules joined other forces in late-1970s conservatism, including the growing tax revolt begun in California, and the fight against quotas in making distinctions on the basis of race, affirmed by the Supreme Court in the *Bakke* case earlier in 1978.

The mobilization by New Right elites on Christian schools, and subsequently on abortion, belies the retrospective story of grassroots protest to *Roe*—what the liberal evangelical historian Randall Balmer has termed "the abortion myth"[39]—and shows how brokers reorient the priorities of parties and movements in order to forge effective alliance on common terms. New Right elites framed threats to white evangelicals in ways that pushed them toward conservatism, and brought together their lives amid the institutions of civil society—church and private school—with basic questions about the state and its power to tax. Beginning in the Reagan administration, that ideological linkage would become a more explicitly partisan one.

The new constellation did not simply emerge from clever language, with new frames somehow creating new realities on the ground. Nor, to use language from another vantage point, was it simply a story of organization or institution building alone: understanding purposive action necessitates understanding the purposes that motivate activists. Rather, conservatives primarily outside the evangelical subculture sought to take advantage of the expanded issue agendas and new partisan cleavages brought about in

---

in Regional Change and Continuity, ed. Robert P. Steed, Laurence W. Moreland, and Tod A. Baker (Tuscaloosa: University of Alabama Press, 1990), 21–33; Earl Black and Merle Black, *Politics and Society in the South* (Cambridge, Mass.: Harvard University Press, 1987), 252.

[37] See Vesla M. Weaver, "Frontlash: Race and the Development of Punitive Crime Policy," *Studies in American Political Development* 21 (2007): 230–65.

[38] See generally Thomas Byrne Edsall with Mary D. Edsall, *Chain Reaction: The Impact of Race, Rights, and Taxes on American Politics* (New York: Norton, 1991).

[39] Randall Balmer, *Thy Kingdom Come: How the Religious Right Distorts the Faith and Threatens America* (New York: Basic Books, 2006), 17.

the sixties and seventies, and awaken a useful political constituency in ways compatible with the rest of American conservatism. Paul Weyrich stated the case explicitly: "What caused the movement to surface was the federal government's moves against Christian schools. This absolutely shattered the Christian community's notion that Christians could isolate themselves inside their own institutions and teach what they pleased. The realization that they could not then linked up with the long-held conservative view that government is too powerful, and this linkage was what made evangelicals active. It wasn't the abortion issue; that wasn't sufficient. It was the recognition that isolation simply would no longer work in this society."[40]

It is no surprise that the climactic battle in forming the Christian Right came on the issue of school desegregation. In the decades following *Brown* but especially after the Civil Rights Act and Voting Rights Act had begun the serious work of dismantling Jim Crow, federal courts, administrative agencies, and Congress sought a variety of new remedies, from consent decrees and structural injunctions to conditional grants, all designed to compel integrated schools despite the intransigence of state and local officials.[41] These efforts to create what the Supreme Court in 1968 called "a system without a 'white' school and a 'Negro' school, but just schools"[42] expanded beyond the public schools to encompass private education.

White parents throughout the South responded by opening church-based schools to educate their children. These "seg academies" often began in a hurry after a desegregation order, with a God and country rally led by a minister, and sometimes began operation in a matter of weeks. Many of the "seg academies" were legally part of the churches that sponsored them. The churches already had buildings for Sunday schools, bank accounts—complete with a 501(c)(3) determination from the IRS—and networks of congregants from which to draw students. Between 1970 and 1980, the number of students in the old Confederacy attending non-Catholic religious schools quadrupled, roughly from 150,000 to 600,000. A journalist in the mid-1980s, after visiting conservative Protestant schools in thirty states, concluded that about a quarter exclusively enrolled white students, and a further half had minority enrollment below 3 percent, with more diversity, in general, outside the South.[43]

[40]Paul Weyrich, "Comments," in *No Longer Exiles: The Religious New Right in American Politics*, ed. Michael Cromartie (Washington, D.C.: Ethics and Public Policy Center, 1993), 26.

[41]See Hugh Davis Graham, "Since 1964: The Paradox of American Civil Rights Regulation," in *Taking Stock: American Government in the Twentieth Century*, ed. Morton Keller and R. Shep Melnick (Washington, D.C.: Woodrow Wilson Center Press, 1999), 187–218.

[42]*Green v. County School Board of New Kent County*, 391 U.S. 430 (1968), 442.

[43]Outside the South, by contrast, enrollment rose by about two-thirds during the decade. Paul F. Parsons, *Inside America's Christian Schools* (Macon, Ga.: Mercer University Press, 1987), xiii, 114; overall enrollment data from the National Center for Educational Statistics.

Observers and historians have clashed on the degree to which racial animosity, or simply the desire to educate children outside the Godless and permissive public schools, motivated the seg academies. The schools outside Jackson, Mississippi, operated by the racist Citizens Council clearly fall into a different category from those less intimately tied to a desegregation order. Parents often spoke of their desire to restore traditional forms of order and discipline. While Christian schools often mentioned the banning of prayer in public schools as a motivating factor, the Supreme Court struck down school prayer in *Engel v. Vitale* in 1962, and the boom in Protestant schools began only at the end of the decade.[44] In the words of a Memphis reverend,

> Integration wasn't it. We've been integrating in Memphis for years. Our kids were the first to be bused, that's what it's all about. I would never have dreamed of starting a school, hadn't it been for busing. Well, our people were concerned and we prayed about it. Now I've been in the ministry for 25 years and this was the only time the Lord ever got me up in the night. And he said "Get the Book, I want to show you what to do." I opened the Book and I found the answer. Oh, the thing was so clear. The first time it fell open in the New Testament, the second time in the Old. This was a Tuesday night and the following night I made a report to the church and we decided to start. We had six months to get ready. . . . I found that 25 to 40 percent of the kids were agnostics. Part of the school's mission is to bring them to the faith. At least a thousand kids in the last three years have made public decisions for Christ in the school.[45]

The legal justification for denying tax exemptions to discriminatory schools emerged (as did many initiatives for affirmative action) from the

[44]See Peter Skerry, "Christian Schools Versus the I.R.S.," *Public Interest*, Fall 1980, 26. On the history of school prayer, see Joan DelFattore, *The Fourth R: Conflicts over Religion in America's Public Schools* (New Haven: Yale University Press, 2004); Aaron Haberman, "Civil Rights on the Right: The Modern Christian Right and the Crusade for School Prayer" (PhD diss., University of South Carolina, 2006), chap. 3; and, from a future U.S. senator, Benjamin Sasse, "The Anti-Madalyn Majority: Secular Left, Religious Right, and the Rise of Reagan's America" (PhD diss., Yale University, 2004). School prayer was a remarkably poor issue around which to build a transdenominational political coalition: it was, above all, a Protestant issue, cuing long-running sectarian disputes on which version of the Lord's Prayer was to be recited and whose translation of the Bible read. In the early meetings of the Moral Majority, Paul Weyrich consistently emphasized abortion, well aware that school prayer would prove divisive. Dueling prayer amendments in the 1980s, sponsored by Jesse Helms and Orrin Hatch, respectively, confirmed that the issue divided rather than bound together religious conservatives. Cf. James McClellan, "Kicking the Amendment Habit," *Benchmark*, April 1984, 1–3.

[45]David Nevin and Robert E. Bills, *The Schools That Fear Built: Segregationist Academies in the South* (Washington, D.C.: Acropolis Books, 1976), 30; cf. Jack White, "Segregated Academies," *Time*, 15 December 1975, 60.

Department of Health, Education, and Welfare under Robert Finch in the Nixon administration. Nixon reluctantly agreed to support the right of the Internal Revenue Service to deny tax exemption, both to avoid a court fight and to stave off attacks from a select committee in the Senate led by Walter Mondale.[46]

In order to receive 501(c)(3) status, the IRS subsequently required schools, including the churches that operated them, to certify and to publish in the local paper a statement that they did not discriminate on the basis of race. However, it did not further investigate. Even for separately incorporated schools largely reliant on tuition, but especially for schools that were legally part of the sponsoring churches, loss of tax exemption would have been a crippling blow as potential donors would lose a powerful incentive to give. Under the new policy, the IRS did revoke the tax-exempt status of Bob Jones University. Until 1971, Bob Jones openly refused to admit African American students, after which point it forbade them to date white students. Yet few other schools actually admitted that they discriminated on the basis of race, even if they opened their doors in the wake of desegregation and had few, if any, minority students.

Importantly, the Nixon, and not the Carter, administration established the precedent that the IRS, an administrative agency, had the power to review tax-exempt status absent specific congressional authorization. Therefore, while critics of the 1978 proposals often elided the distinction between the IRS's legal authority and the rules used to promulgate it, the underlying administrative ruling dates to 1970—an important distinction in understanding how desegregation politics moved into religious politics. In turn, this history points up the differences between Nixon's triangulations in the Southern Strategy, whose brinksmanship in the White House and policymaking in the agencies often pointed in opposite directions, and the subsequent party-group alliance forged against big government.

Following a scathing report from the U.S. Commission on Civil Rights and further litigation, Jerome Kurtz, commissioner of the IRS in the Carter

[46]David Whitman, "Ronald Reagan and Tax Exemptions for Racist Schools," Kennedy School of Government Case 15–0609, 1984, 6–12. HEW had responded to litigation seeking denial of tax exemptions for "seg academies" in Mississippi; a three-judge court in Washington had denied tax exemptions to all new private schools in the state. See *Green v. Kennedy*, 309 F.Supp. 1127 (1970). This separate regime for Mississippi, operating under direct control from the federal courts, remained in place throughout the long interbranch fights over policy in the other forty-nine states. Earlier, Nixon had said that "Whites in Mississippi can't send their kids to schools that are 90 percent black; they've got to set up private schools. There is no statutory authority now for denying tax exemptions for legitimate private schools." On the Mississippi case, see Joseph Crespino, "Civil Rights and the Religious Right," in *Rightward Bound: Making America Conservative in the 1970s*, ed. Bruce J. Schulman and Julian E. Zelizer (Princeton: Princeton University Press, 2007), 90–105.

administration, promulgated a new set of rules designed to revoke exemptions for schools formed as white-flight havens from the public schools.[47] The rules created a new class of "reviewable schools" formed or expanded at the time of and "related in fact to" local school desegregation, *and* whose minority student population was less than 20 percent "of the minority school age population in the community served by the school."[48] A further series of tests centered around programs to recruit minority students; they allowed reviewable schools making strides toward integration to remain tax-exempt, with determinations rendered by IRS headquarters rather than regional offices. In addition, the final rules contained language designed to spare Catholic schools from being classified as reviewable.[49]

Like many liberal initiatives in the fiscally straitened 1970s, the rules stressed stringent regulatory review by activist bureaucracies and aggressive, quantifiable benchmarks, rather than big-ticket public programs inside the budget.[50] They emphasized statistical discrimination and disparate outcomes across groups, rather than seeking to prove bias at the individual level. The immensely detailed regulations would surely have invited lawsuits from schools denied their tax exemptions. Federal district judges would have served as the final arbiters of tax-exempt status for reviewable schools, and consent decrees the modus operandi for resolving disputes.[51]

Early in 1979, Jerry Falwell, with help from Paul Weyrich, formed the Moral Majority. The proposed IRS rules posed an immediate threat to Falwell and his ministry, and to other leading evangelicals, especially independent Baptists. As regulations forbade them from endorsing candidates directly using their 501(c)(3) charities, they needed a new legal instrumentality, and formed Moral Majority to coordinate their efforts.[52]

Falwell ran a seg academy. It would almost certainly have run afoul of the IRS guidelines, and put in jeopardy the tax-exempt status of Falwell's

[47] For the legal history, see Virginia Davis Nordin and William Lloyd Turner, "Tax Exempt Status of Private Schools: *Wright, Green,* and *Bob Jones,*" *Education Law Reporter* 35 (1986): 329–49. The Civil Rights Commission report is in Subcommittee on Oversight of the House Committee on Ways and Means, *Tax Exempt Status of Private Schools*, Serial 96–11 (Washington, D.C.: Government Printing Office, 1979), 236–51.

[48] For the draft rules, see Subcommittee on Oversight, *Tax Exempt Status of Private Schools*, 41–51. The relevant minority was the one covered in court desegregation plans.

[49] The language referred to "long-standing practice of a religion or religious denomination which is not itself racially discriminatory."

[50] R. Shep Melnick, "From Tax-and-Spend to Mandate-and-Sue: Liberalism after the Great Society," in *The Great Society and the High Tide of Liberalism*, ed. Sidney M. Milkis and Jerome Mileur (Amherst: University of Massachusetts Press, 2005), 387–410.

[51] Cf. *Griggs v. Duke Power Co.*, 401 U.S. 424 (1971).

[52] Maxwell Glen, "The Electronic Ministers Listen to the Gospel According to the Candidates," *National Journal*, 22 December 1979, 2142–45. See also Jerry Falwell, *Listen, America!* (Garden City, N.Y.: Doubleday, 1980).

entire empire: *The Old-Time Gospel Hour*, Thomas Road Baptist Church, the Liberty Bible College, Lynchburg Christian Academy. In 1967, the same year as the local public schools desegregated, Lynchburg Christian Academy opened its doors. The local paper called it "a private school for white students," and the city's black ministers, in a statement, "deplored the use of the word 'Christian' in the title of a school which excludes Negro and other non-white people." As of the fall of 1979, Lynchburg Christian Academy had an all-white faculty, and only 5 African Americans among the 1,147 students, even as the 1980 census reported that Lynchburg was nearly a quarter black.[53] By the criteria that the IRS promulgated, Thomas Road would almost certainly have lost its 501(c)(3) status, and with it the fundraising machine that had propelled Falwell for a quarter century. The state threatened Falwell—and he responded in kind.

Falwell was not alone. As desegregation went national, controversies over busing in northern schools began to nationalize issues about "white backlash," and create meaningful opportunities for northern and southern evangelicals to join together against intrusive efforts to force desegregation in church schools. The leaders of the Moral Majority retained deep ties to the traditional evangelical subculture but in the context of a broader geographic and ideological conservative appeal.[54]

The majority of Moral Majority state chairmen were Baptist ministers whose churches operated schools. For at least of ten of them, the timing of their opening would have triggered review. They include not only Shades Mountain Christian School in Birmingham, Alabama, and Garland Christian Academy outside Dallas but also Temple Christian Academy in Omaha and Pine Creek Christian Schools in Newark, Delaware.[55] Other leading

[53]William Martin, *With God on Our Side: The Rise of the Religious Right in America*, rev. ed. (New York: Broadway Books, 2005), 70–71; "Politicizing the Word," *Time*, 1 October 1979, 62. Michael Sean Winters, *God's Right Hand: How Jerry Falwell Made God a Republican and Baptized the American Right* (New York: HarperOne, 2012), 167, notes that Falwell's children had just reached school age at the time.

[54]On these themes, see Darren Dochuk, *From Bible Belt to Sunbelt: Plain Folk Religion, Grassroots Politics, and the Rise of Evangelical Conservatism* (New York: Norton, 2011); and Lisa McGirr, *Suburban Warriors: The Origins of the New American Right* (Princeton: Princeton University Press, 2001), esp. chap. 6.

[55]I rely on Robert C. Liebman, "Mobilizing the Moral Majority," in *The New Christian Right: Mobilization and Legitimation*, ed. Robert C. Liebman and Robert Wuthnow (New York: Aldine, 1983), 61, but his research is incomplete; it does not, for example, identify Tim LaHaye, whose school system was by then separately incorporated. Moral Majority state chairs in Florida, Iowa, Nevada, Ohio, Oklahoma, and South Carolina also operated schools whose timing would have triggered review; the Capitol City Baptist School in Jackson, Miss., would also have triggered review if the *Green* case had been resolved. The Tucson (Ariz.) Christian School, which opened in 1973, would have triggered review if it expanded substantially around the time that the Tucson Unified School District implemented its desegregation plan in 1978. Precisely because the IRS never succeeded in collecting data about enrollment

figures of the nascent Christian Right also operated schools whose timing would have triggered review. In San Diego, Tim LaHaye, the Moral Majority chair for California, had opened Christian High School in 1965, the same year that the San Diego School Board passed a resolution urging racial balance in city schools; in the mid-1980s, it had 6 African Americans in a student body of 650. In Florida, D. James Kennedy, an influential Presbyterian televangelist, had opened Westminster Academy in 1971, a year after a federal district court mandated a comprehensive desegregation plan for Broward County schools and just as newly elected governor Reubin Askew marshaled the state's resources to integrate public schools.[56]

In 1965, Falwell warned the members of his church against letting worldly concerns interfere with soul winning: "Believing the Bible as I do, I would find it impossible to stop preaching the pure saving gospel of Jesus Christ, and begin doing anything else—including fighting communism or participating in civil rights reforms."[57] In time, however, Falwell recanted his position, and began to test out the political waters with a series of "I Love America" rallies on the steps of state capitols in 1976. Yet it was the controversy over reviewable schools that pushed him directly into politics.[58]

The IRS episode politicized white churches, giving them a powerful narrative that cast evangelicals, rather than African Americans, as victims, and wedding them to a program devoted to fighting entrenched liberalism. As testimony before the Ways and Means Committee shows, opposing the IRS rules hardly required silence on race or anger at taxes: New Right elites forged those connections. James Wood of the Baptist Joint Committee for Religious Liberty, later a leading moderate in the Southern Baptist Convention's inerrancy controversies, took the traditional Baptist position of "a free church in a free state." He framed his objections in terms of the Free Exercise and Establishment Clauses, and claimed that the safe-harbor provisions for Catholic schools made invidious distinctions. Crucially, he argued that the rules furthering "an altogether meritorious public policy" might be legal if applied only against schools without formal ties to a church. Wood reflected a long tradition in American Baptism, one that struggled to

---

by race and ethnicity, forming a list of Christian Right leaders at risk from the proposed regulations would require site-by-site reconstructions of enrollment. That said, such data would add immensely to these conclusions, which rely solely on timing.

[56] Parsons, *Inside America's Christian Schools*, 117; *Allen v. Board of Pub. Instruc. of Broward City, Fla.*, 312.F.Supp. 1127 (1970); William R. Amlong, "As Mild-Mannered as Clark Kent . . . But Don't Let That Fool You," *St. Petersburg Times*, 20 September 1971, 21; Susan Anne Cary, "The History of Coral Ridge Presbyterian Church: 1959–1994" (MA thesis, Florida Atlantic University, 1994), chap. 4.

[57] The full text can be found in Young, *God's Bullies*, 310–17, quote at 313.

[58] Frances FitzGerald, "A Disciplined, Charging Army," *New Yorker*, 3 May 1981, 53–141; see also "Why Fundamentalists Are Conservative," *Journal-Champion*, 13 October 1978, 2.

reconcile racial liberalism with church autonomy. His were not the ingredients of productive alliance with a conservative party.[59]

The New Right, by contrast, told a story about taxes and bureaucrats. The pithiest statement came from a Georgia Republican a month into office. Newt Gingrich asked, "Why do bureaucrats persist in going farther than the Congressional authority and the Constitution allow? Partly I think bureaucrats forget what their job is supposed to be. The IRS should collect taxes—not enforce social policy." Similarly, Robert Dornan of Orange County, California, a Viguerie darling, took the language of rights, and put it in the service of tethering agencies' behavior: "There is an inherent right there of people that our society and our Congress has decided is tax exempt. They are not granting anything, and it isn't a question of [the IRS] granting anything." Ronald Reagan weighed in on a similar theme, during his weekly radio broadcast. His talk combined subterfuge about the regulations themselves—his notes never mention anything about desegregation or reviewable schools—with a stark choice, on "a pocketbook issue," between "parents or the agencies & depts. of the Fed govt."[60]

The response to the rules was overwhelming. The IRS received more than a quarter of a million letters against the proposed rules, and the White House nearly as many.[61] In August 1979, Congress inserted riders into the appropriations bill for the Treasury Department to prevent the IRS from implementing the proposed regulations. For members of Congress, the issue developed into an instance of concentrated costs and diffuse benefits: the religious lobby fought hard against the rules, while proponents such as the NAACP and ACLU had less clout outside their core ideological allies, and other battles to fight. The Carter administration, which had bad relations with Capitol Hill anyway, never expanded the fight beyond the agency level. In these terms, the outcome should come as no surprise.

The shape of support in each chamber suggest how deracializing the IRS rules led to a broader coalition including the entire Republican Party. In the House, the Ashbrook and Dornan amendments attacked the Carter administration's rules alone, blocking the use of taxpayer dollars for any IRS rules on exemption not in place as of 22 August 1978.[62] In the Senate,

[59] Subcommittee on Oversight, *Tax Exempt Status of Private Schools*, 538–41.

[60] Subcommittee on Oversight, *Tax Exempt Status of Private Schools*, 1264–65, 971–83; Connaught Coyne Marshner, *Blackboard Tyranny* (New Rochelle: Arlington House, 1978), 234; Ronald Reagan, *Reagan, In His Own Hand: The Writings of Ronald Reagan That Reveal His Revolutionary Vision for America*, ed. Kiron K. Skinner, Annelise Anderson, and Martin Anderson (New York: Free Press, 2001), 354–55.

[61] Martin, *With God*, 173.

[62] The Dornan amendment was slightly broader, but the highly similar amendments simply provided members with two opportunities for position-taking. John Ashbrook, an extremely conservative Ohio congressman who challenged Richard Nixon for the 1972 nomination, was linked more to the Old than the New Right.

the Helms amendment, by contrast, forbade the IRS from *any* spending to review private-school tax exemptions, which would have not only scuttled the proposed rules but also thrown the Bob Jones case into jeopardy. The conference committee then adopted the House language.

In the House, where the Republican Study Committee had worked hard to draw attention to the IRS regulations, the amendments were proposed by staunch conservatives from outside the South, and the decidedly one-sided floor debate focused on themes of bureaucracy and taxes. The Ashbrook amendment passed overwhelmingly on a vote of 297 to 63 with the support of every Republican save one (Jeffords of Vermont), as a sizable fraction of northern Democrats ducked the vote. The debate on the more sweeping Helms proposal, sponsored by the Senate's leading New Right racial conservative, revolved around race. In a colloquy, archliberal Howard Metzenbaum asked Helms "to advise the Senator from Ohio as to the percentage of black students, if at all, he has encountered in these so-called Christian schools." In reply, Helms mentioned "three or four" black students at a school in Kinston where he had delivered the commencement address. "But," he added, "there has been no instance of a black child whose application was denied."[63] The Senate adopted the Helms amendment on a forty-seven to forty-three vote that cued older racial dimensions; twelve Republicans, led by New York's Jacob Javits, who had earlier failed to strike the Ashbrook amendment from the Senate bill, voted no. A mere three Democrats from outside the greater South supported the Helms amendment; only one Democrat from the old Confederacy opposed it.[64] The Senate, in other words, treated the amendment in traditional terms of racial politics, while in the House it linked to antigovernment conservatism.

The Republican platform in 1980 pledged to "halt the unconstitutional regulatory vendetta launched by Mr. Carter's IRS Commissioner against independent schools."[65] If the Constitution was being violated, however, a Republican administration had done the deed: the delegation to an administrative agency originated under Nixon.

The subsequent history veers from direct political mobilization to a different part of the right's revival. Racially tinged opposition to government meddling found a common carrier with incipient legal conservatism. The Reagan administration sought to reinstate Bob Jones's tax-exempt status, although an injunction prevented it from doing so. Trent Lott, a Republican

[63] *Congressional Record—Senate*, 5 September 1979, 22908.

[64] Lawton Chiles of Florida objected to making tax policy through a floor amendment on an appropriations bill. The Republicans voting "no" on the Helms proposal were Hayakawa of California, Weicker of Connecticut, Percy of Illinois, Matthias of Maryland, Boschwitz and Durenberger of Minnesota, Javits of New York, Bellmon of Oklahoma (for the same reasons as Chiles), Packwood of Oregon, Heinz of Pennsylvania, Chafee of Rhode Island, and Stafford of Vermont.

[65] "Republican Party Platform of 1980," http://www.presidency.ucsb.edu/ws/?pid=25844.

Representative from Mississippi, wrote to Reagan at the end of 1981 asking for Bob Jones to get its tax exemption restored. Reagan scrawled a note that "I think we should." Lott hoped ultimately to restore exemptions for "seg academies" in his state, even though that would have required a separate court order.

At the same time, conservative lawyers in the Justice and Treasury Departments, led by Reagan's civil rights chief, William Bradford Reynolds, reviewed the welter of conflicting precedents. Over the advice of career appointees in both the Civil Rights Division and the Solicitor General's office, they concluded that the denial of exemption, absent specific congressional authorization, represented unconstitutional action by the IRS.[66] By an eight to one vote, the Supreme Court in 1983 disagreed; only William Rehnquist adopted the position that the Reagan administration controversially espoused. The administration then returned to applying the earlier rules, which certified the tax exemptions of those schools claiming nondiscrimination on the basis of race—and revoked exemptions for those that did not.[67]

Conservative Protestantism has changed in the decades since the controversy raged. For many white evangelicals, their individualistic worldview still leads them to shy away from anything more than person-to-person solutions for collective ills such as racism and its accumulated legacy. Yet since the 1980s, white evangelicals outside the still-distinctive subculture of the rural South have converged with other Americans in their attitudes toward integrated neighborhoods and interracial marriage.[68]

[66]Stuart Taylor, Jr., "Reagan—Not the Law—Shifted on Bias and Taxes," *New York Times*, 17 January 1982, WR4; Stuart Taylor, Jr., "Reagan Tax Exemption Bill Assailed," *New York Times*, 2 February 1982, A18; Raymond Wolters, *Right Turn: William Bradford Reynolds, the Reagan Administration, and Black Civil Rights* (New Brunswick, N.J.: Transaction Publishers, 1996), 466–86; Lincoln Caplan, *The Tenth Justice: The Solicitor General and the Rule of Law* (New York: Knopf, 1987), chap. 5.

[67]*Bob Jones University v. United States*, 461 U.S. 574 (1983). While the rhetoric to the Christian Right emphasized religious freedom, rather than the more abstruse question of legislative delegation, the Reagan administration never supported the First Amendment claims. Even Bob Jones's lawyer admitted at oral argument that Congress could, indeed, constitutionally deny a tax exemption; Anthony Lewis, "Passing the Buck," *New York Times*, 14 October 1982, A31. See also Whitman, "Ronald Reagan"; Wolters, *Right Turn*, 471; Nordin and Turner, "Tax Exempt Status," 336–38; Aaron Haberman, "Into the Wilderness: Ronald Reagan, Bob Jones University, and the Political Education of the Christian Right," *Historian* 67 (2005): 234–53. Haberman notes that mainstream Christian Right leaders consistently backed Bob Jones despite unease with its ban on interracial dating. In a final coda to the ideological shifts across parties, movements, and branches of government, a five-member Supreme Court majority in 1984 dismissed for lack of standing a suit that sought to extend the *Green* rules from Mississippi to the entire nation. See *Allen v. Wright*, 468 U.S. 737 (1984). On a former "seg academy," see Kevin Sieff, "Star Recruit's Job: Erode a Racist Legacy," *Washington Post*, 12 December 2011, A1.

[68]Michael O. Emerson, *Divided by Faith: Evangelical Religion and the Problem of Race in America* (Oxford: Oxford University Press, 2000); Robert D. Putnam and David Campbell,

This account is not meant to indict the Christian Right with original sin from the IRS controversy, or to take the 1970s out of a very particular cauldron of race, religion, and politics. Rather, the story of the "seg academies" shows how policy entrepreneurs used outside threats to mobilize extant networks, and negotiated the shoals of race as they formed an alliance based explicitly on common notions of limited government and traditional morality. In the process, churches formed the para-organizations they would use in electoral politics, and the Republican Party found itself a new constituency and a powerful frame, devoid of specifically racial appeals, that united religious and economic conservatives.

Abortion: Creating an Evangelical Issue

The controversy over Christian schools served as the catalyzing event to mobilize evangelicals, and to bring them inside a conservative orbit that unified their religious fears with anger at taxes and bureaucrats. Once the Bob Jones case had run its course, however, the controversy dissipated. The abortion issue, by contrast, emerged more slowly and with a smaller institutional imprint in its early years. The fierce and successful evangelical counterreaction against the sexual revolution fed into a broader critique, one that took for conservative ends the feminist dictum that "the personal is political."

American religion reeled from the tremendous social dislocations of the sixties; parishioners young and old had left the pews, and the moral consensus undergirding American life seemed, at times, to be coming apart at the seams.[69] In the wake of the mobilizations and countermobilizations of the sixties (on the left) and the seventies (on the right), conservative Christians found they had more in common with one another, in their orientation toward traditional religious practices as well as on matters of personal morality, than they did with liberals inside the same denominational families. "The broader role of the political," as Robert Wuthnow termed it, pushed religious groups apart.[70] Every denomination had to decide whether women (and later gays) could serve as clergy. While liberal religion spoke up against poverty and in favor of the nuclear freeze, the Christian Right's issue bundling embraced Francis Schaeffer's ideas around cobelligerency—putting aside doctrinal disagreements in battle against pressing threats. Yet,

---

American Grace: The Changing Role of Religion in American Civic Life (New York: Simon & Schuster, 2010), 114–15.

[69] For differing perspectives, see Putnam and Campbell, *American Grace*, chap. 4, and Robert O. Self, *All in the Family: The Realignment of American Democracy since the 1960s* (New York: Hill and Wang, 2012), chap. 11.

[70] Robert Wuthnow, *The Restructuring of American Religion: Society and Faith since World War II* (Princeton: Princeton University Press, 1988), 235.

beginning around 1970, even as mainline Protestantism continued its decline, the share of Americans identifying as evangelical began to rise sharply.

The rise of feminism and the pill had already set off a backlash among tradition-minded Americans—even before *Roe* had been decided. Evidence from the General Social Survey shows that both those who converted into and those who remained evangelicals were substantially more likely than other Americans to deem premarital sex "always wrong."[71] Prolife pioneers found fertile ground in the evangelical subculture. Unlike their mainline counterparts in Protestantism, evangelicals still condemned as sin all sex outside marriage: abortion represented ultimate indifference after sex without purpose. Indeed, evangelicals such as Tim and Beverly LaHaye condemned abortion for allowing unwed mothers to engage in irresponsible nonmarital sex without consequences. In 1993, when discussing the options for pregnant unmarried teenagers, they warned that "the last thing they should do is add murder to fornication."[72]

Political entrepreneurs and evangelicals concerned about public indifference to a moral calamity together transformed abortion into an issue that would unite religious conservatives and demonstrate the looming power of the state.[73] The creation of alliance around abortion required forging a threefold set of links connecting evangelicalism, opposition to abortion, and support for the Republican Party. Neither the standard stories in political science, emphasizing polarization and partisan sort, nor secular historians' generalizations about backlash, nor the church histories that treat religious transformation in isolation from political pressures, nor Christian Right figures' own accounts of principled activism entirely capture the tale of a social movement deeply embedded in both office-seeking partisan politics and the complex world of American evangelicalism as it confronted basic questions.

Abortion became a partisan issue only gradually.[74] The story from the right begins even before *Roe*: Pat Buchanan encouraged Richard Nixon to link abortion with the counterculture to court conservative Catholic voters,

[71] Daniel Schlozman and Valerie Lewis, "Nones, Evangelicals, and the Future of the Culture Wars" (paper, American Political Science Association meeting, Washington, D.C., 2–5 September 2010).

[72] Tim F. LaHaye and Beverly LaHaye, *Against the Tide: How to Raise Sexually Pure Kids in an "Anything-Goes" World* (Portland, Ore.: Multnomah, 1993), 208. See also Tim F. LaHaye and Beverly LaHaye, *The Act of Marriage: The Beauty of Sexual Love* (Grand Rapids, Mich.: Zondervan, 1976); Tim F. LaHaye, *The Unhappy Gays: What Everyone Should Know about Homosexuality* (Wheaton, Ill.: Tyndale, 1978). I thank the historian of evangelicalism David Hempton for this point.

[73] On the worldview of antiabortion activists, see Kristin Luker, *Abortion and the Politics of Motherhood* (Berkeley: University of California Press, 1984), chap. 7.

[74] This analysis echoes Linda Greenhouse and Reva B. Siegel, "Before (and After) *Roe v. Wade*: New Questions About Backlash," *Yale Law Journal* 120 (2011): 2028–87.

and the charge gained force with Pennsylvania Republican Hugh Scott's alliteration of George McGovern as the candidate of "acid, amnesty, and abortion." Nixon subjected abortions at military hospitals (later banned under the Hyde Amendment) to the laws of the relevant state, and Buchanan ghostwrote a letter in which the president decried liberalized abortion laws as "impossible to reconcile with either our religious traditions or our Western heritage." Yet Nixon soon stepped back from the foray. After *Roe* was decided, he "directed aides to 'keep out' of the case."[75]

Nor did the leading conservative evangelicals condemn *Roe*. W. A. Criswell, whose pulpit, First Baptist Church in Dallas, was the country's largest, initially praised the decision. "It was only after a child was born and had life separate from its mother," he argued, "that it became an actual person." Jerry Falwell did not preach at all on abortion until 1978.[76] The first record of antiabortion activity from evangelical circles dates to May 1974, and, crucially, involved an assist from a ubiquitous name. The *Christian Crusade Weekly* reported on the establishment of Americans Against Abortion "in association with" the Richard Viguerie Company.[77] The *Weekly* served as mouthpiece for Billy James Hargis, a far right preacher from Tulsa who, despite his own sins of the flesh, had arrived early at below-the-belt conservatism. Hargis had ghostwritten for Joe McCarthy, and evangelized for the stridently fundamentalist Presbyterian Carl McIntire.[78]

The leaders of the New Right sought a durable conservative majority, and saw the abortion issue as a way to win cross-pressured voters. The practitioners of coalitionism understood better than others in the prolife movement, especially Roman Catholics also attuned to social justice issues, how to tap new sources of funds through direct mail and PACs, to relate electoral and policy work, and to forge ad hoc efforts for particular priorities.[79] Paul Weyrich, especially, saw abortion as the glue in a coalition of conservative

[75] Patrick Buchanan, "Assault Book," in *Before* Roe v. Wade*: Voices That Shaped the Abortion Debate before the Supreme Court's Ruling*, ed. Linda Greenhouse and Reva Siegel (New York: Kaplan, 2010), 215–18; David J. Garrow, *Liberty and Sexuality: The Right to Privacy and the Making of Roe v. Wade* (New York: Macmillan, 1994); Dean J. Kotlowski, *Nixon's Civil Rights: Politics, Principle, and Policy* (Cambridge, Mass.: Harvard University Press, 2001), 252.

[76] "Reactions to Abortion Policy," *Word and Way*, 15 February 1973, 15; Martin, *With God*, 193.

[77] Gerald S. Pope, "Editor's Corner," *Christian Crusade Weekly*, 5 May 1974, 2.

[78] "The Sins of Billy James," *Time*, 16 February 1976; George Thayer, *The Father Shores of Politics: The American Political Fringe Today* (New York: Simon & Schuster, 1967), 222–23; *Congressional Record—Senate*, 16 April 1962, 6576–79, which contains a series from the *Oklahoma Courier* read into the *Record* by Gale McGee, a Democrat from Wyoming; Harold H. Martin, "Doomsday Merchant on the Far Right," *Saturday Evening Post*, 28 April 1962, 19–24.

[79] See, from prochoice activists, Lawrence Lader, "Abortion Opponents' Tactics," *New York Times*, 11 January 1978, A19; and Stacey Oliker, "Abortion and the Left: the Limit of 'Pro-Family' Politics," *Socialist Review* 11 (1981): 84.

Protestants and Catholics. Weyrich, a deacon in the Eastern Rite Catholic Melkite church, cared passionately about the issue—but also understood that it was a foundational concern with the power to unite conservative Christians regardless of denomination.

Until the 1980s, Republicans in the electorate favored fewer restrictions on abortion than did Democrats. In the initial 1976 vote on the Hyde Amendment, white Baptists in the House of Representatives were no more likely than Methodists—and almost twenty points less likely than Catholics—to oppose Medicaid funding for abortions. Yet partisan sorting along with the strong prolife views of white evangelicals socialized to politics since the 1970s have shifted many of the earlier patterns. The partisan divide on abortion roll calls in Congress rose more than threefold between 1973 and 1994.[80] These changes originate in elite actions that reoriented both party and movement to serve common purposes.

The moral backlash against the sexual revolution required careful cultivation. Abortion had traditionally been a Catholic concern. The text of the Bible, the authoritative guide in conservative Protestantism, says nothing whatsoever about abortion per se. Rather than defining the beginning of life strictly at conception, it often indicates that God gave life even prior to the womb.[81]

More than any other figure, the popularizing theologian Francis Schaeffer rendered opposition to abortion into an evangelical cause. Schaeffer's Manichean worldview did not encompass the nuances of political activity. Rather, combating humanism—the sanctification of man above God's natural limits—stood as Protestantism's primary responsibility: "the state and humanistically oriented law have no right and no authority to take human life arbitrarily."[82] While Protestants foremost owed individual loyalty to

[80]Greg D. Adams, "Abortion: Evidence of an Issue Evolution," *American Journal of Political Science* 41 (1997): 718–37; Edward G. Carmines and James Woods, "The Role of Party Activists in the Evolution of the Abortion Issue," *Political Behavior* 24 (2002): 361–77; John H. Evans, "Polarization in Abortion Attitudes in U.S. Religious Traditions, 1972–1998," *Sociological Forum* 17 (2002): 397–422; John P. Hoffmann and Sherrie Mills Johnson, "Attitudes toward Abortion among Religious Traditions in the United States: Change or Continuity?," *Sociology of Religion* 66 (2005): 161–82; Maris A. Vinovskis, "The Politics of Abortion in the House of Representatives in 1976," *University of Michigan Law Review* 77 (1978): 1822.

[81]Two professors at Wheaton College began their chapters in a 1980s volume as follows: "Despite a thorough search of the Old Testament, a text that clearly prohibits abortion is not to be found" and "the New Testament makes no mention of abortion." See respectively James K. Hoffmeier, "Abortion and the Old Testament Law," 49, and Victor R. Gordon, "Abortion and the New Testament," 73, both in *Abortion: A Christian Understanding and Response*, ed. James K. Hoffmeier (Grand Rapids, Mich.: Baker, 1987).

[82]Francis A. Schaeffer, *A Christian Manifesto* (Wheaton, Ill.: Crossway Books, 1984), 69. The best biography is Barry Hankins, *Francis Schaeffer and the Shaping of Evangelical America* (Grand Rapids, Mich.: Eerdmans, 2008).

God, Schaeffer urged them toward what he termed cobelligerence with like-minded associates.[83] This systematic—if, to critics, reductionist[84]—attack placed abortion in intellectual context, with easy-to-name villains and a master construct uniting myriad threats under a single label. Schaeffer's views emerged more from logic than Scripture. He worried that abortion would lead inexorably to infanticide and euthanasia and destroy traditional gender roles.

Schaeffer was trained in the 1930s at Westminster Theological Seminary, on the right wing of the Presbyterian movement, and then spent a decade working for Carl McIntire. In 1949, Schaeffer left for Switzerland, where he founded l'Abri, a Christian retreat that attracted American young people searching for answers, and also wrote a series of popularizing books. With his son, Franky, Schaeffer soon joined Everett Koop, a Philadelphia physician who opposed abortion, to produce a book and film series called *Whatever Happened to the Human Race?* that focused particularly on issues of human life.[85] The film juxtaposes the bearded doctor and the goateed theologian with images of aborted fetuses, carnage at Auschwitz, and the biblical site of Sodom bedecked with tombstones for the victims of abortion.[86]

The Schaeffers reached out to many staples of archconservative causes. The list of funders belies any notion of Schaeffer as an Alpine crank: the Pews of Sun Oil (who, through the Christian Freedom Foundation, also seeded Ed McAteer, Weyrich's emissary to Christian schools); Rich DeVos, founder of Amway (and later president of the Council for National Policy);

[83]Francis A. Schaeffer, *The Church at the End of the Twentieth Century* (London: Norfolk Press, 1970), 46–47.

[84]In an influential 1983 essay, the Reformed church historian George M. Marsden termed Schaeffer a "quasi philosopher and evangelist." See his "Preachers of Paradox: The Religious New Right in Historical Perspective," in *Religion and America: Spiritual Life in a Secular Age*, ed. Mary Douglas and Steven Tipton (Boston: Beacon, 1983), 158; and also Richard Pierard, "The New Religious Right: A Formidable Force in American Politics," *Choice*, March 1982, 863–79; and Garry Wills, *Under God: Religion and American Politics* (New York: Simon & Schuster, 1990), 318–32.

[85]Koop served as Surgeon General during the Reagan administration, where his reports on AIDS and abortion deeply disappointed movement conservatives. See C. Everett Koop, *Koop: The Memoirs of America's Family Doctor* (New York: Random House, 1991).

[86]Franky Schaeffer's views emerged less from intellect or faith than the facts of life: an unintentional pregnancy at seventeen with a member of L'Abri (to whom he has been married ever since) led to a child. Franky, now known as Frank, became disillusioned with the intolerance and hucksterism of the Christian Right and converted to Orthodox Christianity. He endorsed Barack Obama and describes himself as "pro-choice" but not "pro-abortion." See Frank Schaeffer, *Crazy for God: How I Grew Up as One of the Elect, Helped Found the Religious Right, and Lived to Take All (or Almost All) of It Back* (New York: Carroll & Graf, 2007); and Frank Schaeffer, "Obama's Minister Committed 'Treason' but When My Father Said the Same Thing He Was a Republican Hero," *Huffington Post*, 16 March 2008, http://www.huffingtonpost.com/frank-schaeffer/obamas-minister-committed_b_91774.html.

and Bunker Hunt (also the leading funder of the John Birch Society). Tapes reached, among others, Jack Kemp and Paul Laxalt, the Catholic Nevada senator who was Ronald Reagan's best friend in Congress.

For a generation of conservative Protestant religious leaders inside and outside the seminaries, Schaeffer provided an intellectual toolkit. These leaders then adapted and tamed down his arguments. Jerry Falwell distributed sixty-two thousand copies of *A Christian Manifesto* through *The Old-Time Gospel Hour.* "If it hadn't been for Francis Schaeffer," he recalled, "I would have been a pastor in Lynchburg, Virginia, but otherwise never heard of. He was the one who pushed me out of the ring and told me to put on the gloves."[87] More than any other figure, Schaeffer provided the dual voice to which anchoring groups aspire, and that mature alliance often lacks: both internal—in his case, doctrinal—and public witness for political action.[88]

Leveraging Opportunities at Critical Junctures

As this chapter has shown, party-movement alliance melds the very particular with the deeply structural as political entrepreneurs exploited crises in the postwar regime to mobilize evangelicals around conservative politics. The events, principally in the 1970s, examined here, jibe well with an influential recent critique—but with an important difference. David Mayhew has faulted political scientists for emphasizing enduring institutions, forces, and incentives over proximate events in explaining outcomes in American politics. Rather, he posits, the most meaningful explanations emerge from "*interaction* between any such 'underlying' considerations and certain contingent events . . . that allowed the 'underlying' considerations to prevail."[89] Depression and war, his prime suspects among contingent events, of course

[87] Kenneth L. Woodward, "Guru of Fundamentalism," *Newsweek*, 1 November 1982, 88; Daymon Johnson, "Reformed Fundamentalism in America: The Lordship of Christ, the Transformation of Culture, and Other Calvinist Components of the Christian Right" (PhD diss., Florida State University, 1994), 172; Ronald A. Wells, "Schaeffer on America," in *Reflections on Francis Schaeffer*, ed. Ronald W. Ruegsegger (Grand Rapids, Mich.: Zondervan, 1986), 234. For a synthesis, see Michael Lienesch, *Redeeming America: Piety & Politics in the New Christian Right* (Chapel Hill: University of North Carolina Press, 1993), especially chap. 4. The treatment in Tim LaHaye, *The Battle for the Mind* (Old Tappan, N.J.: Fleming-Revell, 1980) might in other contexts count as plagiarism.

[88] Frank Schaeffer, in a 2007 interview, made the parallel that undergirds this book: "My father was someone who was prone to be stubborn and enthusiastic, take a stand, and revel in the battle. If he had converted to the Far Left of his era, say in the early '30s, he might have made a great union leader." See William McKenzie, "Q & A with Frank Schaeffer," *Dallas Morning News*, 4 December 2007 (link no longer online; in collection of the author).

[89] David R. Mayhew, *Parties and Policies: How the American Government Works* (New Haven: Yale University Press, 2008), 343.

define the contours for labor and the Democrats. So, too, the story of evangelicals and the New Right largely bears him out. Explaining evangelicals' changing voting patterns, let alone their influence in the Republican Party, without recourse to particular events would be foolhardy, indeed.

Yet while Mayhew emphasizes sudden and unforeseen shocks to the political system, many events ("things that happen," as he succinctly defines them) should be seen less as discrete disruptive moments than as connected opportunity points that entrepreneurs may exploit to bring together actors in a diffuse political system. The confluence of events in the late 1970s is stunning. The ratification of the Panama Canal Treaties, the second Miami gay rights vote, the passage of Proposition 13, the filibuster of labor-law reform, the defeat of IRS regulations, the publication of Schaeffer and Koop's *Whatever Happened to the Human Race?*, the initial ERA deadline, the initial conservative victory at the Southern Baptist Convention, and the formation of Moral Majority *all* took place between March 1978 and April 1979. Changes in political alignment have often emerged from patterned events that together shift the balance of partisan power; one need not choose between a world of ahistorical realignments or else real-world contingencies one after another.

Instead, once policy windows have opened, to use John Kingdon's metaphor, events that would simply have registered as small-scale shocks may, especially if adroit political entrepreneurs exploit them, register with greater impact and, crucially, interact with one another.[90] That is why the IRS controversy, which connected taxes with social issues, reached so far across the political system. Furthermore, the resultant politics emerge not simply from the political consequences of policy design but from actors' connection of specific controversies with broader ideological concerns and marshalling of new entrants into the system. That is the story of the changing evangelical response to *Roe*.

Moreover, even when entrepreneurs seek to build coalitions, they broker in the context of organizable alternatives. Contrary to New Right brokers' hopes of coalitionism, party returned to lower costs among different high-demanders. Rather than behaving as a set of ad hoc single-issue groups putting pressure on elected officials, the Christian Right became a centerpiece of a new Republican coalition. Hence, far from showing the American political system as disconnected, autonomous, and reactive, many of the events that forged the Christian Right served as centripetal moments, bringing diffuse actors together, politicizing their activities in civil society, and harnessing them to select elites, implement policy, and reconfigure constellations of status and power.

[90] John W. Kingdon, *Agendas, Alternatives, and Public Policies*, 2nd ed. (New York: Longman, 2003).

CHAPTER 5

The Limits of Influence

Populism and the Antiwar Movement

Among the movements have confronted the American party system, two failures have had a particularly sharp impact on American political development. The Populists of the 1890s and the antiwar movement of the 1960s sought far-reaching reorientations in national priorities to accompany more authentically democratic political life.[1] The stories of the two movements stand out for their unrealized possibilities: the rejection of corporate capitalism or overarching American imperialism.

Party regulars successfully repulsed the insurgents at the times of their peak strength, in 1892 and 1968 respectively. The Populists, facing simultaneous uphill battles against western Republicans and southern Democrats, formed a third party and lost. The antiwar movement fought its way to the convention in Chicago, and lost in the hall and in the streets. The consequences of these early failures to find a fit between movement and party proved stark. By the time the Democrats ultimately absorbed the remnants of both movements, they had split apart amid disorganization, and lost their independent capacity to mobilize supporters and extract concessions. In 1896, the Democrats accepted only Populism's Silverite fringe but not its major tenets or leaders, and the movement sputtered out. Even as the reformed Democrats nominated the dovish George McGovern in 1972, the movement itself had split into factions, and the party mobilized voters directly. After atrophy in group capacity, the center could not hold.

[1] For others making the same parallel, see the equally gloomy Bruce Ackerman, "The Broken Engine of Progressive Politics," *American Prospect*, May 1998, 41, and the more positive Terry H. Anderson, *The Movement and the Sixties* (Oxford: Oxford University Press, 1996), 413.

Movement radicals had grown disillusioned and given up on mainstream politics. Moderates could not prune and trim their supporters to meet a party's dictates for alliance as their relative advantage in mobilization disappeared once parties co-opted their supporters.

Nor did either party have much to offer from the political wilderness that followed. Their remnants each powerfully influenced the Democratic Party, toward agrarian and dovish sentiments respectively. The policies, including the income tax and the fiat currency, that the Populists espoused, and the personnel who came of age during the McCarthy insurgency, influenced the party for decades to come. At the level of choices for the American regime, however, neither movement forged partnerships between party and organized autonomous movement, or established institutional residues inside the American state. Their hopes to use party politics as a mean to renew democratic life came to naught.

To be sure, the parallels are inexact, certainly weaker than between the two anchoring alliances. The Populists established a much deeper connection to authentically American values, yet their defeat was the more total. Populists wanted more than a laundry list of policies, many of them ultimately achieved. They wanted an egalitarian polity that substantially circumscribed industrial capitalism. That historical alternative never reappeared in American public life, not even in the New Deal's most radical moment. Instead, populist politics moved rightward across the twentieth century. The antiwar movement, by contrast, met its immediate demand: the Vietnam War ended—even if American imperialism did not. Both movements chafed at conventional, distributive party politics, yet they did so in different ways. Only Populism formed a third party, while the antiwar movement, through party reform, achieved longer-lasting changes in the party structure. One reason comes in the relation of the movement to other agitators for social change. While Populism failed to join with urban workers, the antiwar movement, through the "New Politics," linked with the civil rights movement and, to some extent, the women's movement to dethrone traditional centers of power inside the Democratic Party.

Populism

Populism, the American social movement that most conspicuously and consequentially failed to integrate into party politics, poses a complex and cautionary tale. The agrarian radicals of the Alliance movement challenged large-scale corporations as they emerged in the Gilded Age. If Populism had somehow succeeded, the country's racial and economic history would look very different. It might—despite long odds, not least in the American electoral system—have sustained an agrarian party on the left comparable to the Cooperative Commonwealth Federation in Saskatchewan, which implemented single-payer health care on the provincial level and formed the nucleus of the labor-backed New Democratic Party of Canada.[2]

Yet the dense network of alliances and cooperatives in the late 1880s failed in its bid to form a political program with majority support. The Alliancemen formed a third party in 1892. In the summer of 1896, a rump faction fused with the Democrats under unfavorable circumstances. Their common platform principally advocated the free coinage of silver. These shifts—from movement to third party, and from party-movement to fusion—encompass multiple approaches to the party system, and not only the agrarian radicals themselves but their Silverite sometime-allies.

The Farmers' Alliance emerged from an indigenous egalitarianism concerned with the pernicious effects on democratic life of concentrated wealth. That tradition traced back to Locofocoism in the Jacksonian years, and thence to Jefferson and Paine.[3] More immediately, as transport costs decreased and markets globalized in the decades after the Civil War, deflationary economic policy and depressed agricultural prices had saddled small farmers in the South and West with debt. Greenback arguments for inflationary policies designed to divorce currency from gold appealed widely to small farmers. They found expression in a series of third parties and agrarian movements that culminated in the Farmers' Alliances of the late 1880s. Especially through Charles McCune's subtreasury plan, by which the government would buy grain directly, the Alliance sought to break the exploitative relationships that hurt farmers' livelihood and, in turn, sapped democratic control of the economy and society. As Michael Rogin argued half a century ago, "In America the farmers who stayed on the land played the role of European workers as the major force challenging industrial capitalism."[4]

The Alliance sustained itself through conscious mass movement building on a scale rarely seen in American history; the CIO organizing drives and the civil rights movement of the 1960s serve as the only parallels, and even they had stronger elite leadership and ties to established power. The key figures were lecturers who traveled the country explaining farmers' economic plight. A vast reform press buttressed their efforts.[5] Importantly,

[2] Seymour Martin Lipset, *Agrarian Socialism: The Cooperative Commonwealth Federation in Saskatchewan*, rev. ed. (1950; repr., New York: Anchor Books, 1968).

[3] Chester McArthur Destler, *American Radicalism, 1865–1901: Essays and Documents* (1946; repr., New York: Octagon Books, 1963); Thomas Goebel, "The Political Economy of Populism from Jackson to the New Deal," *Studies in American Political Development* 11 (1997): 109–48.

[4] Michael Paul Rogin, *The Intellectuals and McCarthy: The Radical Specter* (Cambridge, Mass.: MIT Press, 1967), 187.

[5] See, feeling out the party system, William A. Peffer, *The Farmer's Side: His Troubles and Their Remedy* (New York: Appleton, 1891), pt. 3, chap. 5.

the Alliance in the South emphasized the common economic problems of blacks and whites, especially tenant farmers, and opposed Jim Crow and efforts to restrict the suffrage. Although the Southern Alliance was not integrated, many white Populists worked closely with the Colored Farmers' Alliance, and the CFA held official representation in the People's Party.[6]

The Alliance, therefore, began as a grassroots, locally oriented movement of social protest. The transition from movement to third party took place in stages. In 1890, Alliancemen "hastily devised third parties," and that December the different Alliance federations met and laid out their program in the Ocala Demands, but without the instrument of a political party.[7] In 1891, six Alliancemen in the House refused to back a major-party candidate for Speaker and began to caucus separately. The party was formally founded at a meeting of sympathetic organizations, including the various Alliances and the Knights of Labor, in the spring of 1892. It nominated a full slate of candidates under a common banner for the 1892 elections, and adapted the Ocala Demands into the formal Omaha Platform.[8] After the preferred presidential candidate, Leonidas Polk of North Carolina, died in early 1892, the party nominated James Weaver, an old Greenbacker. Few southerners supported a former Union general, and he carried only five western states. Had Polk lived, he might stemmed the tide of defection in the South and, perhaps, served as the plausible fusion candidate in 1896 that the People's Party conspicuously lacked.

The Ocala Demands aimed directly at the interests, banks and railroads foremost among them, that impinged on farmers' lives and threatened their liberties. The Populists called for a vastly reconfigured approach to fundamental problems of production and finance, organized around a mixed economy that melded market, cooperative, and state.[9] They supported the free coinage of silver, to be sure, but in the context of providing subtreasuries for low-interest loans to benefit poor farmers, including those trapped in tenancy, reclaiming railroads' land for homesteaders, abolishing national banks, banning futures contracts on agricultural products, enacting a graduated income tax, and, as a procedural goad toward those substantive priorities, directly electing U.S. senators.

[6]Lawrence Goodwyn, *Democratic Promise: The Populist Moment in America* (New York: Oxford University Press, 1976), 194–206; C. Vann Woodward, *Tom Watson: Agrarian Rebel* (1938; repr., Savannah, Ga.: Beehive Press, 1973); Tom Watson, "The Negro Question in the South," *Arena*, October 1892, 540–50.

[7]John D. Hicks, *The Populist Revolt: A History of the Farmers' Alliance and the People's Party* (Minneapolis: University of Minnesota Press, 1931), 179; Carl C. Taylor, *The Farmers' Movement, 1620–1920* (New York: American Book Company, 1953), chap. 9.

[8]"Populist Party Platform of 1892," http://www.presidency.ucsb.edu/ws/index.php?pid=29616.

[9]Charles Postel, *The Populist Vision* (Oxford: Oxford University Press, 2007), chap. 4.

For students of social movements, Populism often serves as a cautionary tale on the dangers of power.[10] The People's Party simultaneously faced the challenges of maintaining movement infrastructure to mobilize supporters, and of forging a majority in the Electoral College. It did neither. After the disappointing showing in the 1892 election, the party needed support to maintain itself, and issues to resonate with voters. Sectionalism worsened the challenge as the movement found no single party with which to push alliance. In the West, robber barons controlled the railroads, and the railroads controlled the Republican Party. In the South, Populists such as Marion Butler often made common cause with black-and-tan state Republican parties to oppose Bourbon Democrats, racially exclusionary and dominated by a narrow, wealthy planter class. Yet the People's Party also bumped up against deep Democratic loyalties. Charles McCune presciently warned that "the Alliance is a school in which principles are taught and agreed upon, and the destruction of the Order would be fatal to the reform movement. Those who would destroy the Order to build up the party would kill the goose that laid the golden egg"—and then fulfilled his prophecy when he could not break with the Democrats to support Weaver.[11]

The possibilities for the People's Party to adopt a broad agenda became increasingly arduous. The mine owners' hope of restoring silver to its former value clashed with Populist orthodoxy arguing for reflation and a fiat currency. In the midterm elections of 1894, the party retreated substantially in the South while winning in the West mainly when candidates emphasized silver. The movement base atrophied, and the lure of Silverite campaign money increased. Herman Taubeneck, the Populists' national chairman, and Ignatius Donnelly, the lead organizer, took it in order to keep the party a going concern. Once the movement had transformed itself into an organized party, it needed an issue agenda with immediate payoff. As a Kansas state senator asked, "Why a single issue—free coinage? Not because it would benefit the people more than any other reform measure but because it is the only question that the great majority of the people are really interested in."[12] The party soon divided between fusionists seeking to ally with the Democrats and "mid-roaders" favoring an independent path.

Critically, Populism failed to connect with urban workers, a necessity to break out of the periphery and gain for the party a national majority. In the wake of economic depression and political repression, Populism found

[10] Goodwyn, *Democratic Promise*, and, especially, Michael Schwartz, *Radical Protest and Social Structure: The Southern Farmers' Alliance and Cotton Tenancy, 1880–1890* (New York: Academic Press, 1976), serve as good cases in point.

[11] "The Final Answer," *National Economist*, 26 December 1891, 1.

[12] Hicks, *Populist Revolt*, 313; Destler, *American Radicalism*, 44; Goodwyn, *Democratic Promise*, 458.

no ready ally for a multi-issue, farmer-labor third party along the lines of, for instance, the 1924 La Follette coalition. In 1892, Frances Willard of the Woman's Christian Temperance Union made an ambitious attempt to bring together the WCTU, Prohibition Party, suffragists, the dry Knights of Labor, and Populists (in a phrase that would reappear, she even dubbed her amalgam "the New Politics"), but—unsurprisingly, given the gulfs among such disparate reformers—failed to effectuate the fusion.[13] Their agrarian background and difficulties in coalition formation ill prepared Populist leaders to explain how a program based on individual autonomy and inflationary money would serve the interests and advance the values of industrial workers anxious to increase their real purchasing power.

The labor movement was particularly conservative and sectarian in the 1890s. The sympathetic Knights of Labor and its producerist vision lay in tatters. Samuel Gompers and the voluntarist AF of L evinced no interest in national politics. The state and its corporate backers had shattered the nation's first serious industrial union, the American Railway Union under Eugene Debs, in the 1894 Pullman strike. Yet Debs had not yet taken up the banner of socialism. Had Populism flowered a decade earlier, it could—however unstably—have made common cause with, and perhaps even aided the transition into national politics of, the Knights. A decade later and the Socialist Party could conceivably have served as a partner.[14]

At the same time, the shift from movement to party had deleterious consequences. Populism posed starkly the dangers for a movement of embedding itself in purpose-built rather than preexisting social institutions. As the lure of office and the demand for immediate victory took precedence over the slower work of movement building, the Alliance press grew weaker and the system of popular education that had led to strong elite influence on voters in the late 1880s atrophied. Populist leaders still claimed to represent

[13] See "Fight on a Platform," *Chicago Daily Tribune*, 25 February 1892, 5, which includes Willard's proposed language for the People's Party platform; Mary Earhart, *Frances Willard: From Prayer to Politics* (Chicago: University of Chicago Press, 1944), chap. 14; Rebecca Edwards, *Angels in the Machinery: Gender in American Party Politics from the Civil War to the Progressive Era* (Oxford: Oxford University Press, 1997), 98–99. Southern Populists found women's suffrage objectionable.

[14] Gretchen Ritter, *Goldbugs and Greenbacks: The Antimonopoly Tradition and the Politics of Finance in America* (Cambridge: Cambridge University Press, 1997); James Peterson, "The Trade Unions and the Populist Party," *Science and Society* 8 (1944): 143–60; Richard Franklin Bensel, *The Political Economy of American Industrialization, 1877–1900* (Cambridge: Cambridge University Press, 2000); Leon Fink, *Workingmen's Democracy: The Knights of Labor and American Politics* (Urbana: University of Illinois Press, 1983), chap. 2; Robin Archer, *Why Is There No Labor Party in the United States?* (Princeton: Princeton University Press, 2007), esp. chap. 5; James R. Green, *Grass-Roots Socialism: Radical Movements in the Southwest, 1895–1943* (Baton Rouge: Louisiana State University Press, 1978).

a mass base, but it had evaporated.[15] Into this environment came "The Silver Question." Once advocates of the white metal established themselves inside the Democratic Party in the winter of 1896, Populism's fate was effectively determined. The American Bimetallic League (known initially as the National Silver Convention and ultimately as the American Bimetallic Union) was formed at a conference in 1889. Although paid for almost entirely by a small group of mine owners in Nevada and Idaho (including William Randolph Hearst), the funders deliberately kept themselves in the shadows and installed as chairman A. J. Warner, a former Union Army colonel and Democratic representative from Ohio. These unabashed single-issue activists initially sought a pressure group strategy aimed at persuading Congress and the public. In 1890, Congress largely along regional lines approved the Sherman Silver Purchase Act, which authorized limited government purchase of silver.

As the Panic of 1893, the American manifestation of a global downturn, spread through the economy and the Cleveland administration repealed the Silver Purchase Act, the ABL (i.e., the mine owners) sought to redefine the agenda and increase concern about silver such that it would be the central issue in national politics—and, by extension, therefore, the line of cleavage between the parties. A network of silver clubs and nationwide lectures, not unlike the Alliance's, spread the Silverite gospel around the country. The ABL issued pro forma endorsements in 1894. The key transformation took place the following year. The group followed a two-pronged strategy designed both to garner support for silver among Democrats—with an agrarian base amenable to inflationary policy, the party more likely to accept alliance—and to "wean the Populists away from their other doctrines and commit them to support a program in which silver should be the only item of consequence."[16]

Along the way, the ABL promoted a Silver Party as a way to attract potential supporters repelled by the Democratic or Populist label, but never seriously developed the idea, since it raised the same issues of race, sectionalism, and ancestral partisan loyalty that vexed Populists themselves, especially in the South. As a blunt account of the Silver Party's convention explained, "The Southern people cling to the Democratic party, owing to their fear

[15] See, e.g., Scott G. McNall, *The Road to Rebellion: Class Formation and Kansas Populism, 1865–1900* (Chicago: University of Chicago Press, 1988).

[16] William Henry Batty, "The American Bimetallic League and the Fight for Free Silver: A Study of the Organized Silver Movement in the United States" (MA thesis, Southern Illinois University at Edwardsville, 1974), 56; Hicks, *Populist Revolt*, 343. The leading propaganda was W. H. Harvey, *Coin's Financial School* (Chicago: Coin, 1894). For a recent take, which emphasizes machinations around silver to the exclusion of Populism's broader context, see Samuel DeCanio, "Populism, Paranoia, and the Politics of Free Silver," *Studies in American Political Development* 25 (2011): 1–26.

of Negro supremacy, and advocate carrying on of the free silver movement within the party organization."[17]

Instead, silver provided a perfect issue for Democrats to outflank the People's Party—even as they, too, failed to build a national majority from their new coalition.[18] Silver offered some level of monetary flexibility. It would not, however, threaten the essential elements in Bourbon Democratic rule newly entrenched in the South through a series of restrictive state constitutions enacted in the 1890s: control over small farmers, as in the subtreasury plan; or the racial caste system reified in Jim Crow.[19] Unlike many Populists, the Democratic politicians, such as Ben Tillman, who spoke out on behalf of poor whites and free silver harbored no sympathy for African Americans or their plight in the southern tenancy system.

A conference in Memphis in June 1895 brought southern and western Silverite Democrats together with a smattering of dissident Republicans and fusionist Populists. From that conference formed the Bimetallic Democratic National Committee, crystallizing the sectional and partisan linkages that would create single-issue fusion. As William Jennings Bryan argued with less than his usual hyperbole, "it was largely through the efforts of these men that the silver Democrats gained control of the national convention." In short order, state conventions throughout the South and West ratified prosilver platforms; some also adopted unit rules to bind their delegations in advance of the national convention.[20]

If the Silverites helped to set the national agenda, Bryan achieved the coup de grâce. He tricked the People's Party into holding its convention after the Democrats, ensuring the major party first-mover advantage. Instead of forcing the Democrats to decide whether to accept a sympathetic third-party challenger—as they had with Horace Greeley, after the Liberal Republicans had chosen him in 1872—the Populists, with some dissent from the mid-roaders, agreed to hold their convention last, under the notion that they might attract the Silverite dissidents from both major camps. Further restricting the Populists' choice, the Silver Party agreed to meet in St. Louis on the same days. Had the People's Party been able to choose first—and, admittedly, it had no perfect candidate—it might have been able to exercise substantially more independent influence. Instead, it merely ratified Bryan,

[17] "Silver Men in a Row," *Chicago Tribune*, 20 July 1895, 4.

[18] See J. Rogers Hollingsworth, *The Whirligig of Politics: The Democracy of Cleveland and Bryan* (Chicago: University of Chicago Press, 1963), chaps. 2 and 3.

[19] Theodore Saloutos, *Farmers' Movements in the South, 1865–1933* (Berkeley: University of California Press, 1960), chap. 9.

[20] William Jennings Bryan, *The First Battle: A Story of the Campaign of 1896* (Chicago: W.B. Conkey, 1897), 162; James A. Barnes, "Myths of the Bryan Campaign," *Mississippi Valley Historical Review* 34 (1947): 374–75.

the electrifying orator who, in the age of the two-thirds rule, appealed alike to the South and to Silverite delegations from the Midwest and the West.[21]

Bryan was, to use the terms of latter-day political science, less a broker than an issue entrepreneur, an ambitious young man who with silver found his calling. As Ignatius Donnelly later remarked caustically, "We put him to school and he wound up by stealing the schoolbooks." Bryan expressed the Populists' anger at industrial power, but without providing even the rudiments of a theory to explain it. If their instinctive belief in social mobility and agrarian democracy forestalled Populists from developing a systematic theory of urban labor, neither would they claim, with Bryan in the Cross of Gold speech, that "the man who is employed for wages is as much a businessman as his employer."[22]

The American Bimetallic Union had, by putting forth the issue of silver and organizing allies in the Democratic camp, set the issue agenda and, by timing the conventions, also set the slate of candidates. Once Bryan had been chosen, the Populists had little choice. Their cause had its champion, and their group-specific appeals had lost their sway. The American Bimetallic Union immediately came out for Bryan and his running mate, Arthur Sewall, a Maine shipbuilding magnate with Silverite tendencies. Its Silver Party served principally as a bridge for western Republicans to support Bryan; a survey with a prescient question about "prior political loyalties" identified three-quarters of the delegates as ex-Republicans.[23]

Although a few mid-roaders advocated for an independent ticket, the People's Party at its convention in St. Louis similarly acquiesced with the nomination of Bryan and the formation of fusion tickets in areas where Populists had run strongly. The mid-roaders achieved a Pyrrhic victory by nominating Tom Watson, a radical former congressman from Georgia, as the Populist vice presidential candidate, rather than going along with Sewall. The decision to nominate Watson without gaining any influence inside the Bryan camp led, for a potential anchoring group, to the worst of all possible outcomes: loss of support for the candidate from centrist voters worried about the radical specter without corresponding political gains from increased movement support, or even the possibility of policy benefit down the road. The McKinley campaign emphasized Watson's role; a campaign poster shows Watson driving the silver wagon as urban workmen

[21] Henry Demarest Lloyd, "The Populists at St. Louis," *Review of Reviews* 14 (1896): 298–303; Stanley L. Jones, *The Presidential Election of 1896* (Madison: University of Wisconsin Press, 1964), 71; Woodward, *Tom Watson*, 255; Richard Franklin Bensel, *Passion and Preferences: William Jennings Bryan and the 1896 Democratic National Convention* (Cambridge: Cambridge University Press, 2008).

[22] Hicks, *Populist Revolt*, 356; speech reprinted in Bryan, *First Battle*, 199–206.

[23] Bryan, *First Battle*, 252.

stand in line at an empty shop whose goods they can no longer afford.[24] In the end, most supporters of the People's Party as expressed in the Omaha Platform ended up backing Bryan, simply because the election posed so starkly issues of wealth and corporate power. As Henry Demarest Lloyd, who had sought to unite Populism and socialism in Chicago, wrote of the choice, "they cannot afford to side with money against men."[25]

To be clear, it is worth separating out the summer and fall of 1896 as critical junctures. Had Populism somehow failed as a movement and Bryan become the president, a new model for party-movement interaction might have evolved, emphasizing strongly—even more than with organized labor in the New Deal and afterward—the incorporation only of movement moderates acceptable to other partisan elites. Nevertheless, such a counterfactual was highly unlikely. William McKinley's campaign, led by the industrialist Mark Hanna, set quotas by industry for contributions, and put its vast resources to good effect. While McKinley surrogates attacked Bryan and translated broadsides into new immigrants' native tongues, delegations from across the land boarded subsidized railroad trains to visit the genial Republican on his front porch in Canton, Ohio.[26] The poet Vachel Lindsay well evoked the balance of forces. "The ultimate fantastics / Of the far western slope / And of prairie schooner children / Born beneath the stars" stood no chance against "Hanna of Ohio / Rallying the roller-tops / . . . And plutocrats in miles / With dollar signs upon their coats / Diamond watchchains on their vests and spats on their feet."[27]

The realignment of 1896, thus, principally captures a *nonevent*—a thwarted, Populist-led challenge to industrial capitalism. The new alignment demobilized and divided agrarian radicals in the South and West both from one another, and from the urban working class. It forestalled a welfare state, and ensured pliant courts that would use the Commerce and Due Process Clauses to defend corporate personhood, enjoin labor with crushing injunctions, and restrict the sphere of state action.[28]

[24]In collection of the author.

[25]Lloyd, "Populists," 303.

[26]Herbert Croly, *Marcus Alonzo Hanna: His Life and Work* (New York: Macmillan, 1912), chap. 16.

[27]Vachel Lindsay, "Bryan, Bryan, Bryan, Bryan: The Campaign of Eighteen Ninety Six as Viewed at the Time by a Sixteen-Year-Old, etc.," in *Pols: Great Writers on Politics*, ed. Jack Beatty (New York: Public Affairs, 2004), 31–39.

[28]The classic statement is Walter Dean Burnham, "The System of 1896: An Analysis," in *The Evolution of American Electoral Systems*, ed. Paul Kleppner (Westport, Conn.: Greenwood, 1981), 147–202. See, among many, E. E. Schattschneider, "United States: The Functional Approach to Party Government," in *Modern Political Parties: Approaches to Comparative Politics*, ed. Sigmund Neumann (Chicago: University of Chicago Press, 1956), 197–206; Richard McCormick, "Walter Dean Burnham and 'The System of 1896,'" *Social Science History* 10 (1986): 245–62; Richard Franklin Bensel, *The Political Economy of American Industrialization*

Populists had no ongoing organization with which to pressure the establishment, and rural protest ebbed. The failure of biracial politics in the South cut particularly deeply. To protect themselves from an incipient alliance of poor white farmers and African Americans, Bourbon Democrats radically restricted the franchise. Indeed, the later careers of the leading figures in the People's Party are conspicuous by their absence save for Tom Watson, who turned into a vicious race baiter. In the industrialized North and in the West (especially after Bryanism faded), the Republican Party, closely allied with business interests formed in the wake of the first national-level mergers, racked up impressive margins even in urban centers.

To be sure, the agrarian impulse found expression in the Democrats' ambitious domestic program, enacted in Woodrow Wilson's first term. It produced a constitutional amendment to allow an income tax, the Federal Reserve System, and the Federal Trade Commission. This program would have been unthinkable without William Jennings Bryan, or the decades-long legacy of agrarian demands. Yet this burst of activity represented Democrats' pent-up demands more than it sustained linkages between policy and politics, or between movement and party. The new Farmers' Union, despite some of the old rhetoric, behaved as "more an organized interest group than a movement": it treated farmers as a discrete class, and principally lobbied legislators. Nor did it offer relief to African Americans or to poor white tenant farmers. Leading Democrats in Congress had often cut their teeth opposing Populism at the state level. Progressive Republicans, and third parties in the Upper Midwest, meant that reform had no consistent partisan advocate as coalitions shifted across issues. The Progressive impulse proceeded apart from party or from militant movement agitation.[29]

In 1912, Josephus Daniels, FDR's chief at the navy under Wilson, wrote that "in the Republican Party the reactionaries are in the majority whereas in the Democratic Party they are in the minority." He was right about the shape of post-1896 alignments—yet he demonstrated the limits of the new Democracy. In 1898, he helped to orchestrate a brutal riot in Wilmington,

---

(Cambridge: Cambridge University Press, 2000); Thomas Ferguson and Jie Chen, "Investor Blocs and Party Realignments in American History," *Journal of the Historical Society* 4 (2005): 503–46; and, skeptically, David R. Mayhew, *Electoral Realignments: A Critique of an American Genre* (New Haven: Yale University Press, 2002), 128–40.

[29] Elizabeth Sanders, *The Roots of Reform: Farmers, Workers, and the American State, 1877–1917* (Chicago: University of Chicago Press, 1999), 151. By tracing the roots of enacted legislation, rather than the fate of movement insurgencies, Sanders emphasizes the continuities in agrarian demands. See also Grant McConnell, *The Decline of Agrarian Democracy* (Berkeley: University of California Press, 1953), chap. 4; Gwendolyn Mink, *Old Labor and New Immigrants in American Political Development: Union, Party, and State, 1875–1920* (Ithaca, N.Y.: Cornell University Press, 1986), 118; Saloutos, *Farmers' Movements*, chaps. 12 and 13; Taylor, *Farmers' Movement*, chap. 14.

North Carolina, that overthrew a biracial Populist-Republican alliance. At every Democratic convention down through 1944, he hosted a breakfast in memory of William Jennings Bryan.[30]

For all the twists and turns in this saga of Populism and silver, the basic lesson turns on the essential fact in the American electoral system: potential anchoring groups choosing the third-party strategy must cobble together national majorities, which in turn requires electoral victories across diverse parts of the polity while maintaining some organizational coherence. The 1890s confirm the hazards even in such a banal statement of political fact. As they faced the vested interests of cotton, silver, and finance respectively, the Alliance failed to bring the racially divided South into the People's Party, failed to preserve the Omaha Platform from single-issue Silverites, and failed to appeal to urban workers. The dominant political forces marginalized the movement so that it entered the party system on the weakest possible terms congruent with other elements inside established partisan politics.[31] More than a century hence, few remembered that small towns in the South and West, latter-day bulwarks of conservatism, had once launched the fiercest challenge to industrial capitalism ever to take root on American soil.

The Antiwar Movement

The Vietnam War divided Americans more deeply than any conflict since the Civil War. The antiwar movement wanted more than an end to the war, though having such a discrete aim certainly separates it from all the other potential anchoring groups considered in these pages. It sought a reconfigured participatory democracy that closed the book on imperial expansionism. Yet the sprawling, youth-led movement failed to realign the parties between hawks and doves, or ultimately to institutionalize itself as an ongoing, organized force in the party or in the polity. In 1968, the organized party, led by hawkish regulars, repulsed the insurgency. In 1972, a reformed party embraced the remnants of a fissured movement. Partisan support and movement capacity operated on different timetables. Instead, its legacy and personnel have continued to influence the opportunity structure inside the Democratic Party.[32]

[30]Josephus Daniels, *The Wilson Era: Years of Peace, 1910–1917* (Chapel Hill: University of North Carolina Press, 1944), 11; Michael Kazin, *A Godly Hero: The Life of William Jennings Bryan* (New York: Knopf, 2006), 300.

[31]Cf. Martin Shefter, *Political Parties and the State: The American Historical Experience* (Princeton: Princeton University Press, 1994), chap. 4.

[32]James Sundquist, *Dynamics of the Party System: Alignment and Realignment of Political Parties in the United States*, rev. ed. (Washington, D.C.: Brookings Institution, 1983), 379–83; cf. Robert P. Saldin, *War, the American State, and Politics since 1898* (Cambridge: Cambridge

Movement moderates are also, in the national scene, relative radicals. Defining the movement's contours proves particularly hard in this case. The broader New Left in the late sixties and early seventies embraced causes beyond simply bringing the troops home, and disdained elite-oriented, coalition-based bargaining in favor of authentic direct action on the ground.[33] Nor, for that matter, did most antiwar activists directly involved in party politics identify with the New Left. In that sense, Vietnam serves as a useful prism into the sixties, asking how those who wanted to stop the war approached the American party system. Ultimately they reoriented that system more than they achieved their substantive aims.

The antiwar movement faced a Democratic Party partially sympathetic and partially deeply opposed. This unusual alignment pushed conflict *inside* the party coalition. The fratricide pervading liberalism at the end of the 1960s makes sense, however, only in terms of the polity as a whole: Lyndon Johnson, as he ramped up American involvement in Vietnam, faced huge pressures from what he termed "the right-wing beast" and feared that the conservative coalition of northern Republicans and southern Democrats would block the Great Society if they felt him weak on communism.[34] Even if doves such as John Sherman Cooper and Mark Hatfield opposed the war, most Republican leaders and all of the party's presidential aspirants took a hawkish stance. Many Democrats, however queasy about Vietnam, hesitated to offend a powerful president with whose domestic agenda they agreed.

In the summer of 1967, the peripatetic Allard Lowenstein, a sometime advisor to the Mississippi Freedom Democratic Party and Martin Luther King, Jr., and former president of the National Student Association, launched a crusade to "Dump Johnson." Lowenstein justified his search with two claims:

University Press, 2010), chap. 6. See generally Hugh Heclo, "The Sixties' False Dawn: Awakenings, Movements, and Postmodern Policy-Making," in *Integrating the Sixties: The Origins, Structures, and Legitimacy of Public Policy in a Turbulent Decade*, ed. Brian Balogh (University Park: Pennsylvania State University Press, 1996), 34–63.

[33] See Staughton Lynd, "Coalition Politics or Nonviolent Revolution?," *Liberation*, June 1965, 17–21. On "the movement," see James Miller, *Democracy Is in the Streets: From Port Huron to the Siege of Chicago* (New York: Simon & Schuster, 1987); Charles DeBenedetti, *An American Ordeal: The Antiwar Movement of the Vietnam Era* (Syracuse: Syracuse University Press, 1990); Tom Wells, *The War Within: America's Battle over Vietnam* (Berkeley: University of California Press, 1994); Anderson, *Movement*.

[34] Francis M. Bator, "No Good Choices: LBJ and the Vietnam/Great Society Connection," *Diplomatic History* 32 (2008): 336; and the two-by-two choice set ("no war cum Great Society legislation was, [Johnson] thought, not an available option") in Francis M. Bator, "Reply to Roundtable on Francis M. Bator's 'No Good Choices: LBJ and the Vietnam/Great Society Connection,'" *Diplomatic History* 32 (2008): 366. See also Andrew L. Johns, *Vietnam's Second Front: Domestic Politics, the Republican Party, and the War* (Lexington: University Press of Kentucky, 2010); and Julian E. Zelizer, *The Fierce Urgency of Now: Lyndon Johnson, Congress, and the Battle for the Great Society* (New York: Penguin, 2015), 146–151.

that "current American policy in Vietnam is leading the nation to disaster" and that "you stop [the war] by making our case in the political process and reclaiming the Democratic Party."[35] In other words, he sought for the movement to confront the party system, and, through nomination, to bring the Democrats to meet movement demands. Yet by entering the party system through a primary challenge to, rather than in partnership with, dominant elements in the Democratic coalition, the peace movement did so under weaker terms than anchoring alliances. The "New Politics," far from fixing a trajectory, met ongoing resistance. Battles first fought in 1968, over party rules and the use of American power abroad, divide Democrats still.

To telescope a complex history, Lowenstein's friend, Robert Kennedy, turned him down, and Eugene McCarthy of Minnesota took up the antiwar banner, running largely as a single-issue candidate.[36] For McCarthy, a former Benedictine novitiate and an often diffident campaigner, public life served to confront power with moral principle. "When he talks politics," wrote David Halberstam, "it is not the names of counties and delegates and chairmen he speaks of, it is the abstractions."[37] McCarthy gained endorsement from Americans for Democratic Action. After an agonizing meeting, and over bitter dissents from the needle trade unions (and muffled dissent from the Auto Workers), the keepers of the anticommunist liberal flame sided with the movement over the institutional party.[38] In the New Hampshire primary, McCarthy came within a whisker of an uncommitted slate expected to back the president. Johnson soon withdrew from the race, and halted bombing in North Vietnam. Then Robert Kennedy entered the contest, talking about race and class as well as war, and bullets felled Martin Luther King, Jr., and Kennedy himself.

[35]Quotes in respectively Allard K. Lowenstein and Arnold S. Kaufman, "The Case for Opposing Johnson's Renomination," *War/Peace Report*, November 1967, 6; and Lanny J. Davis, *The Emerging Democratic Majority: Lessons and Legacies from the New Politics* (New York: Stein and Day, 1974), 27.

[36]For general histories, see Lewis Chester, Godfrey Hodgson, and Bruce Page, *An American Melodrama: The Presidential Campaign of 1968* (New York: Viking, 1969); Carl Solberg, *Hubert Humphrey: A Biography* (New York: Knopf, 1984); William H. Chafe, *Never Stop Running: Allard Lowenstein and the Struggle to Save American Liberalism* (New York: Basic Books, 1993); and, more critically, Dominic Sandbrook, *Eugene McCarthy: The Rise and Fall of Postwar Liberalism* (New York: Knopf, 2004).

[37]David Halberstam, "McCarthy and the Divided Left," *Harper's*, March 1968, 40; see also E. W. Kenworthy, "Eugene McCarthy: A Blend of Humility, Arrogance, and Humor," *New York Times*, 30 August 1968, 16; and Jeremy Larner, *Nobody Knows: Reflections on the McCarthy Campaign of 1968* (New York: Macmillan, 1970).

[38]James A. Wechsler, "Behind ADA's McCarthy Vote," *New York Post*, 12 February 1968, 33. An estimate from the ADA convention in May (by which point many of the regulars had walked) showed support for McCarthy at 60 percent, for Humphrey at 25 percent, and for Kennedy at 15 percent. See "ADA Looks Ahead," *New Republic*, 1 June 1968, 8.

The spring and summer of 1968 took their toll on the United States, and on the Democratic Party especially. The vice president, Hubert Humphrey, a liberal stalwart who had publicly supported the administration's Vietnam policy, may well have been the most popular and even the most electable nominee. Forty percent of Democrats in a May Gallup poll backed him, as opposed to 31 percent for Kennedy and 19 percent for McCarthy.[39] However, Humphrey failed to enter a single Democratic primary. He relied instead on nominally uncommitted slates chosen by state committees and conventions, with input from voters indirect or nonexistent. In many states, the unit rule forced all delegates, sometimes even down to the level of the county convention, to vote with the majority no matter their personal views. To antiwar activists, these rules reflected deeper ills in American political life: they substituted majority will for individual conscience.[40]

After McCarthy supporters in Connecticut extracted a mere nine of forty-four delegates, they challenged party procedures through a self-appointed Commission on the Democratic Selection of Presidential Nominees, under the nominal chairmanship of Harold Hughes, governor of Iowa. The commissioners met only once, in a suburban Chicago living room; the staff set the agenda and wrote the report. It emphasized an open process with opportunity for all Democrats to participate freely at every level, and further recommended that the convention impose these standards for 1972 and refuse to seat offending delegations.[41]

The searing spectacle of the 1968 Democratic convention marked a kind of climax to the decade's drama—"the before and after marker of your life," said the feminist writer Gloria Steinem. A bitterly divided convention nominated Humphrey as antiwar forces repeatedly protested biased

[39]Nelson W. Polsby, *The Consequences of Party Reform* (Oxford: Oxford University Press, 1983), 23. Contrary to myth, Humphrey would almost certainly have won the nomination even if Kennedy had lived. RFK might well have joined the ticket, leading to—at least in the short run—very different rules of the game for social movements and the constituent elements in the Democratic coalition. See Nelson W. Polsby, "What If Robert Kennedy Had Not Been Assassinated?," in *What If? Explorations in Social-Science Fiction*, ed. Nelson W. Polsby (Lexington, Mass.: Lewis, 1982), 144–52.

[40]See, from erudite (if not always politically astute) McCarthy supporters, Elizabeth Hardwick, "Chicago," *New York Review of Books*, 26 September 1968, 5–7; William Styron, "In the Jungle," *New York Review of Books*, 26 September 1968, 11–13; Arthur Miller, "The Battle of Chicago: From the Delegates' Side," *New York Times Magazine*, 15 September 1968, 29–31, 122–28; and, thoughtfully, Murray Kempton, "The Decline and Fall of the Democratic Party," *Saturday Evening Post*, November 1968, 19–20, 66–79.

[41]Christopher Lydon, "McCarthy People Quit Ct. Convention, Frustrated over Delegates to Chicago," *Boston Globe*, 23 June 1968, 9; William Borders, "Connecticut McCarthy Backers Take Bailey's Offer of 9 Votes," *New York Times*, 3 July 1968, 12; "The Democratic Choice: A Report of the Commission on the Democratic Selection of Presidential Nominees" (n.p., 1968); Chester, Hodgson, and Page, *American Melodrama*, 394–401; Byron E. Shafer, *Quiet Revolution: The Struggle for the Democratic Party and the Shaping of Post-reform Politics* (New York: Russell Sage Foundation, 1983), 14–25.

proceedings. The convention had no use even for moderate doves. For all its grassroots support, no winning coalition inside the party could incorporate the movement at the presidential level. Mayor Richard J. Daley's police and the National Guard fired tear gas on protesters in Grant Park. Connecticut Senator Abraham Ribicoff excoriated "Gestapo tactics in the streets of Chicago," and television viewers lip-read Daley's unprintable reply. To radicals in the antiwar movement, Chicago cemented their view that the conventional political system offered no hope to change U.S. policy. To moderates, it reflected disappointment; millions of antiwar voters stayed home in November. Above all, Chicago discredited the regulars and their claims to democratic legitimacy.[42]

Vietnam exercised little influence in a fall campaign dominated by issues of "law and order." Voters saw little difference on the war between the major-party candidates, especially in contrast to the über-hawkish George Wallace.[43] Humphrey inched toward the center, offering a highly qualified plan to stop bombing of North Vietnam. McCarthy finally endorsed his fellow Minnesotan the Sunday before the election. Humphrey's late surge was not enough. After his narrow defeat, the movement split in different directions. In 1968, at the time of its maximum national influence, the movement met a hostile national party.

Party reform emerged from the joint downstream effects of the civil rights and antiwar movements. In 1964, Lyndon Johnson responded to the Mississippi Freedom Democratic Party's challenge to the lily-white official delegation with a Special Equal Rights Committee of the DNC. It had reported back with six "anti-discrimination standards," including open public meetings and clear descriptions of all public procedures. By voice vote, the 1968 convention approved its recommendation for a committee on Party Structure.[44] More controversially, the convention adopted—at a late hour, by a narrow margin, and in a chaotic vote—the stronger stuff in the Credentials Committee's minority report, based on the Hughes Commission. It completely banned the unit rule for 1972 and called for delegates to be chosen through open procedures.[45]

[42] John Schultz, *No One Was Killed: The Democratic National Convention, August 1968* (1969; repr., Chicago: University of Chicago Press, 2009), 303; see also Theodore H. White, *The Making of the President 1968* (New York: Atheneum, 1969), chap. 9.

[43] Benjamin I. Page and Richard A. Brody, "Policy Voting and the Electoral Process: The Vietnam War Issue," *American Political Science Review* 66 (1972): 979–95; Solberg, *Hubert Humphrey*, chap. 33.

[44] William J. Crotty, *Decision for the Democrats: Reforming the Party Structure* (Baltimore: Johns Hopkins University Press, 1978), 72–76. In 1968, African Americans held only six-tenths of one percent of seats on state Democratic committees in the old Confederacy. See also Max Frankel, "Delegate Fights Transform Party," *New York Times*, 28 August 1968, 1.

[45] Shafer, *Quiet Revolution*, 25–40. Text of both resolutions in *The Presidential Nominating Conventions 1968* (Washington, D.C.: Congressional Quarterly, 1968), 197–98.

A new panel met in early 1969 to merge these two charges. It was chaired first by the dovish South Dakota Senator George McGovern, and later by Donald Fraser, a Minnesota congressman. McCarthy veterans, led by Eli Segal and Anne Wexler, directed the process, and largely modeled recommendations on the Hughes panel. Although the report merely encouraged primaries or caucuses, and was entirely compatible with state-level convention systems (it forbade direct selection of delegates by state party committees), commission staff steered state parties toward primaries with explicit candidate preference.[46]

As its origins attest, many ingredients of McGovern-Fraser appear familiar from other arenas of policymaking in the Rights Revolution: openness and transparency in all public dealings; new opportunities for participation and demands for inclusiveness by underrepresented constituencies; equal numerical representation across groups, especially race but also age and gender; affirmative action for the historically underrepresented; extensive, detailed rulemaking; and primacy for these nationally standardized claims over traditional procedures, or the prerogatives of states.[47] Whether or not party elites have, indeed, reestablished control over presidential nomination, the new Democratic power brokers are, critically, very different *kinds* of elites—more diverse, more cosmopolitan, more skeptical of power for its own sake—than the regulars who nominated Hubert Humphrey. In style if not substance, the antiwar movement affects the organizational party still.[48]

Policymaking proceeded largely separate from an increasingly fractured movement as the all-volunteer army replaced the draft and the troops finally headed home. Congress reasserted itself. Decentralized floor procedures circumvented the old barons, especially on the Armed Service Committees.

[46]The weakened "regulars" never formulated a systematic counterproposal that resolved the tensions in McGovern-Fraser. See Austin Ranney, "The Democratic Party's Delegate Selection Reforms," in *America in the Seventies: Problems, Policies, and Politics*, ed. Allen P. Sindler (Boston: Little, Brown, 1977), 160–206; Penn Kemble and Josh Muravchik, "The New Politics & the Democrats," *Commentary*, December 1972, 78–84; Richard C. Wade, "The Democratic Party, 1960–1972," in *History of U.S. Political Parties*, ed. Arthur M. Schlesinger, Jr. (New York: Chelsea House, 1973), 2827–65; and Shafer *Quiet Revolution*, pt. 2. Cf., sympathetic to reformers, David Plotke, "Party Reform as Failed Democratic Renewal in the United States," *Studies in American Political Development* 10 (2006): 223–88. For context, see Sam Rosenfeld, "A Choice, Not an Echo: Polarization and the Transformation of the American Party System" (PhD diss., Harvard University, 2014), chap. 4.

[47]*Mandate for Reform: A Report of the Commission on Party Structure and Delegate Selection to the Democratic National Committee* (Washington, D.C.: Democratic National Committee, 1970), 38–48.

[48]Cf. Marty Cohen, David Karol, Hans Noel, and John Zaller, *The Party Decides: Presidential Nominations Before and After Reform* (Chicago: University of Chicago Press, 2008); Jeane J. Kirkpatrick, *The New Presidential Elite: Men and Women in National Politics* (New York: Russell Sage Foundation, 1976).

Yet the doves' leadership concentrated among individualistic senators from the periphery, liberal Republicans as well as many Democrats, ill suited to grease wheels and build durable coalitions. Nor did they broker with protestors in the streets. Only Alaska's aged Ernest Gruening had maintained close ties with the student-led movement—and he lost his seat in the 1968 primary.[49]

After it initially confronted the party system, much of the antiwar movement became *more* radical, splitting apart rather than knitting together an alternative coalition.[50] Rather than developing a clear organizational structure to negotiate with the party, the movement splintered. None of its divided parts had the wherewithal on its own to sustain itself, let alone to extract concessions from Democratic elites. Without grassroots infrastructure that politicizes extant networks, movements prove vulnerable to collapse, and the antiwar movement followed the pattern. Views on the war became solvent more than glue, and debates on tactics and strategy divided a dizzying array of factions. Each seemed to occupy only its precise point on the ideological spectrum, from Americans for Democratic Action, to the single-issue Moratorium encompassing the McCarthy veterans more sympathetic to the New Left, to the New Politics at the fringes of the Democratic camp, to the Mobilization Committee to End the War ("the Mobe"), which advocated direct action, to the violent Weather Underground. While the moderates took advantage of the changed opportunity structure, for the radicals, the sixties had proven that "the basic institutions of liberal politics—the unions, the convention system, the mass media and the Democratic Party itself—are undemocratic," and that change came only in the streets.[51]

George McGovern, an early opponent of the war, took advantage of the new rules to claim the Democratic nomination in 1972. By then, the independent movement had largely collapsed. The center of the party had shifted as New Politics elements took advantage of the postreform system. A credentials fight even denied Richard J. Daley and his slate their delegate seats.[52] The party had become open to the antiwar cause. Unlike in 1968,

[49] Ernest Gruening, *Many Battles: The Autobiography of Ernest Gruening* (New York: Liveright, 1973), chap. 27.

[50] On protest activity and congressional policy, see Paul Burstein and William Freudenburg, "Changing Public Policy: The Impact of Public Opinion, Antiwar Demonstration, and War Costs on Senate Voting on Vietnam War Motions," *American Journal of Sociology* 84 (1978): 99–122; and Doug McAdam and Yang Su, "The War at Home: Antiwar Protests and Congressional Voting, 1965 to 1973," *American Sociological Review* 67 (2002): 696–721.

[51] Jack Newfield, "More Mood Than Movement," *Nation*, 28 July 1969, 71. See also Francine du Plessix Gray "The Moratorium and the New Mobe," *New Yorker*, 3 January 1970, 32–42; Sam Brown, "The Politics of Peace," *Washington Monthly*, August 1970, 24–46.

[52] Rowland Evans and Robert Novak, "The Dethroning of Daley," *Washington Post*, 12 July 1972, A27.

however, the movement no longer had resources to offer for meaningful alliance. McGovern drew on his deep antiwar record to mobilize supporters directly, rather than brokering through movement elites.[53] At the same time, his primary victory was a one-off; it is hard to imagine any Democratic nominee since proclaiming in an acceptance speech "that never again will we send the precious young blood of this country to die trying to prop up a corrupt military dictatorship abroad."[54] Nor can the antiwar movement claim long-lasting infrastructure in or out of electoral politics. While many citizens' groups such as the Natural Resources Defense Council, MALDEF (Mexican American Legal Defense and Educational Fund), and a passel of public interest law foundations emerged from the sixties, the peace movement boasts no parallel institutional residue to oppose not just particular foreign involvements, but aggressive use of imperial power.[55]

Vietnam had larger effects on the party system and American foreign policy. The conflict shattered any kind of Cold War consensus. Presidents sought advantage from their actions abroad, and new actors in Congress, the media, and think tanks stood ready to pounce.[56] The neoconservatives who had backed Hubert Humphrey and Scoop Jackson largely switched to support Ronald Reagan, often out of disgust at student excesses.[57]

To be sure, Democrats have become less comfortable with aggressive use of American power across the developing world, a sentiment stronger at the party's grassroots and in Congress than within the party's foreign policy elite. Vietnam's clearest echoes came in the 1980s, when the Boland Amendment prohibited U.S. funding of right-wing rebels in Central America. As George Miller, a liberal House member, said, "Some of us came here to stop Vietnam. And here is our chance to stop the new one." More often,

[53] Bruce Miroff, *The Liberals' Moment: The McGovern Insurgency and the Identity Crisis of the Democratic Party* (Lawrence: University Press of Kansas, 2007). For a New Left take on McGovern, see David Kolodney, "McGovern and the Left: Time for a Stand," *Ramparts*, September 1972, 6–9 and 71–72.

[54] George McGovern, "Address Accepting the Presidential Nomination at the Democratic National Convention in Miami Beach, Florida," www.presidency.ucsb.edu/ws/index.php?pid=25967.

[55] Under McGeorge Bundy, the Ford Foundation poured vast resources into ambitious domestic grantmaking in community action and public-interest law. Its international funding avoided similarly controversial grantees that challenged the garrison state and its well-heeled backers. Whether this outcome should be understood as historically contingent or a hard limit in Cold War liberalism is a more complicated question. See Kai Bird, *The Color of Truth: McGeorge Bundy and William Bundy, Brothers in Arms* (New York: Simon & Schuster, 1998), 390–91.

[56] I. M. Destler, Leslie H. Gelb, and Anthony Lake, *Our Own Worst Enemy: The Unmaking of American Foreign Policy* (New York: Simon & Schuster, 1984).

[57] See, e.g., Jeane Kirkpatrick, "Neoconservatism as a Response to the Counter-Culture," in *The Neocon Reader*, ed. Irwin Stelzer (New York: Grove Press, 2004), 235–40.

however, ambivalence reigned. As Democrats have sought to burnish their toughness, biographical details often trumped larger concerns about America's role in the world. The Democrats in 2004 nominated John Kerry, who came to prominence in Vietnam Veterans Against the War, yet never mentioned his antiwar past, and tried to straddle divides over the war in Iraq, rather than marking out a clear antiwar stand.[58]

Finally, the McCarthy campaign brought into electoral politics an extraordinary political generation, whose names have appeared in linotype and on Twitter alike, and whose impact has ranged far beyond antiwar activism. Two stories among them seem particularly emblematic. David Mixner served both as the only young person on McGovern-Fraser, and as a bridge between New Leftists in the Mobe and more moderate antiwar activists. In 1992, he became, for Bill Clinton, the first openly gay member of a presidential campaign's National Executive Committee; he described the first meeting as "like attending a class reunion." Lanny Davis, a Lowenstein acolyte in the National Student Association, became a powerful lobbyist and served as a special counsel and frequent television flack for Bill Clinton. His client list has included dictators in Honduras, Equatorial Guinea, Côte d'Ivoire, and Bahrain—precisely the sorts of strongmen whose support from the United States during the 1960s aroused such ire among young people demanding radical changes in American policy.[59]

While the counterfactual of public life without them is hard to judge, these journeys seem now as distant from early activism as the saga of the AFL-CIO regulars, determined to resist communism and support LBJ, must have struck students in Chicago as they looked from Grant Park back to Haymarket and Pullman.[60] In a twist on the New Right dictum that personnel is policy, they, more than any formalized partnership or skeptical outlook toward American power, represent the antiwar movement's legacy to the Democratic Party.

The Populists and the antiwar movement met bad luck, made bad choices, and faced bad timing. To ascribe their failures only to layers of contingent circumstance, however, misses the huge difficulties in building

[58] Miroff, *Liberals' Moment*, 269; Marvin Kalb and Deborah Kalb, *Haunting Legacy: Vietnam and the American Presidency from Ford to Obama* (Washington, D.C.: Brookings Institution Press, 2011); Dan Balz, "For Clinton and Kerrey, a New Set of Questions," *Washington Post*, 18 January 1992, A1.

[59] On the McCarthy network, see Davis, *Emerging Democratic Majority*; Jerry Tallmer, "The McCarthy Team—and How It Grew," *New York Post*, 18 March 1968, 6; Miroff, *Liberals' Moment*, chap. 13; David Mixner, *Stranger among Friends* (New York: Bantam Books, 1996), 217; Elisabeth Bumiller, "Public Defender of a High-Profile Private Life," *New York Times*, 3 September 1998, B2; Ginger Thompson and Eric Lipton, "Lobbyist's Client List Puts Him on the Defensive," *New York Times*, 30 December 2010, A10.

[60] See Joseph Hill, "Political Amnesia," *Commonweal*, 4 October 1968, 6–7.

and sustaining ongoing alliance. Movements, including these two, confront substantial organizational and strategic dilemmas. Parties have incentives to flee in pursuit of the median voter, and at the same time to pick over movements' carcasses and mobilize directly on terms congruent with other powerful elements in the party coalition. The book's two major cases, hence, stand out by contrast against the moments when potential anchoring groups failed to reorient American politics, instead depositing their remnants somewhere in the fractious Democratic Party.

PART II
Maintaining Alliance

CHAPTER 6

The Price of Alliance

Labor and the Democrats Meet Postwar Realities

In Part II, the narrative shifts its comparisons. The next four chapters look further along in the life cycle from insurgency to institutionalization, examining parties and anchoring groups as they renegotiate their ties even long after the movements' initial emergence. As their foundational commitments fray, groups may no longer even qualify as movements in the sense used in Chapter 2. Yet their political impact, rooted in and circumscribed by their initial confrontations with the party system, continues for decades to come.

Mature alliance poses challenges for groups and parties distinct from those at the moment of confrontation with the party system: to socialize new cohorts even without a defining cause; to find new issues for changing times; to garner enthusiasm among elected officials willing to shoulder the public-good costs of alliance; to maximize impact despite dwindling numbers; to balance supporters' pecuniary and ideological rewards; to regroup amid electoral defeat and its recriminations; for group leaders, to maintain their specific influence over supporters; above all, to find a fit between the anchoring group's vision and other veto-wielding actors inside the party coalition.

Although in different ways across changing political contexts, these themes recur through failed and successful incorporation alike. For organized labor and for the Christian Right, groups found the space to press agendas congruent with parties' other key actors and their electoral ambitions. New instrumentalities formalized partnership with parties that stabilized oft-stormy relations. Parties responded with policy benefits, through Keynesian growth policies and conservative judicial appointments, that appealed across their coalitions while sheltering movements and their priorities even in rough waters. For abolition-republicanism after the Civil War, by contrast, stable partnership proved elusive. Group capacity atrophied, while policies to support southern blacks ran afoul of the Republicans' core backers in northern capital. Together, the sagas of the three alliances demonstrate how movements can, or cannot, hold their place alongside other constituent elements inside political parties.

Postwar Disappointments

In the early postwar years, alliance between organized labor and the Democratic Party assumed the form it has followed in all the decades since. Possibilities closed, and electoral and policy partnership became routinized. During the Roosevelt years, divides in the union movement and between the parties rarely matched. By the time the AFL and CIO merged in 1955, labor and northern Democrats had largely achieved that congruence, albeit at considerable cost. This chapter narrates that story; Chapter 7 brings the saga of labor and the Democrats to the present.

Democrats and labor each accommodated the key priorities of the other side given limited possibilities: for the Cold War and for the private welfare state. Given the enormous threats to the Democrats' majority and to unions' viability that a rupture would have entailed, each side compromised to preserve alliance. The long-term costs, particularly for a labor movement cocooned in its generous private benefits, were considerable. The alternatives for party and group alike offered few attractive possibilities. The failure of Operation Dixie to organize the South, the expulsion of the left unions from the CIO after they failed to endorse Harry Truman, and the dismemberment of the American Labor Party in New York followed ineluctably from the realities of postwar politics. The private welfare state, which emerged from the interpretation by the prounion NLRB of the antiunion Taft-Hartley, by contrast, seems decidedly more contingent. Together, the extrusions of the left and the shift from universalism to particularism defined a stable alliance far less expansive even than what Sidney Hillman had initially envisioned when he built CIO-PAC in 1944.

With the death of Franklin Roosevelt, an era ended. The competing factions inside the Democratic Party that had coexisted while he lived and while war still raged soon broke apart as Harry Truman threaded the complexities of Cold War abroad and the conservative coalition at home. On the right, southern Democrats thwarted his domestic agenda and bolted in 1948 to support Strom Thurmond on a states' rights ("Dixiecrat") ticket. On the left, Henry Wallace's Progressive Party drew the bulk of its support from communists and the CIO unions that they dominated. The CIO threw its support behind Truman, and expelled the unions that refused to fall into line. As the failure of universal health insurance occluded public possibilities and the restrictions on unions in the Taft-Hartley Act, passed over Truman's veto, began to bite, unions, first in the CIO and then in the AFL, set up their own health and pension plans, and the Democrats acquiesced so as to protect their allies' institutional bases.

Peacetime after victory in Europe and Japan proved an enormous disappointment to labor-liberals. However small Truman may have looked in comparison with his predecessor, the conservative coalition of Republicans and southern Democrats swallowed all liberal initiatives. Roosevelt's Economic Bill of Rights raised great hopes, but went nowhere. In a parallel with the Obama years, conservative congressional majorities thwarted a liberal president propelled by the diverse urban vote. The comprehensive Wagner-Murray-Dingell bill, with health insurance as its centerpiece, the top priority for the AFL as well as the CIO, never stood a chance. Congress instead funded hospital construction.[1] Although a series of incremental ("salami-slicing") amendments expanded Social Security coverage and benefits, they still fell far short of replacing workers' prior earnings. The conservative coalition repeatedly watered down the Employment Act of 1946. It began with a mandate for full employment and a nod to tripartite bargaining, and ended principally by strengthening economic capacity in the executive branch. Rather than building up capacity for the federal government to enhance workers' skills and promote employment for all, a commercial Keynesian growth politics more amenable to business rigidly separated macroeconomic from social policy, and sidelined structural critiques of persistent joblessness that proposed national-level planning or institutional fixes in the labor market.[2]

[1] Paul Starr, *The Social Transformation of American Medicine* (New York: Basic Books, 1982), 348–51; Monte S. Poen, *Harry S. Truman versus the Medical Lobby: The Genesis of Medicare* (Columbia: University of Missouri Press, 1979); James E. Murray, "Paying Our Way," *Commonweal*, 7 June 1946, 182–85; "Week in Review," *Progressive*, 7 October 1946, 3.

[2] Stephen K. Bailey, *Congress Makes a Law: The Story behind the Employment Act of 1946* (New York: Columbia University Press, 1950); Margaret Weir, *Politics and Jobs: The Boundaries of Employment Policy in the United States* (Princeton: Princeton University Press, 1993), chap. 2. These hurdles doomed further attempts to promote full employment through massive federal intervention. Two efforts with strong support from African Americans and progressive unionists, and only tepid approval from the AFL-CIO and many mainstream liberal economists, stand out: the Freedom Budget for All Americans prepared by Leon Keyserling for A. Philip Randolph and Bayard Rustin in 1966, and the early drafts of the Humphrey-Hawkins Act in 1976 and 1977, which included provisions for the federal government to act as employer of last resort. See *A "Freedom Budget" for All Americans: Budgeting Our Resources, 1966–1975, to Achieve Freedom from Want* (New York: A. Philip Randolph Institute, 1966); "Full Employment Is the Answer: An Interview with Congressman Augustus F. Hawkins," *Adherent*, 2 July 1975, 6–19; Helen Ginsburg, "Congressional Will-o'-the-Wisp," *Nation*, 5 February 1977,

Labor relations in peacetime proved contentious as the no-strike pledge expired and business began to flex its muscle. A month-long Labor-Management Conference achieved nothing. The economy retreated sharply as the wartime boom ended and factories reconverted. Real GDP in 1946 contracted fully 10.9 percent. With the end of meaningful price controls, accelerated by congressional unwillingness to extend the mandate of the Office of Price Administration, unions struck for higher wages that would maintain real purchasing power. By November 1946, inflation had reached an annualized rate of 18.1 percent.

The horrible macroeconomy produced the expected result in the 1946 midterms as Republicans gained thirteen seats in the Senate and fifty-seven in the House, assuming control of both chambers. The following summer, over Truman's veto, a coalition of Republicans and southern Democrats enacted the Taft-Hartley Act. The law severely curtailed unions' autonomy and removed many of their most powerful weapons to organize workplaces, confront employers, and link politics to the job site. It enjoined unions from a series of unfair labor practices where the Wagner Act had restricted only employers, forbade secondary boycotts and jurisdictional strikes, banned foremen and other front-line supervisors from unionizing, and, in Section 14(b), allowed states to enact "right-to-work" legislation that banned the union shop.[3] Yet, from the vantage of party-group alliance, the unions' calamitous defeat also marked the critical moment when northern Democrats, Truman, the AFL, and the CIO finally achieved common priorities. It was not the grand coalition that sustained Roosevelt in 1936, nor did it crack the Solid South or, save for a few too-brief moments, sustain a national majority, but it did sustain mutual exchange between party and movement decade after decade.

138–43; A. H. Raskin, "A Tougher Approach to Jobs," *New York Times*, 20 November 1977, F1; *Full Employment and Balanced Growth Act of 1978: Report Together with Minority, Supplemental, and Additional Views* (Washington, D.C.: Government Printing Office 1978); "Full Employment," *CQ Almanac 1978* (Washington, D.C.: Congressional Quarterly, 1978), 272–79; and Timothy N. Thurber, *The Politics of Equality: Hubert H. Humphrey and the African American Freedom Struggle* (New York: Columbia University Press, 1999), esp. 235–43.

[3]Harry A. Millis and Emily Clark Brown, *From the Wagner Act to Taft-Hartley: A Study of National Labor Policy and Labor Relations* (Chicago: University of Chicago Press, 1950), pt. 3, offers an excellent summary of the bill's provisions. See also Alonzo L. Hamby, *Beyond the New Deal: Harry S. Truman and American Liberalism* (New York: Columbia University Press, 1973); Archibald Cox, "Some Aspects of the Labor-Management Relations Act, 1947," *Harvard Law Review* 61 (1947): 1–49; Nelson Lichtenstein, "Taft-Hartley: A Slave-Labor Law?," *Catholic University Law Review* 47 (1997): 763–89; and Fred A. Hartley, Jr., *Our New National Labor Policy* (New York: Funk & Wagnalls, 1948).

Operation Dixie and the South

Like abolition-republicanism and Populism before it, the CIO sought to overthrow the South's cottonocracy, redistribute power within the region, and build a national majority. It, too, failed. With a secure regional base in northern and midwestern cities, and with greater support from pivotal players inside the party, alliance survived. Still, the consequences for American political development proved enormous. Had unions somehow entrenched themselves in the South, civil rights and labor rights might have nurtured one another in a politicized American workplace, with individual rights to protection against discrimination complementing strengthened rights to bargain collectively, and Democrats holding onto an organizational redoubt in southern politics. That future, however tantalizing, found its failure overdetermined.[4]

The CIO saw the South as a linchpin to escape the low-wage competition that threatened its bargaining power with employers, and build for its nationwide political activities a more durable base than its geographic concentration in the industrial heartland allowed. In early 1946, it launched an ambitious Southern Organizing Committee with a million-dollar commitment. Dubbed Operation Dixie, the drive soon foundered amid severe internal weakness.[5] Its leader, Van Bittner, was an unimaginative UMW hand on loan from the Steelworkers. The organizers, mostly native-born southern whites (and no African Americans whatsoever), had little training. Although the CIO had spent a decade assiduously building connections between work and politics, Bittner insisted on a job-conscious strategy, with "no extra-curricular activities—no politics—no PAC—no FEPC, etc." He declined contributions from a mostly African American group, led by Adam Clayton Powell, founded to support the drive, and dissociated himself from the left unions that had organized in the South's urban "rough industries," such as tobacco, canning, meat

[4]See Michael Goldfield, "The Failure of Operation Dixie: A Critical Turning Point in American Political Development?," in *Race, Class, and Community in Southern Labor History*, ed. Gary Fink and Merle E. Reed (Tuscaloosa: University of Alabama Press, 1994), 166–89; Robert Rodgers Korstad, *Civil Rights Unionism: Tobacco Workers and the Struggle for Democracy in the Mid-Twentieth-Century South* (Chapel Hill: University of North Carolina Press, 2003); Michael K. Honey, "Operation Dixie, the Red Scare, and the Defeat of Southern Labor Organizing," in *American Labor and the Cold War: Grassroots Politics and Postwar Political Culture*, ed. Robert W. Cherny, William Issel, and Kiernan Walsh Taylor (New Brunswick, N.J.: Rutgers University Press, 2004), 216–44.

[5]"CIO Launches Organizing Drive, 'Operation Dixie,'" *Business Week*, 27 April 1946, 92; Milton Mackaye, "The CIO Invades Dixie," *Saturday Evening Post*, 20 July 1946, 12, 94–99.

packing, and oil refining, where African Americans and whites worked side by side amid harsh conditions.[6]

By March 1947, overall contributions had run a third behind pledges. Northern industrial unions dissembled, employers realized they could wait out the CIO, and a death spiral accelerated. In the end, overall southern CIO membership remained the same in 1946 as in 1949, at about four hundred thousand workers. In textiles, which employed more southerners than the region's other industries combined, Operation Dixie netted a mere ten thousand members. George Meany opened a competing AF of L drive with an attack on the CIO as "an organization that has openly followed the Communist line," but the AFL, too, failed to meet its goals.[7]

It was unfertile ground. The region, evidence from a series of polls from 1937 to 1943 shows, favored labor unions less than any other.[8] In 1953, eight of the eleven states with the lowest union density were in the old Confederacy (alongside Oklahoma and the Dakotas), compared with six in 1939.[9] Operation Dixie threatened the institutional power structure, and it responded in kind. The Democratic Party jointly oversaw a social hierarchy in Jim Crow that divided workers by race and an economic hierarchy that stratified them by class. A potential biracial coalition threatened the entire edifice of Bourbon Democracy.[10] CIO-PAC, through support of the Fair Employment Practices Commission to mandate equal employment by race, attacked all three legs of the stool: race, class, and party. By issuing endorsements from its central office, rather than relying, as the AF of L did, on local labor councils, the CIO threatened to nationalize the battles inside state Democratic parties. Northern liberalism, with African American voters to support it,

[6]"CIO Stands Alone Organizing South," *New York Times*, 19 April 1946, 4; Robert Zieger, *The CIO, 1935–1955* (Chapel Hill: University of North Carolina, 1995), 233.

[7]Barbara S. Griffith, *The Crisis of American Labor: Operation Dixie and the Defeat of the CIO* (Philadelphia: Temple University Press, 1988), 162; F. Ray Marshall, *Labor in the South* (Cambridge, Mass.: Harvard University Press, 1967), 247.

[8]Devin M. Caughey, "The Mass Basis of the 'Southern Imposition': Labor Unions, Public Opinion, and Representation, 1930s–1940s" (paper, American Political Science Association meeting, Seattle, 1–4 September 2011), 17. The critical, and ultimately unanswerable, question is whether successful organizing could meaningfully have changed southerners' views of unions. In this implicit debate, I view preferences as less fixed than does Caughey, but a much more serious constraint than most left labor historians.

[9]Derived from Leo Troy, *Distribution of Union Membership among the States, 1939 and 1953* (New York: National Bureau of Economic Research, 1957), 5. For recalculations by international, which differ somewhat from Troy's published numbers, see Marshall, *Labor in the South*, 267. For another stab at union-by-union data, see Frank T. de Vyver, "The Present Status of Labor Unions in the South—1948," *Southern Economic Journal* 16 (1949): 1–22. All these numbers, based on a combination of union self-reports and NLRB votes, are unreliable, especially in the South.

[10]On the economic logic of suffrage restriction, see Gerald Friedman, "The Political Economy of Early Southern Unionism," *Journal of Economic History* 60 (2000): 407.

would have a place in Democratic factional politics. Alabama, where CIO-PAC endorsed the upcountry populist "Big Jim" Folsom and pushed his candidacy to the steelworkers of Birmingham, offered a particular object lesson.[11]

The mill owners and elected officials of the South perceptively discerned the links among race, class, and partisan change. The Fair Labor Standards Act and Roosevelt's purge campaign had begun to bring southern political and business leaders closer to their conservative northern brethren.[12] A trade paper told the story of a Textile Workers' Union business agent who refused to hold integrated meetings. "I am a white South Carolinian," he explained, "and I believe in what the Democratic party stands for."[13]

To dethrone the southern Democratic establishment, the CIO would have had to enlist in its cause the very leftist unions whose apostasies against Cold War foreign policy drove such a wedge between movement and party. When the Southern Conference on Human Welfare and the Highlander Folk School, preeminent training grounds for a generation of civil rights and labor activists, refused to toe the line on communism, the CIO dropped funding—and frayed ties that could have placed social unionism at the center of civil rights in the South.[14]

For the Trotskyist Art Preis, "The CIO leaders refused to wage political war against the Southern ruling class because that would undermine the whole Democratic Party and put an end to the Democratic Party-labor coalition."[15] This claim overstates the case. The CIO hardly suppressed Operation Dixie to save the southern Democrats who blocked Wagner-Murray-Dingell, passed Smith-Connally and Taft-Hartley, and passionately defended Jim Crow. It desperately wanted them gone. Rather, fealty to northern Democrats, the movement's core supporters in the state, limited domestic militancy. The same CIO could not simultaneously build and

[11] Robert A. Garson, *The Democratic Party and the Politics of Sectionalism* (Baton Rouge: Louisiana State University Press, 1974), esp. chap. 6; Arthur Krock, "Democrats' Rift Perils Party's Whole Future," *New York Times*, 20 January 1946, 65; Arthur Krock, "Again, the Union Armies Move into 'Dixie,'" *New York Times*, 26 April 1946, 20; A. G. Mezerik, "Dixie in Black and White," *Nation*, 19 April 1947, 448–51.

[12] James T. Patterson, *Congressional Conservatism and the New Deal: The Growth of the Conservative Coalition in Congress, 1933–1939* (Lexington: University Press of Kentucky, 1967).

[13] "C.I.O. Dictators," *Textile Bulletin*, 15 June 1946, 53. Similarly, see, from the intellectual godfather of the Dixiecrat bolt in 1948, the prediction of "head-on collision" between the CIO and the South over race: Charles Wallace Collins, *Whither Solid South: A Study in Politics and Race Relations* (New Orleans: Pelican, 1947), 253.

[14] Thomas A. Krueger, *And Promises to Keep: The Southern Conference for Human Welfare, 1938–1948* (Nashville: Vanderbilt University Press, 1967); John M. Glen, *Highlander: No Ordinary School* (Lexington: University Press of Kentucky, 1988), chap. 5; Myles Horton, "The Spark That Ignites," *Southern Exposure*, Spring–Summer 1976, 153–56.

[15] Art Preis, *Labor's Giant Step: Twenty Years of the CIO* (New York: Pioneer, 1964), 377.

fund unionism in the South to overthrow the region's power structure, and behave as a responsible anchoring group closely connected to party and state in the North.

For the CIO center and right, the choice between a southern strategy that courted national disaster and a northern strategy that maintained alliance with the Democrats was an easy one. The CIO could more easily sever itself in two than could a Democratic Party, which, if it purged the southerners outright (far from the limited bolt of 1948), would lose its national majority and reduce itself principally to an urban rump. To repeat a central premise of this book, in the American electoral system, movements face long odds in pushing through their agendas—even when those movements offer both substantial long-term benefits for the party's high-demanders, and the promise of a more stable electoral coalition.

Electing Truman

After the death of Sidney Hillman in the summer of 1946, Jack Kroll, an Amalgamated vice president from Cincinnati, took over the running of CIO-PAC. Ultimate authority flowed back to Phil Murray at CIO headquarters. Murray, a consummate coalition builder, consistently dismissed talk of a third party and protected alliance against whichever unions in the CIO disagreed with Democratic priorities. He had visited Roosevelt in the summer of 1932 as part of a Mine Workers' delegation even as John L. Lewis publicly remained loyal to Hoover, and since 1936 had served in the Pittsburgh Democratic organization. As a delegate, Murray even spoke for Pennsylvania to second Wallace's vice presidential nomination in 1940.[16]

Long into 1948, some liberals still hoped for a third party to supplant the machine- and segregation-ridden Democrats—although, again, exactly how it would have secured majorities in Congress they never explained. The less dreamy-eyed, including most of the CIO's center-right leadership, instead hoped for a Democratic convention draft of Dwight Eisenhower, whose politics still remained opaque.[17] Ike, of course, was no liberal, nor did any other candidate emerge to oppose a president acutely aware that he had to balance his party's competing interests.

[16] David J. McDonald, *Union Man* (New York: E.P. Dutton, 1969), 67–69; *Official Report of the Proceedings of the Democratic National Convention, Held at Chicago, Illinois, July 15th to July 18th, Inclusive, 1940* (Washington, D.C.: Democratic National Committee, 1940), 224–25. Indeed, not until John Sweeney's victory in 1995 would another leader of a national labor federation involve himself so directly in party machinations.

[17] See Jack Kroll, "Ideas for Discussion," *Antioch Review*, Winter 1946 (dismissing a third party); John C. Cort, "Third Party?," *Commonweal*, 26 July 1946, 350–53; Willard Shelton, "The ADA's Dilemma: HST or GOP," *New Republic*, 1 March 1948, 9.

Instead, the Truman campaign mounted appeals to organized labor, and relied on it to deliver votes. "Tammany, Hague, Kelley [*sic*] and the rest of the straight party leaders, while still important . . . are moribund; they cannot be relied on to do the job alone," warned Clark Clifford, the president's top political adviser.[18] Instead, the Truman campaign reoriented to focus, especially in northern cities, on labor and on African Americans. In his us-and-them rhetoric, Truman harked back to Democrats since Andrew Jackson. In coalitional politics, the campaign augured the future.

By the 1948 campaign, logrolls and efforts at coalition maintenance brought together organized labor, the Democratic organization, and black leadership. Democratic state parties across the North, far more than their Republican counterparts, backed civil rights legislation in employment, housing, and school desegregation.[19] Northern liberals, led by the ADA and CIO, won a major victory at the Democratic convention. After a stirring speech from Hubert Humphrey, delegates voted 651½ to 582½ to adopt a minority plank that called on Congress to support Truman's "courageous stand" for full and equal political rights, equal employment, and equal treatment in the armed forces, desegregated by executive order earlier in the year.

As in 1944 when they backed Truman, urban bosses looking toward victory's spoils dictated policy. They followed the lead of the Bronx's Ed Flynn, an FDR favorite, and swung firmly behind the minority plank.[20] Machines, labor unions, and civil rights leaders all had uneasy relations in the postwar decades, but in 1948, their interests aligned. Bucked up by wartime migration, the black vote concentrated in northern swing states—and, as the bosses well realized, risked trouble for Democrats in state and local politics if Dewey-style racially liberal Republicans played their cards right. As an influential account from an African American journalist argued, "The Democratic party can afford to sacrifice the entire 127 electoral votes of the Solid South and win. It cannot, however, hope for success in

[18]Clark Clifford, "Memorandum for the President," 7, http://www.trumanlibrary.org/whistlestop/study_collections/1948campaign/large/docs/documents/pdfs/1-1.pdf.

[19]Brian D. Feinstein and Eric Schickler, "Platforms and Partners: The Civil Rights Realignment Reconsidered," *Studies in American Political Development* 22 (2008): 1–31; cf. Anthony S. Chen, "The Party of Lincoln and the Politics of State Fair Employment Practices Legislation in the North, 1945–1964," *American Journal of Sociology* 112 (2007): 1713–74.

[20]Robert Bendiner, "Rout of the Bourbons," *Nation*, 24 July 1948, 91–93; "50 Top Democrats Back Rights Plank," *New York Times*, 5 July 1948, 26; Harvard Sitkoff, "Harry Truman and the Election of 1948: The Coming of Age of Civil Rights in American Politics," *Journal of Southern History* 37 (1971): 597–616; Winthrop Griffith, *Humphrey: A Candid Biography* (New York: William Morrow, 1965), 150–60. Original and substitute language in Arthur M. Schlesinger, Jr., ed., *History of American Presidential Elections, 1789–1968*, vol. 4 (New York: Chelsea House, 1971), 3182.

a presidential election without the Negro and organized labor."[21] Truman won despite losing four states in the South, a feat no Democrat had ever before accomplished—and yet the Dixiecrat rebellion set in place the regional and ideological realignment that would dominate coming decades.

Through his whistle-stop tour, Truman mounted a full-throated effort to reinvigorate the constituencies of the New Deal, labor high on the list. Although he had vetoed the bill quietly, on the hustings the president frequently reminded audiences of the horrors of Taft-Hartley. It was, he warned a hundred thousand supporters in Detroit's Cadillac Square on Labor Day, "only a foretaste of what you will get if the Republican reaction is allowed to grow."[22] Even as pollsters expected an easy victory for Dewey, at the end of October Jack Kroll at CIO-PAC predicted a Truman win, picking all but six states correctly.[23]

"Labor did it," the president told a friend in the flush of victory. Certainly, its efforts were more impressive than in any prior election. CIO-PAC matched its million-dollar 1944 spending, and Labor's League for Political Education from the AF of L added three hundred sixty thousand to support candidates pledged to repeal Taft-Hartley. CIO-PAC, aware of past errors and anxious not to serve as lightning rod, focused particularly on Congress. It endorsed 215 candidates in the House, of whom 144 prevailed, and knocked off 79 incumbents who voted for Taft-Hartley, including a dozen in primaries. Nine senators who opposed Taft-Hartley lost their seats. Throughout the industrial states, even in states where Wallace failed to make the ballot, congressional Democrats ran ahead of the president.[24]

[21] Henry Lee Moon, *Balance of Power: The Negro Vote* (Garden City, N.Y.: Doubleday, 1948), 141. So, too, the NAACP had stood with the CIO since the late 1930s, but for coalition maintenance inside the broader liberal orbit, made its peace with the still-discriminatory AFL. On NAACP legal strategy, see Risa L. Goluboff, *The Lost Promise of Civil Rights* (Cambridge, Mass.: Harvard University Press, 2007), chaps. 7 and 8. For an expansive view of NAACP-CIO partnership, see Christopher Baylor, "First to the Party: The Group Origins of the Partisan Transformation on Civil Rights," *Studies in American Political Development* 27 (2013): 1–31.

[22] Hamby, *Beyond the New Deal*, 252; Felix Belair, Jr., "Truman Sees Era of Fear in a Republican Victory; Says Labor Is Threatened," *New York Times*, 7 September 1948, 1.

[23] "The Kroll Poll Hits the Bullseye," *Memo from PAC*, 22 November 1948. 8. Kroll picked Truman and Dewey each to win three states ultimately in the other's column.

[24] Anthony Leviero, "Truman Humble in Pledging Service to American People," *New York Times*, 4 November 1948, 1, 7; R. Alton Lee, *Truman and Taft-Hartley: A Question of Mandate* (Lexington: University of Kentucky Press, 1966), 148–53; Hugh Morrow, "The CIO's Political Hotshot," *Saturday Evening Post*, 5 March 1949, 29 and 115–20. For a state-by-state roundup, see "The Week," *New Republic*, 15 November 1948, 6–9. For PAC technique, see the pamphlets "How We Win: Registration," "How We Win: Farmers," "How We Win: Organization," "How We Win: Ringing Doorbells," and "How We Win: Off Years," all far more capable than in 1944 of articulating the nuts and bolts of ongoing campaign work. All from Washington, D.C.: CIO-PAC, 1948. For the CIO program, see "Brother, What a Congress!," *Economic Outlook*, August 1948, 1–8. On varieties of accommodation with local parties, see Fay Calkins,

The election of 1948 marked labor's acceptance as a signature high-demander in the Democratic order, and in the broadly shared prosperity that followed.[25] Without Hillman or the communists, PAC no longer stood out as a lightning rod for attack. CIO, AFL, and party alike accepted a mixed economy, and the unions, in a sharp reversal of Gompersian voluntarism, sought national legislation to bring it about. Harry Truman, more decisively than FDR ever had, chose northern liberals over southern conservatives, and so built the alignment that would enact civil rights and the Great Society. As the fight over the civil rights plank showed, with unions and African Americans providing support to Democratic candidates at the state and local levels, bosses accommodated their priorities. Without that support, the bosses would likely have stayed with their old brethren in the South, rendering the New Deal's achievements vulnerable.

For his part, Harry Truman did what he could without a working congressional majority to reward his friends, and especially Phil Murray's Steelworkers. Presidents, seeking national majorities, typically do not reward group claimants on high-visibility matters of enormous national import. Instead, midlevel figures work through bureaus and agencies to structure group relations with the state. Truman, however, expressly sought to use his presidential powers to the hilt—even illegally, said the Supreme Court, rejecting his 1952 nationalization of the steel industry—to support the USWA. Yet he did so precisely to avoid invoking Taft-Hartley, despite congressional resolutions urging him to do so. The alternative policy for the president was not silence—Roosevelt's formula in the 1937 Little Steel strike—or moral support, but active use of an instrument party and group alike sought to repeal.[26]

The Extrusions of 1948

The CIO high command in 1948 chose alliance with the Democrats over its internal unity, and prepared to expel the left-led unions, with about a fifth of the CIO's membership, that opposed its decision. Had it done otherwise,

---

The CIO and the Democratic Party (Chicago: University of Chicago Press, 1952). The political geography represented something of a throwback. Truman won the nation's thirteen largest cities, but played better in the Farm Belt than in northern suburbs. Victories by less than one point in Illinois, Ohio, and California, which together gave Truman his majority, allowed labor to take credit. Individual-level estimates of the union vote in 1948 typically use recollections from 1952, and should be treated with appropriate caution.

[25] See, e.g., "Our 'Laboristic' President," *Fortune*, December 1948, 84.

[26] See Robert C. Spencer, "Bargaining with the Government: A Case Study in the Policies of Collective Bargaining in the Basic Steel Industry" (PhD diss., University of Chicago, 1955), 121–23.

then a Democratic Party committed to the Cold War would have used the full suite of powers in Taft-Hartley, and probably more, to destroy the entire CIO. By 1947, the pivotal players in the party favored alliance with a noncommunist CIO, but opposed alliance with a CIO that tolerated Reds. Phil Murray, ever pragmatic, placed alliance with the Democrats foremost, as it provided a sympathetic state in which labor could organize, and orchestrated the expulsion of the unions that refused to comply with CIO endorsement of Harry Truman.

Just as in 1940 and again after 1968, divisions over foreign policy impinged on party-group alliance. The American party system structured the alternatives. Frank Emspak, son of a longtime leader in the United Electrical Workers (UE), the largest left-led union, explained the basic conflict as the losing side saw it: "The crisis came in 1947–8 because the progressives and Communists tried to offer an alternative political party that, in part, challenged American imperialism. The Progressive party posed a threat to the CIO's relations to the Democratic party because the Left wanted the CIO to break out of the orbit of the Democrats."[27]

The left-led unions combined two sets of qualities: they organized hard; they built deep loyalties, including interracial loyalties; and, far more than CIO unions organized from above, such as the Steelworkers (to say nothing of most craft unions), they generated shop-floor democracy in day-to-day union business. Without dedicated, dogged communist organizers, there would have been no CIO. But the grassroots democrats were also ruthless factionalists who cut off internal opponents.[28] Presidents of the communist-dominated unions, few actually party members themselves, swayed to Moscow's prevailing winds on foreign policy.

The CIO committed to the Truman foreign policy to secure its place not simply in the partisan constellation but in the postwar order. Its decision emerged from a series of entwined processes: a regime-level choice for the American republic to assume global leadership; a partisan commitment for the Democrats, led by the president, that group allies would have to accommodate in order to remain stably inside the coalition; and a spigot of state patronage, giving prestige to labor leaders, and jobs as advisers to midlevel functionaries.

[27] Frank Emspak, "The Break-Up of the Congress of Industrial Organizations (CIO), 1945–1950" (PhD diss., University of Wisconsin, 1972), 387–88; for framing sympathetic to the center-right, see Zieger, *CIO*, 267. The best general account is David Brody, *Workers in Industrial America: Essays on the 20th Century Struggle*, 2nd ed. (New York: Oxford University Press, 1993), chap. 6.

[28] For a revisionist synthesis, see Eric Arnesen, "Civil Rights and the Cold War At Home: Postwar Activism, Anticommunism, and the Decline of the Left," *American Communist History* 11 (2012): 5–44.

Although the CIO presence overseas was never as completely enmeshed with the state as the AFL operation, the relationship grew closer in 1947 and 1948. James Carey, the CIO secretary-treasurer, who had lost control of the UE to a leftist slate, served alongside the AFL's George Meany on the advisory panel for the Marshall Plan. Aid provided cover for disinflationary policy. It served, too, as a means to support abroad, through expanded export markets and revived mass demand, the same growth-oriented managed capitalism practiced at home. That managed capitalism was not entirely the regime the CIO center-right would have chosen, but it was one whose benefits American labor shared, and that it embraced as a global vision far preferable to the leftist alternative.[29]

Internal politics also played a role in the nature and timing of the purge. Walter Reuther's anticommunist slate won a clean sweep at the 1947 UAW convention, ending a dozen years of fierce factionalism. With victory in the UAW, Murray and the center-right gained breathing room in the federation to avoid being deposed themselves. Reuther swiftly imposed his will. He placed old friends from the Socialist Party and allies from the Association of Catholic Trade Unionists in key positions, and replaced as legal consigliere the leftist Maurice Sugar with the well-connected liberal, Joe Rauh.[30]

Although he kept up the rhetorical commitment to a third party into the postwar years, both as a bluff and as a means to curry favor inside the UAW, Reuther had long since abandoned the Socialist Party of his youth, and fully backed CIO-PAC strategy. In 1938, he supported the reelection for governor of Frank Murphy, the hero of the sit-down strikes. In 1944, he snuffed out efforts by the Michigan Commonwealth Federation to build a

[29] A. H. Raskin, "Murray Cautions Communists in CIO," *New York Times*, 11 May 1948, 8; Val R. Lorwin, "Labor's Own 'Cold War,'" *Labor & Nation*, Winter 1949, 8–9, 64; *Foreign Relations of the United States 1948*, vol. 3 (Washington, D.C.: Government Printing Office, 1974), 867. For global context, see Charles S. Maier, "The Politics of Productivity: Foundations of American International Economic Policy after World War II," *International Organization* 31 (1977): 607–33; and Charles S. Maier, "The World Economy and the Cold War in the Middle of the Twentieth Century," in *The Cambridge History of the Cold War*, vol. 1, ed. Melvyn P. Leffler and Odd Arne Westad (Cambridge: Cambridge University Press, 2010), 44–66. Cf., from an MP on the left of the Labour Party in Britain, Jennie Lee "Comment on Wallace," *Tribune*, 25 April 1947, 5. For the CP view, see William Z. Foster, "Organized Labor and the Marshall Plan," *Political Affairs*, February 1948, 99–109.

[30] Walter P. Reuther, "How to Beat the Communists," *Collier's*, 28 February 1948, 11; Stewart Alsop, "Reuther Cracked Wallace 'Front,'" *Washington Post*, 16 November 1947, B5; Nelson Lichtenstein, *The Most Dangerous Man in Detroit: Walter Reuther and the Fate of American Labor* (New York: Basic Books, 1995), 268–69; Martin Halpern, *UAW Politics in the Cold War Era* (Albany: State University of New York Press, 1988).

state-level labor party.[31] By 1946, he argued for a new party combining the same coalition of unions, minorities, farmers, and independent progressives "who supported Roosevelt"—a dead ringer for a realigned Democratic Party uniting the nation's liberal elements.[32] Reuther, more than Hillman, saw political parties as vehicles for causes rather than sites of power. Where Hillman had played coalition politics directly as he attempted to assemble a majority, combining CIO-PAC with NC-PAC to appeal to progressive-minded professionals, Reuther worried about becoming a public lightning rod, and so aimed to keep the UAW's fingerprints invisible "rather than destroy the broad base that is essential to make a political party an effective instrument to translate sound policy into governmental action."[33]

The extrusion of the CIO's radical fringe followed ineluctably once Henry Wallace and the Communists each decided to support a third-party strategy for 1948. Wallace had served as agriculture secretary in Roosevelt's first two terms, vice president in his third, and commerce secretary until Truman fired him in 1946. Middle-class liberals exalted his cerebral bent, and contrasted him favorably against Truman's seeming fecklessness toward machine bosses (a louder chant at the time than acquiescence to Jim Crow).[34] Wallace was a lifelong ideological work in progress. Between his

[31] Ben Hall, "Detroit PAC Hog-Ties Labor to FDR," *Labor Action*, 8 May 1944, 1; L. Smith, "Michigan Commonwealth Federation: A New Party and Its Problems," *New International*, June 1944, 172–78.

[32] Dudley W. Buffa, *Union Power and American Democracy: The UAW and the Democratic Party, 1935–1972* (Ann Arbor: University of Michigan Press, 1984), 8. For a good example, see Robert Bendiner, "Politics and People," *Nation*, 12 February 1949, 177–78.

[33] Henry Brandon, *As We Are* (Garden City, N.Y.: Doubleday, 1961), 208. The state CIO president, a Reuther protégé, reportedly said in 1948 that "I now think that in the interests of simplifying the mechanics of voting, that the CIO should endorse only Democrats, endorse no one for any office where a Democratic candidate is unacceptable." See Stephen B. Sarasohn and Vera H. Sarasohn, *Political Party Patterns in Michigan* (Detroit: Wayne State University Press, 1957), 53.

[34] New Deal agriculture policy, which Wallace forged through logrolls for a "marriage of corn and cotton," aimed to reduce farmed acreage and primarily benefited large commercial farmers; it kept entirely intact the systems of sharecropping and Jim Crow through which the planter class dominated the South. In February 1935, Wallace fired a passel of left-wing lawyers and administrators—some communists, although none so identified at the time—in the Agricultural Adjustment Administration. The liberals wanted stronger protections for evicted tenants and sharecroppers, who had begun to organize in the integrated Southern Tenant Farmers Union. The Cotton Section feared that interference in "private labor disputes" would prove "a serious political blunder," in particular with Roosevelt's steady ally, Joseph T. Robinson of Arkansas, the Senate majority leader. Ironically, two purge victims, Lee Pressman and John Abt, left their positions as CIO and ACWA counsels respectively to serve on Wallace's campaign. See David Eugene Conrad, *The Forgotten Farmers: The Story of Sharecroppers in the New Deal* (Urbana: University of Illinois Press, 1965), 146; Peter H. Irons, *The New Deal Lawyers* (Princeton: Princeton University Press, 1982), chap. 8; Lawrence J. Nelson,

early years cross-breeding corn in Iowa and his retirement cross-breeding chickens in Westchester County, Wallace left the Republican, Democratic, and Progressive Parties each in turn.[35]

As the Cold War intensified in 1947, battle lines hardened in dueling para-organizations. Anticommunist liberals, including Eleanor Roosevelt, Hubert Humphrey, and a passel of intellectuals originally on the right wing of the Socialist Party, joined together in Americans for Democratic Action.[36] Leftists formed the Progressive Citizens of America. Murray forbade CIO leaders from supporting either group. Late in 1947, the Communist Party determined to back a third party, as a base from which to attack the Marshall Plan. The Communist-dominated PCA reconstituted itself as the Progressive Party, and Wallace prepared to accept its nomination.[37]

Once such an elemental threat to alliance had come into play, the CIO responded sharply. In January 1948, the CIO Executive Board by a vote of thirty-three to eleven deemed it "politically unwise to inject a third party into the political scene in 1948." Murray soon authorized contacts with the liberals of ADA. The left unions, which had always melded democratic centralism with respect for shop-floor independence, finally pleaded for local autonomy—exactly the argument made by AFL craft unions unwilling to remove color bars to membership. Save for the Transport Workers' Mike Quill, who switched sides, the dissenters were precisely the same when the

---

"The Art of the Possible: Another Look at the 'Purge' of the AAA Liberals in 1935," *Agricultural History* 57 (1983): 416–35; William R. Amberson, "The New Deal for Share-Croppers," *Nation*, 13 February 1935, 185–87; Henry A. Wallace, "No Final Answer to the Farm Problem," *U.S. News & World Report*, 8 January 1954, 40–43.

[35]The best contemporary account of Wallace is Gardner Jackson, "Henry Wallace: A Divided Mind," *Atlantic Monthly*, August 1948, 27–33. For his later reflections, see Edwin A. Lahey, "The Chicken Raiser—A Man Who Used to Be Mr. Henry Wallace," *Chicago Daily News*, 31 March 1951, 30.

[36]On ADA ideology, see Arthur M. Schlesinger, Jr., "The Third Force in America," *ADA World*, 19 February 1948, 2–3; and statement and membership list in "130 Liberals Form a Group on Right," *New York Times*, 5 January 1947, 5. See also Adam Clymer, "The Union for Democratic Action: Key to the Non-Communist Left" (AB thesis, Harvard College, 1958); Steven M. Gillon, *Americans for Democratic Action: The ADA and American Liberalism, 1947–1985* (New York: Oxford University Press, 1987).

[37]Joseph A. Loftus, "2 C.I.O. Leaders Shun an Anti-Red Group," *New York Times*, 28 February 1947, 4; Milburn Akers, "The P.C.A. Convention," *Nation*, 24 January 1948, 92; Alfred Friendly, "Reds Picked Wallace to Run, May Quit Him," *Washington Post*, 2 May 1948, M1; Edwin A. Lahey, "Red-C.I.O. Feud over Wallace Grows," *Chicago Daily News*, 17 May 1948, 1; Victor Lasky, "Who Runs Wallace?," *Plain Talk*, June 1948, 1–13; Eugene Dennis, *The Third Party and the 1948 Elections* (New York: New Century, 1948), chap. 2; and, for context, Joseph R. Starobin, *American Communism in Crisis, 1943–1957* (Cambridge, Mass.: Harvard University Press, 1972), 174–77; and Harvey A. Levenstein, *Communism, Anti-Communism, and the CIO* (Westport, Conn.: Greenwood, 1981), 260–66.

board voted in August to endorse Truman—and all saw their internationals expelled.[38]

To be clear, fealty to CIO policy on endorsement of Truman alone determined expulsion from the CIO in the fall of 1949. A center-left coalition that included communist-linked elements controlled the United Packinghouse Workers of America, the most thoroughly racially integrated union in the CIO. The union papered over internal differences with a resolution simply "endorsing the CIO policy on political action," without naming or amplifying that policy, and escaped completely unscathed.[39]

Neither the Wallace supporters who stayed until the end nor the CP ever resolved how an electoral system based around a first-past-the-post voting system and the Electoral College would allow a small third party meaningfully to move the Democrats leftward. Afraid of losing their own grasp on their membership, leaders of most left-led internationals declined to push endorsement, and only three formally backed Wallace. The great and the good of the New Deal—Harold Ickes, Frances Perkins—signed their names to an October ADA statement accusing the Progressives of "a betrayal of free people throughout the world," alongside domestic policy "merely an imitation of the Democratic party." Wallace won only 1.16 million votes, half of them from New York City, far fewer than the ten million his supporters had deemed possible in the spring, and behind even the total for Strom Thurmond's Dixiecrats. As Lee Pressman, the leftist CIO general counsel who resigned his post under pressure from Murray, later recalled, "There was a hell of a lot of romanticizing at the time."[40]

At its 1949 convention, the CIO formally began expulsion proceedings against the unions whose leaders opposed endorsing Truman. They had, Murray charged, "supported the foreign policy of the Soviet Union against the United States."[41] The IUE, a new union in the electrical industry, half of whose unionized plants held defense contracts, received a CIO charter

[38] Louis Stark, "CIO's Board Votes Against 3d Party, for Aid Plan, 33–11," *New York Times*, 23 January 1948, 1; Louis Stark, "Truman Endorsed, 35–12, by CIO Board," *New York Times*, 1 September 1948, 1; "UE Leaders Defend Rights of Intl. Unions at CIO Exec. Board Meeting," *UE News*, 31 January 1948, 3; "Green, Reuther to Address Convention," *ADA World*, 29 January 1948, 1.

[39] *Proceedings, Fifth Constitutional Convention of the United Packinghouse Workers of America, C.I.O.* (Chicago: United Packinghouse Workers of America, 1948), 289–98.

[40] Murray Edelman, "The Labor Vote in '48: An Analysis," *Nation*, 23 October 1948, 461–65; Curtis D. MacDougall, *Gideon's Army* (New York: Marzani & Munsell, 1965), 1:283 and 3:613–15; Arthur M. Schlesinger, Jr., "Who Was Henry A. Wallace: The Story of an Indomitably Naive Public Servant," *Los Angeles Times*, 12 March 2000, BR3. For a typical statement from an anticommunist New Dealer, see Sumner Welles, "Progressive Party," *Washington Post*, 17 August 1948, 15.

[41] *Final Proceedings of the 11th Constitutional Convention of the Congress of Industrial Organizations* (Washington, D.C.: CIO, 1949), 278. The formal language against Communists at 240.

in place of the expelled UE. The left unions, unable to enforce NLRB contracts, fell victim to raiding and decertification.[42] Once hostilities broke out in Korea, Wallace, a farmer once more and never again a political force, at last denounced the Soviet Union as a threat to international peace. The Communists, too, never looked back. In June 1953, the emasculated CP criticized its own naïveté in attempting to a build a third party without support from the mass of organized labor, and instead sought, by now quite unsuccessfully, to push the Democrats left.[43]

American Labor Party and the Third-Party Dream

The American Labor Party in New York pushed the boundary between partisan ally and third party as far as any anchoring group ever has. Yet the essential fact of alliance still held: movements successfully leverage ties to mainstream parties only so long as parties accept their presence inside the system. Thanks to a quirk of New York law, multiple parties may endorse the same candidate.[44] A third-party strategy based around cross-endorsement

[42]Only two tenaciously retain their independence. On the UE, see Ronald L. Filippelli and Mark McCulloch, *Cold War in the Working Class: The Rise and Decline of the United Electrical Workers* (Albany: State University of New York Press, 1995); and James J. Matles and James Higgins, *Them and Us: Struggles of a Rank-and-File Union* (Englewood Cliffs, N.J.: Prentice Hall, 1974). On the ILWU, see John S. Ahlquist and Margaret Levi, *In the Interests of Others: Organizations and Social Activism* (Princeton: Princeton University Press, 2013).

[43]"Resolution on the Situation Growing out of the Presidential Elections (Final Text)," *Political Affairs*, July 1953, 5–16.

[44]In the nineteenth century, parties printed their own tickets, with no state restrictions on multiple ballot lines. After Populists used the technique, elites denied newly formed parties the ability to print ballots with candidates of their choosing, often in the context of codifying the Australian ballot. These laws ripped from third parties in a first-past-the-post system their best opportunity to cobble together different voter blocs into majorities. (Progressive reforms, often seen simply as antiparty, in this respect reinforced duopoly within the context of one-party dominance; the key point is that they manipulated the rules to insulate elites against protest. See Walter Dean Burnham, *Critical Elections and the Mainsprings of American Politics* [New York: Norton, 1970], 74–76.) Across the North and West, where they held majorities, Republicans cracked down on multiple ballot lines—as did southern Democrats, though their attacks on political competition encompassed stronger stuff. In New York, however, cross-endorsement allowed Republicans to overcome their party's weakness in New York City by running on additional ballot lines, a strategy unchanged from Seth Low down to Michael Bloomberg. In 1911, under unified Democratic control in Albany, Tammany Hall passed a bill (muscled through the two chambers by Al Smith and Bob Wagner, and approved even by a reform-minded state senator from Dutchess County named Franklin D. Roosevelt) to ban fusion. However, a Republican-dominated court threw it out—a decision that paved the way for the ALP. Although fusion remains legal in ten states, nowhere else has it led to robust minor-party politics. See "Levy Election Bill Passed by Senate," *New York Times*, 30 June 1911, 6; "Levy Law Illegal in Blocking Fusion," *New York Times*, 11 October 1911, 1; and, generally,

seems to offer an escape from the harsh realities in the first-past-the-post American electoral system that ordinarily doom small parties. The ALP gained its own ballot line, controlled by the needle trade unions. It cross-endorsed Roosevelt for president while following its own path in state and local politics. However, it never institutionalized itself as an office-seeking party apart from its backers. In the postwar years, this attempt to break out of the strictures of alliance, too, met its limits. The ALP fell apart by 1948, succeeded by the fiercely anticommunist Liberal Party.

Although radicalism spilled over into third parties elsewhere during the Depression years, the ALP, in the nation's most populous and wealthiest state, cut closer to the heart of the New Deal order.[45] It consciously attempted to influence national as well as state politics, and to base itself in the labor movement. In 1937 for Fiorello LaGuardia, the liberal but nominally Republican mayor, and in 1940 and 1944 statewide for Roosevelt, the party provided more votes than the winner's ultimate margin of victory. The ALP emerged from a moment when ethnic solidarities reinforced ideological loyalties, and its votes came predominantly from Jewish neighborhoods, far more than the needle trades' membership would suggest.[46]

At the suggestion initially of Frances Perkins, Roosevelt in early 1936 conceived to use New York's fusion laws and create a ballot line for the president. Elinore Herrick, a social worker whom Wagner had brought to Washington to serve at the NLRB, ran the campaign. The ALP provided six Roosevelt electors for a joint slate, including David Dubinsky and Sidney

---

Howard A. Scarrow, "Duverger's Law, Fusion, and the Decline of American 'Third' Parties," *Political Research Quarterly* 39 (1986): 634–47; and Peter H. Argersinger, "'A Place on the Ballot': Fusion Politics and Antifusion Laws," *American Historical Review* 85 (1980): 287–306.

[45] See George L. Cassidy, "New York Headquarters of ALP Is New Mecca for Leaders in 3rd Party Drive," *Progressive*, 15 January 1938, 1.

[46] In 1944, precinct-level support for Roosevelt correlated with Jewish neighborhood composition at .70 on the ALP line and .80 on the liberal line. See William Spinrad, "New York's Third Party Voters," *Public Opinion Quarterly* 21 (1957): 549; Jews as measured in a 1935 report from the American Jewish Committee. The ILGWU's membership declined from 80 percent Jewish in 1920 to half that in 1935 as the second generation took better jobs. See Beth S. Wenger, *New York Jews and the Great Depression* (New Haven: Yale University Press, 1996), 15. For context, see Deborah Dash Moore, *At Home in America: Second Generation New York Jews* (New York: Columbia University Press, 1981), chap. 8. The definitive history of Jews in the American (or even the New York) labor movement remains unwritten. See, from three vantage points right to left, Selig Perlman, "Jewish-American Unionism, Its Birth Pangs and Contribution to the General American Labor Movement," *Publications of the American Jewish Historical Society* 41 (1952): 297–337; Gus Tyler, "The Legacy of the Jewish Labor Movement," *Midstream*, March 1965, 54–65; and Irving Howe, *World of Our Fathers: The Journey of the East European Jews to America and the Life They Found and Made* (1976; repr., New York: Schocken Books, 1989), chaps. 9–11.

Hillman, and nearly a tenth of his vote.[47] The ALP served as a halfway house for voters desirous to support Roosevelt, but unwilling to pull a Democratic lever. Through the ALP, Fiorello LaGuardia backed Roosevelt while continuing to blast Tammany.

Ideological fights dogged the ALP as it attempted to form a permanent organization. In 1940, then-isolationist Communists fought to stop Roosevelt's renomination, but the needle trades prevailed. In 1944, despite efforts by LaGuardia and Roosevelt to mediate, the right wing under David Dubinsky and his protégé, Alex Rose of the Hatters Union, bolted to found the Liberal Party. The right wing wanted no part of Hillman's plan to use the ALP as the New York arm of CIO-PAC.[48] The left held greater sway in the ALP than in CIO-PAC. Rather than endure yet another schism, the Amalgamated (Hillman's old union) in January 1948 resigned without a fight as the party prepared to endorse Wallace. Henceforth, the ALP followed the CP line slavishly. A 1947 law restricted cross-endorsement to parties willing to accept a nonregistrant on their ballot line. It tolled the death knell to any attempt at fusion with an unwilling political party. The ALP finally expired in 1956.[49]

The Rose-Dubinsky "Libs" for decades traded policy (and, by the end, even patronage) for votes. As Jews assimilated and garment work declined, its influence ebbed; wags termed it neither liberal nor a party. In 2003, the Liberals finally lost their ballot line.[50] Starting in 1998, a new Working

[47]Steven Fraser, *Labor Will Rule: Sidney Hillman and the Rise of American Labor* (Ithaca, N.Y.: Cornell University Press, 1991), chap. 13; Leon Nathan Satenstein, "The American Labor Party of New York" (AB thesis, Harvard College, 1939), 73 and 188.

[48]Fraser, *Labor Will Rule*, 517–23; Hugh A. Bone, "Political Parties in New York City," *American Political Science Review* 40 (1946): 272–82; Warren Moscow, *Politics in the Empire State* (New York: Knopf, 1948), 112; Leo Egan, "ALP Right Wing Secedes, Starts Roosevelt Drive; Chiefs Bitter at Mayor," *New York Times*, 31 March 1944, 1; David Dubinsky and A. H. Raskin, *David Dubinsky: A Life with Labor* (New York: Simon & Schuster, 1977), 274–77; Gilbert Green, "The Dubinsky Social Democrats," *Communist*, July 1943, 633–41; Maurice Isserman, *Which Side Were You On? The American Communist Party during the Second World War* (Urbana: University of Illinois Press, 1982), 210.

[49]Martin Shefter, *Political Parties and the State: The American Historical Experience* (Princeton: Princeton University Press, 1994), 216–20; "Albany Bill Curbs 'Splinter' Parties," *New York Times*, 5 March 1947, 21; James A. Hagerty, "Communists Take Full ALP Control," *New York Times*, 8 January 1948, 1; Alan Wolfe, "The Withering Away of the American Labor Party," *Journal of the Rutgers University Library* 31 (1968): 46–57.

[50]The Libs often endorsed Republicans at the state level, including Nelson Rockefeller, John Lindsay, Jacob Javits, and even Rudolph Giuliani while consistently, save for John Anderson in 1980, backing Democratic presidential nominees. See Adolf A. Berle, *Navigating the Rapids, 1918–1971: From the Papers of Adolf A. Berle*, ed. Beatrice Bishop Berle and Travis Beal Jacobs (New York: Harcourt Brace Jovanovich, 1973), 586; Fred Ferretti, "A Rose Is A. Rose Is a Boss," *New York*, 8 December 1969, 51–55; Robert D. McFadden, "Raymond B. Harding, 77, Liberal Party Power Broker, Dies," *New York Times*, 16 August 2012, A16.

Families Party, backed by a coalition of unions, held a ballot line and sought to revive the old ALP spirit, even as it faced the vexed old dilemmas of cross-endorsement. The party largely formalized the delegation of "the ground game" to the unions. In factional and liberal New York City, it built coalitions with community groups and won mandatory paid sick leave, and a living-wage ordinance. Although the party did not endorse in the primary, the mayoral victory in 2013 of its longtime supporter Bill de Blasio would have been impossible without the infrastructure that it built. Among statewide Democrats willing also to cut deals with their own dissident copartisans and with moderate Republicans, however, it struggled to find leverage points that would redirect policy and power.[51]

Just as the New Right would learn in its strategy of "coalitionism," even as brokers bring new electorates into politics and transform issue agendas, in a nationalized and majoritarian electoral system they cannot structure political conflict. ALP had achieved the classic trade of votes for policy—and with clearer credit for its contributions than anchoring groups ordinarily receive. Yet cross-endorsement is no substitute for proportional representation or for formal coalition government. The ALP achieved its victories only on sufferance—that is, on terms that other high-demanders would accept. When the parties deemed the ALP a threat rather than a boon to their core electoral purposes, they killed it. To its supporters, the American Labor Party had crossed the threshold to become a full-fledged party—but it was a mirage. Cross-endorsement redirects the dilemmas of alliance in a majoritarian system; it does not solve them.

The Private Welfare State

Postwar retrenchment in its bargaining power led unions, with the mass-production industries of the CIO in the vanguard, to embrace private provision of health and pension benefits. By the time unified Democratic control returned in 1949, Taft-Hartley had weakened labor's position in the private sector. Unsurprisingly given the conservative coalition's numbers, Congress failed to overturn Taft-Hartley, or—in what would have been an even heavier lift—to pass Wagner-Murray-Dingell. Without a liberal majority in Congress, the victory of 1948 offered nothing more than had Roosevelt's

[51] See Ben Smith, "Is Party Over for the Working Families Party before It Starts?," *New York Observer*, 3 November 2003, 1; Greg Sargent, "First among Thirds," *American Prospect*, May 2006, 37–40; Ted Fertik, "Which Working Families Party?," *Jacobin*, 23 May 2014, https://www.jacobinmag.com/2014/05/which-working-families-party/; Ted Fertik, "The Working Families Party and Cuomo," *Jacobin*, 6 June 2014, https://www.jacobinmag.com/2014/06/the-working-families-party-and-cuomo/.

win in 1944.[52] Unions placed their organizational maintenance ahead of their goals for the polity as they adopted private health and pension plans. Democrats acquiesced, lest they lose a critical ally on whom their electoral success depended.

The private welfare state retarded public programs, notably health insurance for the nonelderly. Cocooned in generous benefits negotiated at the bargaining table, organized labor offered only general support. At the same time, increasingly cumbersome layers of public and private benefits along with their clients and claimants restricted possibilities for comprehensive programs.[53] These policy feedbacks severed the institutional complementarities across economic management, social provision, and political contest that the early CIO had assiduously cultivated.

Wartime contracts negotiated under the no-strike pledge spurred the adoption of fringe benefits. The Revenue Act of 1942 imposed a tax on excess corporate profits, which companies avoided by depositing earnings into tax-free pension plans. Under the Little Steel formula, the National War Labor Board strictly limited wage increases, but considered fringe benefits, including health insurance, pensions, shift premiums, and vacation pay under separate and more lenient terms.[54] Adding fringe benefits avoided confrontations with unions, and shocks to aggregate demand alike.

[52] Daniel Bell, "The Taft-Hartley Fumble," *Fortune*, May 1949, 189–91; Gerald Pomper, "Labor and Congress: The Repeal of Taft-Hartley," *Labor History* 2 (1961): 323–43; Hamby, *Beyond the New Deal*, chap. 14; Tracy Roof, *American Labor, Congress, and the Welfare State, 1935–2010* (Baltimore: Johns Hopkins University Press, 2011), chap. 2.

[53] For variants on this theme, with differing roles for labor and party, structure and agency, see Michael K. Brown, *Race, Money, and the American Welfare State* (Ithaca, N.Y.: Cornell University Press, 1999), esp. chap. 4; Alan Derickson, "Health Security for All? Social Unionism and Universal Health Insurance, 1935–1958," *Journal of American History* 80 (1994): 1333–56; Marie Gottschalk, *The Shadow Welfare State: Labor, Business, and the Politics of Health Care in the United States* (Ithaca, N.Y.: ILR Press, 2000); Jacob S. Hacker, *The Divided Welfare State: The Battle over Public and Private Social Benefits in the United States* (Cambridge: Cambridge University Press, 2002); Jennifer Klein, *For All These Rights: Business, Labor, and the Shaping of America's Public-Private Welfare State* (Princeton: Princeton University Press, 2003); Jill Quadagno, *The Transformation of Old Age Security: Class and Politics in the American Welfare State* (Chicago: University of Chicago Press, 1988), esp. chap. 7; Hugh Mosley, "Corporate Social Benefits and the Underdevelopment of the American Welfare State," *Contemporary Crises* 5 (1981): 139–54; Beth Stevens, "Blurring the Boundaries: How the Federal Government Has Influenced Welfare Benefits in the Private Sector," in *The Politics of Social Policy in the United States*, ed. Margaret Weir, Ann Shola Orloff, and Theda Skocpol (Princeton: Princeton University Press, 1988), 123–48; Beth Stevens, "Labor Unions, Employee Benefits, and the Privatization of the American Welfare State," *Journal of Policy History* 2 (1990): 233–60; Michael A. McCarthy, "Political Mediation and American Old-Age Security Exceptionalism," *Work and Occupations* 41 (2014): 175–209.

[54] John T. Dunlop, "An Appraisal of Wage Stabilization Policies," in *Problems and Policies of Dispute Settlement and Wage Stabilization during World War II*, U.S. Department of Labor Bulletin 1009 (Washington, D.C.: Government Printing Office, 1950), 166–67; Klein, *For All These Rights*, chap. 5; Stevens, "Blurring the Boundaries," 130–34; Nelson Lichtenstein, "Industrial

Tripartite pension and health plans solved problems of organizational maintenance. Although the CIO favored universal public provision in principle, private benefits offered immediate rewards. Union leaders played a direct role in administering benefits, and could claim victory—and forestall intraunion rivals—even when slack demand or fears of inflation prevented substantial increases in wages. "By keeping up the drive on both fronts we are more likely to get action," a CIO publication declared disingenuously at the end of 1948.[55]

The new plans typically combined under a single trusteeship defined-benefit pension plans (some contributory, some noncontributory) and employer-funded health plans. They diffused quickly as CIO unions negotiated against the same oligopolistic employers, above all in the supply chain from coal to steel to autos. The 1950 "Treaty of Detroit" between Reuther's UAW and General Motors signaled the new pattern. It offered guaranteed wage increases, company-funded pensions, and health insurance in exchange for five years of labor peace.[56] Unorganized workers in the same industries generally received similar welfare-capitalist benefits, as employers lost the ability in national markets to undercut union labor. Nor, for all the ideological strife, was the tactic restricted to the CIO right. The UE and ILWU followed precisely the same strategy; the Longshoremen won a particularly generous welfare plan in their 1948 contract.[57]

For the AFL, pensions simply represented "deferred wages," unaccompanied by the grand talk about security in which the CIO sometimes indulged. In the building trades, employers typically competed in regional labor markets against nonunion competitors, and could not simply pass on cost increases.[58] In short order, AFL unions, too, grew to accept fringe

---

Democracy, Contract Unionism, and the National War Labor Board," *Labor Law Journal* 33 (1982): 524–31; Donna Allen, *Fringe Benefits: Wages or Social Obligation?* (Ithaca, N.Y.: Cornell University, 1964), chap. 6.

[55] "Two-Way Drive for Social Security," *Economic Outlook*, December 1948, 1. See also "CIO Pension Gains Mean Victory for All," *Economic Outlook*, December 1949, 89–96; Harry Becker, "UAW-CIO and the Problem of Medical Care," *American Journal of Public Health* 41 (1951): 1112–17.

[56] Daniel Bell, "The Treaty of Detroit," *Fortune*, June 1950, 53; Michael J. Piore and Charles F. Sabel, *The Second Industrial Divide: Possibilities for Prosperity* (New York: Basic Books, 1984), 78–84.

[57] F. Beatrice Brower, *Company Group Insurance Plans* (New York: National Industrial Conference Board, 1951), chap. 8; A.D.H. Kaplan, *The Guarantee of Annual Wages* (Washington, D.C.: Brookings Institution, 1947), chap. 2; Sanford Jacoby, *Modern Manors: Welfare Capitalism since the New Deal* (Princeton: Princeton University Press, 1997); Clark Kerr and Lloyd Fisher, "Conflict on the Waterfront," *Atlantic Monthly*, September 1949, 17–23.

[58] John Dunlop, "The Industrial Relations System in Construction," in *The Structure of Collective Bargaining: Problems and Perspectives*, ed. Arnold Weber (New York: Free Press of Glencoe, 1961), 260; *Pension Plans under Collective Bargaining: A Reference Guide for Trade Unions* (Washington, D.C.: American Federation of Labor, 1953); Charles L. Dearing, *Industrial Pensions* (Washington, D.C.: Brookings Institution, 1954), esp. chap. 4.

benefits, generally starting with health and then adding pensions. By the eve of merger in 1954, they were virtually universal in the CIO and covered a majority in the AFL as they spread rapidly through the construction industry. The Teamsters, largest union in the merged federation, negotiated a pension plan in 1955.[59]

Taft-Hartley mandated joint labor-management control over unionized workers' pension and health-and-welfare funds, so as to prevent union bosses, John L. Lewis in particular, from agglomerating power—or potentially disturbing management—through their control over capital. Nevertheless, the legislation repeated verbatim language from the Wagner Act to permit bargaining over "wages and other conditions of employment." Although the House bill expressly prohibited bargaining over fringe benefits, Robert Taft axed the ban. He wanted above all the votes to override a presidential veto.

Labor's allies held a majority of four to one on the NLRB in the wake of Taft-Hartley. In April 1948, in the *Inland Steel* case, they confirmed that pension benefits, as "emoluments of value" equivalent to wages, fell under employers' duty to bargain in good faith. The NLRB explicitly cited the legislative history to show that the right it created coexisted comfortably with the constricted labor regime of 1947.[60]

This history suggests that the private welfare state is a more close-run, contingent outcome, and more deeply imbricated in the cross-institutional vagaries of party-group alliance, than most treatments allow. Notably, it might not have happened had the conservative coalition held an even stronger hand. If labor's congressional support had been even slightly weaker in 1947, Taft would have acceded to the House bill, and foreclosed private bargaining. He reproachfully questioned "how far we should go in the matter of public welfare funds" given the existence of Social Security.[61]

[59]Coverage rates are inexact, as government data reported only the number of covered employees, without a denominator, and must be compared to overall estimates of union membership. See "Employee-Benefit Plans Under Collective Bargaining, Mid-1950," U.S. Department of Labor Bulletin No. 1017 (Washington, D.C.: Government Printing Office, 1951); Evan Keith Rowe, "Health, Insurance, and Pension Plans under Union Contract," *Monthly Labor Review*, September 1955, 993–1000; and Leo Troy, *Trade Union Membership, 1897–1962* (New York: National Bureau of Economic Research, 1965), 8.

[60]77 NLRB 4 (1948). The *WW Cross* decision two months later summarily extended the logic to health and welfare plans. 77 NLRB 1162 (1948). John Davis Lodge, a moderate Republican from Connecticut, proposed a House amendment explicitly to protect bargaining rights over "pension plans, group insurance plans, hospitalization benefits," but after brief debate, it was voted down sixty-two to ninety-four. With most members not voting and no roll call, it is impossible to estimate directly a pivot on private provision. See *Congressional Record*, 17 April 1947, 3633–34.

[61]Raymond Munts, *Bargaining for Health: Labor Unions, Health Insurance, and Medical Care* (Madison: University of Wisconsin Press, 1967), 11.

Foreclosing negotiated private benefits would have forced an all-in bet on public provision—or even on some kind of corporatist accommodation to coordinate beyond the company level. To be sure, unions—with the UAW and USWA particularly critical cases—risked losing bargaining power and some intermediary role in the workplace without the ability to negotiate over nonwage compensation. Companies in core sectors might well have responded with lavish benefits from above to cement workers' loyalty. Or else labor would have deteriorated so much, in either numbers or clout, that it would not have been an effective partner even to northern Democrats in Congress.

Still, a ban on private bargaining in Taft-Hartley might ultimately have pushed labor to keep its social democratic commitments as core strategy across internationals—and not just an ideological obligation from the UAW. In the Great Society, the AFL-CIO might have pushed harder for universal health coverage, and for structural responses to unemployment and poverty. While it is hard to predict the outcome of that bet, given what Wilbur Mills or the American Medical Association might have allowed, the possibility remains that not only a stronger but, paradoxically, a politically weaker labor movement in 1947 might in the long run have strengthened the egalitarian capacities of the American state. Instead, from the policy space between overriding Truman's veto only of a bill that kept the door open for negotiated benefits, and the failure to repeal in 1949, emerged the postwar private welfare state.

Unlike the politics of 1965, 1978, and 2009, Congress had no direct role in the settlement of 1948 and 1949. When the Democratic leadership tried to repeal Taft-Hartley, it failed. The House in 1949 had barely 170 northern Democrats, and a conservative coalition in full flower. Explicit congressional authorization for bargaining over benefits, a particular priority for the regionally concentrated and ideologically tinged CIO, would have been as much a nonstarter as Wagner-Murray-Dingell or a full employment bill. The administrative state and not Congress gave labor *Inland Steel*. Nor was the Truman administration's behavior terribly surprising given the constraints it faced. In acceding to labor's wishes for private bargaining, it traded away only possibilities at a future liberal hour. The gains accruing to a party high-demander came immediately, while the costs for ideal policy (including, assuming some feedback, concomitant political losses) manifested themselves long in the future.

As the possibilities for universalism diminished, organized labor retreated toward programs that supplemented rather than supplanted the private welfare state. Across policy arenas, a categorical welfare state served residual populations outside the primary labor market, whether for reasons of age, disability, or severe disadvantage. After a generation, the postwar social contract ultimately receded, and the costs became clear. Corporations abandoned welfare capitalism. Individuals assumed increased risks, with health care coverage hollowed out or cut and defined-benefit plans eliminated. The results divided the Democrats' own supporters. Social provision stratified "into a unionized segment that until recently enjoyed an almost Western European level of social welfare protection, and a still larger stratum, predominantly young, minority, and female, that was left out in the cold."[62]

AFL and CIO

In the wake of Taft-Hartley, the AFL and CIO each moved closer to the other. The CIO shed its radical fringe. The AF of L, for its part, had already begun to step away from voluntarism during the New Deal years. It tepidly supported the Social Security and Fair Labor Standards Acts. William Green first backed some kind of government-administered health and sickness insurance in 1938, and the AFL endorsed Wagner-Murray-Dingell in 1943.[63] The federation entered electoral politics in the wake of Taft-Hartley. Its policy to isolate the CIO, and so preserve the federation's own prerogatives, had failed. Even traditionalists had reason to discard voluntarism: Taft-Hartley's prohibitions on jurisdictional strikes and secondary boycotts incensed building trade unions zealous of their prerogatives.

At the 1947 convention, the federation formed Labor's League for Political Education to reward its friends and punish its enemies. Because opposition to Taft-Hartley was "the sole test for L.L.P.E endorsement of an incumbent Congressman running for re-election," LLPE essentially supported only northern Democrats. The AF of L took a purely voluntarist claim, centered around labor's efforts to stand on its own two feet without undue interference, and used it to buttress the party faction that backed the full agenda of labor-liberalism. In 1952, the federation finally issued a formal

[62] Nelson Lichtenstein, "From Corporatism to Collective Bargaining: Organized Labor and the Eclipse of Social Democracy in the Postwar Era," in *The Rise and Fall of the New Deal Order, 1930–1980*, ed. Steve Fraser and Gary Gerstle (Princeton: Princeton University Press, 1989), 144. For data, see *Employee Benefit Research Institute Databook on Employee Benefits*, http://www.ebri.org/publications/books/?fa=databook. For context, see Michael Katz, *The Price of Citizenship: Redefining the American Welfare State* (2001; repr., Philadelphia: University of Pennsylvania Press, 2008), chap. 7. On similar, but not identical, dynamics, see David Rueda, "Insider-Outsider Politics in Industrialized Democracies: The Challenge to Social Democratic Parties," *American Political Science Review* 99 (2005): 61–74.

[63] George Gilmary Higgins, *Voluntarism in Organized Labor, 1930–1940* (Washington, D.C.: Catholic University of America Press, 1944); T. Charles McKinney, "The Role of Organized Labor in the Quest for Compulsory Health Insurance, 1912–1965" (PhD diss., University of Wisconsin, 1969), 103–6; Daniel B. Cornfield and Holly J. McCammon, "Approaching Merger: The Converging Public Policy Agendas of the AFL and CIO, 1938–1955," in *Strategic Alliances: Coalition Building and Social Movements*, ed. Nella Van Dyke and Holly J. McCammon (Minneapolis: University of Minnesota Press, 2010), 79–98.

presidential endorsement at its convention, in support of Adlai Stevenson. It had become a nonevent. Neither pure voluntarists nor third-party stalwarts saw fit to raise any hackles whatsoever. AF of L propagandists even rewrote history to claim that with LLPE, labor had "now returned to the policy of Gompers."[64]

In November 1952, William Green and Phil Murray, old coal miners at the helm of the two national labor organizations, died within weeks of each other. New leadership paved the way for merger. George Meany, a gruff Bronx-born plumber and longtime union bureaucrat, took the helm at the AFL. Walter Reuther muscled out Allan Haywood, a Steelworkers functionary, at the CIO. After its wartime growth, the AFL had more than twice the membership of its younger rival. Arthur Goldberg, Steelworkers and CIO counsel, negotiated a merger under terms sympathetic to the AFL, and coined the new name: AFL-CIO.[65]

As insurgency gave way to stability in labor relations, unions found legitimacy not only in the Democratic Party but in the postwar consensus as it forged a broadly shared prosperity. Labor had found its place as an anchoring group whose legitimacy in party affairs—if not always its preferred candidates and policies—even internal opponents largely respected. For the Democrats, too, although the terms of partnership would be tested and renegotiated over the decades, the essential trade of votes for ideological patronage, and its form through the AFL-CIO, had now been set. Instead, as Chapter 7 shows, questions rooted in labor's institutional prerogatives and weakening membership and in the Democrats' priorities during brief windows of liberal possibility, have animated alliance in the long shadow of postwar compromise.

The Cold War made anticommunism a sine qua non for alliance while the conservative coalition stopped liberal legislation in its tracks. As they

[64]"The Record They Stand On!" (Washington, D.C.: Labor's League for Political Education, 1948); *Report of the Conference of National and International Unions on Educational and Political Matters* (Washington, D.C.: American Federation of Labor, 1947); Philip Taft, *The A.F. of L. from the Death of Gompers to the Merger* (New York: Harper, 1959), 322; Morton Leeds, "The AFL in the 1948 Elections," *Social Research* 17 (1950): 207–18; *Report of Proceedings of the 1952 Annual Convention of the American Federation of Labor* (Washington, D.C.: American Federation of Labor, 1952), 511; Mary Zon, "Labor in Politics," *Law and Contemporary Problems* 27 (1962): 235; George Meany, *Political Education Is an A.F of L. Tradition* (Washington, D.C.: Labor's League for Political Education, 1953), 6.

[65]A. H. Raskin, "The New Labor Leaders—A Dual Portrait," *New York Times Magazine*, 21 December 1952, 13, 18–19; Daniel Bell, "Labor's New Men of Power," *Fortune*, June 1953, 155–62; "Head of the House," *Time*, 21 March 1955, 20–23; A. H. Raskin, "A.F.L and C.I.O. to Unite Today; Discords Arising," *New York Times*, 5 December 1955, 1; Joseph C. Goulden, *Meany* (New York: Atheneum, 1972), chap. 9; John Herling, "Where Does Big Labor Go from Here?," *Collier's*, 20 January 1956, 54–61. The definitive record, with documents, remains Arthur J. Goldberg, *AFL-CIO: Labor United* (New York: McGraw-Hill, 1956).

interacted, the chances for alternatives ranging from third party to pure voluntarism closed. Above all, the postwar years walled off possibility after possibility to the left. The failures of Operation Dixie, the Wallace campaign, and the American Labor Party, and the expulsion of the left-led unions all sharply demarcated the boundaries of alliance, with few attractive alternatives for the movement in the realm of reasonable possibility. The rise of the private welfare state truncated its universalistic possibilities, instead substituting a new kind of voluntarism made possible through an approving state and an enticing suite of tax benefits. Taft-Hartley stifled labor militancy. In subsequent decades, the consequences from these strictures would come clear. The partnership forged in the New Deal and cemented in the Fair Deal endures, but no longer holds the influence in society or polity to which anchoring groups and majority parties together aspire.

What's Changed—And What Hasn't: A Coda

"Are we coming to the time," asked the labor historian David Brody in 1993, "when the CIO—at least in its original incarnation—will become the kind of historical subject that the Knights of Labor is today?"[66] The New Deal political economy has collapsed, with its obituary written a thousand times over. Union membership, at 11.1 percent of the American workforce in 2014—and 6.6 percent of the private-sector workforce—stands at the lowest level since before the Depression. Deindustrialization and globalization have decimated the old CIO. In hard-rock mining, coal, steel, autos, electrical work, and textiles, unions with far more retirees than active members have turned inward to preserve benefits won in palmier days.

All the same, the CIO era continues profoundly to shape the present moment. Since 1949, unions have failed time and again to change American labor law, victim of Congress and the Senate filibuster in particular. These debates suck back in nearly every particular to the vortex of the New Deal and Fair Deal. The parties, their core positions unchanged, fight about the same policies on state power over collective bargaining as they did in 1947.

In their most recent attempt to change labor law, unions sought through the Employee Free Choice Act to restore card check, the original certification method after passage of the Wagner Act. The early NLRB simply accepted signed cards as evidence of support from the majority of a given bargaining unit. This procedure gave street-level bureaucrats tremendous autonomy, which they typically used to favor the CIO. In early 1939, however, their opponents were closing in, and Representative Howard W. Smith of Virginia began a wide-ranging investigation. Republicans feared that

[66] Brody, *Workers in Industrial America*, 154.

union power threatened American business, southern Democrats that it threatened Jim Crow, and the AF of L that the NLRB, unchecked, would severely weaken the federation. The NLRB quickly voted to require a secret-ballot election if employers demanded one, which they almost invariably did. Taft-Hartley in 1947 then explicitly wrote in a provision for the employer to request a secret ballot.[67]

To take another prominent piece of Taft-Hartley, the Republican platform in 2012 offered support for "the right of states to enact Right-to-Work laws" and ultimate enactment of national right-to-work. Democrats, by contrast, promised "to vigorously oppose 'Right to Work.'" It is hard to think of any other legislation in American history that has engendered such direct partisan animus so many decades after passage. Yet after 1980, the Democratic platform would never again favor repealing Section 14(b) itself.

State-level data, too, suggest the long reach of the New Deal alignment. Every single state that had right-to-work voted for George W. Bush in 2004. Of the states without right-to-work, all but Alaska voted at least once for Bill Clinton or Barack Obama. Yet except for Idaho in 1986, Oklahoma in 2001, and, in much more nationalized circumstances, Indiana and Michigan in 2012, as conservatives redoubled attacks on the opposing anchoring group, all these right-to-work laws passed between 1944 and 1963, decades before the current geographical cleavages became prominent in national politics. Similarly, increases in union density during the CIO years continue to predict partisan preferences decades later. For states outside the South, the correlation between percentage-point increase in union density from 1939 to 1953 and Democratic share of the two-party vote actually rose from 0.40 in 1960 to 0.52 in 2012.[68] In other words, antiunion alignments in the 1940s presaged polarized politics. The CIO era still casts a long shadow over partisan conflict.

[67]The decision is at 13 NLRB 526 (1939), and follows precedent from the National Mediation Board. See Louis Stark, "Labor Board Quits Card Certification," *New York Times* 14 July 1939, 5; James Gross, *The Reshaping of the National Labor Relations Board: National Labor Policy in Transition, 1937–1947* (Albany: State University of New York Press 1981), esp. 85–86, 261–63; David Brody, "Labor Elections: Good for Workers?," *Dissent*, Summer 1997, 71–77; Millis and Brown, *From the Wagner Act*, 133; Gerald Mayer, "Labor Union Recognition Procedures: Use of Secret Ballots and Card Checks" (Washington, D.C.: Congressional Research Service, 2007). Evidence from Canada, at a time when five provinces required secret-ballot vote and five allowed card check, indicates that card check explains about a quarter of the gap in union density between the United States and Canada. See Susan Johnson, "The Impact of Mandatory Votes on the Canada-U.S. Union Density Gap: A Note," *Industrial Relations* 43 (2004): 356–63.

[68]The comparable figures including the South (eleven states in Confederacy) are 0.17 and 0.53. Data from Troy, *Distribution of Union Membership* and uselectionatlas.org. For a similar analysis, see John Ahlquist, "Public Sector Unions Need the Private Sector, or Why the Wisconsin Protests Were Not Labor's Lazarus Moment," *Forum* 10 (2012): article 7: 1–17, doi:10.1515/1540–8884.1499.

CHAPTER 7

Alliance through Adversity

Labor and the Democrats since the Merger

"It's unions like yours," Barack Obama told the United Auto Workers in February 2012, "that forged the American middle class—that great engine of prosperity, the greatest that the world has ever known."[1] The alliance between organized labor and the Democrats endures. Amid labor weakness and partisan polarization, its terms of trade remain intact eight decades after the CIO entered politics. Increasingly, however, alliance seems defined more by enemies from without than by decisive victories. This chapter surveys mature alliance since the AFL-CIO merger in 1955. Two patterns have interacted. Ties between labor and the Democrats have seen a heyday in the Great Society era, rupture after 1968, and revival starting in the 1980s. Unions' own fortunes have undergone secular decline, especially sharp beginning in the late 1970s. Labor faces now less the question of acceptance in party councils, the issue that bedevils movements when first they confront the party system, than of effectiveness, as the movement tries to maintain influence, despite its straitened circumstances, across party, polity, and regime.

To speak generally, alliance operates at three successive levels: inside a party, in a polity, and in a political regime. At the first level, movement elites trade their supporters' votes, time, money, and networks in exchange for policy commitments from the party. At the second, when the party achieves a majority, it realizes those policy commitments by giving the

[1] Speech to the UAW Community Action Program Legislative Conference, 28 February 2012, http://www.uaw.org/page/president-obamas-speech-2012-uaw-community-action-program-legislative-conference-actual-transcr.

group programmatic benefits. At the third, parties and their group allies, during extraordinary junctures, restructure the rules and stakes of the political game and expand its boundaries.

Mature alliance between labor and the Democrats has succeeded inside the party. Labor continues to provide political resources to Democrats, buttressed by well-defined institutional complementarities between group and party. Antilabor southern Democrats, the great confounders of alliance, have largely passed from the scene. As James Sundquist summarized a generation ago, "When the New Deal *alignment* is strengthened, the New Deal *coalitions* are weakened."[2] The schisms that roiled alliance as hard hats battled flower children have receded. The long tradition of pure Gompersian voluntarism, at home and abroad, has passed into obsolescence.

Yet in the polity labor has broken through only rarely, and then only on areas of broader liberal, and not group-specific priority. Abner Mikva, a well-regarded Chicago representative, made the essential point in 1975: "They're just not able to get the horses on an issue that speaks only to labor."[3] In narrow policy windows with unified Democratic control and a seeming mandate for liberal policies, changes in labor law have systematically been shunted aside for presidential priorities with multiple constituencies. By the time labor law came onto the legislative calendar, any window to overcome the Senate filibuster, the repeated veto point, had already closed. The politics of 1965, 1978, and 2009 appear nearly identical. American labor law in the private sector is less friendly to trade unions than in any other advanced democracy save Japan.[4] Old weaknesses in labor law have, like a time capsule, reasserted themselves as union membership inexorably declines.

At the broadest level, labor no longer forms part of a constituent political regime. Instead, rising inequality and much sharpened opposition from the Republican Party and its own matrix of supporters in business and the rejuvenated conservative movement push the old allies still closer together around mutual need as much as opportunity. The wider the lens the weaker seems labor-liberalism.[5]

[2] James Sundquist, *Dynamics of the Party System: Alignment and Realignment of Political Parties in the United States*, rev. ed. (Washington, D.C.: Brookings Institution, 1983), 448, italics original.

[3] Alan Ehrenhalt, "The AFL-CIO: How Much Clout in Congress?," *CQ Weekly Report*, 19 July 1975, 1153.

[4] Bruce Western, *Between Class and Market: Postwar Unionization in the Capitalist Democracies* (Princeton: Princeton University Press, 1997), 194–95.

[5] For treatments of alliance focusing on party, polity, and political regime respectively, see Taylor E. Dark III, *The Unions and the Democrats: An Enduring Alliance*, updated ed. (Ithaca, N.Y.: Cornell University Press, 2001); Tracy Roof, *American Labor, Congress, and the Welfare State, 1935–2010* (Baltimore: Johns Hopkins University Press, 2011); and Nelson Lichtenstein, "Labour, Liberalism, and the Democratic Party: A Vexed Alliance," *Relations Industrielles—Industrial Relations* 66 (2011): 512–31.

Labor-Liberalism at the Zenith

After the merger in 1955, the new AFL-CIO set to work as the keystone of the liberal coalition, busily mastering the intricacies of policy and politics alike. Yet its agenda remained circumscribed by unions' embrace of the private welfare state, and internal prerogatives to direct their own affairs. An effective legislative department under Andrew Biemiller, a socialist turned ADA liberal and later a protégé of Sam Rayburn as a Democratic representative from Milwaukee, took charge of assembling coalitions for labor-liberal priorities. Often it operated indirectly through coalitions or front groups, choosing voices closer to wavering members—mainline Protestant ministers, say—to lobby directly. The UAW often went further in these coalitions than George Meany would countenance for the AFL-CIO. On the electoral side, a new Committee on Political Education (COPE) merged together CIO-PAC and LLPE. While the CIO required political contributions, the merged federation, like the AFL, issued voluntary dollar quotas for internationals, and remitted nearly all the money to state federations, for both political outreach and education to members. Not surprisingly, ex-CIO unions gave more generously, and the Auto Workers most of all.[6]

The labor-Democratic partnership varied in character across space in the 1950s and 1960s, more than in the volatile New Deal and Fair Deal years, or in the more nationalized political environment that emerged in the 1980s. State COPEs followed the AFL's decentralized practices and issued congressional endorsements themselves, without need for approval from Washington. Patterns of influence varied from old-style accommodation between machines and the building trades to support for programmatic liberals.[7] In many states without right-to-work laws, reformers sympathetic to progressive unions, with Hubert Humphrey the paradigmatic example, supplanted political machines or revived sclerotic parties.

In presidential politics, the AFL-CIO endorsed Adlai Stevenson in 1956 with even less ardor than the unions had shown in 1952, and strongly backed Estes Kefauver, a Tennessee liberal, for vice president. Four years later, after Hubert Humphrey withdrew following losses in the West Virginia and Wisconsin primaries, John F. Kennedy won over most union leaders in a charm offensive brokered by Arthur Goldberg. Despite his disappointment

[6]Under Taft-Hartley, electioneering required direct solicitation, carried out under drives to "Give a Buck for COPE." See the financial totals for 1960 in Alan Draper, *A Rope of Sand: The AFL-CIO Committee on Political Education, 1955–1967* (New York: Praeger, 1989), 81–91.

[7]Hence Greenstone's classic account primarily compares across space (Detroit, Chicago, and Los Angeles) rather than time. See J. David Greenstone, *Labor in American Politics* (New York: Knopf, 1969), esp. chaps. 8 and 9, and the figure on 396. On COPE, see "Labor and Politics," COPE Publication 59 (Washington, D.C.: Committee on Political Education, 1960); and "A Few Words about COPE," COPE Publication 86 (Washington, D.C.: Committee on Political Education, 1962).

with the vice presidential selection of Lyndon Johnson (chosen to placate the South), Walter Reuther tamped down liberal hopes for a floor fight at the convention. The platform endorsed full employment and health insurance for the aged, and included sweeping language on labor rights: "the traditional goal of the Democratic Party—to give all workers the right to organize and bargain collectively—has still not been achieved."[8]

To abstract from the back-and-forth, far more than in the Truman nomination of 1944, stable expectations around the exchange of policy for votes conditioned the choice. Johnson, despite his flaws, was a far superior alternative than Jimmy Byrnes, the southerner on offer as vice president sixteen years earlier. So, too, the Hillman role as broker had expanded to encompass a panoply of big union presidents and their political advisers, all shuttling across state delegations, union allies, and the liberal networks around ADA. As they mingled and drank in sweaty hotel suites, they held credible commitments to speak on behalf of, and to deploy in electoral work, their members and supporters. The struggle to regain that legitimacy in party councils would dominate postreform politics after 1968.[9]

For all the initial skepticism, Johnson's presidency marked the apogee of the labor-Democratic partnership, with benefits for both sides. LBJ courted the AFL-CIO based on common priorities: full employment, civil rights, hawkish foreign policy. To secure labor's preferred vice president, Hubert Humphrey, in 1964, Reuther steamrollered his friend, Joe Rauh, the UAW's lawyer in Washington, to enforce Johnson's decision awarding the Mississippi Freedom Democratic Party a mere two at-large convention seats—which they refused to accept.[10] More than any other group leader before or

[8]Kennedy double-crossed Joe Rauh with a promise to nominate Humphrey "or another Midwestern liberal" for the vice presidency. Johnson had allowed the Landrum-Griffin bill, which increased union disclosure requirements, to come to a Senate vote in 1959. David Dubinsky, a Johnson ally, was dispatched to sooth George Meany. On labor and the Johnson selection, the fullest account (with Irish blarney) comes in Kenneth P. O'Donnell and David F. Powers with Joe McCarthy, *"Johnny, We Hardly Knew Ye": Memories of John Fitzgerald Kennedy* (Boston: Little, Brown, 1970), chap. 7. See also Arthur M. Schlesinger, Jr., *A Thousand Days: John F. Kennedy in the White House* (Boston: Houghton Mifflin, 1965), 50–52; David Dubinsky and A. H. Raskin, *David Dubinsky: A Life with Labor* (New York: Simon & Schuster, 1977), 290–94; and, for good recent treatments, Kevin Boyle, *The UAW and the Heyday of American Liberalism* (Ithaca, N.Y.: Cornell University Press, 1995), 141–46; and Michael E. Parrish, *Citizen Rauh: An American Liberal's Life in Law and Politics* (Ann Arbor: University of Michigan Press, 2010), 143–45. "Democratic Party Platform of 1960," http://www.presidency.ucsb.edu/ws/?pid=29602.

[9]This argument is central to Dark, *Unions and the Democrats*, chap. 3.

[10]Murray Kempton, "Conscience of a Convention," *New Republic*, 5 September 1964, 5–7; John Dittmer, *Local People: The Struggle for Civil Rights in Mississippi* (Urbana: University of Illinois Press, 1994), 288–302. From an MFDP leader, see Jack Minnis, "The Mississippi Freedom Democratic Party: A New Declaration of Independence," *Freedomways*, Spring 1965, 264–78. See also the transcripts in Anne Cooke Romaine, "The Mississippi Freedom

since, a peak personal relationship fortified the bonds: Johnson and Meany, LBJ tallied in his presidential diaries, held forty-nine meetings and eighty-two telephone calls.[11]

The merged federation, including even its progressive unions, held a better external than internal record on race. At the behest of A. Philip Randolph of the Brotherhood of Sleeping Car Porters, the most prominent black trade unionist and a longtime member of the Socialist Party, the AFL-CIO pledged nondiscrimination on the basis of race—but did little to goad or sanction the constituent internationals.[12] The AFL-CIO in 1959 neutered Randolph's proposal to "liquidate" segregated locals, and in 1961, to its immediate regret, even censured Randolph for his attacks on union practices. While the federation steered clear of the March on Washington for Jobs and Freedom that Randolph and his protégé, Bayard Rustin, organized in August 1963, Reuther served as the only white speaker without a religious connection, and the UAW picked up the tab for buses, signs, and the sound system.[13]

Legislatively, the Civil Rights Act of 1964 marked a particular triumph. The AFL-CIO successfully incorporated into Title VII a ban on racial discrimination for all employers, not just unions or recipients of government contracts. Less surprisingly, it also won protections against "superseniority" agreements to speed integration in historically white occupations. The UAW lent the Leadership Conference on Civil Rights its only full-time staff, steered by Biemiller, Rauh, and the NAACP's Clarence Mitchell. As Richard

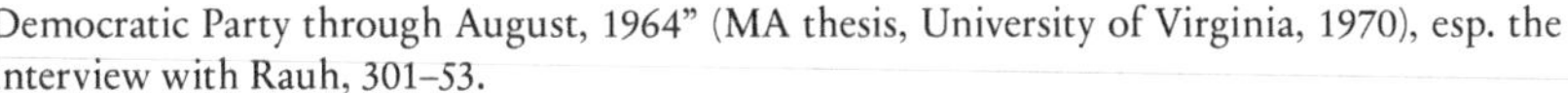

Democratic Party through August, 1964" (MA thesis, University of Virginia, 1970), esp. the interview with Rauh, 301–53.

[11]Joseph C. Goulden, *Meany* (New York: Atheneum, 1972), 369–70.

[12]Herbert Hill, *Racism within Organized Labor: A Report of Five Years of the AFL-CIO, 1955–1960* (New York: Labor Department of the National Association for the Advancement of Colored People, 1961); August Meier and Elliott Rudwick, *Black Detroit and the Rise of the UAW* (New York: Oxford University Press, 1979), 215–22.

[13]Jervis Anderson, *A. Philip Randolph: A Biographical Portrait* (New York: Harcourt Brace Jovanovitch, 1972); Dick Bruner, "The Negro Bids for Union Power," *Nation*, 8 March 1960, 209–11; A. Philip Randolph, "Why Negro and White Labor Chiefs Have Not Always Seen Eye to Eye," *Pittsburgh Courier*, 14 May 1960, 12; A. H. Raskin, "A.F.L.-C.I.O. Faces 'Jim Crow' Fight," *New York Times*, 20 September 1959, 1; Stanley Levey, "A.F.L.-C.I.O. Chiefs Score Randolph," *New York Times*, 13 October 1961, 1; A. Philip Randolph, "For an Economic and Political Revolution Against Racism," *New America*, 24 September 1963, 5. Note that Randolph, like others in the SP, was an implacable anticommunist; see, e.g., A. Philip Randolph, "The Menace of Communism," *American Federationist*, March 1949, 19–20. On Rustin's aims to bring blacks and labor together in the Democratic Party, see Bayard Rustin, "From Protest to Politics: The Future of the Civil Rights Movement," *Commentary*, February 1965, 25–31; updated in Bayard Rustin, "The Blacks and the Unions," *Harper's*, May 1971, 73–81. For a rejoinder from the New Left, see Julius Jacobson, "Coalitionism: From Protest to Politicking," *New Politics*, Fall 1966, 47–65.

Bolling, the bill's whip in the House, said afterward, labor "had the muscle; the other civil rights groups did not."[14]

At the same time, civil rights built on the New Deal legacy of procedural legitimacy through administration and law, not its legacy of politicizing the job site. Title VII layered on individual-level protections against discrimination, but without shoring up the older system of labor-market governance through collective bargaining, or reconfiguring power in the workplace. A labor movement stronger, more attuned to workers' individual rights than unions' own institutional prerogatives, and more sensitive to the intersections across class, race, and maybe even gender might have molded a very different set of labor market institutions from anything on offer in the 1960s, and offered more compelling collective solutions for the subsequent era of stagnating wages and rising inequality.[15]

In 1965, Lyndon Johnson delayed a bill that would have repealed Section 14(b) of the Taft-Hartley Act, the provision allowing state right-to-work laws, until he had passed Medicare and the Voting Rights Act. Everett Dirksen, the minority leader and a protégé of Robert Taft's, proposed a constitutional amendment allowing states to retain a malapportioned legislative branch, and also led the filibuster on 14(b). Labor led the coalition (nominally

[14]Goulden, *Meany*, 322; Joseph L. Rauh, Jr., "The Role of the Leadership Conference on Civil Rights in the Civil Rights Struggle of 1963–64," in *The Civil Rights Act of 1964: The Passage of the Law That Ended Racial Segregation*, ed. Robert Loevy (Albany: State University of New York Press, 1997), 49–75, originally written in 1964. For the legal issues, see William B. Gould, "Employment Security, Seniority, and Race: The Role of Title VII of the Civil Rights Act of 1964," *Howard Law Journal* 13 (1967): 1–50. On the integration of southern unions, see Alan Draper, *Conflicts of Interest: Organized Labor and the Civil Rights Movement in the South, 1954–1968* (Ithaca, N.Y.: ILR Press, 1994), 62–74.

[15]Katherine Van Wezel Stone, "The Legacy of Industrial Pluralism: The Tension between Individual Employment Rights and the New Deal Collective Bargaining System," *University of Chicago Law Review* 59 (1992): 575–644; Michael J. Piore, "Can the American Labor Movement Survive Re-Gomperization?," in *Proceedings of the Thirty-Fifth Annual Meeting of the Industrial Relations Research Association* (Chicago: Industrial Relations Research Association, 1982), 30–39; Michael J. Piore and Sean Safford, "Changing Regimes of Workplace Governance, Shifting Axes of Social Mobilization, and the Challenge to Industrial Relations Theory," *Industrial Relations* 45 (2006): 299–325; Nancy MacLean, *Freedom Is Not Enough: The Opening of the American Workplace* (New York: Russell Sage Foundation, 2006); William E. Forbath, "Civil Rights and Economic Citizenship: Notes on the Past and Future of the Civil Rights and Labor Movements," *University of Pennsylvania Journal of Labor & Employment Law* 2 (2000): 697–718. For such an alternative legal strategy, see the still-bracing Pauli Murray, "The Right to Equal Opportunity in Employment," *California Law Review* 33 (1945): 388–433. Long after the window for any move like it had closed, a few contemporary liberals called for adding protection of the right to organize under Title VII. See Richard Kahlenberg and Moshe Marvit, *Why Labor Organizing Should Be a Civil Right: Rebuilding a Middle-Class Democracy by Enhancing Worker Voice* (New York: Century Foundation Press, 2012); and Ned Resnikoff, "Rep. Keith Ellison Wants to Make Union Organizing a Civil Right," *MSNBC*, 19 July 2014, http://www.msnbc.com/msnbc/keith-ellison-union-organizing-civil-right.

chaired by a civil liberties lobbyist) against the Dirksen amendment, and prevailed with seven votes to spare. Meany refused to allow the Dirksen amendment as a price for winning on right-to-work. "Well, as badly as I want 14(b) repealed," he told the AFL-CIO convention, "I do not want it repealed that badly."[16] It was a rare test of unmediated group priorities; neither Johnson nor the congressional leadership would have interfered had labor decided otherwise, nor would the marginal senators have rebelled against voting for a popular amendment. Meany rejected a logroll that would have severely weakened urban Democrats in state capitols, and chose the long-run interests of his partisan allies.

Although repeal of 14(b) had a comfortable majority behind it, barely half the chamber—far less than the two-thirds then required—voted to invoke cloture in October 1965. Six liberal Republicans voted to cut off debate; twenty-one Democrats, all but two from right-to-work states, to continue it. The lobbying effort, insiders argued, had been flawed. Nor, although it would have been a heavier lift by far, had the AFL-CIO signed on at the beginning of the session, to lower the filibuster threshold, as the NAACP and UAW favored.[17]

Even during the Great Society, fringe benefits negotiated at the bargaining table shaped labor's political strategy in alliance. Pecuniary interests and desire to support the domestic initiatives of the partisan ally went hand in hand. The design of Medicare sealed up a gash in the private welfare state. While health-and-welfare plans could insure working adults and their families, retirees faced hardships in paying medical bills, and a system of union-provided hospitals such as the UMW's made no sense in almost any other industry. Nelson Cruikshank, the director of social insurance activities, had worked on the AFL side since 1944. In 1947, he advocated "a genuine comprehensive health insurance program on the national level." By 1960, he merely predicted that "the principles of social insurance will be applied to the cost of medical care for older people."[18] The ILGWU, UAW, and USWA largely funded a Senior Citizens for Kennedy campaign focused around health insurance for the aged. The unions soon assumed responsibility alongside the

[16] *Proceedings of the 6th Constitutional Convention of the AFL-CIO* (Washington, D.C.: AFL-CIO, 1965), 26.

[17] "Why Labor Didn't Get All It Wanted from Congress," *U.S. News & World Report*, 25 October 1965, 93–98; Gilbert J. Gall, *The Politics of Right to Work: The Labor Federations as Special Interests, 1943–1979* (Westport, Conn.: Greenwood, 1988), 187–88; Archie Robinson, *George Meany and His Times: A Biography* (New York: Simon & Schuster, 1981), 245–46; Neil MacNeil, *Dirksen: Portrait of a Public Man* (New York: World, 1970), 264–67.

[18] Cf. Nelson H. Cruikshank, "Issues in Social Security," *American Federationist*, February 1947, 28; and Nelson H. Cruikshank, "The Social Security Challenge of the Next 25 Years," *American Federationist*, August 1960, 5.

DNC for the National Committee of Senior Citizens, the grassroots coalition that organized retirees to push for Medicare.[19]

Labor remained loyal to Lyndon Johnson until the end. Using twenty million dollars from the Agency for International Development, the Asian-American Free Labor Institute trained twenty-seven hundred Vietnamese labor officials and paid for offices in fifteen provinces. Virtually every union save the UAW muscled its delegates for Hubert Humphrey at the disastrous Chicago convention—and "after the shambles of the Democratic convention," Meany said later, "we were all Humphrey had."[20] Unions tamped down sentiment for George Wallace in their ranks; a massive "Wallace Desk" at the UAW decried his "Fascist implications," while a COPE pamphlet excoriated the backwardness of "George Wallace's Alabama." Nevertheless, the gap between white union members and nonmembers' Democratic vote share declined from twenty-one points in 1964 to thirteen points in 1968, and Humphrey narrowly lost a swath of industrial states—and the presidency.[21]

Walter Reuther, at the country's largest union, had grown steadily more disillusioned with Meany, but remained unwilling, for all his ties to the movement left, to break with the president on Vietnam. Soon after Johnson announced he would not seek another term, Reuther inched toward a more dovish position on Vietnam. The UAW disaffiliated from the AFL-CIO, which it would rejoin only in 1981 to build a united front against Reaganism. The now-established former CIO unions had no desire to edge closer to a new generation's rather different insurgencies, and they remained inside the federation. Reuther died two years later. The UAW more than any other union in the postwar period sought to build a majority by linking industrial workers with minorities and middle-class liberals. Yet as its lonely departure showed, for all its accomplishments the UAW proved less a bellwether than a social-democratic outlier. The old CIO center could not hold.[22]

[19] Martha Derthick, *Policymaking for Social Security* (Washington, D.C.: Brookings Institution, 1979), 115–23; Henry J. Pratt, *The Gray Lobby* (Chicago: University of Chicago Press, 1976), esp. chap. 6.

[20] Quoted in Haynes Johnson and Nick Kotz, "Politics and Labor's 'Machine,'" *Washington Post*, 12 April 1972, A8.

[21] David J. Sousa, "Organized Labor in the Electorate," *Political Research Quarterly* 46 (1993): 745; Lewis Chester, Godfrey Hodgson, and Bruce Page, *An American Melodrama: The Presidential Campaign of 1968* (New York: Viking, 1969), 708. Nixon won New Jersey, Ohio, Illinois, and Wisconsin by less than four points, with a margin less than half of Wallace's total vote. If Humphrey had swept them, he would have had an Electoral College majority; if he had won Ohio or Illinois and one other state, the election would have gone to the House.

[22] See A. H. Raskin, "Divided Labor: Reuther on His Own," *New York Times*, 19 May 1968, E4; Goulden, *Meany*, chap. 15; Nelson Lichtenstein, *The Most Dangerous Man in Detroit: Walter Reuther and the Fate of American Labor* (New York: Basic Books, 1995), chap. 19; Boyle, *UAW*, chaps. 9 and 10 and the theoretical treatment at 4–7.

Growth in the Public Sector

The greatest breakthroughs for labor in the postwar decades occurred in the public sector. Between 1959, when Wisconsin inaugurated state-level collective bargaining with public employees, and 1979, employees in thirty-three states and in the federal government gained the right to bargain collectively. After membership tripled from the mid-1960s through the mid-1970s, 37 percent of public-sector workers held union membership in 1979, a figure that has remained essentially flat in the decades since even as membership rates in the private sector have tumbled threefold.[23]

Since 1935, private-sector unionism has been, save state right-to-work provisions, an all-or-nothing affair governed by uniform federal law. In the public sector, however, labor relations (except for federal employees) remain almost entirely a matter of state law. Workers' rights to establish bargaining organizations, to negotiate over wages, benefits, and working conditions, and to force binding arbitration or to strike diverge widely across states and, in many states, across occupational categories: teachers, firefighters, police officers, civil servants.[24] The public employee unions form a far more heterogeneous lot even than the CIO unions that organized a generation before—or than their critics often allow.[25] They range from AFSCME, a powerhouse extremely close to the Democratic Party, to the National Education Association, which combines liberal politics with continued scruples against calling itself a union, to assorted conservative independent unions of public safety officers willing to buck progressive nostrums.

The public unions' ideological orientations and jurisdictional fault lines—between federal and state civil servants, between urban and rural letter carriers, and (roughly) between urban and suburban teachers—all emerged before the unions won the right to bargain collectively. Through the first half of the twentieth century, fledgling groups, some identifying as trade unions and some as professional associations, held limited rights to lobby elected officials and to consult with management. In the federal government, William Howard Taft reluctantly signed the Lloyd-La Follette Act of 1912, which guaranteed to federal workers (most of them in the post

[23] Richard B. Freeman, "Unionism Comes to the Public Sector," *Journal of Economic Literature* 24 (1986): 47; "Union Membership, Coverage, Density, and Employment among Public Sector Workers, 1973–2013," http://unionstats.gsu.edu/Public-Sector-Workers.htm.

[24] For a survey of state policies, see Richard C. Kearney and Marice M. Mareschal, *Labor Relations in the Public Sector*, 5th ed. (Boca Raton: CLC Press, 2014), chap. 3. For an overview, see B.V.H. Schneider, "Public-Sector Labor Legislation: An Evolutionary Analysis," in *Public Sector Bargaining*, 2nd ed., ed. Benjamin Aaron, Joyce M. Najita, and James L. Stern (Washington, D.C.: Bureau of National Affairs, 1988), 189–228.

[25] For a comprehensive critique, see Daniel DiSalvo, *Government Against Itself: Public Union Power and Its Consequences* (New York: Oxford University Press, 2015).

office) the right to join any organization that foreswore the right to strike, and to petition Congress—but not to bargain collectively.[26] Although contract-like arrangements appeared in agencies such as the Tennessee Valley Authority, the New Deal left that basic status quo untouched.

Earlier legacies crippled public unions during the New Deal years. The Boston Police Strike of 1919 raised the specter of Hobbesian disorder.[27] The union, newly chartered by the AFL, blundered its way into a strike—and the state, through the governor, Calvin Coolidge, seized its opening, crushing the union and banning its members from public service for life. Had the strike taken place in 1934, it might have catalyzed public support to shift state policy. As it was, like the Pullman strike in 1894, it came too early, and hardened opposition. The AFL revoked the charters it had granted to police unions only months before. Given blowback from a hostile state, the federation again concluded, it would organize only skilled craftsmen in the private sector.[28]

Franklin Roosevelt opposed collective bargaining for public employees. In a 1937 letter to Luther Steward, president of the National Federation of Federal Employees, he explained that "the very nature and purposes of Government make it impossible for administrative officials to represent fully or bind the employer. . . . The employer is the whole people, who speak by means of laws enacted by their representatives in Congress."[29] Roosevelt, never a great personal champion of trade unions, faced little pressure; the titans of American labor evinced little interest in his reply to an ineffectual group of white-collar federal employees. He expressed his personal views divorced from coalitional imperatives. If such a message had exposed Roosevelt to the wrath of the AFL or the CIO, he would hardly have sent it.[30]

As old-style machines and their patronage politics retreated, their departure heralded a new model for public employment that treated employees

[26] Harvey Walker, "Employee Organizations in the National Government Service: The Period Prior to the World War," *Public Personnel Studies* 10 (1940): 67–73; for context, see Stephen Skowronek, *Building a New American State* (Cambridge: Cambridge University Press, 1982), chap. 6.

[27] See Francis Russell, *A City in Terror: 1919, the Boston Police Strike* (New York: Viking, 1975); Joseph Slater, *Public Workers: Government Employee Unions, the Law, and the State, 1900–1962* (Ithaca, N.Y.: ILR Press, 2004), chap. 1.

[28] Even the liberal *New Republic* joined the chorus of fear; see "The Police Strike," *New Republic*, 24 September 1919, 218. As small, ill-timed strikes of hardly militant public workers whose consequences conservative politicians exploited, the Boston Police and PATCO strikes parallel each other.

[29] Sterling D. Spero, *Government as Employer* (New York: Remsen Press, 1948), 346; see also Margaret C. Rung, *Servants of the State: Managing Diversity & Democracy in the Federal Workforce, 1933–1953* (Athens: University of Georgia Press, 2002).

[30] This logic follows David Karol and Chloe Thurston, "Exploring Party Position Change at the State Level: Abortion, Partisanship and Religion in the California State Assembly, 1967–2000" (paper, Midwest Political Science Association meeting, Chicago, 3–6 April 2014).

as something other than the bosses' human spoils—but that new model depended on the regime's dominant political coalitions.[31] The left alternative had closed. The CIO expelled the United Public Workers of America, a small, left-led union, in 1949 and the UPWA formally dissolved in 1953.[32] As Joseph McCartin suggests, the purge gave elected officials space to open bargaining, since public workers had shown themselves loyal against communism.[33] Paradoxically, if the UPWA had had greater success in organizing public workers, then Taft-Hartley, which already banned communists from public service, might well have imposed more draconian restrictions that would have doomed any future upsurge in public unionism at either the federal or state level.

The Hatch Acts of 1939 and 1940 show the conservative alternative, insulating public employees from electoral politics rather than empowering them to participate. After scandals at the Works Progress Administration, the conservative coalition united with rural progressives to stop New Deal agencies from mobilizing their workers. The Hatch Acts forbade federal employees, along with state and local employees with salaries paid by federal grants, from taking "any active part in political management or in political campaigns."[34] They had little effect on the most politically potent public-sector unions, whose members' salaries come from state and local coffers: AFSCME, teachers unions, and uniformed services. Under different conditions, the ideology and coalition behind the Hatch Acts might have continued into the postwar regime. In the 1960s, by contrast, the alternatives to bossism looked to pluralist liberalism.

The first major victories for collective bargaining took place in the 1950s. In Philadelphia under Joe Clark and Richardson Dilworth, in New York City under Robert Wagner, son of the crusading senator, and, for the first

[31]Thus, Martin R. West's incisive account, refracting partisan considerations through the lens of public-choice theory, to my mind pays too little heed to coalitional alternatives across time. See his "Bargaining with Authority: The Political Origins of Public-Sector Collective Bargaining" (paper, Policy History Conference, St. Louis, 29 May–1 June 2008).

[32]See Rhonda Hanson, "United Public Workers: A Real Union Organizes" and "United Public Workers: The Conscience of the Capitol" in *The Cold War Against Labor*, vol. 1, ed. Ann Fagan Ginger and David Christiano (Berkeley, Calif.: Meiklejohn Civil Liberties Institute, 1987), 172–86 and 389–98, respectively.

[33]Joseph A. McCartin, "Bringing the State's Workers In: Time to Rectify an Imbalanced US Labor Historiography," *Labor History* 47 (2006): 77.

[34]*Report of the Special Committee to Investigate Senatorial Campaign Expenditures and Use of Governmental Funds in 1938* (Washington, D.C.: Government Printing Office, 1939); David L. Porter, *Congress and the Waning of the New Deal* (Port Washington, N.Y.: Kennikat Press, 1980), chap. 6. Although Benjamin Cohen and Thomas Corcoran recommended a veto, with an alternative proposal to ban private funding of political parties and completely replace it with public appropriations, Roosevelt ultimately signed the bill. See Sidney M. Milkis, *The President and the Parties: The Transformation of the American Party System since the New Deal* (New York: Oxford University Press, 1993), 137–40. Since the 1970s, a series of relatively uncontroversial reforms have reduced the Hatch Acts to a shell.

time at the state level, in 1959 in Wisconsin under Gaylord Nelson, public employees gained the right to bargain—although not to strike.[35] While the nuts-and-bolts treatments of bargaining units and union security differed, collective bargaining rights in each case emerged directly from party-group alliance. Programmatic liberals sympathized with ideological claims that all workers deserved representation. Courts had retreated from old arguments, accepting both the associational freedom of public employees, and the compatibility of legislative sovereignty with negotiated arrangements around the bargaining table.[36] At the same time, elected officials sought new bases of coalitional support to strengthen their tenuous holds on power as machines retreated.[37]

More than responses to movement building from without, along the lines of the CIO a generation earlier, the initial grants of bargaining rights resemble Republican alliances more than Democratic ones, with leaders looking outward to strengthen ties with supporters. It was a transitional moment in American politics. Traditional organizations had receded in many areas, but the group-based advocacy explosion had not yet transformed the Democratic Party.

The Kennedy administration, fulfilling a promise to postal workers the president had made on the campaign trail, in January 1962 promulgated Executive Order 10988, giving the vast majority of civilian federal employees the rights "to form, join and assist any employee organization or to refrain from such activity." Order 10988 emerged as a substitute for an ill-formulated bill in Congress that met the ire of senior officials in the civil service. The bill had little chance of passage, but a version might well have succeeded as veto points receded in the coming years.[38]

Bargaining for public employees that had begun as a response to liberal politicians' dilemmas soon spread quickly as federalism served as opportunity point more than veto point. Republicans who had learned to bargain with unions in the private sector saw few difficulties in extending

[35] Slater, *Public Workers,* chap. 6; Ida Klaus, "Labor Relations in the Public Service: Exploration and Experiment," *Syracuse Law Review* 10 (1959): 183–202.

[36] See Joseph E. Slater, "The Court Does Not Know 'What a Labor Union Is': How State Structures and Judicial (Mis)constructions Deformed Public Sector Labor Law," *Oregon Law Review* 79 (2000): 981–1032.

[37] Wagner had not yet broken with Tammany at the time he established collective bargaining, but support from public employee unions allowed him to win the 1961 primary despite opposition from all five county Democratic organizations. See Martin Shefter, *Political Crisis/Fiscal Crisis: The Collapse and Revival of New York City* (New York: Basic Books, 1985), 74.

[38] Martin Halpern, *Unions, Radicals, and Democratic Presidents: Seeking Social Change in the Twentieth Century* (Westport, Conn.: Greenwood, 2003), chap. 5; Irving Bernstein, *Promises Kept: John F. Kennedy's New Frontier* (New York: Oxford University Press, 1991), 211–17. A provision in the Civil Service Reform Act of 1978, notably uncontroversial for its inclusion just months after the failure of private-sector labor law reform, set the right to organize in statute.

organization into public work; in 1968, Ronald Reagan signed a collective bargaining law for local employees in California. As a 1966 report to Nelson Rockefeller of New York from five experts in labor relations explained, "The right to sovereignty is scarcely an apt term to apply to a system of representative democratic government, such as our own, which is responsive to the electorate. It is more realistic to inquire as to the manner in which public employees can participate in establishing their employment terms within the framework of our political democracy. . . . It is elementary justice to assure public employees, who are estopped from using the strike, that they have the right to negotiate collectively."[39]

In turn, the cautious professionals who had led public-sector employee organizations soon found themselves replaced by more aggressive leaders, often supported by blue-collar and nonwhite members who wanted a larger piece of the pie. In the largest wildcat strike in American history, postal workers struck in the spring of 1970. The resultant settlement created an independent Postal Service, and offered immediate wage hikes to workers, amnesty to all strikers, and mandatory arbitration.[40] The same years saw the rise of teacher unionism. The National Education Association began to sign contracts with school districts and edge close to the Democrats in national politics, even as it stayed out of the AFL-CIO, while the pugnacious, hawkish Albert Shanker leveraged his power base in New York to dominate the smaller American Federation of Teachers.[41]

AFSCME grew to become the most important union in party-group alliance, as the Mine Workers and the Auto Workers had been before them, and a faithful friend to the Democratic Party. AFSCME was founded as a small AFL union of civil servants and grew rapidly after Jerry Wurf, a voluble New Yorker, deposed his mentor, Arnold Zander, as the union's president

[39] "Governor's Committee on Public Employee Relations: Final Report," 31 March 1966, 15 and 20.

[40] Aaron Brenner, "Striking Against the State: The Postal Wildcat of 1970," *Labor's Heritage*, Spring 1996, 4–27; Murray B. Nesbitt, *Labor Relations in the Federal Government Service* (Washington, D.C.: Bureau of National Affairs, 1976), chap. 17. On the differences between PATCO—a strike by a small union with clear leadership and an identifiable target—and a massive wildcat, see John Walsh and Garth Magnum, *Labor Struggle in the Post Office: From Selective Lobbying to Collective Bargaining* (Armonk, N.Y.: M.E. Sharpe, 1992), 176–79.

[41] Marjorie Murphy, *Blackboard Unions: The AFT and the NEA, 1900–1980* (Ithaca, N.Y.: Cornell University Press, 1990); for contrasting portraits of the AFT, David Selden, *The Teacher Rebellion* (Washington, D.C.: Howard University Press, 1985); and Richard D. Kahlenberg, *Tough Liberal: Albert Shanker and the Battles over Schools, Unions, Race, and Democracy* (New York: Columbia University Press, 2011); critically, Terry M. Moe, *Special Interest: Teachers Unions and America's Public Schools* (Washington, D.C.: Brookings Institution Press, 2011); and, for a general introduction, Jane Hannaway and Andrew J. Rotherham, eds., *Collective Bargaining in Education: Negotiating Change in Today's Schools* (Cambridge, Mass.: Harvard Education Press, 2006).

in 1964. After the UAW left the AFL-CIO in 1968, Wurf, who stayed inside to leverage allies as often as he could, played the role of chief internal dissident to Meany.

More than any other union, AFSCME copied the militant tactics of the civil rights movement. "I AM a Man," proclaimed sanitation workers, almost all black, who struck for recognition in Memphis in the spring of 1968. Martin Luther King, Jr., was killed in Memphis; the city finally settled only after Lyndon Johnson directed mediation. "This wasn't a usual labor-management scrap," Wurf later recalled. "It was a freedom struggle, and we had to call on the national black leadership for help."[42] Wurf made AFSCME into a political union whose priorities meshed with those of the Democratic Party's emergent liberalism, based more around funding and delivering government programs than on reshaping the political economy.[43] AFSCME has long operated the largest PAC among unions. Wurf's successor, Gerald McEntee, a canny Philadelphian, moved still closer into the Democratic orbit as a presidential kingmaker.

Alliance in Turmoil

Party-group alliance has followed its own trajectory autonomous from economic change. Three shifts in the late 1960s, all centered around the executive branch, ruptured the union-Democratic partnership: a weakened role for labor in the postreform nominating process, divides over foreign policy in the wake of Vietnam, and new issues on the policy agenda.[44] Yet all three divides ultimately healed.

Internal changes in the Democratic Party weakened unions' voice. The late 1960s and 1970s saw steep declines in traditional party organizations at the local level, with which Central Labor Councils had long coordinated electoral activities.[45] As Chapter 5 shows, the post-1968 rules established by the McGovern-Fraser Commission defined party politics in terms of

[42]Quoted in Fred C. Shapiro, "How Jerry Wurf Walks on Water," *New York Times Magazine*, 11 April 1976, 59–60. See also Michael K. Honey, *Going Down Jericho Road: The Memphis Strike, Martin Luther King's Last Campaign* (New York: Norton, 2007); and Larry Isaac and Lars Christiansen, "How the Civil Rights Movement Revitalized Labor Militancy," *American Sociological Review* 67 (2002): 722–46.

[43]See Jerry Wurf, "The Revolt of the Public Worker," *Progressive*, December 1970, 31–34; "Public Workers' Powerhouse," *Time*, 21 May 1973, 94; "'Once They Join This Damn Union, We Protect Their Rights,'" *Civil Liberties Review*, Summer 1975, 105–24; Marick F. Masters, "AFSCME as a Political Union," *Journal of Labor Research* 19 (1998): 313–49.

[44]I have taken the list from Andrew Battista, *The Revival of Labor Liberalism* (Urbana: University of Illinois Press, 2008), 22.

[45]David R. Mayhew, *Placing Parties in American Politics* (Princeton: Princeton University Press, 1986).

individual conscience rather than collective accommodation, and group interest in terms of demographics rather than organization. These changes enabled reformers to dominate outsider-led primaries and caucuses, and ensured full representation at conventions on the basis of race, gender, and, initially, age—but, crucially, not economic class.

This new understanding of representation left no place for brokers like George Meany or Alexander Barkan, the acerbic political director at COPE, or for their style of politics. Labor has understood representation in collective rather than individual terms. Union elections have always used the bloc vote (casting an entire delegation's vote for the majority preference), typically without a poll beforehand to inform union presidents' choices. Yet the Meany-Barkan forces never formulated a serious response grounded in bargaining, mutually sustaining relationships, and accommodation of interests.[46]

In 1972, for the first and only time since the merger, the AFL-CIO refused to endorse in a presidential election.[47] Richard Nixon had deliberately

[46] See, e.g., "Labor Boycotting McGovern Reforms," *Washington Post*, 21 September 1969, 1. When asked in the spring of 1975 whom he wished to see elected as president the following year, Meany replied "Harry Truman." "Washington Wire," *Wall Street Journal*, 23 May 1975, 1.

[47] In another development that year, followers of the dissident Trotskyite, Max Shachtman, who also refused to support McGovern, won control of the Socialist Party USA, renamed it Social Democrats USA (SDUSA), and placed themselves as the programmatic vanguard for AFL-CIO traditionalism and implacable anticommunism. Some Shachtmanites ultimately joined their neoconservative brethren in the Republican Party. Others clung to an older vision, in which the labor movement and Democratic Party together spoke for the broad, patriotic working class. The other leading socialist faction, led by Michael Harrington and ultimately known as the Democratic Socialists of America (DSA), had a different vision: to make labor *primus inter pares* as an anchoring group in the left-oriented movement constellation sustaining the Democratic Party. For all their harrumphing about a mass base, SDUSA and the DSA had memberships barely in the thousands. All the same, members of the two groups dominated most union political shops, and the major ideological players for decades can be counted in the sponsorships for their respective dinners. John Sweeney's housecleaning of the AFL-CIO headquarters put DSA folks in what were once SDUSA offices. See Battista, *Revival of Labor Liberalism*, 74–79; Michael Harrington, "A Call to American Socialists," *Nation*, 13 November 1972, 454–55; James Ring Adams, "Battle Royal among the Socialists," *Wall Street Journal*, 8 December 1972, 12; *The American Challenge: A Social Democratic Program for the Seventies* (New York: Social Democrats USA and Young People's Socialist League, 1973); for a list of SDUSA-linked unions, the sponsors in "Trade Union Greetings to *New America*," *New America*, August 1975, 11; "Kirkland Commends the S.D. for Defending Freedom," *New America*, August 1981, 3; Justin Vaïsse, *Neoconservatism, The Biography of a Movement*, trans. Arthur Goldhammer (Cambridge, Mass.: Harvard University Press, 2010), esp. chap. 3; Seymour Martin Lipset, "Neoconservatism: Myth and Reality," *Society* 25 (1988): 29–37; Michael Massing, "Trotsky's Orphans," *New Republic*, 22 June 1987, 18–22; Michael Harrington, *The Long-Distance Runner: An Autobiography* (New York: Henry Holt, 1988); Maurice Isserman, *The Other American: The Life of Michael Harrington* (New York: Public Affairs, 2000), chaps. 10 and 11.

played up labor's divisions, cultivating the building trades and praising their patriotism as bulwarks of the Silent Majority.[48] Meany, who had favored Henry M. "Scoop" Jackson of Washington at the convention, cited as a proximate cause George McGovern's vote in 1965 against invoking cloture on 14(b).[49] In the spring of 1971, however, Meany had indicated his sympathy with all the leading candidates save John Lindsay, the mayor of New York. Rather, as Jerry Wurf, McGovern's closest labor ally, assayed, "The real concern was participation and access."[50]

Meany despised *how* McGovern had won: through direct appeals in primaries. The South Dakotan had gone outside the traditional delegate brokers, and owed other constituencies, including even the UAW—but not the AFL-CIO. In 1968, COPE had worked alongside state and local parties to deploy Humphrey's field operation, and had even negotiated for his half-hour television infomercials. The youthful McGovern campaign would have none of that back-and-forth. As Meany told the Iron Workers, "these people running the show repeatedly indicated their contempt, and I mean contempt, for the trade union movement and the people we represent."[51]

Moreover, new cleavages placed aging labor leaders (Meany was born in 1894) apart from the New Politics. "We listened to the gay lib people—you know, the ones who want to legalize marriages between boys and boys and legalize marriages between girls and girls," Meany reported after the convention. "We heard from the abortionists, and we heard from the people

[48]Jefferson Cowie, "Nixon's Class Struggle," *Labor History* 43 (2002): 257–83; William Gould, "Moving the Hard-Hats In," *Nation*, 8 January 1973, 41–43.

[49]While the AFL-CIO rightly regarded the vote as critical—and had also used it to torpedo Arizona liberal Morris Udall's campaign for House majority leader in 1971—McGovern represented a right-to-work state (as did Udall). He had amassed a far better voting record on labor issues than had Lyndon Johnson, backing COPE on sixty-three of seventy-two key votes. The UAW's chief lobbyist claimed that McGovern would have supported repeal of 14(b) if his vote had been the decisive one. See Anthony Champagne, Douglas B. Harris, James W. Riddlesperger, Jr., and Garrison Nelson, *The Austin/Boston Connection: Five Decades of House Democratic Leadership, 1937–1989* (College Station: Texas A&M Press, 2009), 142 and 169; Frank Wallick, "What's McGovern REALLY Like?," *UAW Solidarity*, September 1972, 2.

[50]Jerry Wurf, "What Labor Has Against McGovern," *New Republic*, 5 August 1972, 21–23; Paul Wieck, "Some COPE, Some Don't," *New Republic*, 30 June 1973, 10–12. McGovern received endorsements principally from unions that opposed the Vietnam War, although the ILGWU and Communications Workers of America backed him despite their hawkish policies. See Peter B. Levy, *The New Left and Labor in the 1960s* (Urbana: University of Illinois Press, 1994), 253. A short-lived group called Labor for Peace even brought together the old CIO center (UAW, ACWA) and left (UE, ILWU) along with AFSCME in opposition to the war. See Steve Murdock, "The Unions Find Consensus," *Nation*, 10 July 1972, 11–14.

[51]Stephen C. Schlesinger, *The New Reformers: Forces for Change in American Politics* (Boston: Houghton Mifflin, 1975), chap. 4; Bruce Miroff, *The Liberals' Moment: The McGovern Insurgency and the Identity Crisis of the Democratic Party* (Lawrence: University Press of Kansas, 2007), 189.

who look like Jacks, acted like Jills, and had the odor of johns about them."[52] Al Barkan dismissed the "Harvard-Berkeley Camelots," and bemoaned that "this great party of mine this year of 1972 seems to be taken over by a lot of kooks and nuts."[53]

Divisions on foreign policy placed the AFL-CIO leadership far to the right of a Democratic Party increasingly skittish about the use of force aboard, and sensitive about human rights abuses committed by American-backed regimes. The federation followed what it termed "free trade unionism," an undiluted AF of L voluntarism for the Cold War age. Its internal opponents—most loudly in the UAW—found it a fig leaf for sometimes unsavory American interests. The concept had three major components. Unions must be independent of the government, "they must not be subordinated to any political party," and they must hold rights to organize themselves and to strike.[54] These distinctions, often in the eye of the beholder, drew a *cordon sanitaire* against unions deemed too close to communist parties. Especially in Latin America, they favored relatively privileged workers organized in state-sanctioned trade unions.

Foreign policy gave the AFL-CIO a distinctive mission beyond the scope of the constituent international unions to justify its organizational resources and to build its prestige. Meany, "a leader of labor leaders,"[55] understood his clients to be the union presidents whose bloc votes kept him in office. The internationals could largely run their affairs as they pleased. In the less dense space of foreign policy, the leadership could exercise its own unconstrained prerogatives, and exercise its claims to legitimacy. Insistence on free trade unionism abroad cemented labor as an independent actor vital to any society that valued liberty.

The powerful AFL-CIO International Department operated almost entirely autonomously. It reported directly to the presidency, outside the Executive Council, and its budget never appeared in the federation's consolidated accounts. The swashbuckling Jay Lovestone, a Lithuanian-born ex-communist who swung hard right, led the department from 1945 onward de facto, and from 1963 to 1974 de jure. At his memorial service, a

[52]Maurice Isserman attributes the line to the closeted Shachtmanite, Tom Kahn. Kahn's friend and ally, Rachelle Horowitz, points to Al Barkan. See Isserman, *Other American*, 298; and Rachelle Horowitz, "Tom Kahn and the Fight for Democracy: A Political Portrait and Personal Recollection," *Democratiya* 11 (2007): 250.

[53]Theodore H. White, *The Making of the President 1972* (New York: Atheneum, 1973), 38; Gordon Gottlieb, "Barkan Assails Changed Party," *Milwaukee Sentinel*, 3 August 1972, 16.

[54]Michael Kerper, *The International Ideology of U.S. Labor* (Gothenburg: University of Gothenburg Research Section, 1976), 42.

[55]The line, from Theodore Kheel, a labor mediator, appears in Nick Kotz, "Can Labor's Tired Leaders Deal with a Troubled Movement?," *New York Times Magazine*, 4 September 1977, 9.

mourner wrote, "There were more CIA men than there were labor men." The defenders of voluntarism abroad, who sought to export a philosophy of trade unionism independent of an overweening state, became themselves dependent on the state to spread that very message. By 1985, the department's forty-one-million-dollar budget, almost all from government grants, accounted for half of AFL-CIO spending. In Poland and Nicaragua, where communists oppressed free trade unions, the federation criticized the Reagan administration from the right.[56]

Business Mobilization and Labor Retreat

A policy time capsule has opened. Labor's opponents in business and the conservative movement mobilized, and the Republican Party exploited old weaknesses, to the detriment of labor-liberalism. Republicans have become, to use Samuel Lubell's phrase, the "sun party" without changing—indeed, while reinforcing—the basic axis of partisan cleavage.[57] Theories of policy development over time say rather little about the recurrence of older debates amid changed circumstances.[58] To complement ideas of critical junctures with increased lock-in costs, institutional layering, and multiple streams of change, the time capsule serves as useful metaphor: something preserved within a system, and ready to emerge from hibernation should circumstance allow. Yet when the time capsule opens, everyone sees it with fresh eyes.

Weaknesses in the New Deal labor settlement lay dormant for decades. Beginning with the celebrated memo from Lewis Powell—then a Richmond attorney; soon to become an associate justice of the Supreme Court—to the U.S. Chamber of Commerce in 1971, business, like conservative evangelicals,

[56] Ted Morgan, *Jay Lovestone: A Covert Life* (New York: Random House, 1999), 369; Harry Bernstein, "AFL-CIO Unit Accused of Snooping Abroad," *Los Angeles Times*, 22 May 1966, G20; Victor G. Reuther, *The Brothers Reuther and the Story of the UAW* (Boston: Houghton Mifflin, 1976), esp. 183–88 and 419–24; Irving Brown, *Labor in International Affairs* (Washington, D.C.: Institute for the Study of Diplomacy, Georgetown University, 1984); Massing, "Trotsky's Orphans"; Aaron Bernstein, "Is Big Labor Playing Global Vigilante?," *Business Week*, 4 November 1985, 92–96; Daniel Cantor and Juliet Schor, *Tunnel Vision: Labor, the World Economy, and Central America* (Boston: South End, 1989), 45. For an intellectual history, see Nicolas Guilhot, *The Democracy Makers: Human Rights and International Order* (New York: Columbia University Press, 2005), esp. chap. 2.

[57] See Samuel Lubell, *The Future of American Politics*, 2nd ed. (Garden City, N.Y.: Doubleday, 1956), 212.

[58] See Paul Pierson, *Politics in Time: History, Institutions, and Political Analysis* (Princeton: Princeton University Press, 2005); Karen Orren and Stephen Skowronek, *The Search for American Political Development* (Cambridge: Cambridge University Press, 2004); and John W. Kingdon, *Agendas, Alternatives, and Public Policies*, 2nd ed. (New York: Longman, 2003).

mounted a "defensive offensive," vying to regain influence against labor and environmental and consumer groups. To UAW president Doug Fraser, it was, as he wrote in a prescient 1978 letter, "one-sided class war."[59] This mobilization was a kind of spearhead for shifts reorienting the U.S. economy toward the logic of the market and tolerance of inequality. They weakened the New Deal order's reinforcing linkages across economics, politics, and society.[60] Deunionization lay at the very heart of these processes. It accounts, estimates say, for about a quarter of the increase in wage inequality from 1973 to 2007.[61]

More generally, a friendlier configuration of partisanship and power might have pushed back harder against the slow growth and concentration of wealth at the top that redefined the political economy. A stronger labor movement might well have meant a different Democratic Party, less beholden to corporate interests and more willing to push back against forces that have stalled economic progress for the party's core constituents. The rapprochement between party and movement would have interacted not with labor decline but with a movement strong enough to influence the polity and perhaps even the political regime.[62] Such a counterfactual, however, diverges in important ways from the business mobilization and labor weakness manifest starting in the 1970s.

In 1978, labor law reform fell two votes short in the Senate. The bill would have expedited contested representation elections (without card-check), promulgated nationwide rules defining bargaining units, substantially increased fines on "rogue" employers, and allowed unions access to employees to deliver their messages. The Carter administration used its political capital on the Panama Canal Treaties, and never attempted the full-court press to persuade southern Democratic friends. In opposition, the

[59]The Powell memo, "Attack on American Free Enterprise System," can be found at http://law.wlu.edu/deptimages/Powell%20Archives/PowellMemorandumTypescript.pdf. For context, see Kim Phillips-Fein, *Invisible Hands: The Making of the Conservative Movement from the New Deal to Reagan* (New York: Norton, 2009), chap. 7. Text of Fraser's letter in Jefferson Cowie, "'A One-Sided Class War': Rethinking Doug Fraser's 1978 Resignation from the Labor-Management Group," *Labor History* 44 (2003): 307–14. See also David S. Broder, "UAW's Strategy: Discipline for Democrats," *Washington Post*, 15 October 1978, C7.

[60]See Frank Levy and Peter Temin, "Inequality and Institutions in 20th Century America," in *Economic Evolution and Revolution in Historical Time*, ed. Paul Rhode, Joshua Rosenbloom, and David Weiman (Palo Alto: Stanford University Press, 2011), 357–86. Cf. Jacob S. Hacker and Paul Pierson, *Winner-Take-All Politics: How Washington Made the Rich Richer and Turned Its Back on the Middle Class* (New York: Simon & Schuster, 2010).

[61]Bruce Western and Jake Rosenfeld, "Unions, Norms, and the Rise of U.S. Wage Inequality," *American Sociological Review* 76 (2011): 513–37.

[62]See especially Thomas Byrne Edsall, *The New Politics of Inequality* (New York: Norton, 1985); and Larry M. Bartels, *Unequal Democracy: The Political Economy of the New Gilded Age* (New York: Russell Sage Foundation, 2008).

U.S. Chamber of Commerce, the new Business Roundtable, the National Federation of Independent Business, and Reed Larson's New Right–linked National Right to Work Committee all joined forces, flying planeloads to Washington to mobilize against the bill. Richard Lugar and Orrin Hatch, then young conservative *enfants terribles*, mounted an effective floor attack. As the labor journalist A. H. Raskin wrote presciently, "that single crucial battle marked the end of a thirty-year entente cordiale."[63]

Nevertheless, in the relatively freewheeling Senate of the 1970s, the vote reflected regional political economies as well as party. In contrast to business unity on what it deemed core class interest, neither party entirely coalesced around the electoral consequences that flowed from the balance between labor and capital. Unlike the vote over Taft-Hartley thirty-one years before or the Employee Free Choice Act thirty-one years after, cross-pressured legislators saw fewer consequences in labor-market institutions flowing back to change political power. On the critical fourth cloture attempt, fourteen Republicans voted to end the filibuster, all but two from liberal states in the Northeast or Pacific Northwest. Seventeen Democrats voted nay, all but two from the old Confederacy, while only one southern Democrat (James Sasser of Tennessee) supported cloture.[64] By 2015, all but

[63] A. H. Raskin, "Big Labor Strives to Break Out of Its Rut," *Fortune*, 27 August 1979, 33; Sar A. Levitan and Martha R. Cooper, *Business Lobbies: The Public Good and the Bottom Line* (Baltimore: Johns Hopkins University Press, 1984), chap. 7; James A. Gross, *Broken Promise: The Subversion of U.S. Labor Relations Policy, 1947–1994* (Philadelphia: Temple University Press, 1995), chap. 12; Robert W. Merry and Albert R. Hunt, "Business Lobby Gains More Power as It Rides Antigovernment Tide," *Wall Street Journal*, 17 May 1978, 1; Juan Cameron, "Small Business Trips Big Labor," *Fortune*, 31 July 1978, 80–82; James W. Singer, "There's Little Joy in Laborville," *National Journal*, 26 August 1978; Peter G. Bruce, "Political Parties and the Evolution of Labor Law in Canada and the United States" (PhD diss., Massachusetts Institute of Technology, 1988), 174; Thomas Ferguson and Joel Rogers, "Labor Law Reform and Its Enemies," *Nation*, 6 January 1979, 1, 17–20; *National Right to Work Newsletter* 20 January 1978, 22 May 1978, 24 July 1978.

[64] 124 *Congressional Record* 17568, 14 June 1978. John Sparkman of Alabama "was widely considered ready" to be the sixtieth vote if the leadership could find a fifty-ninth. See Harrison R. Donnelly, "Cloture Backers Still Two Votes Shy of Goal," *CQ Weekly Report*, 17 June 1978, 1521. The likeliest suspect was Dale Bumpers of Arkansas, but he ultimately voted against cloture to protect himself against a challenge from the right in 1980. Two days before the key vote, in the Democratic runoff for the state's other seat, David Pryor, the governor and a moderate who had tacked right on labor issues, won 55 percent against Jim Guy Tucker, a liberal representative who had supported labor-law reform—after a near tie in the primary two weeks prior. Bill Clinton, cruising to his first gubernatorial election victory, shared an interest in defeating Tucker, whom he "viewed as his main competition as the rising star of state Democratic politics." Clinton introduced Pryor to his consultant, Dick Morris, and regularly consulted on the campaign Morris devised, which harshly attacked Tucker as the pawn of unions. In a 1981 interview, Stuart Eizenstat, Carter's domestic policy adviser, said that Pryor's win "may have cost unions passage of labor law reform." See Steven Lee Lapidus, "Politics, Lobbying and the Labor Reform Act of 1977–78" (BS thesis, Cornell University,

four of the seats whose senators voted across against their party's majority had changed hands.

Just as the failure of labor-law reform heralded a shift from plateau to decline for unions in the private sector, so, too, the 1970s shifted public-sector unionization from growth to plateau, as supporters grew ambivalent and opponents emboldened. Attempts to enact a federal statute guaranteeing all public employees the right to bargain collectively never even emerged from committee.[65] The fiscal crises that hit once growth sputtered and inflation ticked up forced confrontations between elected officials and unions. In New York, Seattle, San Francisco, and Atlanta, moderate Democratic mayors elected with the support of public employee unions confronted them over wages. As Maynard Jackson, the first black mayor of Atlanta, who broke the strike of AFSCME-affiliated garbage workers by hiring permanent replacements, asked in 1977, "Is it liberal to make a predominantly black city financially unsound?"[66]

Anger at legions of overpaid public employees protected by fat contracts fed into issue bundling on the right. California's antitax crusader Howard Jarvis in 1978 proclaimed that "we're not going to permit public employee unions to run this country."[67] So, too, the conservative legal movement seized on old doctrines of sovereignty to argue that public employee unions perverted the traditional functions of government.[68] The counterattacks in 2011 and beyond drew amply on the original backlash. In response, public employees have had to look upward for more money, to state capitols and, above all, to Washington. The politics of public employee unionism divided. Priorities at the national level grew largely congruent. As states

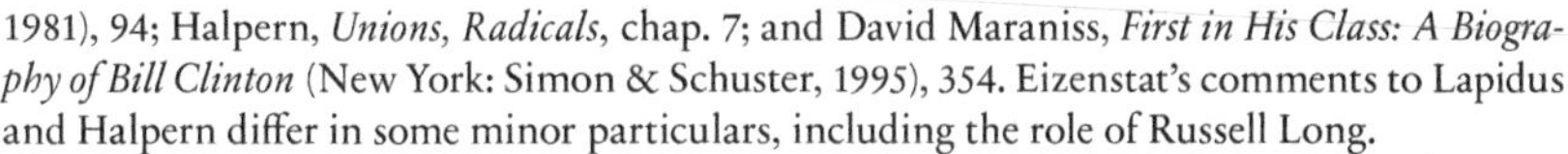

1981), 94; Halpern, *Unions, Radicals*, chap. 7; and David Maraniss, *First in His Class: A Biography of Bill Clinton* (New York: Simon & Schuster, 1995), 354. Eizenstat's comments to Lapidus and Halpern differ in some minor particulars, including the role of Russell Long.

[65]Joseph A. McCartin, "'A Wagner Act for Public Employees': Labor's Deferred Dream and the Rise of Conservatism, 1970–1976," *Journal of American History* 95 (2005): 123–48; James C. Hyatt, "Unions Are Stepping Up Efforts to Secure Bargaining Rights for Public Employees," *Wall Street Journal*, 6 August 1974; "Congressman Clay Tells Public Employee Groups to Unite on Federal Labor Law Hill Will Enact," *Government Employee Relations Report*, 14 April 1975, B12–B15.

[66]Tom Mathews, "Atlanta: The Strikebreaker," *Newsweek*, 25 April 1977, 29. See also Shefter, *Political Crisis*, 163–66; Joseph McCartin, "'Fire the Hell Out of Them': Sanitation Workers' Struggles and the Normalization of the Striker Replacement Strategy in the 1970s," *Labor* 2 (2005): 67–92; Marc Levinson, "Public Employees in Trouble," *Nation*, 10 September 1977, 208–10.

[67]McCartin, "Bringing the State's Workers In," 84.

[68]The locus classicus, from a member of the ultraconservative Mont Pelerin Society, is Sylvester Petro, "Sovereignty and Compulsory Public-Sector Bargaining," *Wake Forest Law Review* 25 (1974): 25–165; popularized, with a foreword from Jesse Helms, in Ralph de Toledano, *Let Our Cities Burn* (New Rochelle, N.Y.: Arlington House, 1975). Echoes reappear in DiSalvo, *Government Against Itself*.

and cities faced limited resources, however, confrontations between public workers and their employers have often divided Democrats and emboldened Republicans.

Labor policy, unlike the story for deregulation and financialization, reflected old divisions made salient, rather than a new consensus. If the defeat of labor law reform signaled stasis in existing laws, a second turning point marked their hollowing out. In August 1981, Ronald Reagan invoked Taft-Hartley to order striking controllers from PATCO (the Professional Air Traffic Controllers' Organization) back to work. When they refused, he fired all 11,345 strikers, banned them from federal service for life, and put replacement workers on the job. The particulars of the PATCO story hardly reflect deliberate confrontation. The union, badly led, blundered into the strike, and had even endorsed Reagan the prior year. Reagan, the former president of the Screen Actors' Guild, himself praised unions as "some of our freest institutions," and drew a bright line between strikes in the public and private sectors. When the replacement contractors voted in a new union in 1987, the Reagan administration signed a contract with it.[69]

Nevertheless, PATCO effectively ended public-sector militancy, and strongly signaled to employers in the private sector that they could replace strikers without serious consequences. Strike activity nosedived sixfold from 1984 to 2010—and work stoppages often now reflect workers' weakness, not their strength. In contrast to the postwar decades, strike rates no longer increase in boom times, nor do strikes raise workers' pay.[70] Above all, the decisive PATCO strike marked an end to unions' guarantee of legitimation, in public life and on the job site.

Reagan broke no new legal ground in the PATCO strike. Instead, the postwar labor regime ushered in by Taft-Hartley planted the seeds for employer mobilization against labor power.[71] The early labor board proscribed employer interference in representation elections for workers to "decide whether collective bargaining or individual bargaining will better advance

[69] Ronald Reagan, "Remarks in Chicago, Illinois, at the Annual Convention and Centennial Observance of the United Brotherhood of Carpenters and Joiners," 3 September 1981, http://www.presidency.ucsb.edu/ws/index.php?pid=44193; Joseph A. McCartin, *Collision Course: Ronald Reagan, the Air Traffic Controllers, and the Strike That Changed America* (Oxford: Oxford University Press, 2011); Richard B. Freeman and Eunice Han, "The War Against Public Sector Collective Bargaining in the US," *Journal of Industrial Relations* 54 (2012): 387.

[70] Jake Rosenfeld, *What Unions No Longer Do* (Cambridge, Mass.: Harvard University Press, 2014), chap. 4.

[71] See Rich Yeselson, "Fortress Unionism," *Democracy*, Summer 2013, 68–81; Rich Yeselson, "The Supreme Court and Taft-Hartley's Legal Land Mines," *Democracy*, 25 June 2013, http://www.democracyjournal.org/arguments/2013/06/the-supreme-court-and-taft-hartleys-legal-land-mines.php; and Nelson Lichtenstein, "Taft-Hartley: A Slave-Labor Law?," *Catholic University Law Review* 47 (1997): 763–89.

their own interests."[72] Taft-Hartley, however, legislated employers'—but not unions'—rights to free speech, mandated representation elections rather than card checks, barred the NLRB from employing economic analysts as well as lawyers, rendered ineligible for coverage workers with even minimal supervisory responsibility, failed to require representation elections within a timely manner, and reframed representation decisions as contests not over the nature of workers' organization but between unions and management. Nor did labor law ever cover independent contractors—a growing category as clever employers met the new American workplace—or ban striker replacements.

As the policy time capsule opened, the troubled NLRB, far from merely evincing policy drift or de facto retrenchment, actively exploited weaknesses in old statutes.[73] In the 1980s, under Donald Dotson, whom Reagan nominated as chair after PATCO, it took a sharp turn to the right, investigating union finances, reversing representation elections often on technicalities, and giving companies free passes for what would once have been deemed unfair labor practices. The troubled agency, far from serving as a refuge of neutral competence, has become beset with bickering between de facto designees of unions and management. Often, it has operated without a quorum.[74] The 1984 Democratic platform asked, in language far more subtle and plaintive than the typical convention fare, "What would happen if Mr. Reagan is reelected? Will the National Labor Relations Act be converted into a tool that limits working men and women and empowers only their employers?"[75] The subsequent decades have told the sorry answer.

Aided by a burgeoning "union avoidance" industry encompassing lawyers, consultants, and industrial psychologists, employers dramatically stepped up efforts to fight unions. Because companies must remit only back pay with interest less any other earnings workers have received in the

[72] Paul Weiler, "Promises to Keep: Securing Workers' Rights to Self-Organization under the NLRA," *Harvard Law Review* 96 (1983): 1813.

[73] See Jacob Hacker, "Privatizing Risk without Privatizing the Welfare State: The Hidden Politics of Social Policy Retrenchment," *American Political Science Review* 98 (2004): 243–60; and Wolfgang Streeck and Kathleen Thelen, "Introduction: Institutional Change in Advanced Political Economies," in *Beyond Continuity: Institutional Change in Advanced Political Economies*, ed. Wolfgang Streeck and Kathleen Thelen (Oxford: Oxford University Press, 2005), 1–39.

[74] See Cynthia L. Estlund, "The Ossification of American Labor Law," *Columbia Law Review* 102 (2002): 1527–1612; James J. Brudney, "Isolated and Politicized: The NLRB's Uncertain Future," *Comparative Labor Law & Policy Journal* 26 (2004): 221–60; from a longtime Democratic appointee to the Board, Wilma Liebman, "Decline and Disenchantment: Reflections on the Aging of the National Labor Relations Board," *Berkeley Journal of Employment and Labor Law* 28 (2007): 569–89; Joan Flynn, "A Quiet Revolution at the Labor Board: The Transformation of the NLRB, 1935–2000," *Ohio State Law Journal* 61 (2000): 1361–1455.

[75] "Democratic Party Platform of 1984," http://www.presidency.ucsb.edu/ws/?pid=29608.

meantime, without further penalties for lawbreaking, they face extremely weak disincentives when they break labor laws.[76] Unfair labor practice charges against employers more than doubled between 1970 and 1980 even as certification elections declined. Organizing rates have fallen far below replacement levels for union workers. Only 0.2 percent of U.S. workers per year have organized under NLRB elections during the past decade, with about twice as many in private-sector card-check elections. Changing these trends would involve expenditures per union member in the thousands every year. All the same, a 2005 survey found that 53 percent of nonunion employees would favor a union on the job. If such figures were somehow to become reality, unions would represent 58 percent of the American workforce.[77] Responses from unions aim to circumvent the limits in the NLRB system. Neutrality agreements expressly limit the role of union-avoidance consultants, and card-check campaigns circumscribe their use. In other cases, they shift organizing into the public sector (or, in a few instances, the Railway Labor Act), where different rules apply. Now even those enclaves have become contested, as labor's emboldened opponents set their eyes on the public sector.

Politics from Kirkland to Sweeney

Just two months before his death at eighty-five in 1979, George Meany relinquished his post to his deputy and former speechwriter, Lane Kirkland, a well-connected Washingtonian from an old South Carolina family known for his elegant dinner parties.[78] One might see the 1980s as a kind

[76]Richard B. Freeman and James L. Medoff, *What Do Unions Do?* (New York: Basic Books, 1984), chap. 15; Weiler, "Promises to Keep," 1780; R. C. Longworth, "Business Is Booming for 'Union Avoidance,'" *Chicago Tribune*, 20 September 1979, 12; Tom Nicholson, "The Union-Busters," *Newsweek*, 28 January 1980, 67; John Logan, "The Union Avoidance Industry in the United States," *British Journal of Industrial Relations* 44 (2006): 651–75; Kate Bronfenbrenner, "No Holds Barred: The Intensification of Employer Opposition to Organizing," EPI Briefing Paper 235 (Washington, D.C.: Economic Policy Institute, 2009), 23–24. For a how-to from the leading management-side law firm, see Jackson Lewis, *Winning NLRB Elections: Avoiding Unionization through Preventive Employee Relations Programs*, 4th ed. (Chicago: CCH, 1997). Links between conservative politics and aggressive union busting deserve greater scholarly scrutiny.

[77]Richard B. Freeman and Joel Rogers, *What Workers Want*, updated ed. (Ithaca, N.Y.: ILR Press, 2006); Richard B. Freeman, "Do Workers Still Want Unions? *More Than Ever*," EPI Briefing Paper 182 (Washington, D.C.: Economic Policy Institute, 2007); Henry S. Farber and Bruce Western, "Can Increased Organizing Reverse the Decline of Unions in the United States? Lessons from the Last Quarter-Century," in *The Changing Role of Unions: New Forms of Representation*, ed. Phanindra V. Wunnava (Armonk, N.Y.: M.E. Sharpe, 2004), 323–61.

[78]Robert B. Reich, *Locked in the Cabinet* (New York: Knopf, 1997), 98–100; "Lane's Friends," *Nation*, 19 January 1980, 37–40; Kathy Sawyer, "Lane Kirkland: Made in America, and Proud to Wear the Union Label," *Washington Post*, 15 July 1984, K1; A. H. Raskin,

of Brezhnev era. The long-serving leader kept the ship afloat, but without fixing the rot below the water line. While Kirkland corralled the UAW, UMW, and Teamsters back into the AFL-CIO, membership as a share of the private-sector workforce tumbled by more than half during his sixteen-year tenure, from 21.2 percent to 10.3 percent.

Relations with the Democratic establishment improved after Kirkland sidelined Al Barkan and party leadership passed from the prickly Jimmy Carter to Tip O'Neill, the labor-liberal House Speaker. O'Neill sought to recreate against Reaganism's assaults "thirty of the greatest, fruitful, and beneficial years a democracy ever had. We did it together, labor and the Democrats working together." The relationship deepened under his feisty successor, Jim Wright, for whom the AFL-CIO "functioned as a kind of informal adjunct of the Democratic leadership."[79] Union PAC spending almost doubled in real terms from the 1978 to the 1988 cycles, increasing from 5.1 to 7.3 percent of total campaign spending.[80] These dollars brought goodwill from congressional Democrats, but failed to increase labor's own infrastructural capacities, or to arrest union decline or build broad social programs.[81] Kirkland's major success, a toothless law providing sixty-day notice for plant closing, passed without Reagan's signature (and with nineteen Republican votes in the Senate), cushioned the blow of economic change rather than seeking to shape it.[82] Again, operational partnership fell short of change in the polity or the political regime.

Achieving influence in presidential nomination proved a harder nut to crack. No strategy has clearly maximized labor influence in the postreform

---

"Unionist in Reaganland," *New Yorker*, 7 September 1981, 50–113; Elaine Sciolino, "Kirkland Wins Acclaim for Success Abroad, but Faces Criticism at Home," *New York Times*, 15 December 1989, A24. On Kirkland's vision, see *The Changing Situation of Workers and Their Unions* (Washington, D.C.: AFL-CIO, 1985) and the essays, from a carefully chosen cast, in Seymour Martin Lipset, ed., *Unions in Transition: Entering the Second Century* (San Francisco: Institute for Contemporary Studies, 1986).

[79] Adam Clymer, "Labor Now also Counsels Candidates," *New York Times*, 21 July 1982, A13; Kathy Sawyer, "Big Labor Going High Tech in Battle for Votes of Working People," *Washington Post*, 9 September 1982, A8; Warren Brown, "Democrats and AFL-CIO Leaders Hold a Love Fest," *Washington Post*, 18 November 1981, A8; Thomas Ferguson and Joel Rogers, *Right Turn: The Decline of the Democrats and the Future of American Politics* (New York: Hill and Wang, 1986), esp. chap. 5; and Barbara Sinclair, *Majority Leadership in the U.S. House* (Baltimore: Johns Hopkins University Press, 1983), 122.

[80] Democrats consistently received more than 90 percent of PAC spending, with Teamsters the largest GOP givers. See Marick F. Masters, Robert S. Atkin, and John Thomas Delaney, "Unions, Political Action, and Public Policies: A Review of the Past Decade," *Policy Studies Journal* 18 (1989): 475; James W. Endersby and Michael C. Munger, "The Impact of Legislator Attributes on Union PAC Contributions," *Journal of Labor Research* 13 (1992): 79–97.

[81] Cf. Dark, *Unions and the Democrats*, 152–56.

[82] James Drew and Steve Eder, "Without Warning: Flaws, Loopholes Deny Employees Protection Mandated by WARN Act," *Toledo Blade*, 15 July 2007, 1.

primary process, in victory or defeat. In 1980 and since 1992, international unions have endorsed on their own timetables and in response to their own sometimes peripheral concerns. This middle ground between neutrality and endorsement by the AFL-CIO reflects labor's ongoing influence—but also its fragmentation.

In 1980, as a hawkish aide wrote to Al Barkan, labor "felt closer to Kennedy on the economic issues and closer to Carter on the environmental and foreign policy issues." Although the Auto Workers, Farm Workers, AFSCME, and Machinists all backed Kennedy, most other unions remained loyal to the president. In 1984, the federation issued its only endorsement before the nominee had been settled. Walter Mondale, a redoubtable liberal who had done battle with Hubert Humphrey to purge communists from the Minnesota Democratic Farmer-Labor Party, attracted support from union leaders right to left. Yet a top-down approach failed to rally a rank and file swelled with Reagan Democrats. In 1988, with a lackluster field, the AFL-CIO voted, again for the only time, to bar international unions (although not their affiliates; Michael Dukakis made particular use of AFSCME locals) from issuing preprimary endorsements.[83]

By 1992, the party wanted victory. The Democratic Leadership Council, a party faction that brought funders and Sunbelt politicians together to support free trade and hefty defense budgets, aimed to limit the influence of both old-style liberals and identity politics, and pushed its former chair, Bill Clinton.[84] The cycle marked a low point for labor influence. The more politically astute unions, led by Gerald McEntee of AFSCME, held their distaste for a right-to-work governor and backed Clinton.[85]

In 1995, the Service Employees' International Union president, John Sweeney, and his New Voice ticket—the descendants of the CIO-Reuther tradition, refracted through a more positive appraisal of the sixties—dethroned the AFL-CIO's old guard on a platform to expand organizing, and rebuild labor's clout. The 1994 Republican takeover of the House had

[83]Timothy Stanley, *Kennedy vs. Carter: The 1980 Battle for the Democratic Party's Soul* (Lawrence: University Press of Kansas, 2010), 108–10; Bernard Weinraub, "Mondale Woos His Party's Conservative Wing," *New York Times*, 15 November 1983, A20; Harold Meyerson, "Labor's Risky Plunge into Politics," *Dissent*, Summer 1984, 285–94; Marianne Hare, "Organized Labor and the Mondale Campaign," *Labor Center Review*, November 1985, 11–14; David Shribman, "Divided and Dispirited as Iowa Caucuses Near, Organized Labor Just Isn't Organized Politically," *Wall Street Journal*, 19 January 1988, 70.

[84]The DLC, based in sectors and regions with weak labor movements, had little in common with AFL-CIO traditionalists, although a few lineages can be traced through the Coalition for a Democratic Majority. The DLC was, in Samuel P. Huntington's terms, a group of the party's New Affluent not its New Deal wing. See Huntington, "The Visions of the Democratic Party," *Public Interest*, Spring 1985, 73; cf. Ferguson and Rogers, *Right Turn*, 4–9.

[85]Todd S. Purdum, "Union Members Do Footwork of Candidates," *New York Times*, 4 April 1992, 9; Julie Kosterlitz, "Labor's Pit Bull," *National Journal*, 2 August 1997, 1549–51.

finally galvanized discontents into action, just as the devastating 1942 midterms sparked the formation of CIO-PAC. The fall of the Soviet Union in 1991 paradoxically weakened the right wing, as it took off the table the claims to Americanism that free trade unionism had long provided. Sweeney's victory culminated a decade of organizing among the "outs," bringing together—in bloc vote, just like the unreformed Democratic conventions—the old CIO unions, SEIU, AFSCME, and, critically, enough discontents among traditionalists (for instance, Painters, Locomotive Engineers, Boiler Makers)—to eke out a narrow victory.[86]

The fight was, the Sweeney-aligned journalist, Harold Meyerson, wrote, "the last battle between the upstart New Left, now a bunch of 50-year-olds, and the entrenched Old Left, now pushing 70."[87] In its wake, the divides between party and group healed as the Sweeney team rejuvenated labor's electoral work—but membership, after flat years in the late nineties boom, continued its inexorable decline. To return to the three levels of alliance, it was political revival without roots in the polity or a political regime.

The New Right had consciously imitated the left's techniques—and labor sought to recover the playbook, focusing on intense door-to-door mobilization. The political analyst Charlie Cook in 2000 contrasted labor's new political operation with the 1994 efforts as "like comparing a Model T with a Ferrari." Ninety-two percent of union voters in presidential battleground states received a pamphlet about the election in 2000 and 2004; eighty-eight percent did so in 2008 and 2012. By 2008, the SEIU spent $55.5 million, AFSCME $39.9 million and the AFL-CIO $36.5 million. Increasingly, their efforts coordinated with other actors in the Democratic penumbra, such as MoveOn.org, Planned Parenthood, and the NAACP.[88]

Yet corporate spending by labor's opponents, which had held steady with labor's rising spending until 2002,[89] shot sharply upward in 2004, aided by new nominally independent expenditures under various provisions of the tax and electoral laws. In 2009, when the Supreme Court in *Citizens United* allowed unlimited independent expenditures, labor could finally spend

[86] See the vote in *Proceedings of the 21st Constitutional Convention of the AFL-CIO* (Washington, D.C.: AFL-CIO, 1995), 217–30.

[87] Harold Meyerson, "Mother Jones Returns," *LA Weekly*, 3 November 1995, 23; Leslie Kaufman and Bob Cohn, "Union Solidarity Forever? Not This Year," *Newsweek*, 22 May 1995, 64.

[88] Steven Greenhouse, "Despite Defeat on China Bill, Labor Is on the Rise," *New York Times*, 30 May 2000, A1; Peter L. Francia, "Assessing the Labor-Democratic Alliance: A One-Sided Partnership?," *Polity* 42 (2010): 297–99; Julie Kosterlitz, "For Labor: No More Playing Defense," *National Journal*, 24 August 1996, 1799–1801; Peter L. Francia, *The Future of Organized Labor in American Politics* (New York: Columbia University Press, 2006), 54 and 75; Herbert B. Asher, Eric S. Heberlig, Randall B. Ripley, and Karen Snyder, *American Labor Unions in the Electoral Arena* (Lanham, Md.: Rowman & Littlefield, 2001), 103; Steven Greenhouse, "Unions Recruit New Allies to Fight for the President," *New York Times*, 5 November 2012, A10.

[89] Francia, *Future of Organized Labor*, chap. 4.

from the general treasury, reversing the ban enacted by Taft-Hartley—but so could corporations.

While unions reach an ever smaller share of the American electorate, the effects of union membership on voting have changed little in recent decades. Since the 1960s, members of union households have been more likely to vote than nonmembers—since the 1980s by a margin of approximately ten percentage points, a figure that increased marginally during the Sweeney years. The effects are notably larger in the private sector, where union members' education levels are lower, but where membership is shrinking. One estimate finds that deunionization has reduced U.S. voter turnout by about three percentage points, working through both individual and contextual mobilizing effects.[90] Among voters, Democrats have had a consistent advantage. Since 1980, voters in union households have consistently preferred Democratic candidates by margins between eleven and sixteen percentage points greater than voters in nonmember households.[91] In multivariate analysis, both party identification and, although somewhat less powerfully, union membership help to predict vote choice.[92] These findings make sense given the framework presented here: in mature alliance, voters' group interests often merge to become partisan loyalties, and both identities reinforce each other.

In the aggregate, does labor effectively shift political behavior, or fail to "get its electoral house in order"? The question is subjective, but factors

[90] Jan E. Leighley and Jonathan Nagler, "Unions, Voter Turnout, and Class Bias in the U.S. Electorate, 1964–2004," *Journal of Politics* 69 (2007): 430–41; and Jake Rosenfeld, "Economic Determinants of Voting in an Era of Union Decline," *Social Science Quarterly* 91 (2010): 379–96. See also Sousa, "Organized Labor"; Benjamin Radcliff and Patricia Davis, "Labor Organization and Electoral Participation in Industrial Democracies," *American Journal of Political Science* 44 (2000): 132–41; and Benjamin Radcliff, "Organized Labor and Electoral Participation in American National Elections," *Journal of Labor Research* 2 (2001): 405–14. Effects are greater in off-cycle elections; see Sarah F. Anzia, *Timing & Turnout: How Off-Cycle Elections Favor Organized Groups* (Chicago: University of Chicago Press, 2013). Mobilization and contact by the Democratic Party has moved up the SES gradient over time (see Andrea Louise Campbell, "Parties, Electoral Participation, and Shifting Voting Blocs," in *The Transformation of American Politics: Activist Government and the Rise of Conservatism*, ed. Paul Pierson and Theda Skocpol [Princeton: Princeton University Press, 2007], 87), but we do not know the distributional impacts of union contacting, especially to non–union members.

[91] Data from William Form, *Segmented Labor, Fractured Politics: Labor Politics in American Life* (New York: Plenum Press, 1995), 270, and exit polls at CNN.com. The 2012 exit poll showed only a nine-point gap in Democratic presidential support for Obama's youth-led victory. The Peter D. Hart survey for the AFL-CIO, which historically has found larger union effects, showed an eighteen-point gap. See David Moberg, "Unions Played Major Unsung Role in Obama Victory," *In These Times*, 13 November 2012, http://inthesetimes.com/working/entry/14154/unions_play_major_little_noted_role_in_obama_victory. No systematic data relate international union affiliation, or work in the public or private sector, to individual political behavior; a high-quality survey could shed real light.

[92] Sousa, "Organized Labor," 747; Asher et al., *American Labor Unions*, 142.

militate toward the former conclusion. Union members are more male than female, and disproportionately in the top three income quintiles. In an increasingly important cleavage, they are also generally older. At the same time, the implications behind the oft-asked question seem misplaced. Since Labor's Non-Partisan League, unions have sought in their political work to mobilize more than their membership alone—just as the Christian Right aspires to represent more than adherents of any leader's particular sect. These claims to legitimacy, and the partisan alliances that nurtured them, made anchoring groups, rather than pressure groups. Doubling down only on mobilizing members, in a kind of electoral retreat into a "monopoly" rather than a "voice" face, surrenders the claims to represent all American workers that have long propelled the more universalist elements in labor-liberalism.

Dilemmas of Contemporary Unionism

The decline of the right wing in American labor has profoundly shifted the terms of trade in party-group alliance. Kirkland hewed to a Gompersian line, and refused to address party functions himself, leaving the task to his deputies or the international presidents. Sweeney delivered the AFL-CIO endorsement from the rostrum at every Democratic convention in his tenure.[93] As the two parties' supporters sort themselves out ideologically and cross-pressured voters move to their natural homes, engendering the new pathologies of polarization, they edge the Democrats closer to the dream of a unified liberal party that animated Labor's Non-Partisan League and CIO-PAC. With core role-of-government questions at the fore, harmony on the social issues, and foreign policy invisible, the anchoring group, for the first time since 1968—or, given the yawning gaps between professed aims and unions' own employment practices in the 1950s and 1960s, perhaps ever—pushed from the left on economic issues with high internal ideological cohesion, relatively few crosscutting pressures, and no party factions specifically opposed to its agenda, particularly outside the contested arena of education policy. Yet this limited electoral cohesion belies deeper weaknesses, amid stagnant wages and declining union membership, in the polity and in the political regime.

Trade loomed less large inside the Democratic coalition. From 1970 onward, the AFL-CIO, and principally its industrial unions, opposed

[93] Arch Puddington, *Lane Kirkland: Champion of American Labor* (New York: John Wiley, 2005), 305; "The Democratic Convention Wednesday," *Chicago Tribune*, 28 August 1996, 2; Nancy Cleeland, "Revitalized Unions Pour Money, Labor into Democratic Campaigns," *Los Angeles Times*, 14 August 2000, 1; "Convention Notebook," *Baltimore Sun*, 30 July 2004, 6A; "John J. Sweeney, President, AFL-CIO, Remarks to the Democratic Convention," http://www.prnewswire.com/news-releases/john-j-sweeney-president-afl-cio-remarks-to-the-democratic-national-convention-64955517.html.

increased trade liberalization, with little success either in blocking trade pacts (although it occasionally won procedural victories to limit negotiating authority) or in helping displaced workers. The passage of NAFTA in 1993 marked a particular low point.[94] Since the 1990s, however, big industrial unions have declined within the federation. Globalization changed, too. Round-by-round and country-by-country deals susceptible to lobbying pressure paled in comparison as the free flow of financial capital and the entrance of China into world markets reshaped the global economy. Again, quiescence inside alliance hardly equals group victory.

Polarization across multiple issue domains and the changing composition of the union workforce have also meant rapprochements with various citizens' groups with whose agendas Meany bore no truck and Kirkland practiced a studied distance.[95] Although their internal records still remain checkered, cultural and postmaterial issues have been largely subordinated in union politics. The heads of the Service Employees International Union and the American Federation of Teachers are both out lesbians. The UAW endorsed a cap-and-trade system to price carbon in 2009, and the Sierra Club and Steelworkers spearheaded a Blue-Green Alliance for infrastructure spending and sustainable jobs.[96]

Immigration, which has bedeviled labor since the Chinese Exclusion Act, too, seemed to resolve itself. In 2009, AFL-CIO and Change to Win unions alike signed onto a plan to "adjust the status" of undocumented immigrants, limit temporary work programs, and allow an independent commission to set immigration levels based on labor demand.[97] The International

[94] I. M. Destler, "Trade Politics and Labor Issues: 1953–1995," in *Imports, Exports, and the American Worker*, ed. Susan M. Collins (Washington, D.C.: Brookings Institution Press, 1998), 389–422; James Shoch, "Grappling with Globalization: The Democratic Party's Struggles over International Market Integration," in *What's Left of the Left: Democrats and Social Democrats in Challenging Times*, ed. James Cronin, George Ross, and James Shoch (Durham, N.C.: Duke University Press, 2011), 210–37; Frederick W. Mayer, "Labor, Environment and the State of U.S. Trade Politics," *Law and Business Review of the Americas* 6 (2000): 335–46.

[95] Two carefully worded examples: In 1990, a special panel on abortion reaffirmed "the rights of all persons to privacy, to personal belief, and to self-determination in all matters of religion, thought, conscience, and family." In 1993, the convention resolved to oppose measures "which reduce the rights of people based on their sexual orientation." Puddington, *Lane Kirkland*, 272; *Proceedings of the 20th Constitutional Convention of the AFL-CIO* (Washington, D.C.: AFL-CIO, 1993), 183.

[96] Steven Greenhouse, "Steelworkers and Sierra Club Unite," *New York Times*, 8 June 2006, http://www.nytimes.com/2006/06/08/us/08labor.html; Jane McAlevey, "Blues and Greens: Get It Together!," *Nation*, 7 May 2012, 15–20; "BlueGreen Alliance," www.bluegreenalliance.org. The membership includes the USW, UAW, SEIU, and AFT, as well as the Sierra Club, Natural Resources Defense Council, and Union of Concerned Scientists. The Blue-Green unions stayed largely neutral in the fight over the Keystone XL pipeline from the Alberta tar sands to Louisiana, backed by the Laborers and Teamsters and opposed by environmentalists.

[97] Ray Marshall, *Immigration for Shared Prosperity* (Washington, D.C.: Economic Policy Institute, 2009), especially the principles summarized at 51–54. See also Brian Burgoon, Janice

Department largely left power politics. It retrenched, renamed itself as the Solidarity Center, and reframed its work from "free trade unionism" to "social movement unionism."[98]

On race, the balance between internal openness and the impact of exogenous change has been less positive. In 2012, Lee Saunders, Gerald McEntee's longtime deputy, assumed the presidency of AFSCME, the public employee union and reliable supporter of Democrats, and became the first-ever African American to lead a major union. The decline in unionized industry hit African Americans especially hard. From 1983 to 2013, union density among employed black men dropped from 31.6 percent to 14.8 percent (in the least-affected demographic group, white women, it declined from 13.3 to 10.3 percent). The mass-production industries that had opened so many doors in the age of the CIO contracted severely. Nor could African American women consolidate gains in the labor market won in the 1960s and 1970s. In the private sector, deunionization among African American women substantially worsened racial wage gaps in earnings after 1980.[99] In the public sector, even as the share of workers in unions has remained flat, outsourcing of low-wage work and declining employment in agencies with disproportionately black workforces, such as the U.S. Postal Service, have hurt union membership among African Americans.[100]

The broken NLRB system has interacted with increasing hostility from the right. Unions have responded to this harsh environment in different ways. In 2005, the labor movement split yet again, with disputes over jurisdiction far more important than ideology. After the AFL-CIO rejected its proposals to merge smaller internationals and pour resources into new organizing drives, the Service Employees International Union led several other internationals, including the conservative-leaning Carpenters and Teamsters, out of the AFL-CIO, and formed a new federation called Change to Win. The SEIU organized more than a million workers in the decade following Andy Stern's accession to the presidency in 1996, from security guards to home health aides to janitors, typically in powerful mega-locals.

Fine, Wade Jacoby, and Daniel Tichenor, "Immigration and the Transformation of American Unionism," *International Migration Review* 44 (2010): 933–73.

[98] Barbara Shailor, "A New Internationalism: Advancing Workers' Rights in the Global Economy," in *Not Your Father's Union Movement: Inside the AFL-CIO*, ed. Jo-Ann Mori (London: Verso, 1998), 145–55; Jay Mazur, "Labor's New Internationalism," *Foreign Affairs*, January 2000, 79–93; *Justice for All: A Guide to Worker Rights in the Global Economy*, 3rd ed. (Washington, D.C.: Solidarity Center AFL-CIO, 2009).

[99] Kate Bronfenbrenner and Dorian T. Warren, "Race, Gender, and the Rebirth of Trade Unionism," *New Labor Forum* 16 (2007): 143; Bureau of Labor Statistics, "Union Affiliation of Employed Wage and Salary Workers by Selected Characteristics," last modified 24 January 2014, http://www.bls.gov/news.release/union2.t01.htm; Rosenfeld, *What Unions*, chap. 5.

[100] Louis Uchitelle, "Labor's Lost; For Blacks, a Dream in Decline," *New York Times*, 23 October 2005, C1; Timothy Williams, "Public Sector Sheds Jobs; Blacks Are Hit Hardest," *New York Times*, 29 November 2011, A16.

The sharp-elbowed union sought alternatives to the NLRB system by cutting deals with management for labor peace, and redefining bargaining units, especially at the periphery of the contracting state.[101]

In "blue America," coalitions at the local and state levels turned to political action. They aimed to shore up workers in the public sector and make an end-run around labor law in the private sector, especially on behalf of hard-to-organize populations earning low wages: day laborers, home-care workers, fast-food workers. Through tactics such as wage ordinances, zoning laws, contract requirements, and designation of public employees, they seek opportunities to leverage party-group alliance and organize outside of the broken NLRB framework. Often, they aim not to recruit dues-paying members, but to catalyze attention and change regulations.[102]

The new coalitions, often going by the label "alt-labor," resemble their counterparts in the Christian Right, with separate arms for voter registration and issue organizing; for civic and political work; and, as a political action committee, for overt electioneering. They typically tap philanthropic foundations (only sometimes aware of the political purposes at play) for support where possible, and have found difficulty in generating the kind of self-sustaining revenue model or long-term viability that union dues from automatic check-off have long ensured. Although accounts often tiptoe around the issue by speaking of replacing "moribund" or "hidebound" leadership, in practice social movement unionism has typically meant displacing the building trades in Central Labor Councils. Successes, from Buffalo to Miami to Los Angeles, have generally come in cities with relatively weak incumbent internationals and fewer entrenched turfs.

Nevertheless, even if mobilization produces victories that benefit low-wage workers in particular jurisdictions or industries, extant strategies and organizational repertoires may well prove incapable of institutionalizing any upsurges in militancy or outpourings of popular support.[103] As in the

[101] Harold Meyerson, "Labor's Civil War," *American Prospect*, June 2005, 45–50; Steve Early, *Civil Wars in US Labor: Birth of a New Workers' Movement or Death Throes of the Old?* (Chicago: Haymarket Books, 2011); Max Fraser, "The SEIU Andy Stern Leaves Behind," *Nation*, 5 July 2010, 20–24; for a theoretical model, see John S. Ahlquist, "Who Sits at the Table in the House of Labor? Rank-and-File Citizenship and the Unraveling of Confederal Organizations," *Journal of Law, Economics, and Organization* 28 (2012): 588–616.

[102] Richard C. Shragger, "Mobile Capital, Local Economic Regulation, and the Democratic City," *Harvard Law Review* 123 (2009): 482–540; Freeman and Rogers, *What Workers Want*; Josh Eidelson, "American Workers: Shackled to Labor Law," *In These Times*, June 2012, 20; Steven Greenhouse, "A Union in Spirit," *New York Times*, 11 August 2013, BU-1; Steven Greenhouse, "Advocates for Workers Raise the Ire of Business," *New York Times*, 17 January 2014, B1; Benjamin I. Sachs, "The Unbundled Union: Politics Without Collective Bargaining," *Yale Law Journal* 123 (2013): 148–207.

[103] See Dorian T. Warren, "A New Labor Movement for a New Century" (PhD diss., Yale University, 2005), 322; Rosenfeld, *What Unions*, chap. 2; Harold Meyerson, "Labor Without Unions," *Los Angeles Times*, 8 December 2014, A13.

nineteenth century, workers have found collective voice outside the trade union legally sanctioned as exclusive bargaining agent—but, just like their forebears, these new organizational forms stand vulnerable to drift, decay, or collapse.[104] Unless presidents put labor law before their other domestic priorities, cloture rules shift decisively, or liberals gain a more sustained opportunity for major legislation than they have had for many decades, changing the NLRB regime through statute to allow unions to organize more easily, or to permit something other than the full-fledged suite of unionism established by the Wagner Act, seems highly unlikely. In straitened circumstances, alliance must look to different policy responses across the American state.

Alliance in the Obama Years

In 2008, amid the longest primary season since 1984, unions split along lines of identity and affinity more than ideology or sectoral interest. AFSCME and both teachers' unions, leading public-sector unions close to the party establishment, alongside most of the building trades with their older, whiter memberships, plumped for Hillary Clinton. The dissident Change to Win unions almost all endorsed Barack Obama, a fellow organizer seeking new models for winning victories. The leading industrial unions stayed out of the two-candidate battle.[105]

The Obama administration showed the fruits and frustrations of mature alliance. In one important but aberrant case, it shaped economic policymaking writ large. Through messy industrial policy of the kind that New Democrats had long abhorred, the administration diverted federal funds to keep General Motors and Chrysler from liquidation, and ordered packaged bankruptcies for the two companies. Contracts slashed pay rates for new hires and cut benefits for all workers. The administration protected the United Auto Workers' pension plan for retirees, which took nonvoting stock in exchange for a no-strike pledge. In a favorite New Right dictum, personnel was policy: a task force led by Steven Rattner, a private-equity titan with liberal views, and Ron Bloom, who had done time at both the United Steelworkers and on Wall Street, convinced the administration's economic heavyweights.[106]

[104]On these themes, see David Montgomery, *Workers' Control in America: Studies in the History of Work, Technology, and Labor Struggles* (Cambridge: Cambridge University Press, 1979), 171.

[105]See "Labor Endorsements in the Race for the 2008 Primary Campaigns," http://www.gwu.edu/~action/2008/labor/laborendorse08.html.

[106]Steven Rattner, *Overhaul: An Insider's Account of the Obama Administration's Emergency Rescue of the Auto Industry* (Boston: Houghton Mifflin Harcourt, 2010); Noam Scheiber, "Manufacturing Bloom," *New Republic*, 2 December 2009, 18–21; Bill Vlasic, "Two-Tier Pay Now the Way Detroit Works," *New York Times*, 13 September 2011, A1. Bloom and Rattner had each

Other executive actions aided labor. An executive order in 2014 forced companies that apply for federal contracts to disclose violations of labor law during the three prior years, and banned them from forcing employees into mandatory arbitration. In party-line votes, the NLRB allowed nursing assistants to form their own bargaining units, and adopted new rules consolidating appeals, standardizing hearings, and delaying litigation on initial elections. Yet these changes and others on the table—for instance, allowing unions access to voters' telephone and email addresses in NLRB elections—change only on the margins the underlying conditions that frustrate union organizing: limited enforcement powers, cumbersome procedures, unequal resources.[107]

Health care reform, the president's signature initiative, bore the imprints of the Service Employees International Union. Its president, Andy Stern, was the single most frequent visitor to the White House during Obama's first year in office. SEIU members, much less affluent than most unionists, gain from taxpayer-backed health insurance exchanges and expansions in Medicaid: they may bargain over wages rather than benefits. Unions with legacy costs from fringe benefits fared worse. The final bill included an indirect tax on high-priced health plans, phased in beginning only in 2018—that is, beyond the length of nearly all extant contracts. In implementation, unions especially of lower-middle-skilled workers (the Laborers, for instance) feared that employers would force workers into the law's new insurance exchanges, again threatening the hard-won health-and-welfare funds. The AFL-CIO ultimately put its muscle behind the bill, but attempts to oust the bill's Democratic opponents in the House—twenty-one of thirty-four of whom hailed from right-to-work states—amounted to nothing in a Republican year.[108]

---

done time at Lazard Frères, which, since Felix Rohatyn worked with municipal unions in New York's fiscal crisis, has been the investment bank most sympathetic to union concerns.

[107] Dave Jamieson, "Labor Board Eases Path to Unions for Health Care Workers," *Huffington Post*, 30 August 2011, http://www.huffingtonpost.com/2011/08/30/labor-board-unions-health-care-workers_n_942485.html; Emily Bazelon, "Obama Is on a Pro-Labor Roll," *Slate*, 7 August 2014, http://www.slate.com/articles/news_and_politics/jurisprudence/2014/08/obama_executive_order_on_mandatory_arbitration_huge_news_for_workers_rights.html; Steven Greenhouse, "Labor Board Adopts Rules to Speed Unionization Votes," *New York Times*, 22 December 2011, B5; Brian Mahoney, "NLRB Boosts Unions' Organizing Leverage," *Politico*, 12 December 2014, http://www.politico.com/story/2014/12/national-labor-relations-board-unions-rule-113528.html.

[108] Jeff Zeleny, "White House Visitor Log Lists Stars and C.E.O.'s," *New York Times*, 31 October 2009, A11; "The Medicaid Program at a Glance" (Henry J. Kaiser Family Foundation, June 2010); Jenny Gold, "'Cadillac' Insurance Plans Explained," *Kaiser Health News*, 18 March 2010, http://kaiserhealthnews.org/news/cadillac-health-explainer-npr/; Sam Stein, "Barack Obama, Campaign Manager: How the 2008 Playbook Passed Health Care," *Huffington Post*, 13 May 2010, http://www.huffingtonpost.com/2010/05/13/barack-obama-campaign-man_n_574665

The Employee Free Choice Act in 2009 followed an old script. The bill resurrected many of the provisions from the 1978 labor-law reform and added increased penalties for employers and an option for signed cards ("card check") rather than secret-ballot NLRB elections. Again, labor acquiesced as its top priority lost space on the congressional calendar. EFCA had *no* Senate Republican support whatsoever. The House, where the bill almost certainly had a majority, hung fire so as not to expose conservative Democrats to a tough vote. Only between July 2009 and January 2010, with the Senate tied up with work on the massive Affordable Care Act, did Democrats have sixty votes in the Senate. Even then it is unclear whether a bill offering expedited NLRB elections alone, stripped of card-check, would have had the votes.[109]

Whether or not a bill could possibly have snuck through the narrow window, however, the outcome should appear as no surprise whatsoever: openings to the left that overcome the usual veto points shut remarkably quickly in American politics. As with its predecessors back to 1935, when Roosevelt pushed the Social Security Act—even as pressure from below and Robert Wagner's tactical mastery passed the NLRA—the president put his own policy initiatives first. The White House wanted health care reform. Most liberals spent the fall of 2009 pushing for a government-run entrant in the health insurance exchanges ("the public option"), rather than EFCA. As ever, labor did a better job in putting its weight behind and molding to its advantage major progressive legislation in which other stakeholders had interests, than in persuading the broader left to advocate for a change in labor law.

Unions Embattled

Unions representing workers in the public sector represent labor's most successful redoubt, now making up half of American unionists. As industrial unions have retreated, public-sector unions have powered alliance at the

.html; Jonathan Martin and Steven Greenhouse, "Unions' Misgivings on Health Law Burst Into View," *New York Times*, 12 September 2013, B1. Opponents calculated from final vote, http://clerk.house.gov/evs/2010/roll165.xml.

[109] Blanche Lincoln of Arkansas and Ben Nelson of Nebraska were questionable and became more so as the year progressed. See Dorian Warren, "The Unsurprising Failure of Labor Law Reform," in *Reaching for a New Deal: Ambitious Governance, Economic Meltdown, and Polarized Politics in Obama's First Two Years*, ed. Theda Skocpol and Lawrence R. Jacobs (New York: Russell Sage Foundation, 2011), 191–229; Kevin Bogardus, "Harkin: Kennedy's Illness Stalled Card-Check," *Hill*, 11 September 2009, 12 and 15; Jeanne Cummings, "Labor Helps Kill Its Own Top Priority," *Politico*, 26 January 2010, http://www.politico.com/news/stories/0110/32041.html.

national level: AFSCME, NEA, AFT, and, with a membership split down the middle between public and private sectors, SEIU. Beginning after the 2010 elections, Republicans mounted attacks in states with strong public-sector unions where they held unified control. They adopted the tough anti-union tactics long common in the private sector, sharply limiting collective bargaining on wages, benefits, and pensions, and restricting other union priorities such as worker's compensation, project labor agreements on construction jobs, and rules on wage theft and overtime pay. It was a fight about power, aiming to defang the Democratic Party's strongest supporters. The restrictions on public-sector unions sought not only to balance budgets, but, as both sides explicitly acknowledged, to attack a critical Democratic support base. The Republican Party had traveled far from the days when Nelson Rockefeller and George Romney worked easily with unions in office. Antiunion legislation from the American Legislative Exchange Council, a Washington-based group founded in the heyday of the New Right and funded largely by corporations, provided templates for ambitious Republican lawmakers.[110] The old Gompersian responses against a hostile state—cultivating issue-specific allies or simply negotiating contracts and winning concessions across the bargaining table—make little sense when precisely the hostility of the state is at issue.

The heartland of American industry saw the most dramatic confrontations. In Madison, Wisconsin, protesters surrounded and occupied the capitol building, attempting to stop legislation that would slash public employees' benefits, limit collective bargaining to wages, and eviscerate unions' infrastructural power by denying them automatic check-off and forcing annual certification elections. The protesters failed, and the governor, Scott Walker, survived a recall with an identical share of the vote, against the same weak candidate, as in his initial election.[111] Opponents of a similar bill in Ohio (which also targeted the uniformed services) followed a more successful strategy: voters nullified it by a margin of more than three to two. Indiana and, amazingly, Michigan passed right-to-work legislation prohibiting the union shop in the private sector, following the first serious push in half a century.

The Great Recession decimated public budgets whatever states' rules on bargaining or level of unionization. Yet workers in blue states as well as red agreed to givebacks through collective bargaining. Nor do most

[110]On ALEC, see Alan Greenblatt, "What Makes ALEC Smart," *Governing*, October 2003, 30–34; Alan Greenblatt, "Right-Minded," *Governing*, December 2011, 32–36; Ed Pilkington and Suzanne Goldenberg, "ALEC Facing Funding Crisis from Donor Exodus in Wake of Trayvon Martin Row," *Guardian*, 3 December 2013, http://www.theguardian.com/world/2013/dec/03/alec-funding-crisis-big-donors-trayvon-martin.

[111]On the consequences, see Steven Greenhouse, "The Wisconsin Legacy," *New York Times*, 23 February 2014, BU1.

public-sector workers, with a relatively compressed wage scale, earn more than their counterparts in the private sector, except at the lowest skill levels, although they do have higher job security. While public pension plans in many states, red as well as blue, face funding shortfalls, legislative decisions (and the markets' performance), not agreements hashed out around the bargaining table, principally determine their funding. In the 1970s, labor militancy triggered the initial backlash against public-sector unions, but the recent legislation emerged after a decade when strikes had remained at an historic ebb.[112]

Hostility from the right and tight state budgets have limited unions' leverage in seeking even limited rapprochement with Republicans at the state and local levels, and sometimes forced public unions into competition over limited dollars. As they split, the Change to Win unions hoped for a more flexible relationship with the parties, but bitter hostility from Republicans increasingly precluded even tactical deals on priorities for particular internationals outside the uniformed services.[113] In a sign of the new alignments, the American Federation of Teachers, for decades a superhawkish union in federation politics (some even bruited its president, Sandra Feldman, as an alternative to Sweeney in the late 1990s),[114] became the poster child for the liberal public employee unions.

Belying predictions from political-economy models and conservative pundits alike, divisions between public-sector workers in the competition for scarce dollars often loom larger than fissures between unions in the public and private sectors. In states such as California, powerful unions representing prison guards have protected the carceral state, in many cases against other unionized public workers in health and education. When they go beyond bread-and-butter collective bargaining and take tough-on-crime stands, police unions often scramble the usual alliances. For their part, the building trades, the most conservative unions in the private sector save the Teamsters, rely on large-scale public contracts that pay the

[112]For overviews, see Freeman and Han, "War Against Public Sector Collective Bargaining"; Robert Hebdon, Joseph E. Slater, and Marick F. Masters, "Public Sector Collective Bargaining: Tumultuous Times," in *Collective Bargaining under Duress: Case Studies of Major North American Industries* (Ithaca, N.Y.: ILR Press, 2013), 255–95; and, from a liberal think tank, Gordon Lafer, "The Legislative Attack on American Wages and Labor Standards, 2011–2012," EPI Briefing Paper 364 (Washington, D.C.: Economic Policy Institute, 2013). On pensions and wages, see Alicia H. Munnell, *State and Local Pensions: What Now?* (Washington, D.C.: Brookings Institution Press, 2012); and Jeffrey Keefe, "Are Public Employees Overpaid?," *Labor Studies Journal* 37 (2012): 104–26. On public-sector work as "safe harbor" but also "backwater" amid private-sector inequality, see John D. Donahue, *The Warping of Government Work* (Cambridge, Mass.: Harvard University Press, 2008).

[113]Harold Meyerson, "Union Seeks Republicans," *American Prospect*, 21 October 2002, 25–29; Chris Maher, "SEIU Campaign Spending Pays Dividends," *Wall Street Journal*, 16 May 2009.

[114]Jonathan Mahler, "Labor's War Winds," *Forward*, 31 October 1997, 7.

prevailing wage—even as the Republican platform pledges to repeal the Davis-Bacon Act.[115]

Nor have the same currents escaped the allied party. Barack Obama speaks powerfully of inequality, but embedded in a narrative only glancing at labor's role. Mayors like Cory Booker in Newark and Rahm Emanuel in Chicago—even if far more gingerly than their GOP counterparts—positioned themselves as defenders of the public fisc against greedy unions in their employ, especially teachers seemingly uninterested in students' success. While the New Democrats of the eighties and nineties aimed at the corpus of New Deal liberalism's accumulated commitments, the new reformers stake their claims to moderation much more specifically on confrontation with organized labor, personified by teachers, in particular.[116] To be sure, the presidential nomination of such a figure without some kind of accommodation with labor would seem highly unlikely. Unions control powerful resources, and their agenda converges with the party's economic liberals, themselves feeling out new possibilities in the Obama era. Still, the fissures may portend not just continued drift away from commitments to economic justice, but a sharper rift between party and anchoring group than has been since at the national level since the age of a far stronger labor movement.

For its part, the Supreme Court, by a five to four vote in the 2014 case of *Harris v. Quinn*, banned on First Amendment grounds the mandatory collection of agency fees, which cover the costs of collective bargaining, from "partial-public employees" who decline to join a union. The decision applied principally to low-wage home-care workers, predominantly women, whom state legislatures designated as public employees to allow them to form coherent bargaining units. The decision's logic, however, put the collection of agency fees for all public employees at risk. While strong organizing would blunt the effect from a nationwide ban, without agency fees unions would face an additional barrier to collecting funds.[117] More than at

[115] Joshua Page, "Prison Officer Unions and the Perpetuation of the Penal Status Quo," *Criminology & Public Policy* 10 (2011): 735–70. On police unions, see respectively the conservative defense in Matthew Hennessy, "A City on the Brink," *City Journal*, 21 December 2014, http://www.city-journal.org/2014/eon1221mh.html; and the leftist attack in Shawn Gude, "The Bad Kind of Unionism," *Jacobin*, Winter 2014, 41–44. Cf. Steven Malanga, "The Emerging Political Divide Between Public and Private Unions," *Wall Street Journal*, 25 October 2014, 11.

[116] See, e.g., Laurel Rosenhall, "Schism Opens among Dems," *Sacramento Bee*, 24 December 2010, A1; Joel Klein, "A Watershed for Democrats and Unions," *Wall Street Journal*, 16 September 2012, A19; Motoko Rich, "Teachers' Unions Wooing GOP, Too," *New York Times*, 25 September 2012, A1; Libby Nelson, "How the Democrats alienated teachers' unions," *Vox*, 16 May 2014, http://www.vox.com/2014/5/16/5683260/how-the-democrats-alienated-teachers-unions.

[117] For contrasting perspectives, see Jake Rosenfeld, "The Supreme Court Did Not Just Kill Public Sector Unions," *Politico*, 30 June 2014, http://www.politico.com/magazine/story/2014/06/the-supreme-court-did-not-just-kill-public-sector-unions-108432.html; and Cynthia Estlund

any time since 1937, *Harris* demonstrated, the Supreme Court represents a deep threat to American labor. In a partisan era, however, what it decides about labor unions depends on which party controls the presidency and the Senate. State and local policies toward unions trace back to national-level partisan politics.

Daniel Patrick Moynihan, whose journey from left to center to left paralleled that of his friends in American labor, told the 1981 AFL-CIO convention, two months after PATCO, that "you can't always outvote them, Lane, but you can outlast them."[118] The current moment tests that proposition. Alliance emerges from partisan *majority.* Groups and parties trade electoral muscle for ideological patronage. Groups, at the same time, become dependent on the state to secure their hard-won benefits. Once these lock-in costs have been paid, alliance may continue without majority, provided the cleavages it engendered continue to forestall any alternatives for group and party alike. At other times, with abolition-republicanism after the Civil War the most notable example, those cleavages may lose salience and alliance will disintegrate.

In this instance, however, mutual dependence amid a polarized macro environment keeps party and group allied as they face common opponents. No other actors have emerged as labor's equal inside the Democratic Party. The postmaterialist groups, for all their success in changing public mores, have failed to establish equal organizational capacity. The liberals among superrich funders have fickly changed tactics and para-organizations from cycle to cycle. Nor has the labor movement a clear alternative. A third party is out of the question. Going it alone as a pressure group requires some kind of willing partner on the other side. Yet only majority transforms organizational partnership into influence in the polity and the political regime. For labor leaders with the broadest visions, the union-Democratic alliance was always the means toward a social end, and not simply a strategy for the representation of interests. The means endure but the end still hovers, in a famous phrase from the New Deal decade, somewhere over the rainbow.

and William E. Forbath, "The War on Workers," *New York Times*, 3 July 2014, A23. On public unions' response, see David Moberg, "Has AFSCME Found the Cure to Harris v. Quinn?," *In These Times*, 16 July 2014, http://2fwww.inthesetimes.com/working/entry/16963/has_afscme_found_the_cure_to_harris.

[118] *Proceedings of the 14th Constitutional Convention of the AFL-CIO* (Washington, D.C.: AFL-CIO, 1981), 8.

CHAPTER 8

From the Moral Majority to Karl Rove

Since the Christian Right burst onto the scene in the late 1970s, white evangelical voters have become the heart of the Republican coalition, making up almost 40 percent of GOP voters in the 2012 presidential election. Movement influence inside the party remains robust; nominees on national tickets must hold strong prolife views. Movement bastions such as the Southern Baptist Convention orient themselves around national political cleavages. The story has paradoxes, too. The movement, which once sought to "put God in Washington," has had far more success and influence in wielding a veto inside the Republican Party than in shaping the polity as a whole. As observers left and right have noted, the movement's goals remain unfulfilled: by most measures, the United States has become less religious in recent decades.[1] Abortion remains legal and school prayer illegal. For the movement, the trajectory on homosexuality seems headed inexorably in the wrong direction. Like organized labor in mature alliance, the Christian Right has learned that allies protect priorities against counterattack even when majorities prove elusive, but struggled to translate influence in the allied party into change in the polity. Its concrete policy victories have occurred in courts and in the states more than in national legislation.

In the political regime, evangelicals have assumed increasing public prominence, but the cultural consensus they once felt behind them has eroded, and they increasingly seek shelter from the dictates of pluralism. As the movement has increasingly portrayed itself as a beleaguered minority more than a majority, its "defensive offensive," to use Nathan Glazer's

[1]Mark Chaves and Shawna Anderson, "Continuity and Change in American Religion, 1972–2008," in *Social Trends in American Life: Findings from the General Social Survey since 1972*, ed. Peter V. Marsden (Princeton: Princeton University Press, 2012), 212–39.

phrase, has used party as shield just as much as sword.[2] After the failure to impeach Bill Clinton, even Paul Weyrich, a far less prominent presence than in the New Right's heyday, questioned the benefits of active engagement in politics in a "decadent" society, fretting that "we have probably lost the culture war."[3] The paradox of institutionalization in politics—"we got our people elected," as Weyrich put it—without cultural hegemony still looms large.

Relatively early in their interaction, the relationship between parties and potential anchoring groups crystallizes. Yet its impact continues long past that moment. Anchoring groups exert *ongoing* influence on major parties, even as those parties shape and constrain their own development. Just as the story of labor and the Democrats continues to shape American politics, the forces that once seemed like such a political earthquake have now become a part of ordinary politics. In 1979, the only thing less probable to many observers than the emergence of the Christian Right might have been its durability. It has remained a vital anchoring group despite long odds.

The staying power of the Christian Right raises a major question for the underlying framework developed in this book: how a movement can succeed, and continue to exercise group-specific influence, even when its leading organizations—Moral Majority, the American Coalition for Traditional Values, and the Christian Coalition—have all collapsed amid financial mismanagement. Yet the paradox resolves itself. Many of the same leaders have reconstituted new groups with sequentially wider religious bases and closer relations with GOP electoral machinery. Person-to-person networks rooted in churches and linkages between elites and masses rooted in direct-mail lists survived the organizational tumult.

Across different periods, the relative importance of actors has shifted: from ideologically oriented brokers seeking policy outcomes, to movement leaders seeking glory or organizational development, to partisan elites desirous to find voters so as to win elections. The New Right sought to supersede

[2]Nathan Glazer, "Toward a New Concordat?," *This World*, Summer 1982, 113. Cf., e.g., Steven P. Miller, *The Age of Evangelicalism: America's Born-Again Years* (Oxford: Oxford University Press, 2014).

[3]Letter reprinted in Paul Weyrich, "An Open Letter to Conservatives," in *Conservatism in America since 1930: A Reader*, ed. Gregory L. Schneider (New York: New York University Press, 2003), 428–31. Weyrich's PAC had fallen on hard times along with other Viguerie-funded groups, and his fulminations against Reagan's moderation won him few friends in the White House. A quixotic effort called National Empowerment Television, with none of the sizzle that Fox News would bring to conservative broadcasting, represented his last major effort. Cf. David Grann, "Robespierre of the Right," *New Republic* 27 October 1997, 20–24; and Susanna Monroney, "Laying the Right Foundations," *Rutherford*, December 1995, 7–11 and 24. Viguerie hatched an idea for a conservative cable network in the early 1980s, but it never got off the ground. See James D. Snyder, "Playing Politics by Mail," *Sales & Marketing Magazine*, 5 July 1982, 46.

political parties with "coalitionism" organized issue by issue. Richard Viguerie and Paul Weyrich saw themselves as "leaders" and deemed evangelicals "the troops."[4] In fact, the "troops" mattered more after 1980 than the early "leaders." The brokers of the New Right were less extruded, in the manner of the CIO left, than superseded. Increasing conservatism in the Republican Party, ideological sorting of voters, and nationalization of southern politics each brought the GOP closer to the priorities of the New Right.

However, the first wave of Christian Right activism was vulnerable: the combination of elite ties and direct-mail fundraising proved brittle when mismanagement from above and apathy from below slowed and diverted the flow of money. The next two iterations of party-movement alliance followed different models. The Christian Coalition sought party building as a strategy for movement ends, while Karl Rove, George W. Bush's political guru, saw movement building as a strategy for partisan ends. In the 1990s, the Christian Coalition sought to take over state and local Republican parties, focusing on organization to the exclusion of policy or movement purpose. And after yet another crisis on the right, the GOP organization sought to build a party-based system to reach evangelical voters. Group elites' control over votes, money, and networks—the sine qua non of alliance—now appears weaker than it has at any point in the up-and-down history of the Christian Right and the Republican Party.

Beyond Moral Majority

The victory of Ronald Reagan in 1980 decisively changed the place of evangelical conservatives in the Republican Party. Movement claims to the contrary, the impact of the Christian Right was hard to find at the mass level, amid a deep repudiation of Jimmy Carter and stagflation. Yet it appeared in the Republican platform, with its planks opposing the IRS regulations and supporting a constitutional amendment "to restore protection of the right to life for unborn children," and in the popular reaction to the Republican landslide.[5] In searing confrontations with Jerry Falwell and Paul Weyrich on ABC's *Nightline* the evening after they lost their Senate seats, Frank Church of Idaho rued that "when I look back upon the foundations of liberty, I wonder where we're headed," and George McGovern of South

[4] Ed McAteer, quoted in Connie Paige, *The Right to Lifers: Who They Are, How They Operate, Where They Get Their Money* (New York: Summit Books, 1983), 182.

[5] Seymour Martin Lipset and Earl Raab, "The Election and the Evangelicals," *Commentary*, March 1981, 25–31; Pamela Johnston Conover and Virginia Gray, *Feminism and the New Right: Conflict over the American Family* (New York: Praeger, 1983), chap. 6; "Republican Party Platform of 1980," http://www.presidency.ucsb.edu/ws/index.php?pid=25844.

Dakota that "the forces of extremism have never been better organized in this country."[6]

The Reagan years were, in many ways, disappointing ones. Support from the president was largely symbolic, limited to White House meet-and-greets and stops at big religious gatherings; Reagan delivered the 1983 "Evil Empire" speech at a National Association of Evangelicals meeting in Orlando. Although he did ban funding for abortions overseas and stop the Legal Services Corporation from pushing for gay rights, Reagan nominated the moderate Sandra Day O'Connor to the Supreme Court and went through a charade of support for constitutional amendments on abortion and school prayer that stood no chance in the Senate.[7] As the Bob Jones case showed, social conservatives found more success inside the Justice Department, where an aggressive team of political appointees deployed legal theories such as originalism to retrench commitments from the Rights Revolution, and build bridges from legal conservatism outward across the state and to movement conservatives in civil society.[8]

Nor, as they approached the work of influencing policy—a very different matter from mobilizing public anger or creating new issue cleavages—were the Christian Right groups terribly effective. Rather than emphasizing party or movement building, or else achieving substantive policy victories, they often focused on high-profile media campaigns alone. The New Right's major early priority in Congress, known as the Family Protection Act and sponsored by Nevada's Paul Laxalt, contained a grab bag of everything from prolife to antitax provisions. Movement leaders faced little internal opposition to spending on dubious programs, or to pushing forward based on optimistic scenarios for revenue. Until 1984, Moral Majority had not even coded its supporters by congressional district.[9]

By the late 1980s, this first wave had run its course as a series of Washington-centered groups encountered serious financial problems and closed their doors. The movement was lucky, however. Party-group ties had by then established themselves outside the peak para-organization, and soon reconstructed themselves. For an insurgency just trying to make its way in the party system, the consequences would have been far more severe.

[6] *Nightline*, ABC News, 3 November 1980.

[7] Sidney Blumenthal, "The Righteous Empire," *New Republic*, 22 October 1984, 18–24.

[8] Al Kamen and Howard Kurtz, "Theorists on Right Find Fertile Ground," *Washington Post*, 9 August 1985, A1; David M. O'Brien, "Meese's Agenda for Ensuring the Reagan Legacy," *Los Angeles Times*, 28 September 1986, E3; Steven M. Teles "Transformative Bureaucracy: Reagan's Lawyers and the Dynamics of Political Involvement," *Studies in American Political Development* 23 (2009): 61–83; Robert Post and Reva Siegel, "Originalism as a Political Practice: The Right's Living Constitution," *Fordham Law Review* 75 (2006): 545–75.

[9] Matthew C. Moen, *The Christian Right and Congress* (Tuscaloosa: University of Alabama Press, 1989), pt. 2.

The party would have been afraid to be associated with movement leaders, and those movement leaders would have lacked the infrastructural capacity to contact supporters. Instead, the same leaders and networks reassembled in new institutional forms.

Midlevel historical figures built institutions away from the public limelight. An evolving series of weekly meetings in Washington have brought activists across "on the same page" across disparate groups and issues.[10] In early 1981, New Right leaders, along with Edwin Feulner of the Heritage Foundation, formed the Council for National Policy, an exclusive invitation-only, off-the-record group to facilitate connections across the insurgent right, and serve as a testing ground for candidates and causes. Through three decades, the CNP has remained, as a 2002 account termed it, "the most powerful conservative group you've never heard of."[11] The CNP brought to the same tables in hotel ballrooms New Rightists (Paul Weyrich, Richard Viguerie, Howard Phillips), evangelical pastors (Tim LaHaye, Pat Robertson, D. James Kennedy, Paige Patterson, James Dobson), legal conservatives (William Bradford Reynolds, John Bolton), movement funders (Joe Coors, Nelson Bunker Hunt, Rich DeVos), supply siders (George Gilder, Paul Craig Roberts), the far right (Gary North, R. J. Rushdoony, Robert Welch), and Republican stalwarts (John Ashbrook, Jesse Helms, James McClure).[12] This umbrella group has outlasted most of the para-organizations that its initial members led and remained a conservative bulwark.

In 1986, the Moral Majority shifted into a new group called the Liberty Federation, while the Religious Roundtable, Christian Voice, the National Christian Action Center, and the American Coalition for Traditional Values all closed their doors. Richard Viguerie himself slid into irrelevance; he

[10]Thomas Medvetz, "The Strength of Weekly Ties: Relations of Material and Symbolic Exchange in the Conservative Movement," *Politics & Society* 34 (2006): 343–68.

[11]Marc Ambinder, "Inside the Council for National Policy," *ABC News*, 2 May 2002; see also Adam Clymer, "Conservatives Gather in Umbrella Council for a National Policy," *New York Times*, 20 May 1981, A17. The New Right found models and targets not only in left-liberalism, but in the centrist establishment, and designed the CNP along the lines of other influential gatherings (often underwritten with Rockefeller money), including the Bilderberg Group and the Council on Foreign Relations. On this comparison, see Sidney Blumenthal, *The Rise of the Counter-Establishment: From Conservative Ideology to Political Power* (New York: Times Books, 1986); John B. Judis, "The Twilight of the Gods," *Wilson Quarterly* 15 (1991): 43–55; and Andrew Rich, *Think Tanks, Public Policy, and the Politics of Expertise* (Cambridge: Cambridge University Press, 2004).

[12]Weyrich papers, unprocessed accretion of 12/88. See also the steering committee list reprinted in *Group Research Report*, 26 February 1982, 7; and members listed in Edward Ericson, "Behind Closed Doors at the CNP," *Church and State*, June 1996, 4–7. A notable omission from the membership list: neoconservatives, often Jewish and, for all their hawkishness, still generally moderate on role-of-government and church-state questions. The only identifiably Jewish name on a 1988 membership list is that of Jack Abramoff, who had preceded Ralph Reed as president of the College Republicans.

attacked the popular Reagan administration, mounted a failed bid to serve as lieutenant governor of Virginia, and lost his technological edge to other shops, many run by his former associates. The Unification Church, founded in South Korea by Sun Myung Moon and famous for mass weddings over which Moon presided, bought his headquarters at an inflated price—in essence, a bailout.[13] Although admittedly indirect and observational rather than experimental, some evidence indicates that direct mail reached saturation and recipients tossed all the pieces into the trash.[14] Nevertheless, vendors still held the records, on magnetic tape reels and later in ever-richer computer files, even when the groups themselves disappeared, and sold them to new groups and campaigns that reestablished ties with donors.

The Reagan campaign mounted a massive mobilization effort for the 1984 campaign. Although the president was never terribly devout (Pat Moynihan quipped that "I absolutely believe President Reagan when he says he does not want to establish a state religion—that would require him to attend services"[15]), and even supported the Equal Rights Amendment and signed a liberalized abortion law early in his years as governor, his image-makers for decades constructed a portrait of devotion, emphasizing Reagan's personal relationship with God. In a 1976 interview, Reagan claimed that "yes, I have had an experience that could be described as 'born again.'"[16] They redoubled their efforts for a campaign that wrapped the Gipper in gauzy

[13] Molly Moore and Tom Sherwood, "PACs Balk at Viguerie Mailing Fees," *Washington Post*, 22 March 1985, A1; David Brooks, "Please, Mr. Postman: The Travails of Richard Viguerie," *National Review*, 20 June 1986, 28–32; Lloyd Grove, "The Graying of Richard Viguerie," *Washington Post* 29 June 1989, D1; and Alan Pell Crawford, "Reactionaries' Reaction," *Nation*, 20 February 1989, 231–36. On the Unification Church, which mixed a complex theology that accorded Moon near-messianic status, with anticommunist and profamily politics, and a desire to achieve influence, see "New Christian Group Jumps into Right-Wing Lobbying," *Group Research Report*, 28 February 1979, 5; Edward E. Plowman, "Is Morality All Right?," *Christianity Today*, 2 November 1979, 76–85; Bill McKenzie, Ken Ruberg, and Jim Leach, "Theocracy from the Right: The Reverend Sun Myung Moon and the American Political Process," *Ripon Forum*, January 1983, 8–14; Michael Isikoff, "Church Spends Millions on Its Image," *Washington Post*, 17 September 1984, A1; Dinesh D'Souza, "Moon's Planet," *Policy Review*, Spring 1985, 28–49; John B. Judis, "Rev. Moon's Rising Political Influence," *U.S. News & World Report*, 27 March 1989, 27–28.

[14] Matthew C. Moen, "From Revolution to Evolution: The Changing Nature of the Christian Right," *Sociology of Religion* 55 (1994): 345–57; cf. R. Kenneth Godwin, *One Billion Dollars of Influence* (Chatham, N.J.: Chatham House, 1988).

[15] Paul Taylor, "Falwell Hits Mondale on Religion; Democrat's Actions Called 'Hypocrisy,'" *Washington Post*, 10 September 1984, A6.

[16] "Reagan Seeks Return to Absolutes," *National Courier*, 6 August 1976, 6. See also William Rose, "The Reagans and Their Pastor," *Christian Life*, May 1968, 23; and, from an associate of Pat Robertson, Bob Slosser, *Reagan Inside Out* (Waco, Tex.: Word Books, 1984), chap. 1, which suggests that the Holy Spirit worked through Reagan. For a framework, see Hugh Heclo, "Ronald Reagan and the American Public Philosophy," in *The Reagan Presidency: Pragmatic Conservatism and Its Legacies*, ed. W. Elliot Brownlee and Hugh Davis Graham (Lawrence: University Press of Kansas, 2003), 17–39.

Americanism. At the Republican convention in Dallas, Christian Right leaders offered the opening prayer (from James Robison) and the closing benediction (from W. A. Criswell). "If we ever forget that we are a nation under God," Reagan told a massive prayer breakfast the morning after adjournment, "we are a nation gone under."[17]

The American Coalition for Traditional Values (pronounced "active"), an umbrella para-church group, did the bulk of the work on the ground. Its executive committee included the major televangelists across denomination, as well as leading figures in the SBC and the Assemblies of God; a board of three hundred prominent ministers coordinated voter registration and get-out-the-vote work. Its leader was Tim LaHaye, a graduate of Bob Jones, pastor of a church outside San Diego with a potentially reviewable school, antigay advocate, recent past president of the Council for National Policy, and prolific author.[18]

At a White House reception in July 1984, Reagan told ACTV's leaders that "what you are doing is important, is necessary, and is right." Lee Atwater, Reagan's chief political aide for the South, credited ACTV with registering four and a half million voters.[19] Yet ACTV served more as a deliberately targeted adjunct to the Reagan campaign than a force with ongoing aims of its own. It collapsed in 1986 after the exposure of its funding from the Unification Church.[20]

The Southern Baptist Convention: "In It for the Long Haul"

The conservative takeover of the Southern Baptist Convention beginning in 1979 fused cleavages inside the nation's largest Protestant sect with those in national politics, and provided the Republican Party with stable support

[17] Richard V. Pierard, "Religion and the 1984 Election Campaign," *Review of Religious Research* 27 (1985): 105; Richard V. Pierard, "Reagan and the Evangelicals," in *Fundamentalism Today: What Makes It So Attractive?*, ed. Marla J. Selvidge (Elgin, Ill.: Brethren Press, 1984), 47–61; Blumenthal, "Righteous Empire"; V. S. Naipaul, "Among the Republicans," *New York Review of Books*, 25 October 1984, 5–17.

[18] Darren Dochuk, *From Bible Belt to Sunbelt: Plain Folk Religion, Grassroots Politics, and the Rise of Evangelical Conservatism* (New York: Norton, 2011), 234; John Leland Berg, "An Ethical Analysis of Selected Leaders and Issues of the New Religious Right" (PhD diss., Baylor University, 1985), 159–90.

[19] Daniel J. Galvin, *Presidential Party Building: Dwight D. Eisenhower to George W. Bush* (Princeton: Princeton University Press, 2010), 135; Bruce Nesmith, *The New Republican Coalition: The Reagan Campaign and White Evangelicals* (New York: Peter Lang, 1994), 100; Haynes Johnson and Thomas B. Edsall, "North Carolina Contests Spark Registration War," *Washington Post*, 30 September 1984, A1; Beth Spring, "Some Christian Leaders Want Further Political Activism," *Christianity Today*, 9 November 1984, 46; Kenneth L. Woodward with Eleanor Clift, "Playing Politics at Church," *Newsweek*, 9 July 1984, 52.

[20] Carolyn Weaver "Unholy Alliance," *Mother Jones*, January 1986, 14–17 and 44–46.

resting on newly espoused socially conservative positions. As Paul Weyrich recalled, "The problem with Jerry Falwell and some of those people was that they had very short attention spans. But these people are in it for the long haul."[21]

The takeover of the SBC, like the formation of the CIO a half century earlier, interjected partisan politics into the stable operations of a group in civil society that, while it had long had political interests and involvements, had refrained from taking sides on the big questions of national politics. Instead, the two groups developed ideologies—industrial democracy and biblical inerrancy—that spoke both to their distinctive mission, and to the priorities of the allied political party. The anchoring group provided the foot soldiers and stoked the fires in exchange for favorable policies.[22] Had the New Right not developed the issue bundle of positions that defined social conservatism, then shifts toward inerrancy in the SBC would simply have represented yet another theological reorientation, without implications for political coalitions.

"The Holy Bible," states the Baptist Faith & Message, the denomination's statement of beliefs, "has God for its author, salvation for its end, and truth, without any mixture of error, for its matter." To generalize, for conservatives in the SBC, "truth, without any mixture of error, for its matter" meant that each and every word in the Bible is true. For moderates, it meant that the Bible's message is entirely true.[23] Denominational employees and students at seminary must sign agreement with the Baptist Faith & Message, so the question of biblical inerrancy poses no small challenge. Both sides reached back deep into Baptist tradition: the "cons" to a bedrock belief in the Bible's truth, and the "mods" to "the priesthood of all believers"—the freedom, in a noncreedal faith, for all individuals to make their own way with God.[24]

Like so many of the religious cleavages of the seventies and eighties, the divides in the SBC emerged from splits over civil rights. The SBC largely sat out the civil rights struggle led by African American clergy; it finally

[21] Michele McKeegan, *Abortion Politics: Mutiny in the Ranks of the Right* (New York: Free Press, 1992), 169.

[22] While it has taken strong stands on policy and signaled its intentions clearly, as a consequence of its tax-exempt status, the SBC has not, unlike unions, engaged in direct electioneering.

[23] James C. Hefley, *The Truth in Crisis: The Controversy in the Southern Baptist Convention*, vol. 1 (Hannibal, Mo.: Hannibal Books, 1986), 28–30.

[24] Fisher Humphreys, *The Way We Were, How Southern Baptist Theology Has Changed, and What It Means to Us All* (New York: McCracken Press, 1994), esp. chaps. 3 and 11, provides an excellent summary of commonalities and differences across Baptist theologies. See also Arthur Emery Farnsley II, *Southern Baptist Politics: Authority and Power in the Restructuring of an American Denomination* (University Park: Pennsylvania State University Press, 1994); Charles W. Allen, "Paige Patterson: Contender for Baptist Sectarianism," *Review and Expositor* 79 (1982): 105–20; D. G. Hart, "Conservatism, the Protestant Right, and the Failure of Religious History," *Journal of the Historical Society* 4 (2004): 447–93.

endorsed civil rights legislation at its 1965 meeting, but thereafter typically "reaffirmed its general commitment to racial justice in well-worn platitudes," and refused to endorse specific measures.[25] While the scar of race pushed moderates toward political action, conservatives saw moral truths swept up in the maelstrom. They pushed the denomination to jettison its search for contemporary relevance, reaffirm its belief in biblical inerrancy, and stand behind the public policies that they felt such an interpretation demanded.[26]

By the 1970s activist racial liberals held key posts, and they began to push against other forms of hierarchy, notably gender. In the SBC seminaries, theologians began to grapple with the role of women, and the possibilities for multiple voices and even inconsistencies in the Bible. In 1971, the Southern Baptist Convention passed a resolution acknowledging divergent positions, recognizing "the dignity of human life, including fetal life," and calling "on Southern Baptists to work for legislation that will allow the possibility of abortion under such conditions as rape, incest, clear evidence of severe physical deformity, and carefully ascertained evidence of the likelihood of damage to the emotional, mental, and physical health of the mother." The SBC generally accepted *Roe*, and divisions on abortion crosscut sectarian lines. The Baptist Joint Committee, the SBC-led Washington lobby, opposed a prolife constitutional amendment on old Baptist grounds of "liberty of conscience and the separation of church and state."[27]

In 1967, Paul Pressler, a well-connected Houston judge, and Paige Patterson, a third-generation preacher and protégé of influential SBC conservative W. A. Criswell, "the Baptist Pope," met over beignets in New Orleans to despair against encroaching liberalism. While Patterson and Criswell provided the theological basis for the conservative takeover, Pressler was the great tactician and the key link to the conservative movement; he served a term as president of the Council for National Policy.[28]

[25]Mark Newman, *Getting Right with God: Southern Baptists and Desegregation, 1945–1995* (Tuscaloosa: University of Alabama Press, 2001), 192.

[26]When asked in a private conversation whether to take literally the Bible's passages on slavery, Adrian Rogers reportedly answered, "Well, I believe slavery is a much-maligned institution. If we had slavery today, we would not have this welfare mess." To be sure, a leading SBC moderate reports the quotation. See Cecil E. Sherman, "An Overview of the Moderate Movement," in *The Struggle for the Soul of the SBC: Moderate Responses to the Fundamentalist Movement*, ed. Walter E. Shurden (Macon, Ga.: Mercer University Press, 1993), 36.

[27]Paul Harvey, *Freedom's Coming: Religious Culture and the Shaping of the South from the Civil War through the Civil Rights Era* (Chapel Hill: University of North Carolina Press, 2005), 245–50; Paul L. Sadler, "The Abortion Issue within the Southern Baptist Convention, 1969–1988" (PhD diss., Baylor University, 1991), 32; James E. Wood, Jr., "Religious Liberty and Abortion Rights," *Report from the Capital*, January 1974, 2.

[28]On Criswell, see Dick J. Reavis, "The Politics of Armageddon," *Texas Monthly*, October 1984, 162–66 and 235–46; and Paige Patterson, "W.A. Criswell," in *Theologians of the Baptist Tradition*, ed. Timothy George and David S. Dockery (Nashville: Broadman & Holman, 2001),

After years of laying the groundwork, in 1979 the conservatives bused enough supporters to the annual convention to elect an inerrantist president, Adrian Rogers, a Memphis minister. The vote—an equivalent to the 1935 AF of L convention, when John L. Lewis punched the Carpenters' "Big Bill" Hutcheson on his way to forming the CIO—began a wrenching, decade-long process that ended with the conservatives in firm control over the SBC. It was yet another religio-political transformation begun in the pivotal year of 1979.

For the SBC conservatives, biblical inerrancy went hand in hand with New Right politics. At the 1979 convention, James Robison, the antigay Dallas televangelist, preached that "if you tolerate any form of liberalism . . . you are the enemy of God. Satan, my friend, is attacking the word of God. Satan will never concede that the Bible is the divine, inspired, infallible, inerrant word of God."[29] Adrian Rogers was pastor to Ed McAteer, who had worked to organize religious academies. McAteer, in turn, regularly consulted on resolutions with the "mechanic of the New Right," Morton Blackwell, the Reagan administration's emissary to evangelicals. The wives of Paige Patterson and Adrian Rogers served on the advisory board for Beverly LaHaye's Concerned Women for America—alongside Dot (Mrs. Jesse) Helms and Macel (Mrs. Jerry) Falwell.[30] In 1982, the SBC described the fetus as a "pre-born person" and reversed its support for the ERA. In 1988, Adrian Rogers, sent out to all SBC pastors a letter praising George H. W. Bush's pro-life record. A pamphlet from the SBC's Christian Life Commission framed the scriptural themes: "The Bible makes no distinction between the humanity and personhood of the born and unborn."[31]

Given the decentralized structure of the SBC, it took until 1990 for the conservatives to consolidate the dual transformation of religious doctrine and to political alliance. They installed their choices to lead the five

233–56. On Pressler, see John MacCormack, "Southern Baptists' Architect Inspires Either Wrath or Rapture," *Dallas Times Herald*, 8 October 1990, A-4; Paul Pressler, *A Hill on Which to Die: One Southern Baptist's Journey* (Nashville: Broadman & Holman, 1999); and Pressler's interviews with the author and postmillennialist Gary North, in Dennis Ray Wiles, "Factors Contributing to the Resurgence of Conservatism in the Southern Baptist Convention, 1979–1990" (PhD diss., Southwest Baptist Theological Seminary, 1992).

[29] James Robison, "Satan's Subtle Attacks," in *Going for the Jugular: A Documentary History of the SBC Holy War*, ed. Walter B. Shurden and Randy Shepley (Macon, Ga.: Mercer University Press, 1996), 31. See also, from a John Birch Society publication, John Rees, "Conservative Evangelist James Robison: An Exclusive Interview," *Review of the News*, 1 July 1980, 39–48.

[30] Allan J. Mayer, "A Tide of Born-Again Politics," *Newsweek*, 15 September 1980, 28; Stan Hastey, "Reagan's Social Revolution Breathing, but Barely Alive," *Baptist Press*, 28 January 1983; Amy Greene, "SBC Tied to Political Right?," *SBC Today*, October 1987, 3–4.

[31] Sadler, "Abortion Issue," chap. 4; see also Michele Dillon, "Religion and Culture in Tension: The Abortion Discourses of the U.S. Catholic Bishops and the Southern Baptist Convention," *Religion and American Culture* 5 (1995): 159–80.

SBC seminaries—Patterson is now the president of the Southwest Baptist Theological Seminary—and boards and missions on matters ranging from Sunday School curriculum to lobbying. They also forbade churches where women serve as pastors from affiliation with the convention. The "mods" who had not already left the SBC formed the small Cooperative Baptist Fellowship. The SBC pulled out of the Baptist Joint Committee and pivoted sharply in its interpretation of the Establishment Clause. After a job search in which he had to submit in writing his views on inerrancy, abortion, women in the clergy, and capital punishment, Richard Land, who had known Pressler since his high school days, replaced the liberal Foy Valentine at the now-renamed Ethics & Religious Liberty Commission, where he served from 1988 until 2013.

Land and the SBC pushed hard for joint action among conservative Christians, assuming particular prominence since the demise of the Christian Coalition. Paradoxically, the drive to reassert traditional doctrine has sublimated the denomination's distinctly Baptist beliefs: in a noncreedal faith with substantial individual and congregational autonomy, and in "a free church in a free state." Instead, Southern Baptists increasingly resemble other conservative Protestants theologically, and cooperate, in Schaeffer-style cobelligerency, even with Catholics and Mormons. Land coordinated joint action with Catholics against abortion and, with D. James Kennedy, defended the invasion of Iraq as a just war. In 2004, the ERLC launched a massive voter education campaign, "I Vote Values," in concert with the Family Research Council, founded in 1983 by James Dobson and focused especially on gay marriage. The SBC endures as a bulwark of theological and political conservatism.[32]

The Electric Church and Pat Robertson

Many conservative Christian leaders rose to prominence not through the traditional routes of ministering at long-prominent pulpits or assuming leadership at schools of theology, but through the "electric church," as the head of its trade association named the broadcasters who had become

[32] Pressler, *Hill*, 253; Michael M. Soud, "A Critical Analysis of the Criswell College's Effect on the Southern Baptist Convention, 1980–2000" (PhD diss., Southeastern Baptist Theological Seminary, 2003), 163–64; Oran P. Smith, *The Rise of Baptist Republicanism* (New York: New York University Press, 1997); "The So-Called 'Land Letter,'" http://erlc.com/article/the-so-called-land-letter; Julia Duin, "Dobson's Retirement Ends Era for Evangelicals," *Washington Times*, 4 March 2009, A1. "Let's remember," Land said in 1988, that in 1969 when he graduated from college, "homosexuality was a crime that was being prosecuted." Jerry Sutton and James T. Draper, Jr., *A Matter of Conviction: A History of Southern Baptist Engagement with the Culture* (Nashville: B&H, 2007), 275.

increasingly prominent by the 1970s.[33] That social change could have, but did not, form the basis for group-specific mobilization into partisan politics. Instead, Pat Robertson's presidential run, and formation of the Christian Coalition, moved televangelism into the Republican fold.

Television expanded movement activity to embrace a wide spectrum of Pentecostals and charismatics. According to Arbitron estimates, viewership of religious television rose fivefold between the late 1960s and the mid-1980s, from five million to twenty-five million.[34] Whatever viewers actually assimilated from the tube, this audience represented many Americans' exposure to the world of conservative Protestantism—and also a market that the Christian Right sought to tap. And so rose a new breed of pastor. He held a national rather than a local audience; he was a showman as well as a minister, in order to keep viewers' eyes glued so their souls could be saved; and he had to raise money. Paying for TV airtime, whether over the air or, starting in the late 1970s, on satellite or cable, cost serious money, and religious broadcasters—many of them initially disliked the term "televangelists"—relied on the same direct-mail technologies as secular New Right operatives. Richard Viguerie cross-fertilized his work for churches and campaigns, and often used the former to subsidize the latter. Although some Pentecostal televangelists praised the Moral Majority, most steered clear of direct politicking.

D. James Kennedy at Coral Ridge Presbyterian Church, Jerry Falwell at the Thomas Road Baptist Church, Charles Stanley at First Baptist Church in Atlanta, Robert Schuller at the Crystal Cathedral, and Rex Humbard at the Cathedral of Tomorrow all broadcast their churches' services on television; Pat Robertson, Jimmy Swaggart, Oral Roberts, and Jim and Tammy Faye Bakker preached to the airwaves without ongoing bricks-and-mortar churches. Telephone hotlines sought to replace in-person pastoral care and counseling. Yet the televangelists had not created face-to-face communities, with their potential to generate collective action.[35]

Many of these broadcasters came out of the Pentecostal tradition. Pentecostals hold a distinctive set of beliefs around "the experience of an enduement with power called 'Baptism in the Holy Spirit,'" and evidenced with miracles such as glossolalia (speaking in tongues). Theirs is a far more joyful and ecstatic tradition, complete with over-the-top confessionals and

[33] Ben Armstrong, *The Electric Church* (Nashville: T. Potter, 1979).

[34] Jeffrey Hadden, "The Rise and Fall of American Televangelism," *Annals of the American Academy of Political and Social Science* 527 (1993): 113–30. For a longer discussion on audience size, see Jeffrey Hadden and Anson Shupe, *Televangelism: Power and Politics on God's Frontier* (New York: Henry Holt, 1988), 142–59.

[35] Philip Yancey, "The Ironies and Impact of PTL," *Christianity Today*, 21 September 1979, 29–31.

adoring crowds, than the independent Baptism, with its plain worship and regard for the Old Testament, that formed the bulk of Moral Majority.[36]

Adding to the dislocations of the late 1980s, a series of lurid scandals hit televangelists in short succession. By discrediting so many prominent evangelicals, the church scandals closed off a major source of party-group brokers in the movement's initial decade. Without those alternatives foregone amid scandal, one can imagine religious broadcasters occupying a niche like that of Fox News, with special appeal to evangelicals.[37] Jimmy Swaggart, who had launched a public investigation against another Assemblies of God minister, Marvin Gorman, himself had an affair and used prostitutes. Jim Bakker had an affair, and a very uncomfortable Jerry Falwell tried to rescue Heritage USA, the Christian theme park in South Carolina that Jim and Tammy Faye Bakker had begun to develop. Oral Roberts warned that if fundraising for his hospital (which combined faith healing and modern medicine) failed to reach its goals, God would "call him home."

Elite misbehavior triggered consequences in the mass public. The scandals may well have triggered a backlash against religion, associating it with hypocrisy more than virtue. Viewership of religious broadcasting fell by half. After remaining steady at about 7 percent of the population for two decades, the fraction of Americans identifying a religious preference as "nothing in particular" began a steady increase in about 1990, just after the church scandals had broken, to a point where by 2014 about 16 percent of all adults, including almost a third of those born in the 1980s, claim to have no religion.[38]

Like so many critical figures in party-group alliance, Pat Robertson stood at the intersection of multiple political traditions: in his case, the old

[36] Donald W. Dayton, "Theological Roots of Pentecostalism," *Pneuma: The Journal for Pentecostal Studies* 2 (1980): 5. Many Pentecostals are African American. Their views are quite conservative on issues of personal morality, somewhat more so than other African Americans, although not on economic questions. See the profiles in Corwin Smidt, ed., *Pulpit and Politics: Clergy in American Politics at the Advent of the Millennium* (Waco, Tex.: Baylor University Press, 2004); cf. Allison Calhoun-Brown, "The Politics of Black Evangelicals: What Hinders Diversity in the Christian Right?," *American Politics Quarterly* 26 (1998): 81–109. Baptists and Pentecostals each divide on eschatological questions, with pre- and postmillennialists in both camps adhering to differing schemes for the Days of Judgment—and dictates about the relations between church and state, and role for the State of Israel.

[37] The literatures on talk radio, cable news, and televangelism have not established the similarities and differences in the political impacts among conservative media.

[38] Michael Hout and Claude S. Fischer trace the "nones" to antipathy against the Christian Right, but do not specifically implicate the church scandals. "Why More Americans Have No Religious Preference: Politics and Generations," *American Sociological Review* 67 (2002): 165–90; cf. Daniel Schlozman and Valerie Lewis, "Nones, Evangelicals, and the Future of the Culture Wars" (paper, American Political Science Association meeting, Washington, D.C., 2–5 September 2010).

Bourbon political elite, Southern Baptism, and the fast-growing world of charismatic religion. While many leaders of the Christian Right emerged from modest backgrounds, Robertson came from Tidewater aristocracy. His father, A. Willis Robertson III, an archconservative Byrd Democrat, served three decades in the U.S. Senate, where he opposed all civil rights legislation. Pat attended Washington and Lee, and earned undistinguished marks at Yale Law School.

Then Robertson found God. While at the Biblical Seminary in New York, he discovered Pentecostal religion, but was ordained a Southern Baptist. After briefly pastoring a church near Virginia Beach, he founded the Christian Broadcasting Network. CBN bought a series of low-power broadcasters to distribute a mix of televised prayers (Jim and Tammy Faye Bakker hosted a show, before they went off on their own) and "The 700 Club," Robertson's talk show with a mixture of political and religious guests. Beginning in the 1970s, CBN moved aggressively into cable and satellite broadcasting. Direct mail and telephone hotlines allowed CBN to track names and addresses when viewers requested baptisms in the Holy Spirit, prayer, or salvation. Via the Freedom Council, founded in 1981, Robertson used a series of list rentals and shell companies to give the CBN lists to his presidential campaign. These files proved the basis for the Christian Coalition. It is a textbook case in how to politicize extant networks.[39]

Robertson steered largely clear of the early Christian Right. "God isn't a right-winger or a left-winger," he said in 1980. From Virginia Beach, Robertson looked down on the less sophisticated Falwell. From Lynchburg, Jerry Falwell distrusted his rival Robertson's Pentecostal sympathies, and in 1988 pointedly issued an early presidential endorsement to George H. W. Bush. Yet each, in his own way, bridged the divide between traditional Baptist congregations and the new world of televangelism.[40]

The ubiquitous Paul Weyrich had his eye on Robertson, too, and recruited him to head the Council for National Policy in 1985 and 1986. Robertson, who had never held public office, then announced a run for president in 1988. He raised forty-one million dollars in public and matching money through the primary, the highest total for any candidate. The campaign was not an electoral success; Robertson won no state delegation, and came in second only in caucus states. The Swaggart scandal broke two weeks before

[39] David Edwin Harrell, Jr., *Pat Robertson: A Personal, Religious, and Political Portrait* (New York: Harper & Row, 1987), 63; Pat Robertson and Jamie Buckingham, *Shout It from the Housetops* (Plainfield, N.J.: Logos, 1972); Garrett Epps, "Pat Robertson's a Preacher, but His Father Was a Pol," *Washington Post*, 19 October 1986, H1; Charles R. Babcock, "Robertson: Blending Charity and Politics; Tax-Exempt Television Ministry Was Foundation for Campaign," *Washington Post*, 2 November 1987, A1.

[40] William Martin, *With God on Our Side: The Rise of the Religious Right in America*, rev. ed. (New York: Broadway Books, 2005), 259.

Super Tuesday, and Robertson's erratic behaviors hurt his free-spending campaign. The Bush campaign, led by Lee Atwater, mounted a church-by-church strategy in the South aimed at shoring up support in large congregations that were evangelical but not charismatic. Robertson discovered that he had no extant support inside the party apparatus, and emerged from his loss determined to build effective organization, from the grassroots up, that would increase social conservatives' clout inside the Republican Party.[41]

Rise and Fall of the Christian Coalition

The Christian Coalition, formed in 1989, combined the networks created in the Robertson campaign with the savvy of grassroots, partisan organizing. Pat Robertson served as chairman and gave some of the resources of CBN, but the key figure was the executive director, Ralph Reed. Along with Jack Abramoff, later a disgraced lobbyist, and the antitax crusader Grover Norquist, Reed had been a high-profile hell-raiser (with funding from the Unification Church) in early 1980s College Republican politics. He then found religion and went off to Emory for a doctorate in history, where he wrote about evangelical colleges in the nineteenth-century South.[42] Reed had backed Jack Kemp in the 1988 primaries, but by 1990 found himself in Virginia Beach as the decade's most important broker.

The Christian Coalition sought to transform an existing movement into an explicitly partisan setting. Like CIO-PAC under Sidney Hillman, the Coalition emphasized campaign work, influence inside organizational parties, and pressure on targeted lawmakers (and sometimes bureaus and agencies) rather than broad-brush public crusades. Both periods of institutionalization led to greater success within parties than in translating the anchoring alliance into victories in the polity. Such are the paradoxes of mature party-movement alliance.

While the early Christian Right focused on single-issue, national-level campaigns, the Christian Coalition reversed both patterns. In classic

[41] Cory SerVaas and Maynard Good Stoddard, "CBN's Pat Robertson: White House Next?," *Saturday Evening Post*, March 1985, 50; Allen D. Hertzke, *Echoes of Discontent: Jesse Jackson, Pat Robertson, and the Resurgence of Populism* (Washington, D.C.: CQ Press, 1993), 136–51; James M. Penning, "Pat Robertson and the GOP: 1988 and Beyond," *Sociology of Religion* 55 (1994): 327–44.

[42] Benjamin Hart, ed., *The Third Generation: Young Conservative Leaders Look to the Future* (Washington, D.C.: Regnery, 1987), 68. On Reed and his contemporaries, see Nina Easton, *Gang of Five: Leaders at the Center of the Conservative Crusade* (New York: Simon & Schuster, 1999). On funding, see McKenzie, Ruberg, and Leach, "Theocracy from the Right," 10. See also Charles Crossfield, "College Republicans Back on the Front Lines," *Conservative Digest*, November 1982, 11.

models of social movements, discrete local grievances coalesce into national and sometimes transnational causes.[43] Early Christian Right groups, by contrast favored national media exposure over local organizing, and recruited many weak first-time candidates for office. The Christian Coalition saw the limits in those scattershot efforts. It returned to local-level organizing, and carefully meshed its appeals with those of other influencers inside the allied party.

The Christian Coalition mounted a sustained effort to take over state and local Republican committees, the proving grounds for future candidates. This process eased the challenge of getting loyal Republican voters unaffiliated with the movement to back Christian Right stalwarts. While Republicans had been avid party-builders at the national level, many local organizations were largely moribund, and ripe for takeover. In the 1980s, conservative evangelicals had often bypassed local organizations populated, said one activist, by "three Martini Episcopalians." Instead, they waged primary battles. They sometimes appeared, at the local level, as much party faction as anchoring group.[44]

A 1993 guide told activists to "become directly involved in the local Republican committee yourself. This way you can get a copy of the local committee rules and a feel for who's who in the current local Republican committee. You should never mention the name 'Christian Coalition' in Republican circles."[45] Seminars in leadership development covered not only turnout and key races, but the minutiae of Republican delegate selection rules. A 1994 survey for *Campaigns & Elections*, which polled political operatives in each state, found that Christian Right affiliates made up the majority of the Republican state committees in eighteen states, and at least a quarter in a further thirteen; the geographic patterns, concentrated in the South with additional strength in the Rocky Mountain states, should

[43] See, e.g., Sidney Tarrow, "States and Opportunities: The Political Structuring of Social Movements," in *Comparative Perspectives on Social Movements: Political Opportunities, Mobilizing Structures, and Cultural Framings*, ed. Doug McAdam, John D. McCarthy, and Mayer N. Zald (Cambridge: Cambridge University Press, 1996), 41–61.

[44] Mark Caleb Smith, "With Friends Like These: The Religious Right, the Republican Party, and the Politics of the American South" (PhD diss., University of Georgia, 2001); Steve Bruce, *The Rise and Fall of the Christian Right: Conservative Protestant Politics in America, 1978–1988* (Oxford: Clarendon, 1988), 54; William Bole, "The Christian Right Eyes the Republican Party," *Interchange Report*, Winter 1985, 10–12; Rob Gurwitt, "1986 Elections Generate GOP Power Struggle," *CQ Weekly Edition*, 12 April 1986, 802–7; Paige Schneider, "The Impact of the Christian Right Social Movement on Republican Party Development in the South" (PhD diss., Emory University, 2000). Descriptions of these contests resonate with contemporary fights between the party establishment and the Tea Party.

[45] "Building a Christian GOP," *Harper's*, January 1993, 26; see also Barry Horstman, "Christian Activists Using 'Stealth' Campaign Tactics," *Los Angeles Times*, 5 April 1992, 1; and Joe Conason, "The Religious Right's Quiet Revival," *Nation*, 27 April 1992, 541 and 553–59.

be unsurprising, although the survey also reported high influence in a clutch of Upper Midwest caucus states that are unusually permeable to issue activists.[46]

By taking over local parties directly, the Christian Coalition went a step further than the labor movement to attenuate the distance between party and movement, and utilize voice rather than the possibility of exit in party affairs. The National Republican Senatorial Committee even gave the Coalition a sixty-four-thousand-dollar grant in 1994. The flow of dollars marks an important difference between the anchoring alliances, and underscores the Christian Coalition's particular contribution to Republican candidates: not money per se, but access to time and group-specific electoral niches.[47]

The Christian Coalition looked for leadership in the pews rather than the pulpits, often among leaders from the private sector with overlapping ties in business, church, and politics. In contrast to the Moral Majority, which primarily mobilized extant networks of independent Baptists, and to the hybrid strategy of ACTV, the Christian Coalition organized geographically by precinct. This decision, alongside selective outreach to conservative Catholics, helped to diversify its denominational orientation. Only one state chair of the Christian Coalition was a minister; its Michigan state director, a veteran of the Robertson campaign, was Catholic.[48]

The Christian Coalition used as its distinctive method of persuasion the voter guide, to be distributed in church—ideally inside the church bulletin—on the Sunday before election day. The Coalition, to maintain its tax-exempt (although not tax-deductible) 501(c)(4) status, distributed guides on issues such as "Homosexuals in the Military" and "Balanced Budget Amendment" that, while putatively neutral, listed positions as profamily or

[46]John F. Persinos, "Has the Christian Right Taken Over the Republican Party?," *Campaigns & Elections*, September 1994, 21–24. The survey question asked, "What percentage of the governing body of the Republican Party in your state would you estimate is directly affiliated with the Christian Right or with an organization commonly associated with religious conservative causes such as pro-life, home-schooling, and other similar groups?" See also Thomas B. Edsall, "Robertson Urges Christian Activists to Take Over GOP State Parties," *Washington Post*, 10 September 1995, A10; and, emphasizing informal organization, Martin Cohen, "Moral Victories: Cultural Conservatism and the Creation of a New Republican Congressional Majority" (PhD diss., University of California, Los Angeles, 2005).

[47]Duane Murray Oldfield, *The Right and the Righteous: The Christian Right Confronts the Republican Party* (Lanham, Md.: Rowman & Littlefield, 1996), 191; Howard Fineman, "God and the Grass Roots," *Newsweek* 8 November 1993, 42; David Von Drehle and Thomas B. Edsall, "Life of the Grand Old Party," *Washington Post*, 14 August 1994, A1; Brett M. Clifton, "Romancing the GOP: Assessing the Strategies Used by the Christian Coalition to Influence the Republican Party," *Party Politics* 10 (2004): 475–98; Mark J. Rozell and Clyde Wilcox, "Second Coming: The Strategies of the New Christian Right," *Political Science Quarterly* 111 (1996): 271–94.

[48]Ralph Reed, *Active Faith: How Christians Are Changing the Soul of American Politics* (New York: Free Press, 1996), 122; Martin, *With God*, 366.

antifamily.[49] Despite these simple headings, the votes often reflected more complicated dynamics—whether to close debate, say, or to accept a substitute amendment—and critics found them misleading.[50] As a Coalition official said when asked why California voter guide deemed opposition to handgun waiting periods a profamily position, "it is a position that most of our members take because they tend to be conservative in general . . . violence is a problem from the breakdown of society, not from the availability of handguns."[51]

Like many movement leaders—partisan officials, with clearer goals, have tended to be less reflective—Ralph Reed pondered in public the costs and benefits of alliance. In 1995, he warned against traditional relationships of allied interest groups, temptations to be fought only by the distinctive sensibilities that religious people bring to public life: "We will not, we must not, become to the Republicans, what the AFL-CIO, the feminists, and the radical left have become to the Democratic party. They are no longer servants, but power brokers. They no longer seek to heal; they seek influence. We will not become, as people of faith, what they have become—just another special interest group. Politics, for us, is a mission field, not a smoke filled room."[52]

Whatever their purposes, however, Reed and the Christian Coalition certainly behaved as power brokers. The move toward a less sectarian form of religious involvement fed into closer coordination with Republican priorities, and the softer language of rights and opportunity. When asked in 1993 about winning messages for conservative candidates, Reed said to "start with taxes. Working families with children feel over-taxed and under-appreciated by the government."[53] The old standbys of abortion and gay

[49]Justin Watson, *The Christian Coalition: Dreams of Restoration, Demands for Recognition* (New York: St. Martin's, 1997), 58; Frederick Clarkson, "The Christian Coalition: On the Road to Victory?," *Church and State*, January 1992, 4–7; Easton, *Gang of Five*, 287; Joel D. Vaughan, *The Rise and Fall of the Christian Coalition: The Inside Story* (Eugene, Ore.: Resource Publications, 2009), 47. The use of voter guides by ideologically oriented allies has a resonant political history, beginning with a 1944 insert in the *New Republic* by NC-PAC (CIO-PAC's twin for independent-minded liberals, with George Norris and Eleanor Roosevelt as titular heads).

[50]For examples, see Larry J. Sabato and Glenn R. Simpson, *Dirty Little Secrets: The Persistence of Corruption in American Politics* (New York: Crown, 1996), 129–39. For legal issues, see the IRS rules from 2002, Judith E. Kindel and John Francis Reilly, "Election Year Issues," http://www.irs.gov/pub/irs-tege/eotopici02.pdf; and Chris Kemmitt, "RFRA, Churches, and the IRS: Reconsidering the Boundaries of Church Activity in the Political Sphere," *Harvard Journal on Legislation* 43 (2006): 145–80. Note that no church has ever lost its 501(c)(3) status for distributing voter guides.

[51]Roy Beck, "Washington's Profamily Activists," *Christianity Today*, 9 November 1992, 22.

[52]Watson, *Christian Coalition*, 180.

[53]"Mobilizing the Christian Right," *Campaigns & Elections*, October 1993. See also Ralph Reed, *Contract with the American Family* (Nashville: Moorings, 1995), chap. 5.

rights came to be described in family-friendly terms, while school prayer received less emphasis. Reed also sought, without much success, to reach out to African Americans; he saw Christians at "the new back of the bus."[54] In all these ways, evangelicals abandoned the jeremiad for a partisan brand of pluralism.

While a retrospective narrative claimed that George H. W. Bush lost in 1992 because evangelicals stayed home, movement conservatives backed the president. Despite support of family planning during the 1960s that earned him the sobriquet "Rubbers," Bush had remained firm on abortion. Social conservatives on the platform committee added planks to the original draft platform opposing same-sex marriage as well as the inclusion of "sexual preference" in nondiscrimination statutes at any level of government; these were the first mentions of homosexuality in a Republican platform.[55] The elections of 1994, when the GOP recaptured Congress, and 1996 represented the high-water mark for the Christian Coalition. In 1996, the Coalition backed the Republican establishment candidate, Bob Dole, in the primary and claimed membership from a fifth of all delegates.

And then the Christian Coalition, like its predecessors, fell apart. The story combines two familiar elements: mismanagement at the top, and problems with direct mail. Under section 501(c)(4) of the IRS code, the Coalition could not accept contributions from the conservative foundations that propelled other parts of the right. Instead, it had to rely on contributions from wealthy conservatives such as Rich DeVos of Amway, and the mercurial medium of direct mail. In 1997, Ralph Reed left the Coalition to become a GOP political consultant and chair of the Georgia Republican State Committee. Reed's departure followed allegations that his friend, Benjamin Hart,[56] an alum of the Heritage Foundation and Oliver North's PAC, had used shell companies and no-bid contracts to extract vastly inflated fees for direct mail. Fundraising faltered without Hart's hard-hitting letters (revenue dropped from twenty-six million dollars in 1996 to seventeen million in 1997), leaders came and went, and the Coalition, crippled with debt, has never returned to anything like its former prominence.[57]

[54]James M. Perry, "Soul Mates: The Christian Coalition Crusades to Broaden Its Political Base," *Wall Street Journal*, 19 July 1994, A1; Ralph Reed, *Politically Incorrect: The Emerging Faith Factor in American Politics* (Dallas: Word, 1994), chap. 7.

[55]Oldfield, *Right and the Righteous*, 201–3.

[56]See Hart, *Third Generation*, 67–71 and 88–91. For his direct-mail secrets, see Benjamin Hart, *How to Write Blockbuster Sales Letters* (Denver: Outskirts Press, 2006).

[57]Thomas B. Edsall and Hanna Rosin, "IRS Denies Christian Coalition Tax-Exempt Status," *Washington Post*, 11 June 1999, A4; Bill Sizemore, "Fired Official Is a Key Player in Christian Coalition Troubles," *Virginian-Pilot*, 27 July 1997, A1; Liz Szabo, "Christian Coalition Losing Clout," *Virginian-Pilot*, 19 February 2000, A1; Vaughan, *Rise and Fall*, chaps. 14–18.

Toward Partisan Mobilization

Although a Methodist and not an evangelical, George W. Bush moved beyond the personal devotion he shared with McKinley, Wilson, and Carter to drape the White House in a patina of religiosity; his was, an evangelical historian writes, "a faith-based presidency."[58] Far more than in the Reagan years, the Christian Right held policy influence over the Bush administration, which restored the Mexico City policy on funding abortion overseas, and mounted an aggressive push to exempt faith-based programs receiving federal funding from rules on nondiscrimination in hiring.[59] As he attempted to build an ongoing majority for the Republican Party, Bush reached beyond the usual cobelligerents to religiously inclined Americans of all colors and creeds, Hispanics especially, as he reached toward what Gary Gerstle termed "a multicultural coalition of the godly." Through unusually ambitious presidentially led coalition building, Bush and his political strategist, Karl Rove, not only sought new supporters through direct outreach, but in the process aimed to transform their party's anchoring group.[60] The attempt proved largely unsuccessful.

The Bush era began in yet another period of crisis. In the 2000 elections, overall turnout rose—but it fell by approximately six points among white evangelicals.[61] Bush and his political team responded by bringing traditional movement functions in house, and relying on direct appeals rather than group intermediaries. In 2004, Karl Rove led weekly calls directly with evangelical pastors, along with Richard Land and James Dobson. In a year notable for the profusion of nominally independent para-organizations, vastly the largest source of direct mail to evangelicals was the Republican National Committee itself.[62]

[58]Gary Smith Scott, *Faith and the Presidency* (Oxford: Oxford University Press, 2007), 365; see also Alan Cooperman, "Openly Religious, to a Point; Bush Leaves Specifics of His Faith to Speculation," *Washington Post*, 16 September 2004, A1.

[59]See David Kuo, *Tempting Faith: An Inside Story of Political Seduction* (New York: Free Press, 2006).

[60]Gary Gerstle, "Minorities, Multiculturalism, and the Presidency of George W. Bush," in *The Presidency of George W. Bush: A First Historical Assessment*, ed. Julian E. Zelizer (Princeton: Princeton University Press, 2010), 280; Marvin Olasky, "Add, Don't Subtract: How Christian Conservatives Should Engage American Culture," in *The Future of American Conservatism: Conflict and Consensus in the Post-Reagan Era*, ed. Charles W. Dunn (Wilmington, Del.: ISI Books, 2007), 79–100; Sidney Milkis and Jesse H. Rhodes, "George W. Bush, the Republican Party, and the 'New' American Party System," *Perspectives on Politics* 5 (2007): 461–87.

[61]Clyde Wilcox, "Wither the Christian Right? The Elections and Beyond," in *The Election of the Century and What It Tells Us about American Politics*, ed. Stephen J. Wayne and Clyde Wilcox (Armonk, N.Y.: M.E. Sharpe, 2002), 117.

[62]Dana Milbank, "Religious Right Finds Its Center in Oval Office," *Washington Post*, 24 December 2001, A2; Alan Cooperman and Thomas B. Edsall, "Evangelicals Say They Led

One technique, however, came from the bottom up. In response to the court-ordered legalization of same-sex marriage in Massachusetts, grassroots conservatives in thirteen states—despite Rove's initial apprehensiveness—placed referenda on the November ballot to reaffirm marriage as a contract between a man and a woman. The gay marriage referenda, scholars generally concur, boosted turnout among evangelical conservatives, while depressing it among secular liberals. The evangelical share of the overall vote climbed to its 1996 level, and the proportion voting Republican, 79 percent, was the highest ever.[63]

Advocacy on behalf of Bush's judicial nominations united social conservatives with circles around the Federalist Society, whose origins lie in the revival of intellectual conservatism and whose funding comes primarily from supporters of the free market.[64] Three Justice Sunday rallies in 2005, organized by Dobson's Family Research Council, pressured the Senate to confirm Bush's judicial nominees. They featured a mix of religious leaders—James Dobson, Al Mohler of the SBC's Southern Seminary—Republican pols—Tom DeLay, Bill Frist—and movement conservatives—Phyllis Schlafly, Robert Bork.[65] As in the 1980 National Affairs Briefing, a para-organization aimed for influence through high-impact television. Yet the rhetoric had grown more ecumenical, focusing on respect for judicial nominees' private faith, and the goals more immediate.

In 2008, the Christian Right failed to coalesce behind a single candidate. Mike Huckabee, the former governor of Arkansas and a protégé of James Robison, received the most votes from evangelicals, but little support elsewhere in the party or from the old elites. Paul Weyrich backed Mitt Romney; Paul Pressler chose Fred Thompson; Pat Robertson, surprisingly,

---

Charge for GOP," *Washington Post*, 8 November 2004, A1; Scott, *Faith and the Presidency*, 377; J. Quin Monson and J. Baxter Oliphant, "Microtargeting and the Instrumental Mobilization of Religious Conservatives," in *A Matter of Faith: Religion in the 2004 Presidential Election*, ed. David E. Campbell (Washington, D.C.: Brookings Institution Press, 2007), 114–15; Clyde Wilcox, "Of Movements and Metaphors: The Coevolution of the Christian Right and the GOP," in *Evangelicals and Democracy in America*, vol. 2, ed. Steven Brint and Jean Reith Schroedel (New York: Russell Sage Foundation, 2009), 337.

[63]Gregory B. Lewis, "Same-Sex Marriage and the 2004 Presidential Election," *PS: Political Science and Politics* 38 (2005): 35–39; David E. Campbell and J. Quin Monson "The Religion Card: Gay Marriage and the 2004 Election." *Public Opinion Quarterly* 72 (2008): 399–419; for a contrary view, see Alan Abramowitz, "Terrorism, Gay Marriage, and Incumbency: Explaining the Republican Victory in the 2004 Presidential Election," *Forum* 2 (2004): article 3: 1–17, doi:10.2022/1540–8884.1059.

[64]Steven M. Teles, *The Rise of the Conservative Legal Movement* (Princeton: Princeton University Press, 2008).

[65]David D. Kirkpatrick, "In Telecast, Frist Defends His Effort to Stop Filibusters," *New York Times*, 25 April 2005, A14; Sheryl Henderson Blunt, "No 'Justice'?," *Christianity Today*, June 2005, 21.

picked Rudy Giuliani. The eventual nominee, John McCain, gambled and tapped Sarah Palin for the vice presidency. He chose a conservative with a background in the Assemblies of God, a premillennialist commitment to Israel, and strong prolife views.[66] If Republican coalition politics had been different—that is, if the anchoring group had not held an effective veto over the nominee—McCain assuredly would have picked his friend, Joe Lieberman, a prochoice ex-Democrat. McCain's gambit failed, and Palin almost certainly cost the ticket votes.[67]

So, too, in 2012. Rick Perry, the governor of Texas, made a hard play for movement support, but floundered after a series of weak debate performances. Michele Bachmann, a divisive member of the House with a penchant for publicity, credited Francis Schaeffer with her political awakening, and quoted him on the stump, but went nowhere. Evangelical leaders ultimately coalesced behind Rick Santorum, a Catholic who had lost his Senate seat from Pennsylvania, but he won binding primaries in only four states, and never appealed beyond his base. Again, the eventual nominee, Mitt Romney, accommodated movement priorities, including a U-turn on abortion from his days in Massachusetts. Self-described white evangelicals kept their proportional presence in the electorate, and, in a sign of changed cleavages around religion, gave 78 percent support to the first presidential ticket in American history without a Protestant: Romney was Mormon and his vice presidential nominee, Paul Ryan, Roman Catholic.[68]

The larger picture, however, remained unsettled. The two leading issues in social conservatism found their trajectories seemingly dissociated. On gay rights, conservatives faced a choice on whether to fight or surrender given unfavorable trends. A majority of Americans, although less

[66]Tom Kizzia, "Long, Strange Journey to Governor's Office Nears Its Conclusion," *Anchorage Daily News*, 5 November 2006, A1; Ralph J. Hallow, "Palin's Evangelical Faith Drives Pro-Israel View," *Washington Times*, 4 September 2008, A01. On evangelicals, the GOP, and support for Israel, especially since 9/11, see Ron Kampeas, "How the GOP Has Learned to Love Israel Unconditionally," *Jewish Telegraphic Agency*, 28 September 2011, http://www.jta.org/2011/09/28/news-opinion/politics/how-the-gop-has-learned-to-love-israel-unconditionally.

[67]Richard Johnston, Emily Thorson, and Andrew Gooch, "The Economy and the Dynamics of the 2008 Presidential Campaign: Evidence from the National Annenberg Election Study," *Journal of Elections, Public Opinion & Parties* 20 (2010): 271–89.

[68]On Perry, see Forrest Wilder, "Rick Perry's Army of God," *Texas Observer*, August 2011; on Bachmann, see Ryan Lizza, "Leap of Faith," *New Yorker*, 15 August 2011, 54–63; on Santorum, see Alex Altman and Michael Scherer, "The New Christian Right," *Time*, 2 April 2012, 30–33; Erik Eckholm and Jeff Zeleny, "Evangelicals, Seeking Unity, Back Santorum," *New York Times*, 15 January 2012, A1; and Matthew J. Franck, "Rick Santorum's Evangelical Appeal," *Washington Post*, 16 March 2012, http://www.washingtonpost.com/blogs/guest-voices/post/rick-santorums-evangelical-appeal/2012/03/16/gIQA30yvGS_blog.html. On election results, see Laurie Goodstein, "Christian Right Failed to Sway Voters on Issues," *New York Times*, 10 November 2012, A1.

than three-tenths of Republicans and less than a quarter of evangelicals, supported gay marriage as of 2013. Acceptance by mainstream Republicans would constitute a signal defeat for the Christian Right.[69]

On abortion, however, public opinion has remained more or less constant. After their 2010 election victories, which emerged more from a bad economy and anger over health care reform than cultural issues per se, emboldened Republicans seeking support from the base mounted a new offensive against abortion and its providers. The House of Representatives voted to eliminate federal funding for Planned Parenthood. State legislatures moved further. Absolute bans on abortion after twenty weeks—and, in the case of North Dakota, a mere six weeks—tempted judicial review. Clinics faced onerous new restrictions, including mandatory fetal ultrasounds, requirements for operating-room facilities and admitting privileges at local hospitals, and restrictions on insurance coverage for abortion and even contraception.[70]

Yet in a rapid-fire media environment prone to seize on any misstatement, evangelical Republican candidates, on the right in contested primaries, got caught in their words on issues of sex, and especially rape, at the cost of two Senate seats in 2012. In Missouri, Todd Akin claimed that victims of "legitimate rape" rarely get pregnant. In Indiana, Richard Mourdock said that pregnancies following rape "are something that God intended to happen."[71] The statements were more than mere gaffes. When elected officials mobilize evangelicals directly, they must speak to group audiences and broader publics alike, without the aid of brokers on whom they long relied. Even in Red America, the doctrinaire conservatism that the Christian Right did so much to promote as GOP orthodoxy could lead its practitioners astray. The new party-based mobilization still cued old tropes as evangelicals sought their way in Republican politics.

With direct mobilization into the conservative movement has come new space for leading evangelicals to rethink their public witness beyond a few hot-button issues—and even to dream of a cohesive movement at greater remove from the GOP. This is the nascent vision of a "new evangelical center"

[69] "Changing Attitudes on Gay Marriage," Pew Research Religion & Public Life Project, 2013, http://features.pewforum.org/same-sex-marriage-attitudes/download.php.

[70] Juliet Eilperin, "Abortion Returns to National Spotlight," *Washington Post*, 6 July 2013, 1. For a summary of state policies, see "State Policies in Brief, as of August 1, 2014: An Overview of Abortion Laws" (New York: Guttmacher Institute, 2014), http://www.guttmacher.org/statecenter/spibs/spib_OAL.pdf.

[71] "Jaco Report: Full Interview with Todd Akin," *Jaco Report*, KTVI-TV, St. Louis, 19 August 2012, http://fox2now.com/2012/08/19/the-jaco-report-august-19-2012/; Lucy Madison, "Richard Mourdock: Even Pregnancy from Rape Something 'God Intended,'" *CBS News*, 23 October 2012, http://www.cbsnews.com/news/richard-mourdock-even-pregnancy-from-rape-something-god-intended/.

unallied with either political party. Its vision encompasses traditional, pro-life views on abortion as well as, in almost all cases, opposition to gay marriage, but also concern for human rights, global warming, poverty, and nuclear war. It draws strength from a variety of sources, including megachurch pastors (Rick Warren in Orange County, Joel Hunter in suburban Orlando, Gregory Boyd in St. Paul), Calvinist theologians from the Center for Public Justice, and evangelicals involved in international relief work.

The new center explicitly eschews alliance in favor of a public witness "'upstream' from politics," and at greater distance from particular leaders and policies.[72] As Boyd asks, "The distinctly kingdom question is not, How should we *vote*? The distinctly kingdom question is, How should we *live*?"[73] Evangelicalism has been losing ground, surveys show, among those in the millennial generation, increasingly liberal on issues of personal morality other than abortion and unaligned with conservative Protestant denominations.[74] Nevertheless, the evangelical center has its boundaries. Richard Cizik, longtime vice president for governmental affairs at the NAE, quit under pressure in December 2008, after expressing support for same-sex civil unions.

Organizational Form and the Success of Alliance

The interaction between organizational maintenance and partisan coalitions has shaped alliance between the Christian Right and the Republican Party. Groups allied to political parties organize potential electorates, and then negotiate for ideological patronage in exchange for votes, money, and

[72] Stephen Monsma and Mark Rodgers, "In the Arena: Practical Issues in Concrete Political Engagement," in *Toward an Evangelical Public Policy*, ed. Ronald J. Sider and Diane Knippers (Grand Rapids, Mich.: Baker, 2005), 327. See also David P. Gushee, *The Future of Faith in American Politics: The Public Witness of the Evangelical Center* (Waco, Tex.: Baylor University Press, 2008), esp. 88–91; Joel C. Hunter, *A New Kind of Conservative* (Ventura, Calif.: Regal, 2008); Gregory A. Boyd, *The Myth of a Christian Nation: How the Quest for Political Power Is Destroying the Church* (Grand Rapids, Mich.: Zondervan, 2005); Mark Tooley, "Evangelicals Opposing Nukes," *Weekly Standard*, 10 November 2011, http://www.weeklystandard.com/blogs/evangelicals-opposing-nukes_607950.html; Cal Thomas and Ed Dobson, *Blinded by Might: Can the Religious Right Save America?* (Grand Rapids, Mich.: Zondervan: 1999); Frances FitzGerald, "The Evangelical Surprise," *New York Review of Books*, 26 April, 2007, 31–34; and, from a Burkean slant, D. G. Hart, *From Billy Graham to Sarah Palin: Evangelicals and the Betrayal of American Conservatism* (Grand Rapids, Mich.: Eerdmans, 2011). Although it has much in common with ideas in the Catholic church that privilege neither human life nor social justice, the Protestant vision places much less emphasis on social solidarity. Nor should it be confused with the liberal evangelicalism exemplified by Jim Wallis that equivocates on abortion and emphasizes social-justice issues.

[73] Boyd, *Myth of a Christian Nation*, 154, punctuation and italics original.

[74] Schlozman and Lewis, "Nones, Evangelicals."

networks. When peak associations collapse from internal strife before the movement finds a place in the party system, they bring the cause down with them, and the potential electorate dissipates away or else awaits mobilization on substantially different grounds. The Populists demonstrate the proposition. When they fall apart with their place inside the party coalition secure, with other elites waiting in the wings—as Robertson, in a general sense, followed Falwell—and with internal support to keep them inside the party coalition, then the paradox of organizational failure amid movement success gets easily resolved. From the bottom up, the combination of extant church-based organizing with direct-mail lists provided for ongoing movement infrastructure even as particular organizations collapsed. From the top down, the linkages between evangelicals and other elements in the contemporary Republican fold protected the movement from its disorganization.

Over time, however, if the potential electorate becomes better organized—or at least easily identifiable and cohesive—and if partisan allies become better able to mimic group-specific appeals, then the party may move away from the median voter to meet the already formed and mobilized concerns of movement supporters, even if the movement infrastructure, the key intermediary, no longer exercises the same kind of influence. For the figures at the helm of the New Right, who saw the future of conservatism in carefully brokered single-issue coalitions unconnected to vacillating parties, this prospect would come as a surprise. Yet it is also a sign of conservative evangelicals' political maturity.

CHAPTER 9

The Failure of Abolition-Republicanism

In 1860, the antislavery movement stood at the heart of a Republican Party committed to stopping the expansion of slavery into the territories, and abolition gave the party moral ardor. In 1866 and 1867, Radical Republicanism seemed to dominate the party. While it provided the impetus for—although not all the votes behind or, critically, the final versions of—the Civil Rights Act of 1866 and the Fourteenth and Fifteenth Amendments, the anchoring group ultimately failed to build the virtuous circles that sustain long-term alliance, and the party forsook its racially egalitarian lodestar.

Unlike Populism and the antiwar movement and like labor and the Christian Right, abolitionism established itself at the heart of a major party. Successful alliances, however, maintain themselves through the linked processes of state building, movement building, and party building. Through them, anchoring groups entrench themselves and make accommodations with other interests inside the allied parties. Abolition-republicans relied on party alone, and they failed. For unions and the Democrats, the policy-politics connections around the Wagner Act, and Keynesian pump-priming united disparate elements. For the Christian Right and the Republicans, the conservative counterestablishment provided a base around which to organize, and the "tribes of the right" came together around tax cuts. In the postbellum Republican Party, a cross-sectoral appeal to the North and its industries had to fit alongside a cross-racial appeal in the South. It was an impossible order. The anchoring group conflicted with the immediate priorities of stronger, veto-wielding elements in the Republican Party, and it became marginalized and ultimately irrelevant. Implacable Democratic opposition did not alone render African Americans captured by the Republican Party. Rather, the party's internal dynamics marginalized the would-be anchoring group as it failed to build common carriers with dominant elements in the party coalition.[1]

[1]Cf. Paul Frymer, *Uneasy Alliances: Race and Party Competition in America* (Princeton: Princeton University Press, 1999), chap. 3.

Abolition-Republicanism and the Republicans

Nineteenth-century parties, both before and after the Civil War, held enormous advantages in mobilizing voters that their institutionally weakened successors lacked. They controlled the electoral machinery, from funding candidates to mounting campaigns to printing ballots, and they held esteem, even veneration, as essential instruments of democracy. Any ongoing organization would, like the Grand Army of the Republic, have had to cleave to the allied party, more so than its twentieth-century counterparts.

The anchoring group filled a structural demand. A large bloc of voters, geographically concentrated, ideologically distinct, and unattached (in this instance because they had no suffrage—and, for the vast majority, no status as human beings) in the prior party system, stood waiting for targeted appeals. A deeply rooted social movement held special suasion over those voters. Such conditions held in the case of abolition-republicanism even more powerfully than for labor or the Christian Right, yet long-running alliance never established itself. Even if its failure seems inevitable, the basic ingredients of anchoring alliance all existed. The puzzle is why they proved insufficient, and the answer principally lies in coalitional politics. Had northern business behaved differently, the Republican Party would have put far more resources toward the freedmen and their descendants.

Strategies to empower African Americans, rooted in the Republican Party's historic claims to legitimacy from its abolitionist progenitors and supporters, foundered in the contest among competing interests in the business-dominated party. The limits of Reconstruction, to which scholars, especially on the left, have often returned, expressed themselves inside the Republican "sun party" itself.[2] To follow a policy of Radicalism in the South meant nurturing collective action among and giving land to poor farmers as they struggled against rich planters. Yet those same policies alienated northern voters leery of full equality, and gave an opening to labor organizations demanding higher wages, an eight-hour day, and legal recognition

[2]See W. E. Burghardt Du Bois, *Black Reconstruction in America: An Essay toward a History of the Part Which Black Folk Played in the Attempt to Reconstruct Democracy in America, 1860–1880* (New York: Russell & Russell, 1935); David Montgomery, *Beyond Equality: Labor and the Radical Republicans, 1862–1872* (New York: Knopf, 1967); Eric Foner, *Politics and Ideology in the Age of the Civil War* (Oxford: Oxford University Press, 1980), esp. chap. 6; Barrington Moore, *Social Origins of Dictatorship and Democracy: Lord and Peasant in the Making of the Modern World* (Boston: Beacon, 1966), 141–49; cf. the counterfactual in C. Vann Woodward, *The Future of the Past* (New York: Oxford University Press, 1989), chap. 10. Hence, Republicans faced more than a simple encounter between "office-seeking" politicians eager to win the next election unencumbered by too many promises and "benefit-seeking" groups eager to see their policies realized. Rather, highly constrained office seekers chose among benefit seekers. Cf. Anna L. Harvey, *Votes without Leverage: Women in American Electoral Politics, 1920–1970* (Cambridge: Cambridge University Press, 1998).

for cooperatives and unions; and to Greenback sentiment demanding leniency to smallholders. That price was too high to pay.

Northern voters reacted uneasily to racially egalitarian policies; Radicalism's ascendance owed much to the intransigence of Andrew Johnson. Voters in 1866 and 1867 rejected black suffrage in most states where it appeared on the ballot. Only in the national context, where defense of the Union—contemporary debates around the Fourteenth Amendment centered around the provisions limiting officeholding by ex-Confederates—and the reconstitution of southern society on free labor principles came into play, could Radicals avoid immediate pushback from racially conservative northern voters. As they sought "to maintain the Republican party at the high pitch of excitement" on ideological grounds, thus, abolition-republicanism battled both public opinion and other interests in the party coalition.[3]

The possibilities for abolition-republicanism narrowed severely when the Radicals failed to approve land confiscation or a strong Fourteenth Amendment in 1866 and then failed to impeach Andrew Johnson in 1868. In fits and starts as the Third Party System evolved, vested interests reasserted themselves. Members of Congress protected their districts; presidents courted southern capital; courts struck down civil rights legislation that would threaten the right to contract. At each moment, "lock-in" costs to an alternative strategy continued to rise.[4]

Northern Radicals largely negotiated the terms of trade for African Americans, as well as the northern whites who sympathized to a greater or lesser extent with the freedmen. Despite the proliferation of labels to describe various factions, we have no accepted name for this broad mass emerging from earlier social-movement activity and advocating a strongly egalitarian view of free labor ideology. W.E.B. Du Bois used "abolition-democracy," and C. Vann Woodward "the Radical-Abolitionist coalition." Since its ideas were embedded both in party and in the requisites of civic membership, "abolition-republicanism" might come closest to the mark.[5]

Movement's End

The leading abolitionist organizations folded up their tents with their cause seemingly won. The differences from the anchoring alliances in the twentieth century prove instructive. While the CIO and the Moral Majority drew

[3]Hans L. Trefousse, *The Radical Republicans: Lincoln's Vanguard for Racial Justice* (New York: Knopf, 1969), 443; see also Brooks D. Simpson, *The Reconstruction Presidents* (Lawrence: University Press of Kansas, 1998), chaps. 3 and 4.

[4]Paul Pierson, *Politics in Time: History, Institutions, and Social Analysis* (Princeton: Princeton University Press, 2004). 23.

[5]Du Bois, *Black Reconstruction*, 184–85; C. Vann Woodward, *Reunion and Reaction: The Compromise of 1877 and the End of Reconstruction* (Boston: Little, Brown, 1951).

on extant organizational ties and ideological impulses adumbrated but never fully fleshed out in a direct partisan context before alliance crystallized, the abolitionist movement had been in politics for a generation before the Civil War, whether via moral agitation (William Lloyd Garrison), third-party politics (Free Soil), or even violent struggle (John Brown). Its major accomplishment, the end of slavery, had been achieved under a Republican Party initially committed only to stopping its expansion into the territories. Like the League of Women Voters after suffrage half a century later, a long prior history of activism closed off alternatives. The task of institutional transformation toward mature alliance required not creating new, politically aware forms of linkage to partisan actors, like CIO-PAC and the Christian Coalition, but transforming congealed groups and understandings to new ends. They had now to protect the freedmen's interests across sectional divides and in policy venues from voting to schooling.

Fragmented as they faced a cohesive if factional party system, old abolitionists could not trade policy for votes in any meaningful fashion. The Union League movement served briefly in the late 1860s as a para-organization to bring African Americans together with the Freedmen's Bureau and federal troops, but withered after the Radical moment passed.[6] After passage of the Thirteenth Amendment, Garrison sought to disband the American Anti-Slavery Society; his longtime ally, Wendell Phillips, a more thoroughgoing social reformer, managed to forestall dissolution until after ratification of the Fifteenth Amendment. Even then, however, few besides Phillips saw how precarious were the freedmen's circumstances, and most simply celebrated their equal status. Rather than seeking to broker with the Republican Party, Phillips ranged farther afield to advocate also for women's rights and labor rights.[7]

At the same time, the lack of established movement infrastructure left Radical Republicans bereft when they disagreed with their fellow partisans. Instead of working reciprocally, abolition-republicanism began with

[6]Michael W. Fitzgerald, *The Union League Movement in the Deep South: Politics and Agricultural Change during Reconstruction* (Baton Rouge: Louisiana State University Press, 1989). For a rough parallel, see the discussion of the Primrose League in Daniel Ziblatt, *Conservative Political Parties and the Birth of Modern Democracy in Europe, 1848–1950* (Cambridge: Cambridge University Press, forthcoming).

[7]James M. McPherson, *The Struggle for Equality: Abolitionists and the Negro in the Civil War and Reconstruction* (Princeton: Princeton University Press, 1964); Irving H. Bartlett, *Wendell Phillips: Brahmin Radical* (Boston: Beacon, 1961), chaps. 16 and 17; Eric Foner, *Reconstruction: America's Unfinished Revolution, 1863–1877* (New York: Harper & Row, 1988), 448–49; the speeches of Phillips and Garrison respectively, reprinted in Harold M. Hyman, ed., *The Radical Republicans and Reconstruction, 1861–1870* (Indianapolis: Bobbs-Merrill, 1967), 478–84 and 492–95; "The Republican Party, What Wendell Phillips Thinks of It Today," *Boston Herald*, 13 August 1879, 2. The causes Phillips espoused would join haphazardly in a political party a century later, and under the Democratic banner.

partisan leaders and extended principally outward. Thaddeus Stevens, "lacking a political base outside the Republican party," could have no outside game, as latter-day pundits would say, when his proposals for land confiscation went nowhere in Congress.[8] When Charles Sumner blocked Grant's machinations to annex the present-day Dominican Republic in 1870, deeming them quasi-imperialistic paternalism, he found himself in a political wilderness that culminated in endorsement for Horace Greeley, by then no racial egalitarian, in 1872. And when Radicalism waned, appeals to party principle itself became the only, paradoxical strategy.

Nor did abolition-republicans supplement party building with a program of state building that would leave an institutional legacy to render their amended Constitution concrete. While far more expansive than the Progressives a generation later about the society they wanted to build and the constitutional framework that would undergird it, abolition-republicans rested their program for national renewal on state and local organization still patterned after the Jacksonian Democracy; the contrast to the New Deal here proves sharp.[9] Support from only a single political party, without concomitant movement building, state building, or acceptance by the other party of the new rules of the game, rendered abolition-republicanism vulnerable to factional struggle inside that party, for it had no effective means to entrench its position against internal opponents.

The Freedmen and the Gilded Age

The economic relations that undergirded southern society posed the knottiest questions. Any plan to give the freedmen permanent political standing would require some economic basis to resist the encroachment of a revived and determined planter class. Under those circumstances, landless whites, distant from the slaveocracy that free labor ideology had castigated since before the great conflict, seemed like a logical target. "The problem with a class-based strategy," Richard Bensel shrewdly observed, "was that it was difficult to see how it could be limited to the South."[10] A program of comprehensive land confiscation—well beyond that contained in the

[8] Foner, *Politics and Ideology*, 149.

[9] See William G. Shade, "'Revolutions May Go Backwards': The American Civil War and the Problem of Political Development," *Social Science Quarterly* 55 (1974): 753–67. In ways that scholars have only begun to probe, this period serves as a critical counterpoint to Stephen Skowronek, *Building a New American State* (Cambridge: Cambridge University Press, 1982).

[10] Richard Franklin Bensel, *Yankee Leviathan: The Origins of Central State Authority in America, 1859–1877* (Cambridge: Cambridge University Press, 1990), 350. For the New Deal–era solution, see Bruce J. Schulman, *From Cotton Belt to Sunbelt: Federal Policy. Economic Development, and the Transformation of the South, 1938–1980* (New York: Oxford University Press, 1991).

vetoed Freedmen's Bureau Bill of 1866—from rebel plantation holders to former slaves, Union veterans, and even poor white scalawags risked that the new smallholders would withdraw from large-scale cotton production to tend their plots as yeoman farmers, as had occurred in an early experiment on the Sea Islands of South Carolina.[11] Such an effort immediately ran up against northern manufacturers' interests in cheap and plentiful cotton.

So, too, as freedmen sought minimal protections from their toil. Labor contracts defined the contours of life under tenant farming. In 1890, only 14 percent of black farmers in South Carolina and 16 percent in Mississippi owned their land. Croppers, mostly black, sought pay for specific tasks, rather than a lump sum for all their labor, and in the early postwar years looked for the state to stop violations of contract. African Americans banded together to protect these rights, both in Union League Clubs tied to the Republican Party but also through labor organizations. A convention in South Carolina "petitioned the state legislature for land distribution, a legal nine-hour day, and labor commissioners in each county to oversee the claims of rural workers."[12]

Yet similar demands from northern trade unions quickly cut to the bone, as they threatened the inviolability of private contracts. The nascent labor organizations argued against the dangers from concentrated wealth, undermining the basis behind free-labor ideology and threatening the interests of northern manufacturers. Some even began to see soft money, and its ruinous flirtation with default, as a means to bring toiling men together across race and section. The city of Washington during a brief episode of home rule offered particular object lessons on the risks of biracial democracy. "Boss Shepherd," supported by African Americans, spent profligately (notably on a sewer system), endangering bondholders.[13]

African Americans were in the minority in every state except South Carolina and Mississippi, so Republicans needed simultaneously to appeal to a substantial segment of southern whites. Atop the class structure, they looked to old Whigs to bulk up their coalition. As Republicans "hoped for

[11] Foner, *Politics and Ideology*, 108–11. Compare sections 5 and 6 of the vetoed bill with section 11 of the enacted bill, which began restitution of the lands Sherman seized; LaWanda Cox and John H. Cox, eds., *Reconstruction, the Negro, and the New South* (Columbia: University of South Carolina Press, 1973), 45 and 51.

[12] David Montgomery, *Citizen Worker: The Experience of Workers in the United States with Democracy and the Free Market during the Nineteenth Century* (Cambridge: Cambridge University Press, 1993), 126.

[13] Montgomery, *Citizen Worker*; Montgomery, *Beyond Equality*, esp. chap. 9; Robert P. Sharkey, *Money, Class, and Party: An Economic Study of Civil War and Reconstruction* (Baltimore: Johns Hopkins University Press, 1959); Bartlett, *Wendell Phillips*, 363–65; Wendell Phillips, *Who Shall Rule Us? Money or the People?* (Boston: Franklin Press, 1878); "Ring Rule at Washington," *New York Tribune*, 19 April 1873, 3.

cooperation with the economic leaders of the South while seeking to deprive them of political authority," the sort of activist programs that would build the state the Radicals wished to see, with universal schooling and decent infrastructure, ran quickly into trouble.[14] In places like Atlanta, the direct tax costs hit the rising mercantile elites whom Republicans hoped to romance—and so thwarted the partisan efforts to achieve abolition-republican goals.

As the Great Railroad Strike of 1877 demonstrated, labor threatened both parties. Federal troops now protected against the striking urban rabble, not the Ku Kluxer—and labor agitation threatened Republican elites immediately, in their workplaces and even their homes. Occasionally, urban labor parties even upended the traditional partisan cleavages, with demands for shorter workdays and respect for workmen's liberties. Nor did either a financially oriented Democracy or an industrially oriented Republican Party have any interest in the plans for reflation promulgated by Greenbackers from the West—and potentially of interest, as Populism would demonstrate, to poor southerners, as well. Instead, the parties agreed to disagree on the tariff and, especially at the local level, various ethnocultural issues, even as they kept the boundaries of conflict narrowly drawn and protected their joint interests.[15]

Reform, Corruption, and Republicanism

Even more than most movements, the story of abolition-republicanism over time is the saga of a generation as it aged.[16] As so often in gradual political change, generational replacement had a greater impact than the conversion of positions. New issues came to the fore, and energetic young people zealous to help their country and join a great cause—the basic personality type behind so many potential anchoring groups—fretted over profligate government, and promoted civil service reform. Or else they turned to the labor movement or women's suffrage or inward to private pursuits. Old abolitionists still aiming principally to improve the lot of former slaves and their descendants turned to work in civil society, especially in education,

[14] William R. Brock, "Reconstruction and the American Party System," in *A Nation Divided: Problems and Issues of the Civil War and Reconstruction*, ed. George M. Fredrickson (Minneapolis: Burgess, 1975), 88.

[15] See Martin Shefter, *Political Parties and the State: The American Historical Experience* (Princeton: Princeton University Press, 1994), 142–48, and the broad-brush critiques in Matthew Josephson, *The Politicos, 1865–1896* (New York: Harcourt Brace, 1938), and Jack Beatty, *Age of Betrayal: The Triumph of Money in America, 1865–1900* (New York: Knopf, 2007).

[16] See Nancy Whittier, "Political Generations, Micro-Cohorts, and the Transformation of Social Movements," *American Sociological Review* 62 (1997): 760–78.

where they formed, staffed, and funded a string of schools and colleges. Stevens and Sumner died in the saddle of overwork. In the following generation, their commitments echoed only in New England Yankees with older loyalties beyond the emergent politics of large corporations and professional bosses: George Frisbie Hoar of Massachusetts, William Chandler of New Hampshire, and, most effectively, Thomas Brackett Reed of Maine. Their efforts had a twinge of nostalgia, a look back to the party's purer days more than a program for a rapidly industrializing future.[17]

In 1877, dissatisfied with Rutherford B. Hayes's outreach to "the better elements" in the South, Chandler, who for decades served as his party's chief strategist on southern matters, hoped for political gain from a higher purpose "than keeping a political party in power—that of protecting the colored man and saving the Nation from great peril."[18] His rhetoric closely echoed that of Frederick Douglass, who served in a succession of spoils appointments for Republican presidents. He blamed James Blaine's loss in 1884 on a campaign that "made the body more important than the soul; national prosperity more important than national justice."[19]

Patronage-oriented postwar politics appalled a swath of reformers, including plenty of old Radicals. Reformers elevated party to a level rarely reached in a system of interest aggregation—and then castigated it for failing to meet such a high bar. Opponents of Boss Tweed in New York recoiled at similar tales of lined pockets in the South debasing the pure motives that lay behind proper citizenship. Disadvantaged southern populations relied on material incentives; the middle-class-oriented Liberals reacted with horror.[20]

For many, decrees of formal legal equality fulfilled their cause's mission. Horace Greeley's combined Liberal Republican-Democratic platform of 1872, in what would become known as the New Departure, pledged to support the Fourteenth and Fifteenth Amendments—but left all enforcement to the states. To be sure, the old abolitionists generally held firm; about

[17] James M. McPherson, *The Abolitionist Legacy: From Reconstruction to the NAACP* (Princeton: Princeton University Press, 1975), pt. 2; David W. Blight, *Race and Reunion: The Civil War in American Memory* (Cambridge, Mass.: Belknap, 2001), esp. 128.

[18] Stanley Hirshson, *Farewell to the Bloody Shirt: Northern Republicans & the Southern Negro* (Bloomington: Indiana University Press, 1962), 25. On Chandler, see Leon Burr Richardson, *William E. Chandler, Republican* (New York: Dodd Mead, 1940), and the revealing *Letters of Mr. William E. Chandler Relative to the So-Called Southern Policy of Mr. Hayes, Together with a Letter to Mr. Chandler of Mr. William Lloyd Garrison* (Concord, N.H.: Monitor and Statesman, 1878).

[19] Frederick Douglass, "The Return of the Democratic Party to Power" (1885), in *The Life and Writings of Frederick Douglass*, ed. Philip S. Foner (New York: International, 1950), 415.

[20] "A Southern View of the Southern Problem," *Nation*, 7 July 1871, 4–5; George W. Julian, *Political Recollections, 1840 to 1872* (Chicago: Jansen, McClurg, 1884), 330–31. Cf. James Q. Wilson, *The Amateur Democrat: Club Politics in Three Cities* (Chicago: University of Chicago Press, 1962).

three-quarters of them, by James McPherson's estimate, still supported Grant over Greeley. Yet Liberalism would become an important strand in elite opinion, helping to sever the link between influential brokers and their mass constituency.[21] In Du Bois's words, "When, therefore, the conscience of the United States attacked corruption, it at the same time attacked in the Republican Party the only power that could support democracy in the South."[22]

Republicans responded only weakly. "In state after state, men who placed greater weight on organization than on ideology came into or retained power."[23] These professional bosses brokered not between partisans and groups, but among a highly complicated set of actors, encompassing a variety of economic cleavages, claimants for patronage (or graft), and ethno-cultural schisms especially prominent in state politics. Perhaps simply because nobody had the stature to do so, no prominent Republicans laid down the law on the collective harm done to the party from internal strife. Instead, factionalism rendered the Republican program, including the enforcement mechanisms for the Fourteenth and Fifteenth Amendments, vulnerable once new officeholders arrived to distribute spoils for their own purposes. The party attempted a vast program of party building based entirely around the limited resources from patronage and a tax system still based around tariffs and excise revenue. Corruption followed, yet under the circumstances, Republicans had few alternatives.

Northern Republicans failed to support effective party building in the South. Even as the Fourteenth Amendment created national citizenship, the creation of similarly national structures to organize parties would have to wait for another generation, until Matthew Quay in 1888 and, with much more sophistication, Mark Hanna in 1896. Throughout the Radical years, "prominent northern congressmen and party professionals steadfastly declined invitations to join southern Republicans on the campaign trail," and sent insubstantial sums—a mere five thousand dollars per state from the Republican National Executive Committee in the freewheeling 1868 campaign, with even less thereafter—along with proportionately fewer traveling speakers, broadsides, and the like.[24]

Successful party building not only invests in human capital and technology, but also nurtures policies that promise electoral feedback to the party

[21]John G. Sproat, *The Best Men: Liberal Reformers in the Gilded Age* (New York: Oxford University Press, 1968); McPherson, *Abolitionist Legacy*, 33.

[22]Du Bois, *Black Reconstruction*, 624.

[23]Morton Keller, *Affairs of State: Public Life in Late Nineteenth Century America* (Cambridge, Mass.: Belknap, 1977), 552.

[24]Terry L. Seip, *The South Returns to Congress: Men, Economic Measures, and Intersectional Relationships, 1868–79* (Baton Rouge: Louisiana State University Press, 1983), 276, see also 89–97.

as a whole.[25] Pensions for union veterans conceivably could have bundled together patronage, economic development, and racial equality. Yet just as labor and populist agitation failed to materialize at the same points, the one new issue that could have resuscitated the old loyalties blossomed only in the 1880s, as veterans aged and their war wounds made work painful—by which time Republicans' southern strategy had become an orphan.[26] Pensions instead principally allowed Republicans to claim credit as they funneled out the revenues from a high tariff. While many who waved the bloody shirt and pressed the GOP "to pension the boys who wore the blue" also sought to uphold the abolitionist legacy, others used the issue more opportunistically; Joseph Foraker of Ohio, who beat the drum for Benjamin Harrison in the 1888 campaign, had earlier represented clients suing to repeal state-level open access laws.[27]

Party and Failed State Building

Elsewhere across American government, abolition-republicanism failed to build a durable base for African Americans. No administrative bulwark (except for the Bureau of Pensions, which gained power long after Radicalism had sputtered out) gained power to secure partisan achievements. The Freedmen's Bureau, staffed mainly by northern whites and working alongside with Union troops, distributed Republican propaganda from the Union League committees in the 1868 campaign, but expired at the end of that year, doomed by fiscal pressures—the president of the American Iron and Steel Association, in a May 1868 speech, decried "rivers of waste"—the organizational politics of military reconstruction, and opposition from southern whites of all stripes. Systematically hamstrung by Andrew Johnson, the bureau ultimately facilitated resettlement only on abandoned lands, most of them marginal, and enforced labor contracts that often tied black workers to their former masters.[28] State and local taxpayers proved

[25] See, e.g., John H. Aldrich, *Why Parties? The Origin and Transformation of Political Parties in America* (Chicago: University of Chicago Press, 1995), 49–50.

[26] Cf. Theda Skocpol, "Did the Civil War Further American Democracy? A Reflection on the Expansion of Benefits for Union Veterans," in *Democracy, Revolution, and History*, ed. Theda Skocpol (Ithaca, N.Y.: Cornell University Press, 1998), 73–101.

[27] Lawrence Grossman, *The Democratic Party and the Negro: Northern and National Politics, 1868–1892* (Urbana: University of Illinois Press, 1976), 83–84. On Republican ideology in the 1880s, see Keller, *Affairs of State*, 558–64.

[28] Foner, *Reconstruction*, 155–70; George R. Bentley, *A History of the Freedmen's Bureau* (Philadelphia: University of Pennsylvania Press, 1955), 201; William S. McFeely, *Yankee Stepfather: General O.O. Howard and the Freedmen* (New Haven: Yale University Press, 1968), esp. chap. 14; and the documents in Cox and Cox, *Reconstruction, the Negro, and the New South*, 315–30. Bentley pushes the charge of politicization, but in the context of seeing the late 1860s as substantially more Radical than most scholars now conclude.

unwilling to back its work in education (carried out largely by idealistic New England women), which, devoid of state support or administrative capacity, became largely private.[29] Yet whatever the bureau's ambivalent legacy, it was emphatically *not* the NLRB of an earlier alliance: an ongoing federal bureaucracy mediating relations between African Americans and the national state.

After Democrats took control of Congress in 1874, funding for U.S. marshals and district courts in the South dropped sharply. Enforcement of election laws shifted to northern swing states.[30] Limited federal patronage, centered around customs houses and post offices, became a flash point for racially tinged factionalism. Educated blacks had few options for employment outside the public sector, and changing that reality would have required either massive public investment or serious regulation of the labor market.[31]

In Congress, southern members cycled in and out too fast to build seniority. Westerners, often good Radicals when it came to Reconstruction policy, brought the bacon home to their districts; the undercapitalized South received less than its proportional share for rivers and harbors and, especially, railroads.[32] Just like their counterparts in the North and the West, state governments in the South used grants to railroads to secure economic development and bridge coalitional divides. Overinvestment in dubious projects followed, and many of the roads failed. The investment represented, too, an opportunity cost in dollars unspent and effort unexpended on education or land reform that might conceivably have built feedback mechanisms to organized segments among white voters.[33]

Under the 1877 deal that installed Rutherford B. Hayes to the presidency in exchange for keeping federal troops in their barracks, northern Republicans had reached a modus vivendi with conservatives in the South. Redeemer governments won breathing room. They soon dismantled the

[29] McPherson, *Struggle for Equality*, chap. 17.

[30] Everette Swinney, "Enforcing the Fifteenth Amendment, 1870–1877," *Journal of Southern History* 28 (1962): 212; Scott C. James and Brian L. Lawson, "The Political Economy of Voting Rights Enforcement in America's Gilded Age: Electoral College Competition, Partisan Commitment, and the Federal Election Law, *American Political Science Review* 93 (1999): 115–31.

[31] Foner, *Reconstruction*, 348; Keith Ian Polakoff, *Political Parties in American History* (New York: John Wiley, 1981), 220.

[32] Seip, *South Returns*, 222–27.

[33] Richard M. Valelly, *The Two Reconstructions: The Struggle for Black Enfranchisement* (Chicago: University of Chicago Press, 2004), 86–87; Maury Klein, "The Strategy of Southern Railroads," *American Historical Review* 73 (1968): 1052–68; Michael Perman, *The Road to Redemption: Southern Politics, 1869–1879* (Chapel Hill: University of North Carolina Press, 1984); Mark W. Summers, *Railroads, Reconstruction, and the Gospel of Prosperity: Aid under the Radical Republicans, 1865–1877* (Princeton: Princeton University Press, 1984); Thomas Holt, *Black over White: Negro Political Leadership in South Carolina during Reconstruction* (Urbana: University of Illinois Press, 1977).

biracial patronage channels put in place under state Republican administrations, strengthened planters' rights against those of their sharecroppers, and stepped up the voter intimidation and suffrage restriction that would reach fulfillment at the turn of the century. In a very real sense, the end of military reconstruction demonopolized the legitimate use of force in southern life. Nationally, Republicans vacillated among a variety of incompatible strategies. Hayes attempted a reconciliation tour with the South's "better elements," but it alienated remaining Radicals while producing few tangible gains. Chester Arthur episodically reached out to small third parties, whose racial records varied substantially from state to state, but the strategy, unsurprisingly, failed to build stable coalitions.[34]

African Americans themselves remained loyal Republicans (with the occasional deviation in state-level, but never federal-level races) even as their elected numbers and influence declined, and the party's southern policy bobbed and weaved. And while African Americans occasionally considered forming third parties to balance power (much like the independents to whom Chester Arthur reached out), or else joining tactically with the party that offered the most jobs to black supporters, especially as Radical Republicanism slid into corruption, the more politically astute leaders, and the vast majority of voters rejected those efforts.[35]

Democrats never fully accepted the new rules of the game. They remained implacably and intransigently opposed to national-level civil and voting rights legislation or to intervening against the campaign of terror throughout the South. Even after northern Democrats accepted the Fourteenth and Fifteenth Amendments in their jurisdictions and even competed fitfully for African American votes in state elections, they reliably opposed all federal intervention to force universal schools, and, critically, honest elections in the South. National-level unity inside the Democracy emboldened Redeemer governments in readmitted states toward ever more aggressive moves, legal and otherwise, against blacks and their interests. No congressional Democrat from 1866 onward *ever* supported civil rights legislation in a vote on final passage.[36]

Finally, the Supreme Court severely limited use of the new amendments to ensure equal rights and protect citizens from state government. While the New Deal constitutional revolution and the conservative legal movement's

[34] J. Morgan Kousser, *The Shaping of Southern Politics: Suffrage Restriction and the Establishment of the One-Party South, 1880–1910* (New Haven: Yale University Press, 1974), 24–27.

[35] Grossman, *Democratic Party and the Negro*; Peter D. Klingman and David T. Geithman, "Negro Dissidence and the Republican Party, 1864–1872," *Phylon* 40 (1979): 172–82.

[36] J. Morgan Kousser, "The Voting Rights Act and the Two Reconstructions," in *Controversies in Minority Voting Behavior: The Voting Rights Act in Perspective*, ed. Bernard Grofman and Chandler Davidson (Washington, D.C.: Brookings Institution Press, 1992), 150; C. Vann Woodward, "The Political Legacy of Reconstruction," *Journal of Negro Education* 26 (1957): 235.

partial successes in chipping away at the Warren and early Burger Courts parallel one another less closely than do other aspects of anchoring alliance, the postbellum Court tells a different story entirely. Republican-appointed judges, free to exercise a laissez-faire philosophy unrestrained by the exigencies of coalition building, stopped Republican legislation in its tracks. Far from maintaining a political regime that placed them on the bench, the Court, deep in the party period, paradoxically faced all the limits bedeviling postwar Republicans without the motivating forces behind partisan action.[37]

The justices attempted to graft the new amendments and understandings into their ideological and constitutional frameworks. The "constitutional moment"—or "moments"—of the 1860s and 1870s reverberate still.[38] The Court's membership was dominated by politically motivated appointees from Lincoln's early tenure, before he backed emancipation, and, critically, a long string of railroad lawyers committed to orthodox economic doctrine.[39] The judicial retreats emerged also from the weaknesses of Radical Republicans. Their moment in the sun was short and centered around Congress, especially in the House. They never controlled appointments. They had to compromise repeatedly on the language of the Fourteenth Amendment.[40] As he decried the verdict in the Civil Rights Cases, therefore, Douglass looked both back and forward in constitutional interpretation as he spoke of "the object and intention of the adoption of the Fourteenth Amendment."[41]

While the Court, still reeling from *Dred Scott*, was generally quiet in the Radical years, it soon struck back against Reconstruction, gutting the Fourteenth Amendment's Privileges and Immunities Clause in the Slaughter House Cases, decided in 1873.[42] In 1876, it limited prosecutions under

[37] Pamela Brandwein, *Rethinking the Judicial Settlement of Reconstruction* (Cambridge: Cambridge University Press, 2011), 21–22.

[38] Bruce Ackerman, *We the People: Foundations* (Cambridge, Mass.: Belknap, 1991), 44–47 and 78–83; Akhil Reed Amar, "The Bill of Rights and the Fourteenth Amendment," *Yale Law Journal* 101 (1992): 1193–1284; Michael W. McConnell, "The Forgotten Constitutional Moment," *Constitutional Comment* 11 (1994): 115–44.

[39] Howard Gillman, "How Political Parties Can Use the Courts to Advance Their Agendas: Federal Courts in the United States, 1875–1891," *American Political Science Review* 96 (2002): 511–524.

[40] Randall Kennedy, "Reconstruction, the Waite Court, and the Politics of History," in *The Supreme Court and the Civil War*, ed. Jennifer M. Lowe (Washington, D.C.: Supreme Court Historical Society, 1996), 99–102; Jack M. Balkin, "How Social Movements Change (or Fail to Change) the Constitution: The Case of the New Departure," *Suffolk University Law Review* 39 (2005): 27–65.

[41] Frederick Douglass, "The Civil Rights Case" (1883), in Foner, *Life and Writings of Frederick Douglass.*

[42] 83 U.S. 36 (1873). If Lincoln's Chief Justice, Salmon Chase, an old Free Soiler from Ohio, had not been on his deathbed, he might have rounded up another vote, potentially shifting constitutional history. For context, see William E. Nelson, *The Fourteenth Amendment:*

the Enforcement Act to carry out the Fifteenth Amendment. In 1883, it invalidated the Civil Rights Act of 1875, which compelled "full and equal enjoyment" in public accommodation, but not schooling. The infamous *Plessy v. Ferguson* followed in 1896. Many Republicans applied old free-labor principles against state interference to a Gilded Age concerned with the right to contract, and felt relief when the Court finally repealed the Civil Rights Act.[43]

Rather, the story is of a jurisprudential road not taken. The Warren Court, pace various law professors, was never in the cards. All the same, if Radicals rather than railroad lawyers had sat on the bench, then they would assuredly have interpreted the Fourteenth and Fifteenth Amendments more broadly, and Republicans could have begun to enact a "civil rights state" to protect their advantages in the South, especially in states with large black populations.[44] Such a coalition might also have been better able to resist the dominance of northern corporate interests. Instead, the new alignment formed after 1896 and reflected in *Lochner* a decade later fully reconnected the party's backers, judicial philosophy, and electoral imperatives. Again, rather than proceeding to enact itself throughout the American state, abolition-republicanism had to proceed by party—and especially by national party—alone.

The "Force Bill" and the End of Abolition-Republicanism

The last gasp of the Republican commitment to African Americans came with the Federal Elections Bill in 1890 and 1891, when Republicans held unified control of Congress for the first time since the Grant administration. The bill's centerpiece was a system of supervisors empowered to issue writs of election; disputes would be settled by federal courts, making them, rather than state administrators, the arbiters of elections to the House and

---

From Political Principle to Judicial Doctrine (Cambridge, Mass.: Harvard University Press, 1988), chap. 7; Richard L. Aynes, "Constricting the Law of Freedom: Justice Miller, the Fourteenth Amendment, and the Slaughter-House Cases," *Chicago-Kent Law Review* 70 (1994): 627–88; G. Edward White, "Reconstructing the Constitutional Jurisprudence of Salmon P. Chase," *Northern Kentucky Law Review* 21 (1993): 41–116.

[43]Heather Cox Richardson, *The Death of Reconstruction: Race, Labor, and Politics in the Post–Civil War North, 1865–1901* (Cambridge, Mass.: Harvard University Press, 2001), chap. 4; text in "Civil Rights Act of 1875," in Cox and Cox, *Reconstruction, the Negro, and the New South*, 123–25.

[44]Cf. R. Shep Melnick, "The Supreme Court and the Civil Rights State" (paper, Boston Area Research Workshop on History, Institutions, and Politics, 7 April 2011); see also Ellen D. Katz, "Reinforcing Representation: Congressional Power to Enforce the Fourteenth and Fifteenth Amendments in the Rehnquist and Waite Courts," *Michigan Law Review* 101 (2003): 2341–2408.

electors for the presidency. Efforts to secure voting rights without the army or impositions on states' rights, William Chandler understood, required use of the federal courts, armed with Congress's power under Article I Section 4 to fix the "times, places, and manner" for congressional elections.

The bill aimed to fossilize partisan advantage in institutional amber: Republicans had appointed the vast majority of federal judges. Unlike the Supreme Court, district courts generally proved pliant to partisan superiors. "More than twenty negro Representatives from the South will render the Republican control of the future Congresses absolutely secure and safe," claimed a party organ.[45] The plan, moreover, applied nationally, so it could also dethrone urban Democratic machines, if required. This scheme presaged Section 5 of the Voting Rights Act, and avoided the direct targeting of specific jurisdictions for special review; intriguingly, it might also have led, after the civil rights era, to a system of federal rather than state control over the machinery of federal elections.

What opponents termed the "Force Bill" remained stuck in the Senate after a Democratic filibuster. In the House, the Speaker, Thomas Brackett Reed, in February 1890, engineered a series of strongly majoritarian rules changes that eliminated the disappearing quorum and drastically restricted dilatory motions. House passage followed in July, with two Republican opponents and no Democratic supporters.[46]

By the time it took up the Elections Bill in December, the Senate had already passed the McKinley Tariff and the Sherman Silver Purchase Bill. While Harrison had vainly hoped that protectionists would back the Federal Elections Bill as a way to protect growing southern manufactures, their enthusiasm declined precipitously after they won their tariff. Meanwhile, western Republicans, led by Nevada's William Stewart (who, in an earlier incarnation, had framed the Fifteenth Amendment and its Enforcement Act) opposed the bill, both as retaliation for the weak Sherman bill, and because they feared—a new twist on the old cross-regional incongruities—that the courts would interfere out West, as well, disrupting cozy arrangements with mine owners and railroads, and potentially even helping Chinese immigrants and American Indians to vote.[47]

[45] *Congressional Record* 21, 26 September 1890, 10548.

[46] Thomas B. Reed, "The Federal Control of Elections," *North American Review* 150 (1890): 671–80; Richard M. Valelly, "The Reed Rules and Republican Party Building: A New Look," *Studies in American Political Development* 23 (2009): 115–42.

[47] Thomas Adams Upchurch, *Legislating Racism: The Billion Dollar Congress and the Birth of Jim Crow* (Lexington: University Press of Kentucky, 2004), chap. 8. By 1893, Stewart explicitly used opposition to federal election rules as a way to curry favor with potentially prosilver southerners. See his answer to Chandler's query asking why a framer of the Enforcement Act so ardently sought its repeal; *Congressional Record*, 12 December 1893, 164–67.

Democrats mounted elaborate objections to the bill as they sought, ultimately successfully, to pick off wavering Republicans. As debate dragged on, Nelson Aldrich, the Republican floor leader, hoped to gain recognition for a motion to close debate with a simple majority. However, Levi Morton, the vice president, refused to recognize him. If Morton—a conservative Wall Street investment banker and a parliamentary neophyte (and an opponent of Radicalism in the 1860s)—had allowed Aldrich to make his motion, then the modern filibuster would never have come about.[48] As debate dragged on, however, opponents peeled off wavering western Republicans and, by a single vote, the Senate at the end of January 1891 finally moved on to other business. It was the last Republican-led effort to help African Americans that reached the floor.[49]

The key caucus debate, on whether to take up the tariff or election bill first, served as metaphor for a party with higher priorities than black suffrage. George Frisbie Hoar of Massachusetts lost out to Matthew Quay of Pennsylvania. Hoar, a Free Soiler who still wore a frock coat, had picked huckleberries with Thoreau in Concord boyhood. By contrast, Quay, no stranger to the darker arts of politics, had led the Republican effort to dun big business for the 1888 campaign; he noted that, whatever their historical claims, "few if any Negroes had advanced the cause of the party by contributions to its funds."[50]

Meanwhile, new political coalitions enacted de jure suffrage restrictions that doomed the remnants of abolition-republicanism. As the Senate debated in 1890, Mississippi avoided the problem of denying the suffrage to eligible voters: its new constitution barred suffrage from all illiterates unable to understand the state constitution, and imposed a hefty poll tax. The

[48] "Goodby, Closure. Goodby, Force Bill," *New York Herald*, 27 January 1891, 3; Robert McElroy, *Levi Parsons Morton: Banker, Diplomat and Statesman* (New York: Putnam, 1930), esp. 72–73 and 183–94.

[49] "Where the Responsibility Lies," *New York Tribune* 2 January 1891, 4; Richard M. Valelly, "Partisan Entrepreneurship and Policy Windows: George Frisbie Hoar and the 1890 Federal Elections Bill," in *Formative Acts: American Politics in the Making*, ed. Stephen Skowronek and Matthew Glassman (Philadelphia: University of Pennsylvania Press, 2007), 126–49; Richard E. Welch, Jr., "The Federal Elections Bill of 1890: Postscripts and Prelude," *Journal of American History* 52 (1965): 510–26; "The Senate Crisis," *Boston Journal*, 21 August 1890, 1; George F. Hoar, *Autobiography of Seventy Years* (New York: Scribner, 1903), vol. 2, chap. 13; Rayford W. Logan, *The Betrayal of the Negro: From Rutherford B. Hayes to Woodrow Wilson* (1954; repr., New York: Collier Books, 1970), chap. 4.

[50] Hoar, *Autobiography*, 1:70; Richardson, *Chandler*, 413. On the 1888 campaign, see Robert D. Marcus, *Grand Old Party: Political Structure in the Gilded Age, 1880–1896* (New York: Oxford University Press, 1971), chap. 4. After Harrison thanked Providence for his election, Quay replied that "'Providence hadn't a damned thing to do with it,' to which he added that he supposed Harrison would never learn how close a number of men were compelled to approach the gates of the penitentiary to make him President." Alexander K. McClure, *Old Time Notes of Pennsylvania* (Philadelphia: Winston, 1905), 2:573.

Democratic Congress in 1894 overturned the sections of the Enforcement Act of 1870 proscribing poll taxes and literacy tests for voters in federal elections. Only Hoar and Chandler fought seriously against the bill, and nine Republican senators skipped the vote altogether.[51]

Urban workers plumped for the full dinner pail in 1896. Republicans now held their national majority, and entirely from the North and West. Adding elements beyond a notably stable minimum winning coalition risked destabilizing the party. The McKinley administration nodded occasionally to African Americans' economic achievement, but never mentioned their political rights. It deliberately starved black-and-tan state Republican parties that cooperated with Alliancemen against Democrats—even when such cooperation offered the only route to electoral success—and stayed silent after the savage 1898 riot in Wilmington, North Carolina, against a biracial Alliance-Republican municipal government.[52] "That vote means the death of the Republican party," Hoar grimly declared moments after the Senate laid the Federal Elections Bill aside.[53] About the party's electoral prospects he was quite wrong, but as far as its historic commitments utterly correct.

Failed Alliance and the Limits of Party

Republicans failed to consolidate party-led alliance cemented in 1860. This outcome looks different depending on the comparison. In one light, it seems a partial success. Populism never meaningfully entered the party system at all. This comparison suggests the Janus face of failed long-term incorporation. As the twentieth century dawned, the fates of the Abolitionist and Populist insurgencies bookending the Third Party System could seem identical. For both cases but through different channels and to the detriment (especially severe for southern blacks) of different groups, incongruence of race and class across section doomed hopes to reinterpret the egalitarian promise of the founding. For Radicals, a thoroughgoing southern policy threatened northern capital; for Populists, easy money for the periphery repelled the northern worker. The party system, and the interests behind it, seemed incapable of giving voice to those whom moneyed interests—tycoons, industrialists, planters, bankers—exploited or ignored.

[51] Xi Wang, *The Trial of Democracy: Black Suffrage and Northern Republicans, 1860–1910* (Athens: University of Georgia Press, 1997), 256–58; Kousser, *Shaping of Southern Politics*, 139–45; Michael Perman, *Struggle for Mastery: Disenfranchisement in the South, 1888–1908* (Chapel Hill: University of North Carolina Press, 2001).

[52] Charles W. Calhoun, *Conceiving a New Republic: The Republican Party and the Southern Question, 1869–1900* (Lawrence: University Press of Kansas, 2006), chap. 10; Logan, *Betrayal*, 94–95; Valelly, *Two Reconstructions*, 131–32.

[53] "Force Bill Put Aside," *New York Sun*, 6 January 1891, 1.

Analytically, the two cases differ critically. Abolition-republicanism, which could not consolidate its gains into mature alliance, failed from a very different starting point. While support for the freedmen and their descendants would never again serve as "the very definition of Republicanism," abolition-republicanism left for the civil rights movement a time capsule that opened a century hence. To repeat a central premise, simple success or failure to become institutionalized says less about movements' fate—especially for consequential cases—than do their sequential outcomes in the party system as they influence ideological possibilities and leave policy legacies.

Turning the comparison to the anchoring alliances, the decades-long process through which Republicans deserted their heritage helps makes sense of differences between failed and successful cases of mature alliance. Stable, long-running partnership between supporters of an egalitarian republicanism that would benefit the freedmen and the Republican Party was never a likely prospect after the early Reconstruction period, when alliance was most likely to be institutionalized, and when its advocates stood at the peak of their power. (A second Lincoln administration probably delves deeper into counterfactual history than a comparative-institutional study ought to go.[54]) By 1870, serious land reform and federal assistance to southern schools were off the table, and the Fourteenth and Fifteenth Amendments had passed in forms that allowed southern states to ignore them and the Supreme Court to hollow them.

Successful ongoing alliance is a cross-institutional project. Movement infrastructure reaches issue publics, and diffuse state capacity forges policy-politics linkages that make anchoring groups attractive to partisan partners. Together they cement the trade of votes for policy, and raise the costs to exit from the party coalition. Abolition-republicanism, by contrast, relied principally on a program of party building, attempting to meld appeals to Union in the North with support from African Americans in the South. That coalition, however, faced deep challenges from other forces inside the Republican tent, including northern business interests as well as liberal reformers. The New Deal–era Democratic Party withstood fierce internal challenges, but did so in a more sympathetic constellation of alliance supported by the administrative state.

Similarly, while organized labor and conservative evangelicals successfully reinvented themselves as they moved seriously into electoral politics, the transition proved too much for the old abolitionists, as they sought a still-more-wrenching shift in a period when parties served as the preeminent

[54]Cf. Bruce Ackerman, *We the People: Transformations* (Cambridge, Mass.: Belknap, 1998), 275–76, which imagines abolition-republicanism backed by a Republican court, rather than constitutional amendment.

vehicles to mobilize voters. The abolitionists had succeeded in ending slavery and then securing the ballot without regard to color. Amid seeming triumph, only the most uncompromising among them, Wendell Phillips especially, understood the precariousness of African Americans' position in the era of Reconstruction, or the connections among different groups demanding rights, recognition, and spoils. For Frederick Douglass, the yawning gaps between the parties kept him a loyal Republican, however angry he became at the perfidy of Hayes and McKinley. Yet those agitators rarely had the political sense and never had the leverage to shift policies that placated more central elements in the Republican coalition.

The generational and institutional stories here meld. Because the Radicals failed to build a durable base for their political heirs, younger would-be leaders went elsewhere. Again, the contrast with the anchoring alliances in twentieth century proves instructive. Instead, every election after the Civil War, in the formula of the era, became a battle, internal as well as external; alliance never became routinized, nor did the beneficiaries of alliance, African Americans, ever become wholly accepted as players in the game. Although the failures of Reconstruction go far beyond it, precisely the weakness of so many other actors and venues, from scalawag governments to the Supreme Court, refocuses attention on the internal politics of the Republican Party. They reveal, more even than do the successful cases of alliances in ordinary politics, the myriad ways that political parties refract opportunities for structural change in American politics. Radical movements ally with parties only when those parties accept them—and, in the party period, the party deployed its blocking power all too effectively.

CHAPTER 10

Conclusion

The Future of Alliance

Since the dawn of mass politics, Americans seeking fundamental change have joined together in social movements. As these pages have shown, movements may substantially reconfigure the broader political system, especially in the rare, consequential cases when they establish themselves as anchoring groups allied with a major party. Through alliance, anchoring groups solve a dilemma emerging directly from the constitutional structure of the Electoral College, a first-past-the-post electoral system, and federalism: how a movement backed by a minority wields power in a system designed to reward cobbled-together national majorities. When movements with distinctive visions of the American experiment ally with major parties as anchoring groups, they change the contours of politics.

Parties accept alliance only if a winning coalition inside the party, including hard-nosed pragmatists as well as ideological sympathizers, prefers joining with an anchoring group over other paths to ongoing electoral majority. If the pragmatists feel that the anchoring group threatens their core interests, or the party's prospects for victory, they will spurn it. Parties give benefits, in policy and prestige, to movement elites, in exchange for votes and access to money, time, and networks that those elites control. If parties can mobilize movement supporters directly, without paying movement elites' price, they will do so. Hence, movements enter and maintain their place inside political parties only when parties accept them and covet their resources. Otherwise, parties will freeze out their movement allies.

Nor does entrance into a party coalition alone determine eventual movement success. Without policies, cross-cutting ties, and ideological appeals that entrench anchoring groups' position and bring them together with other high-demanding elements inside parties, then movements will prove unable to consolidate the gains won when first they confronted the American party system. In a process that often stretches for decades, party and movement adapt in a process of reciprocal change, as parties assimilate core movement priorities while movements lose their early zeal, radicalism, and naïveté, instead accepting the strategies and compromises of ordinary politics.

To be sure, comparisons such as these have their limits. The alternatives in American party politics emerge from multiple interests as they interact. As Robert Dahl wrote in 1967, "no single group can win national elections—only heterogeneous combinations of groups can."[1] The framework here attempts to makes sense of one set of groups, namely those with origins in social movements. It says rather less about the panoply of other partisan allies, or about *combinations*. Dynamic interactions among multiple sets of high-demanders, with varying goals from playing the party-political game, represent the next frontier for research on parties and their group backers.[2] How, to reverse the vantage points, have existing high-demanders welcomed or thwarted new entrants? What strategies best disrupt existing coalitions—and how should coalition brokers respond? What constellations of group interests have proven more and less stable? How do the preferences of party identifiers, rank-and-file supporters, or grassroots leaders affect elite calculations? How have the answers changed from the party period to the networked party? Above all, such work would move further along the road traveled here: to make sense of political parties as instruments of inclusion and exclusion, conflict and compromise alike.

Labor and the Democrats, the Christian Right and the Republicans

Twice in twentieth-century politics, alliance with an anchoring group has fundamentally reshaped the party system. In the 1930s, the CIO abandoned labor's long-standing philosophy of voluntarism—that is, union men standing on their own two feet to advocate for job-specific benefits—and made common cause with the New Deal, working in politics for social legislation that would help all workers. Three-quarters of a century on, the partnership between labor and the Democrats endures, with a weakened labor movement still beckoning Democrats to economic liberalism, and putting its remaining muscle on the line in the political ground game. In the late 1970s, conservative evangelicals responded to threats and dislocations in the

[1] Robert Dahl, *Pluralist Democracy in the United States: Conflict and Consent* (Chicago: Rand McNally, 1967), 456.

[2] See the framework in David Karol, *Party Position Change in American Politics: Coalition Management* (Cambridge: Cambridge University Press, 2009), 17–22.

wake of the sixties, most notably the Carter administration's attempts to revoke tax exemptions for segregated religious schools, to form a partnership with the Republican Party. The GOP platform supported the Equal Rights Amendment decades before Democrats did so. Yet the party now serves as a bulwark of social conservatism; 40 percent of its votes come from white evangelicals, and a strong prolife stance has become a de facto requirement for the Republican presidential nomination.

In profound ways, the decades-long trajectories of these alliances parallel each other. Both new entrants sharply shocked the political system. Midwived by brokers inside the state, both in Congress and near to transformative presidents, they channeled large-scale popular mobilization into electoral politics. Their civic visions, however nationally unpopular, fused group, partisan, and national purposes, whether of industrial democracy or a Christian America. Each emerged from institutional rupture that politicized longstanding group activity, as the CIO broke away from the AF of L in 1935 and conservatives seized the presidency of the Southern Baptist Convention in 1979. Entry into electoral activity in realigning elections soon followed, with Labor's Non-Partisan League in 1936 and the Moral Majority in 1980. After ambivalent (and, in the case of FDR, occasionally stormy) relations with transformative presidents, canny operatives used party machinery to uphold those presidents' ideological legacies. A decade after the movements' initial forays into politics, new group institutions—CIO-PAC, formed in 1943, and the Christian Coalition, formed in 1989—cemented durable electoral partnerships focused on achievable victories in ordinary politics.

Both alliances have endured moments of soul-searching—when the AFL-CIO high command sat on its hands rather than endorse George McGovern, or when leaders in the Christian Right despaired of politics after the Clinton impeachment. And deunionization and secularization weaken group numbers, especially in labor's ranks, impinge on influence in an increasingly hostile culture, and threaten anchoring groups' hard-won status inside allied parties. Long after all the figures of the New Deal years and most of those from the late 1970s have passed from the scene, these oft-battered alliances continue to shape the political landscape, supporting yet also constraining contemporary political parties.

Party-Group Alliance and Political Life

The ordinary women and men, most unpaid (or else severely underpaid for their formidable talents), who do the day-to-day work of movements and parties alike—reserving meeting halls, setting up folding chairs and putting them away once the speakers depart, calling supporters, persuading neighbors—remain largely invisible in these pages. Understanding elite bargaining and the structure of policy choices means paying too little attention to voices from below, and the ways their preferences and incentives shape priorities at the peak.[3] Assuredly, the view from deep inside union halls and church basements, doorsteps and street corners, would look different from the conference halls and antechambers to power explored here. Yet alliance gives such everyday activists political leverage; whether or not the public as a whole is better represented, these ordinary folks gain powerful advocates and serve as loci for networks of influence in their own communities. Activists have learned to wield influence in remarkably similar ways—even if activists themselves would blanch at the comparison. While the National Right to Work Committee or the People for the American Way could easily mine these pages for details of nefarious bosses making backroom deals, the bosses often have behind them millions whose needs and desires other elites typically dismiss. Party and movement work serves as a school of citizenship in ways that deliberative democrats would cheer, teaching how to reason with others, advocate for change, and work through possibilities to transform American democratic life.[4] Alliance affects not only state policy but the experience of politics for millions of people.

The multiple outcomes for movements in the party system represent far more than simply differing scholarly categories. The New Deal built up institutions that deployed countervailing power, with the labor movement, for all its flaws, at the very core. Cynics may say that the Christian Right seeks only an outdated status quo, and stands arm in arm with mammon. Yet it systematically opposes an educated elite with control over the bulk of the nation's cultural production.[5] They faced foes as implacable as any in American life—corporate power and changing cultural norms—and fought them to something like a draw.

Although the exercise risks presentism, it might be worth imagining what today's party politics might look like devoid of these strong anchoring alliances. Without a politically effective labor movement, the already exceptional American welfare state would likely be smaller yet and even less redistributive, with more modest pensions, less state provision of health care (and, as an immediate matter, no Affordable Care Act in 2010), and a much more limited federal role in governing wages and hours. Other sectors—finance and technology, for instance—would exercise still more influence

[3]For a trenchant version of this critique, see James Green, "Working Class Militancy in the Depression," *Radical America*, November 1972, 3–33.

[4]See respectively Paul Johnston, "The Resurgence of Labor as Citizenship in the New Labor Relations Environment," *Critical Sociology* 26 (2000): 139–60; and Jon A. Shields, *The Democratic Virtues of the Christian Right* (Princeton: Princeton University Press, 2009). Both cases undoubtedly raise complicated questions about self-interest and deliberation.

[5]This is certainly the framework in which the movement views itself. See, e.g., Tim LaHaye *The Battle for the Mind* (Old Tappan, N.J.: Fleming-Revell, 1980), chap. 8.

on matters like taxes and trade inside the Democratic coalition. And overt discussion of class issues would be rarer still.[6]

If the Christian Right had not arisen with its distinct issue priorities and partisan loyalties, one might imagine a one-sided culture war, in which the agenda of secularism and social liberalism faced fewer challenges in American national life, in which conservative Catholics and Protestants still regarded one another with sectarian suspicion, in which the southern move to the right had interacted differently with race and class—and perhaps offered greater space for old-fashioned, moderate Democrats—and in which abortion and homosexuality aroused relatively little public ire, still less of it tied to conservative or Republican politics. Unlike so many of the other attempts here to imagine alternative outcomes, even when they can seem like obscure blind alleys, this speculation is armchair speculation precisely because the counterfactuals differ from political reality so drastically.

Capture, Autonomy, and Actors' Choices

Anchoring groups both impinge on the choices that elected officials face, and face impinged choices as a result of alliance. Both sides, in other words, choose voice over exit. As "capture theory" emphasizes across its variants, movements as well as politicians lose autonomy in the process. Escape from the iron cage proves a more difficult matter, however. To ask whether alliance has "worked," tally up wins and losses, and paraphrase John L. Lewis to declare that alliance, like Israel, has many sorrows, fails to answer the deeper question: whether, given imperfect alternatives in a majoritarian system, another approach to partisan politics would better realize movements' goals for policy and power.[7] Such an alternative often proves elusive under the rules of the game. Even if privileging movement autonomy avoids grubby compromises of power and problems of dirty hands, its real advantages often prove chimerical. Or, as a British trade unionist memorably replied in the 1970s when asked about the relationship between unions and the Labour Party, "Murder yes, divorce never."[8]

[6]As Chapter 6 indicates, the shape of the private welfare state without union political activity is a more complicated question that raises a number of counterfactuals about, for example, corporate liberalism.

[7]Some analysts who oppose a given alliance on normative grounds agree that it has been a shrewd strategy to "infiltrate" the party; in turn, they sometimes overstate the benefits of alliance. See, e.g., Leo Troy, *The Twilight of the Old Unionism* (Armonk, N.Y.: M.E. Sharpe, 2004); and Sara Diamond, *Roads to Dominion: Right-Wing Movements and Political Power in the United States* (New York: Guilford, 1995).

[8]Jack Jones of the Transport and General Workers' Union, quoted by John Monks in Paul Leduc Browne, ed., *Labour & Social Democracy: International Perspectives* (Ottawa: Canadian Center for Policy Alternatives, 2002), 28.

The voluntarist Christopher Tomlins, in celebrating the achievements of early AF of L unions and their "space beyond the reach of the New Deal's administrative state," offers a model for unions to bargain and protest without recourse to the political process.[9] This vision has very little to say about countervailing power beyond a defense of labor's own procedural rights, nor does it posit any special role for the trade union in democratic society. So, too, Tomlins offers total silence on the issue of race. If the NLRA had accepted AFL jurisdictional claims, as Tomlins seems to propose, then racially exclusionary job categories such as those promulgated by the exclusionary railroad unions might well have been the rule across American industry.[10]

For Frances Fox Piven and Richard Cloward, militancy from below amid crisis dissipates after entrenched powers regroup and counterattack. In understanding opportunities amid regime crisis—above all in these pages, the settlement of 1935—such a perspective, which takes as its touchstone the Wobbly strand in the CIO, can prove invaluable. Yet such a perspective critically underdetermines long-term outcomes. Movement leaders become incorporated into politics on vastly different terms, and those terms critically determine long-term success or failure.[11]

The most serious challenge to alliance from inside political science comes from Paul Frymer, who uses the case of African Americans captured inside the Democratic Party to argue against partisan politics as a means to effect social change.[12] Judges and bureaucrats, he argues, better protect unpopular minorities. Frymer explores in depth a uniquely bad period, and the scorecard looks rather different in the hyper-partisan and fitfully

[9]Christopher L. Tomlins, *The State and the Unions: Labor Relations, Law, and the Organized Labor Movement in America, 1880–1960* (Cambridge: Cambridge University Press, 1985), 195.

[10]Tomlins, *State and the Unions*, 102.

[11]Frances Fox Piven and Richard A. Cloward, *Poor People's Movements: Why They Succeed, How They Fail* (1977; repr., New York: Vintage Books, 1979) is the classic position. Frances Fox Piven, *Challenging Authority: How Ordinary People Change America* (Lanham, Md.: Rowman & Littlefield, 2006), esp. chap. 6, restates "the power problem" in light of various institutionalist critiques. Frances Fox Piven, "Structural Constraints and Political Development: The Case of the American Democratic Party," in *Labor Parties in Postindustrial Societies*, ed. Frances Fox Piven (Cambridge: Polity Press, 1991), 235–64, offers a more macrostructural account. Frances Fox Piven and Lorraine Minnite, "Replies," *Nation*, 22 October 2012, 15–17, edges closer toward a joint movement-electoral strategy. See also Mike Davis, *Prisoners of the American Dream* (London: Verso, 1986); and Charles Williams, "The Racial Politics of Progressive Americanism: New Deal Liberalism and the Subordination of Black Workers in the UAW," *Studies in American Political Development* 19 (2005): 75–97.

[12]Paul Frymer, *Uneasy Alliances: Race and Party Competition in America* (Princeton: Princeton University Press, 1999); see also Paul Frymer, *Black and Blue: African Americans, the Labor Movement, and the Decline of the Democratic Party* (Princeton: Princeton University Press, 2008). Frymer has also influenced Piven's recent work; see Frances Fox Piven, Lorraine C. Minnite, and Margaret Groarke, *Keeping Down the Black Vote: Race and the Demobilization of American Voters* (New York: New Press, 2009), chap. 1. Cf. William Julius Wilson, "Race-Neutral Policies and the Democratic Coalition," *American Prospect*, Spring 1990, 74–81.

cross-racial age of Obama. The Democrats in the 1980s were a party adrift. Brutal zero-sum conflicts among party factions and allied groups often revolved around programs such as Aid to Families with Dependent Children deemed to benefit African Americans.[13] Jesse Jackson misstepped in his efforts to build a transracial Rainbow Coalition behind his presidential runs, and the party instead nominated what seemed to be sanctimonious bores. Barack Obama, by contrast, built unlikely bridges among African Americans, upper-middle-class reformers, and youth. Although Frymer specifically indicts Democratic nomination procedures, Obama skillfully exploited the proportional-representation rules inserted on Jackson's behalf after the 1988 campaign.

Frymer contrasts the legal system favorably with the electoral process for the years he examines. Throughout most of American history, however, courts have proven hostile to movements for fundamental social change. They did abolition-republicans no favors and, through the injunction, emasculated labor unions for decades. In the coming generation, liberal legislatures may well spend their time battling back against conservative courts; the Supreme Court's 2013 ruling in *Shelby County v. Holder*, gutting the preclearance formula in the Voting Rights Act reaffirmed by overwhelming congressional majorities, may offer a foretaste of such a future. By contrast, the years when the Rights Revolution marched on in the courts despite conservative electoral resurgence represent an historical anomaly.[14] Nor can courts ordinarily tax, spend, or build coalitions to sustain programs should they suffer public assault. Through their exercise of the appointment power, parties decide—especially in periods of unified government—whether to put on the courts judges receptive to movements, and sometimes-novel legal interpretations they may present. "To put it bluntly," writes Jack Balkin, "when constitutional claims of social movements are presented before courts, it matters a great deal whether the movement's representatives have friends in high places."[15]

More broadly, the very diversity of movements' mistakes and failures points to the limits of capture as a master concept. Policy windows open and close rapidly. Sometimes group capacity atrophies. Movements may

[13]Cf. William Galston and Elaine Ciulla Kamarck, *The Politics of Evasion: Democrats and the Presidency* (Washington, D.C.: Progressive Policy Institute, 1989). Nor were the problems limited to African Americans. Organized labor, too, endured a lean decade in the 1980s—its worst since the 1920s, claims Nelson Lichtenstein. See his *State of the Union* (Princeton: Princeton University Press, 2002), chap. 6. For a thoughtful take on the Democrats' strategic dilemmas, see Tom Wicker, "A Party of Access?," *New York Times*, 25 November 1984, E17.

[14]See R. Shep Melnick, *Between the Lines: Interpreting Welfare Rights* (Washington, D.C.: Brookings Institution, 1994).

[15]Jack M. Balkin, "How Social Movements Change (or Fail to Change) the Constitution: The Case of the New Departure," *Suffolk University Law Review* 39 (2005): 57–58.

fall victim to pressure from partisan elites with peripheral aims—as, for instance, in the 1980s when Beverly LaHaye's Concerned Women for America focused on supporting the right-wing side in Central American civil wars. At other times, however, movements suffer when they disdain coalition politics and fail to defend themselves against group opponents: the AF of L in the late 1930s and early 1940s, dissatisfied with pro-CIO rulings, emboldened labor's opponents to rein in the NLRB, and reaped the whirlwind in the Smith-Connally and Taft-Hartley Acts. Anchoring groups, in short, hold the *opportunity* to leverage power through alliance with political parties.

Differences

For all the parallels between the major cases, they diverged in important ways. During the twentieth century, facets of American politics from presidential nomination to gender roles shifted in basic ways. No change looms larger than the end of Jim Crow. Those shifts affected the environments in which party-group alliance took root, and the choices that actors made. In turn, the transformed political system reoriented the making of alliance itself.

In both cases, party-group alliance elevated group moderates. In national discourse, these figures appear radical. When compared with movement maximalists, the same men and women seem decidedly tame. That said, the extrusion of the postwar years had no parallel in the Christian Right. The same hard limits on incorporation into mainstream politics that bedeviled abolition-republicanism and Populism also hit the CIO. The failure of Operation Dixie to organize the South, the passage of Taft-Hartley, and the expulsion of the Red unions severely limited agitation from the left, or the possibility of a labor-led coalition to end Jim Crow with a class-based appeal to reconstruct southern life. To be sure, the Republican Party's move toward direct mobilization of white evangelicals has marginalized figures important in movement building. Yet the far right—the John Birch Society, the postmillennialists around Gary North and R. J. Rushdoony, the anti-abortion zealots of Operation Rescue—seem even more like fringe figures, rather than avatars of an alternative history. Nor have mainstream conservatives waged nearly so vociferous a campaign as postwar liberals to separate themselves from their radical brethren. Both alliances polarized American politics, but once the boundaries of partisan coalitions resolved themselves, that polarization was decidedly asymmetric.[16]

[16]See Nancy MacLean, "Neo-Confederacy vs. the New Deal: The Regional Utopia of the Modern American Right," in *The Myth of Southern Exceptionalism*, ed. Matthew D. Lassiter and Joseph Crespino (New York: Oxford University Press, 2010), 308–29.

While both movements have extracted important concessions from their allied parties, they differ in the rewards they have sought. Divide-the-dollar compromises work better for bread-and-butter policies than for cultural issues. Abortion is the ultimate example. In a difference more of degree than kind, labor has emphasized a straightforward exchange of votes—and the money, bodies, and networks needed to get votes—for policy. Evangelicals have treated ideological patronage somewhat more broadly, seeking recognition in public and party settings as well as tangible "wins." To generalize, at national conventions, union leaders have tended to worry more about the platform, Christian Right leaders more about the tableau of speakers.[17] As Gompersians and certain strands of Marxists never fail to note, the state sets the rules for unions. Alongside their broader, countervailing power, they face concerns every day over the NLRB, wage-and-hour rules, and oversight of the private welfare state. Although not unlimited, as the 1978 tax-exemption controversy showed, religious actors benefit from their explicit constitutional protection—and yet face deep challenges, as they enter politics, in negotiating the tensions between the sacred and the profane. The status and recognition that successful alliance brings into the public square can itself justify the effort of resources.

Nor have movement contributions to their partisan allies proven identical. Organized labor has contributed far more money directly to Democrats than has the Christian Right (although not, to be sure, rich white evangelicals acting individually) to Republicans. So, too, while both movements have activated networks for their partisan allies, the labor movement deployed no new technological advances in campaigning comparable to direct mail on the right. Jack Kroll in 1948 correctly termed CIO-PAC an "army of doorbell ringers," applying traditional tactics in neighborhoods where Democratic organizations rarely ventured.[18] Its major advance in the machinery of elections, the Political Action Committee, emerged simply as a work-around to congressionally imposed limits rather than a deliberate attempt to remake politics.

Finally, sequence matters. While labor-liberalism emerged from a combination of outside agitation and state action in the Second New Deal only after the repudiation of Hoover, conservatives in the 1970s sought to build a majority where none existed. The election of 1980, in other words, encapsulated the transformations embodied in 1932 and 1936. In this sense, Richard Viguerie and Paul Weyrich required an imagination around political

[17]This conclusion broadly matches Matt Grossmann and David A. Hopkins, "Ideological Republicans and Group Interest Democrats: The Asymmetry of American Party Politics," *Perspectives on Politics* 13 (2015): 119–39.

[18]Quoted in Marvin Persky, "Walter Reuther, the UAW-CIO, and Third Party Politics" (PhD diss., Michigan State University, 1974), 188.

demographics that John L. Lewis and Sidney Hillman, strengthening poles in an existing tent, did not.

On the other hand, a Hawthorne effect may also be at work. Only in 1952, when the AF of L convention finally endorsed a presidential candidate, did labor at last fully accept alliance, with third-party activity a nonstarter and pure pressure group activity insufficient. After a third-party dalliance in 1976, the New Right quickly settled on its basic strategy to mobilize issue publics and bargain with the GOP. As the epigraph from Richard Viguerie indicates, the New Right understood how to balance across Congress and the presidency, influence nominations, use money strategically, form networks of issue groups, and so forth, precisely because it had in New Deal liberalism a role model and worthy adversary.

Future of Alliance

These stories remain even now incomplete. Neither partnership has yet broken apart, or else been buried amid the accumulated weight of new issues and cleavages. While the link between the Christian Right and the GOP seems more fluid, accumulated history will continue to structure the ongoing dialogue between party and movement.

The "repoliticization of U.S. labor relations" has placed unions in the crosshairs.[19] The new class war is fought on Republican turf. Far from fading gently into twilight, unions remain a force inside the Democratic Party. In a kind of linked-fate politics, each actor's future seems to depend on success for the other. Although Democrats have seen success at the presidential level in states with weak unions such as Colorado, Florida, and Virginia, they still cannot win nationally without blue-collar votes in the Rust Belt organized by the CIO eight decades ago. The twin challenges of winning meaningful group-specific victories, especially around labor law, and pushing for policies to help workers more broadly reflects neatly the two major pieces of Second New Deal legislation: the Wagner Act and the Social Security Act.

In the fall of 2011, encampments from the Occupy movement arose in every major American city. "We are the 99 percent!" they proclaimed, in a cry against rising inequality. Without clear demands or effective group leadership and enamored of its decentralized processes that allowed vocal minorities to hijack decision making, the movement failed to survive the clearing of its tents.[20] Occupy never confronted the Democratic Party because it

[19] I have taken the phrase from Nelson Lichtenstein, "Labour, Liberalism, and the Democratic Party: A Vexed Alliance," *Relations Industrielles—Industrial Relations* 66 (2011): 523.

[20] On the perils of unstructured groups, see Jo Freeman, "The Tyranny of Structurelessness," *Ms. Magazine*, July 1973, 76–78, 86–89.

built no infrastructure, nor harnessed any existing infrastructure, on the left or elsewhere, with which to do so.

Yet Occupy dominated the headlines in a way that unions themselves had not for decades. With the NLRB process broken and unlikely to be rescued through labor law or huge sums expended in organizing drives, and public-sector unions vulnerable—and besieged outside of liberal redoubts—unions turned increasingly to protest. Fast-food workers, many of them recent immigrants, unleashed waves of nationwide strikes funded by the SEIU, aiming at better working conditions and a higher minimum wage. Unions searched for a way to translate the energy from the "Fight for $15" into policy victories—and, more difficult still, to translate policy victories into new configurations of power and ideological possibility.[21] In 1935, strike activity gave Robert F. Wagner and John L. Lewis their openings for the Wagner Act, the CIO and, in short order, the labor-Democratic partnership. In an institutionally denser setting and a postindustrial economy, and with their opponents far more mobilized, the endgame for labor now seems far less clear.

The conservative attacks on unions, along with labor's continued strengths in grassroots mobilization, protect alliance between labor and the Democrats, but Republican-led unified government or an emboldened conservative majority on the Supreme Court could drastically weaken union membership. Public unions (and their Democratic allies) see their evisceration in Wisconsin. National right-to-work no longer seems an absurd prospect. Just before the 2012 election, the president of the Amalgamated Transit Union worried aloud that if Republicans "take over the federal government, there will be no such thing as a labor movement."[22]

Nor does the trade of votes for ideological patronage answer the deeper questions of unionism amid the new inequality. As it fights for survival, what distinct, resonant claims can organized labor make when it seeks to speak on workers' behalf? As it fades, what organizations and strategies can replace the trade union as a collective, ongoing voice for workers?[23] And

[21] See, Steven Greenhouse, "A Day's Strike Seeks to Raise Fast-Food Pay," *New York Times*, 1 August 2013, A1; Josh Eidelson, "Fast-Food Strikes Hit Record Numbers, Span 190 Cities," *Business Week*, 5 December 2014, http://www.businessweek.com/articles/2014-12-05/fast-food-strikes-hit-record-numbers-span-190-cities; William Finnegan, "Dignity," *New Yorker*, 15 September 2014, 70–79.

[22] Quoted in Josh Eidelson, "Attacks on Labor Put Unions on the Defense in Election 2012," *Nation*, 2 November 2012, http://www.thenation.com/article/170980/attacks-labor-put-unions-defensive-election-2012; see also Alec MacGillis, "How Obama Won Ohio," *New Republic*, 7 November 2012, http://www.newrepublic.com/blog/plank/109821/how-obama-won-the-ohio-election.

[23] See Richard Yeselson, "Not with a Bang but with a Whimper," *New Republic*, 6 June 2012, http://www.newrepublic.com/blog/plank/103928/not-bang-whimper-the-long-slow-death-spiral-americas-labor-movement; and Timothy Noah, "The Most Challenging Issue Facing

what, without such a voice, are the prospects for an egalitarian welfare state to protect against the hazards and vicissitudes of life?[24]

For its part, the future of the Christian Right and the Republican Party appears in flux as old organizations fade from the scene and the Tea Party assumes the mantle of grassroots conservatism. To be clear, the underlying loyalties of white evangelicals are not up for grabs. Occasional libertarian hopes to the contrary, divorce between party and movement seems off the table. Nor is the party likely to retreat on the core issue of human life. Fully 78 percent of white evangelicals voted Republican in the 2012 presidential election, a figure twenty points higher than the Democrats' share of the vote in union households. More than 40 percent of Republican voters were white and self-identified as evangelicals, and the link between church attendance and voting behavior is strongest at the top of the income distribution.

Since the Christian Coalition began to infiltrate state parties in the early 1990s and on through Karl Rove's efforts during the Bush years to activate evangelical networks directly on behalf of the GOP, the divide between movement and party has attenuated. Rather than brokering through group elites, elected officials have increasingly sought evangelical support directly—at times with the same clumsy framing on gender, sexual orientation, and reproduction that led so many Christian Right leaders into hot water. While the movement has shown an uncanny penchant for rejuvenation, no peak association has arisen to claim the Christian Coalition's mantle. Instead, polarization, sorting, and fears of primary challenges from the right give ambitious conservative politicians their own incentives to back policies far from the national median.

Into the gap, in yet another wave of conservative discontent, rode the Tea Party with its call, harking back deep in grassroots conservative politics, to "take our country back." It reached peak influence in the 2010 midterm elections, when Republicans gained sixty-three seats in the House of Representatives. The Tea Party arose amid the Great Recession, and synthesized conservative anger against fiscal and monetary policy, from bailouts to

---

Liberalism Today," *MSNBC*, 31 August 2014, http://www.msnbc.com/msnbc/the-most-challenging-issue-facing-liberalism-today.

[24] For contrasting perspectives from sometime coauthors favoring near-identical social policies, see Lane Kenworthy, *Social Democratic America* (New York: Oxford University Press, 2014), arguing that "unions are too weak now to have much impact and there is little reason to expect that their decline can be reversed" (132); and Jonas Pontusson, "Once Again a Model: Nordic Social Democracy in a Globalized World," in *What's Left of the Left: Democrats and Social Democrats in Challenging Times*, ed. James Cronin, George Ross, and James Shoch (Durham, N.C.: Duke University Press, 2011), arguing that "building stronger unions must surely be an indispensable part of any effort to move economic and social policies in the United States in an egalitarian direction" (115).

stimulus to Obamacare, into a broader critique against handouts to undeserving recipients, and a country losing its bearings.[25]

Both its substantive concerns and, especially, its mode of organizing separate the Tea Party from the Christian Right.[26] A bare majority of Tea Party activists in a 2011 survey identified as evangelical or born-again. Yet the Tea Party shifted conservative mobilization away from the denomination- and congregation-based organizing that dominated the Christian Right, assigns no special role to authentically religious voices or leaders, and puts particular emphasis on perceived government profligacy. Instead, it combined grassroots energy—from face-to-face Tea Party gatherings—with outside resources—through the antitax conservative establishment—and group-specific influence on supporters—via talk radio and Fox News.[27]

For all its confrontational tactics with the simulacrum of a social movement, the Tea Party behaved, in a polarized age, far more as an aggressive party faction than as a movement grappling with the limits of electoral politics. It swiftly chose the primary as its weapon to dethrone RINOs (Republicans in Name Only) and replace them with more doctrinaire conservatives. In lower-profile House races, Tea Party enthusiasm helped the party; when its Senate nominees faced sharp public scrutiny, Republicans lost winnable races.[28]

The Tea Party and direct mobilization by Republican politicians form two sides of the same coin. Evangelicals have entered, and even come to define, the new Republican core. Ideological and partisan leaders increasingly mobilize them without tapping into other loyalties. Yet this fusion of social and economic conservatives, elite and grassroots alike, simply sharpens the

[25] See, among many, Zachary C. Courser, "The 'Tea Party' as a Conservative Social Movement," *Society* 49 (2012): 43–53; Martin Cohen, "The Future of the Tea Party: Scoring an Invitation to the Republican Party," in *Steep: The Precipitous Rise of the Tea Party*, ed. Lawrence Rosenthal and Christine Trost (Berkeley: University of California Press, 2012), 212–41; and Christopher S. Parker and Matt A. Baretto, *Change They Can't Believe In: The Tea Party and Reactionary Politics in America* (Princeton: Princeton University Press, 2013).

[26] Alan I. Abramowitz, "Grand Old Tea Party: Partisan Polarization and the Rise of the Tea Party," in Rosenthal and Trost, *Steep*, 195–211. See also Ben Smith, "Tea Parties Stir Evangelicals' Fears," *Politico*, 12 March 2010, http://www.politico.com/news/stories/0310/34291.html; and Ed Vitigliano, "Rise of the Teavangelicals," *American Family Association Journal*, January 2011, 20–22.

[27] Theda Skocpol and Vanessa Williamson, *The Tea Party and the Remaking of Republican Conservatism* (Oxford: Oxford University Press, 2012); Kate Zernike, *Boiling Mad: Inside Tea Party America* (New York: Henry Holt, 2010); Wendy K. Tam Cho, James G. Gimpel, and Daron R. Shaw, "The Tea Party Movement and the Geography of Collective Action," *Quarterly Journal of Political Science* 7 (2012): 105–33; Jane Mayer, "Covert Operations," *New Yorker*, 30 August 2010, 44–55.

[28] Michael Sokolove, "Dick Armey Is Back on the Attack," *New York Times Magazine*, 8 November 2009, 24; Michael A. Bailey, Jonathan Mummalo, and Hans Noel, "Tea Party Influence: A Story of Activists and Elites," *American Politics Research* 20 (2012): 1–36.

dilemma of majoritarian politics for minority interests. Coalition brokers, with Ralph Reed a particularly good example, take minority interests and use them to extract concessions to build a majority.[29] Unbrokered and unfettered, the tendencies to appease ideological minorities at the expense of long-term party building can grow extreme. When they control state capitols in polarized America, unified conservative majorities may now launch the kinds of frontal assaults against liberalism untried in the 1980s and 1990s, drastically restricting labor and abortion rights and curtailing means-tested programs. In national politics, however, their attempts to do so may backfire. Far from dreaming of a moral majority, religious conservatives have increasingly emphasized threats to religious liberty from big government, typically through rules on speech or hiring, that encroach on beleaguered communities of faith.[30] As Republicans appeal to an increasingly less white, less Christian, and more gay-friendly electorate and balance the formidable resources from base supporters, they face an old dilemma in American politics without the old restraints.

Social Movements and Political Parties: "The Decisive Political Impact"

In a 1988 essay, Robert Korstad and Nelson Lichtenstein quoted E. P. Thompson, who "once asserted that most social movements have a life cycle of about six years. And unless they make a decisive political impact in that time, that 'window of opportunity,' they will have little effect on the larger political structures they hope to transform."[31] Thompson, a pioneering student of industrial workers, dissenting Protestants, and the state in another empire, captured the extraordinary possibilities that open up when social movements confront the state. In short order, certainly within six years, they succeed or fail in establishing themselves, their immediate aims fulfilled or not. Yet their "decisive political impact" unfolds over a longer time

[29]The now-diminished Reed still dispenses familiar advice: emphasize popular policies that strengthen families. See Julie Bykowicz, "'Stained Glass Ghetto' a Trap for Republicans, Reed Warns," *Bloomberg Government*, 12 December 2012, http://go.bloomberg.com/political-capital/2012-12-12/stained-glass-ghetto-a-trap-for-republicans-ralph-reed-warns/.

[30]See, e.g., McKay Coppins, "Republicans Take Up Cause of Religious Liberty—And Ditch Family Values," *Buzzfeed*, 1 August 2013, http://www.buzzfeed.com/mckaycoppins/republicans-take-up-cause-of-religious-liberty-and-ditch-fam; and Jennifer Haberkorn, "Religious Groups Prep for Hobby Lobby Repeat," *Politico Pro*, 3 July 2014, http://www.politico.com/story/2014/07/hobby-lobby-religious-groups-contraception-mandate-108559.html.

[31]From a speech on the European peace movement, 8 July 1983, cited in Robert Korstad and Nelson Lichtenstein, "Opportunities Found and Lost: Labor, Radicals, and the Early Civil Rights Movement," *Journal of American History* 75 (1988): 811.

span than the "window of opportunity" allows. "Larger political structures" can take decades to reckon with demands first made and opportunities first seized when movements initially confront them, especially when the movements work through the primary linkage institutions in democratic life: political parties.

In any modern democratic polity, only political parties form the government, and exercise whatever modicum of popular control over the state, and its apparatuses to repress and to make war. And so the challenge, as for so many movements in the past, still stands: how to take movement fervor and translate it into durable change. The stories of labor and the Democrats, and the Christian Right and the Republicans speak to the possibilities and limits in American politics: new actors, working in concert with political parties, shifted the trajectories of ideological combat. While their dreams of industrial democracy or a Christian nation, of workers' or moral majorities, remained myriads of eternity, they instead succeeded in integrating themselves into the political system, and helping to define the contours of politics. Those are no small feats.

Index

Page numbers in *italics* refer to tables.

PRINCETON STUDIES IN AMERICAN POLITICS: HISTORICAL, INTERNATIONAL, AND COMPARATIVE PERSPECTIVES

Ira Katznelson, Eric Schickler, Martin Shefter, and Theda Skocpol, Series Editors

---

When Movements Anchor Parties: Electoral Alignments in American History by Daniel Schlozman

Electing the Senate: Indirect Democracy before the Seventeenth Amendment by Wendy J. Schiller and Charles Stewart III

The Substance of Representation: Congress, American Political Development, and Lawmaking by John S. Lapinski

Looking for Rights in All the Wrong Places: Why State Constitutions Contain America's Positive Rights by Emily Zackin

Paths Out of Dixie: The Democratization of Authoritarian Enclaves in America's Deep South, 1944–1972 by Robert Mickey

Fighting for the Speakership: The House and the Rise of Party Government by Jeffery A. Jenkins and Charles Stewart III

Three Worlds of Relief: Race, Immigration, and the American Welfare State from the Progressive Era to the New Deal by Cybelle Fox

Building the Judiciary: Law, Courts, and the Politics of Institutional Development by Justin Crowe

Still a House Divided: Race and Politics in Obama's America by Desmond S. King and Rogers M. Smith

The Litigation State: Public Regulation and Private Lawsuits in the United States by Sean Farhang

Reputation and Power: Organizational Image and Pharmaceutical Regulation at the FDA by Daniel Carpenter

Presidential Party Building: Dwight D. Eisenhower to George W. Bush by Daniel J. Galvin

Fighting for Democracy: Black Veterans and the Struggle against White Supremacy in the Postwar South by Christopher S. Parker

The Fifth Freedom: Jobs, Politics, and Civil Rights in the United States, 1941–1972 by Anthony S. Chen

Reforms at Risk: What Happens after Major Policy Changes Are Enacted by Eric Patashnik

The Rise of the Conservative Legal Movement: The Long Battle for Control of the Law by Steven M. Teles

Why Is There No Labor Party in the United States? by Robin Archer

Black and Blue: African Americans, the Labor Movement, and the Decline of the Democratic Party by Paul Frymer

Political Foundations of Judicial Supremacy: The Presidency, the Supreme Court, and Constitutional Leadership in U. S. History by Keith E. Whittington

The Transformation of American Politics: Activist Government and the Rise of Conservatism edited by Paul Pierson and Theda Skocpol

Disarmed: The Missing Movement for Gun Control in America by Kristin A. Goss

Filibuster: Obstruction and Lawmaking in the U.S. Senate by Gregory Wawro and Eric Schickler

Governing the American State: Congress and the New Federalism, 1877–1929 by Kimberley S. Johnson

What a Mighty Power We Can Be: African-American Fraternal Groups and the Struggle for Racial Equality by Theda Skocpol, Ariane Liazos, and Marshall Ganz

When Movements Matter: The Townsend Plan and the Rise of Social Security by Edwin Amenta

Shaping Race Policy: The United States in Comparative Perspective by Robert C. Lieberman

How Policies Make Citizens: Senior Political Activism and the American Welfare State by Andrea Louise Campbell

Dividing Lines: The Politics of Immigration Control in America by Daniel J. Tichenor

Managing the President's Program: Presidential Leadership and Legislative Policy Formulation by Andrew Rudalevige

Shaped by War and Trade: International Influences on American Political Development edited by Ira Katznelson and Martin Shefter

Dry Bones Rattling: Community Building to Revitalize American Democracy by Mark R. Warren

Disjointed Pluralism: Institutional Innovation and the Development of the U.S. Congress by Eric Schickler

The Forging of Bureaucratic Autonomy: Reputations, Networks, and Policy Innovation in Executive Agencies, 1862–1928 by Daniel P. Carpenter

The Rise of the Agricultural Welfare State: Institutions and Interest Group Power in the United States, France, and Japan by Adam D. Sheingate

In the Shadow of the Garrison State: America's Anti-Statism and Its Cold War Grand Strategy by Aaron L. Friedberg

Stuck in Neutral: Business and the Politics of Human Capital Investment Policy by Cathie Jo Martin

Uneasy Alliances: Race and Party Competition in America by Paul Frymer

Faithful and Fearless: Moving Feminist Protest inside the Church and Military by Mary Fainsod Katzenstein

Forged Consensus: Science, Technology, and Economic Policy in the United States, 1921–1953 by David M. Hart

Parting at the Crossroads: The Emergence of Health Insurance in the United States and Canada by Antonia Maioni

Bold Relief: Institutional Politics and the Origins of Modern American Social Policy by Edwin Amenta

The Hidden Welfare State: Tax Expenditures and Social Policy in the United States by Christopher Howard

Morning Glories: Municipal Reform in the Southwest by Amy Bridges

Imperiled Innocents: Anthony Comstock and Family Reproduction in Victorian America by Nicola Kay Beisel

The Road to Nowhere: The Genesis of President Clinton's Plan for Health Security by Jacob S. Hacker

The Origins of the Urban Crisis: Race and Inequality in Postwar Detroit by Thomas J. Sugrue

Party Decline in America: Policy, Politics, and the Fiscal State by John J. Coleman
The Power of Separation: American Constitutionalism and the Myth of the Legislative Veto by Jessica Korn
Why Movements Succeed or Fail: Opportunity, Culture, and the Struggle for Woman Suffrage by Lee Ann Banaszak
Kindred Strangers: The Uneasy Relationship between Politics and Business in America by David Vogel
From the Outside In: World War II and the American State by Bartholomew H. Sparrow
Classifying by Race edited by Paul E. Peterson
Facing Up to the American Dream: Race, Class, and the Soul of the Nation by Jennifer L. Hochschild
Political Organizations by James Q. Wilson
Social Policy in the United States: Future Possibilities in Historical Perspective by Theda Skocpol
Experts and Politicians: Reform Challenges to Machine Politics in New York, Cleveland, and Chicago by Kenneth Finegold
Bound by Our Constitution: Women, Workers, and the Minimum Wage by Vivien Hart
Prisoners of Myth: The Leadership of the Tennessee Valley Authority, 1933–1990 by Erwin C. Hargrove
Political Parties and the State: The American Historical Experience by Martin Shefter
Politics and Industrialization: Early Railroads in the United States and Prussia by Colleen A. Dunlavy
The Lincoln Persuasion: Remaking American Liberalism by J. David Greenstone
Labor Visions and State Power: The Origins of Business Unionism in the United States by Victoria C. Hattam

CPSIA information can be obtained
at www.ICGtesting.com
Printed in the USA
JSHW020815021122
32432JS00002BA/59